A GOODLY HERITAGE:

ESSAYS IN HONOR OF THE REVEREND DR. ELTON J. BRUINS AT EIGHTY

The Historical Series of the Reformed Church in America
no. 56

A GOODLY HERITAGE

Essays in Honor of the Reverend Dr. Elton J. Bruins at Eighty

Jacob E. Nyenhuis
Editor

William B. Eerdmans Publishing Company
Grand Rapids, Michigan / Cambridge, U.K.

Wm. B. Eerdmans Publishing Co.
255 Jefferson Ave. S.E., Grand Rapids, Michigan 49503 /
P.O. Box 163, Cambridge CB3 9PU U.K.
www.eerdmans.com

Printed in the United States of America

The Reverend Dr. Elton J. Bruins

The Historical Series of the Reformed Church in America

The series was inaugurated in 1968 by the General Synod of the Reformed Church in America acting through the Commission on History to communicate the church's heritage and collective memory and to reflect on our identity and mission, encouraging historical scholarship which informs both church and academy.

Contents

Illustrations

Tables

Acknowledgments

The publication of any book leaves the author or editor in debt to many people. My list is long.

I thank first of all each and all of the contributors, who willingly accepted my invitation to them to prepare an essay for this festschrift in honor of our dear friend and colleague. The alacrity with which some responded was amazing: the ink was barely dry on the letter before I had the first acceptance. Some manuscripts were even submitted prior to the deadline, a character trait that their authors share with our honoree. Others needed a little more time. They tolerated my sometimes slow response and my requests for more information with ever shorter deadlines. They even responded graciously to most, if not all, of my editorial decisions. But best of all, they submitted excellent essays that not only do honor to Elton Bruins, but also represent significant contributions to their field.

I owe a huge debt of gratitude to Karen G. Schakel, Editorial Assistant and Office Manager of the Van Raalte Institute. It would indeed be difficult to find another copy editor with her superb combination of a keen eye for detail, a phenomenal knowledge of the *Chicago Manual of Style*, a strong sense of language and style, love for good writing, doggedness in tracking down missing information, and dedication to excellence. Karen has spared me and all the other contributors from more than one embarrassment by her outstanding work.

Geoffrey Reynolds, director of the Joint Archives of Holland, and Lori Trethewey, secretary of JAH, were generous with their time in tracking down numerous files, scanning photographs, and assisting in many other ways. It has been a special pleasure these past three years to share the Henri and Eleanore Theil Research Center with them.

I am grateful to Joel Lefever, President of the Holland Historic Trust, for permission to publish the collection of Ben Van Raalte's letters from their collection.

I owe a great debt of gratitude to Donald J. Bruggink, General Editor of the RCA Historical Series, for shepherding this project through the RCA Commission on History, as well as for all his advice during the project, his patience with missed deadlines, and for his friendship.

Russ Gasero, Archivist for the Reformed Church in America, who has faithfully done the layout and coding for so many volumes in the RCA Historical Series, has earned my gratitude and admiration especially for his good work on this particular volume.

My colleagues at the Van Raalte Institute have provided support and encouragement to me during this project, answering numerous questions that arose during my editorial work, helping me track down information, and preserving the secrecy that this project has required in order to make the presentation of the book to Elton a genuine surprise for him. I am grateful as well as for the intellectual stimulation they have provided these past six years, through our ongoing conversations at coffee time and all the times between. They have thereby made my semi-retirement enjoyable and fulfilling.

Peter H. Huizenga, has given generous support to this publication, just as he has supported the Van Raalte Institute with his generosity from its founding in 1994 up to the present. He is that rare donor who shows genuine interest in a cause which he has endowed with his funds. He continues to support the work of all of us at the Institute, with frequent notes, telephone calls, and visits. We are all very grateful for his vision and his commitment to preserving our rich heritage.

Last, but by no means least, I offer my deepest gratitude to my beloved wife of over fifty years, Leona. She has supported me with her love and encouragement throughout this project, even when I began to spend ten to twelve hours a day on it toward its end. I am truly blessed to have such a wonderful life partner and best friend.

Jacob E. Nyenhuis

Introduction

When Elton Bruins retired from Hope College in 1992 shortly before his sixty-fifth birthday, it was still the custom for retirees to give a speech at the retirement dinner. For some retirees, even very accomplished teachers, the prospect of giving a swan song before their faculty colleagues struck fear in their hearts. Others relished the opportunity. There was no fear evident on Elton's joyful face as he delivered his retirement speech.

Elton chose Psalm 16:6 as the theme for his carefully-crafted remarks, which of course had been completed well in advance of the dinner. Fifteen years later, these words still stand as witness to how Elton views his life: "The lines have fallen to me in pleasant places; surely, I have a goodly heritage." I therefore chose "A Goodly Heritage" as the title for this collection of essays presented to him in honor of his eightieth birthday on 29 July 2007.

The fifteen essays in this collection were written by former students and long-time friends of Elton, many of us brought to the Van Raalte Institute during his tenure as founding director of the Institute (1994-2002). The essays have been assembled into three categories, all of which reflect the different aspects of Elton's career. Two-thirds of the essays concern church history and theology, as is reasonable, since he spent most of his career in the field of religion, first as a minister in two New York congregations of the Reformed Church in America, then as a professor of religion at Hope College. The other third of the essays essentially represents the field of local history, but they have been separated into two categories. The purpose of this division is to give greater attention to Reverend Albertus C. Van Raalte, D.D., whose life, career, and influence have occupied a large portion of Elton's scholarly research over more than three decades: during that time he accumulated over two thousand files on Van Raalte, and his final major project is the production of an edition, with commentary, of the correspondence between Rev. Van Raalte and Dr. Philip Phelps Jr., principal of the Holland Academy and founder and first president of Hope College. The two essays in this category present important new insights into Van Raalte and his family.

The final category, consisting of three essays, focuses on Hope College and Holland, Michigan. One of the essays, by James C. Kennedy, underscores another aspect of Elton's career—leadership and administration—to which Elton devoted a substantial period of time. He chaired the Religion Department for seven years, was Dean for Arts and Humanities for five, Acting Provost for a semester, and founding Director of the Van Raalte Institute for eight years.

Taken together, the fifteen essays cover a broad range of topics, from religious conflict in the nineteenth century, to the Civil War, to Hope College history, to a noble experiment in unifying community archives, to recent ideological conflict in the field of Reformation history, to contemporary issues in the Reformed Church in America. In each section the essays are arranged in alphabetical order by the last name of the contributor.

Church History and Theology

Introducing the first group, Harry Boonstra's essay presents a comparative study of congregational song in the Reformed Church in America (RCA) and the Christian Reformed Church (CRC). He traces the history of singing, psalmody and hymnody, and song books in the RCA from 1628 to the beginning of the third millennium, ending with a chronology of hymn books approved by the RCA during nearly four centuries in America. The history of the CRC is much shorter (est. 1857) and the control exercised in the development of song books for official use in the denomination is much stricter. The Dutch *Psalmboek* of 1773 was used as long as the Dutch language prevailed in the worship services. Whereas a dozen song books were approved by the RCA after the CRC came into existence, the CRC has approved only four, including three editions of their own *Psalter Hymnal* (1934, 1959, and 1987). A joint hymnal supplement published in 2001 "signals a wonderful rapprochement of the two bodies."

One of two of Elton's former students included among the contributors, Timothy Brown pays homage to his mentor with his essay, crediting him with contributing to Brown's desire to become a preacher. Drawing upon a scene in Acts 8:26-40 (the story of Philip and the Ethiopian eunuch), Brown educes a series of insights that offer wisdom to preachers in the twenty-first century. As pastor-shepherds, preachers take care of their flock, remind them to whom they belong, and pay attention to their needs. As theologians, they "reflect thoughtfully and speak winsomely on behalf of God." And as evangelists, they demonstrate "an irrepressible desire to tell the good news of Jesus Christ to everyone, everywhere."

Donald J. Bruggink argues that "precedent in the Reformed Church in America (RCA) is against the establishment of extra-canonical tests for individual church membership or ministerial office." Any test beyond the Liturgy and Constitution of the Reformed Church in America is deemed "extra-canonical." Bruggink traces the history of the testing of this fundamental principle, from the nineteenth-century controversies over Freemasonry and the Mercersburg Theology of the German Reformed Church to the twentieth-century dispute about the ordination of women. Against that history, he examines the actions of the Synods of 2004 and 2005 with regard to the issue of homosexuality and the trial of Rev. Dr. Norman J. Kansfield.

Eugene Heideman's discourse on Albertus Pieters draws a number of comparisons between Pieters and Elton Bruins, including their origin in Alto, Wisconsin. Pieters spent thirty-two years as a missionary in Japan, where he "pioneered the ministry of newspaper evangelism." After his return to the U.S. in 1923, Pieters was invited to teach at Hope College, but was called in 1926 to Western Theological Seminary as Professor of English Bible and Missions. Although he taught a wide array of courses, his "real love was for biblical theology and history." Heideman explores Pieters's theological views on a number of issues and demonstrates the significant impact that he had upon generations of students and faculty at WTS.

I. John Hesselink brings his well-honed theological skills to his treatment of the role of Scripture and tradition in the world-wide communion of Reformed churches. Noting that "Christians in the Reformed tradition . . . have always affirmed . . . the Reformation principle *sola scriptura*," Hesselink further observes that churches in this tradition, "though generally confessional churches . . . have no one common, binding confession." He examines the various confessions that have been produced over the centuries, noting common motifs and divergent viewpoints. He views the development of contemporary confessions as evidence of the continuing power of the "venerable and popular Reformed slogan: *Ecclesia reformata semper reformanda est!* [A Reformed church must always be reforming]." Although tradition sometimes "overwhelms the *sola scriptura* principle," he concludes that fidelity to the principle remains strong.

Lynn Winkels Japinga tells the story of her use of oral history interviews to help preserve the history of the Reformed Church in America. She interviewed "over eighty RCA ministers, missionaries, and elders," beginning in November 1999. One of her student research assistants subsequently "interviewed about sixty lay and clergy women." The interviews themselves provide an important record of the life and work of these people, most of whom are retired, but Japinga's summary of the interviews and her conclusions about them are a very valuable resource. The interviews make clear "that there is no single story of the denomination," that the people interviewed were often linked to each other through a "web of relationships," and that "denominational history is far more nuanced and complex" than official publications would suggest. She concludes with a number of provocative questions for us to ponder about the future of the church.

Earl Wm. Kennedy, with meticulous documentation, provides an intriguing thesis regarding the reasons for the secession of a number of congregations and individuals from the Reformed Protestant Dutch Church (RPDC; later, the Reformed Church in America, or RCA) to establish a new denomination that became known as the Christian Reformed Church (CRC). He attributes to the writings of a seventeenth-century English Puritan, Richard Baxter (1615-91), a significant influence upon many members and leaders of the RPDC, including Rev. A. C. Van Raalte. The influence of Baxter's *A Call to the Unconverted* alarmed and upset some of the immigrants in Western Michigan, who perceived Baxter's views as unorthodox. His "denial of the doctrine of 'limited atonement' was judged a fatal flaw by some of those involved in the CRC schism." Kennedy traces the development of the controversy and introduces all the major contenders, linking the three major regional parties among the Secessionists in the Netherlands to some of the theological conflicts of seventeenth-century England. Rev.

Van Raalte and the Eastern RPDC were more tolerant of "diversity and inclusiveness, as well as accommodation to the American evangelical environment," than were those who left to form the CRC.

Gregg Mast, another of Elton's former students, explores a decade in the middle of the nineteenth century when conflict over theological teachings of two faculty members of the Mercersburg Seminary of the German Reformed Church derailed a once-promising merger of the GRC with the RPDC (later, RCA). Professors John Williamson Nevin and Philip Schaff sowed "the theological seeds of discord that would cause the denominations to move from altar to divorce in a decade." The stage was set by Nevin's opening sermon, "Catholic Unity," delivered at the 1844 Triennial Convention, and a few months later by Schaff's inaugural address, in which he set forth "his theory of the historical development of the church." Schaff rejected both the American Protestant call for a return to the model of the church of the first century in order to escape "the corruption of the Roman Catholic Church of the Middle Ages" and the Anglican view "that it was the first four or five centuries that needed to form the church, a position which clearly allowed for the apostolic offices." These teachings aroused intense concern among the leaders of the RPDC. Mast's essay demonstrates how difficult it is to effect ecclesiastical unions.

Jacob E. Nyenhuis, striving to emulate Elton's significant study of Third Reformed Church in Holland, Michigan (*The Americanization of a Congregation*), undertakes an analysis of the first English-speaking congregation of the Christian Reformed Church in Holland, Fourteenth Street Church, which was established in 1902. The church went from explosive growth in the early decades to a painful schism in the 1950s, resulting from debate over whether to rebuild on the same site or to move to a new location. Those who remained behind built a new structure, but also had to rebuild their congregation's damaged reputation. Outreach efforts began with foreign missions, then turned toward local evangelism and service to the community. The last quarter century the congregation has dealt increasingly with building cross-cultural understanding, with both successes and failures, as the congregation continues to adapt to the environment in which it is called to minister.

J. Jeffery Tyler recounts the substantial reassessment in recent years of the significance of the Protestant Reformation. He reports that "During the last half-century, scholarship has largely downplayed religion and theology as significant sources of historical change."

Whereas in 1956 Roland Bainton's *The Age of the Reformation* was viewed as a significant contribution to the understanding of modern history, historians largely reject the idea that there was a "world changing 'age of reformation' . . . that ushered in the modern world." They argue, among other things, that "*the* Reformation never existed," that "one must speak in the plural of 'reformations,'" that these "reformations were not limited to the sixteenth century," that governments used the church to exploit and control the populace, that they had little effect on ordinary people, and particularly not on women. For the most part, over the past fifty years social history has been on the ascendance, whereas "historical research that continues to take seriously ideas, religion, and theology" has experienced "decline, resilience, and revival."

The Life and Heritage of Rev. Albertus C. Van Raalte

Jeanne Jacobson leads off with an essay on the Civil War correspondence of Ben Van Raalte that he sent home to his parents from the front during the Atlanta campaign in 1864. Her annotations on the letters identify both many of the leaders and some of the foot soldiers, with a fine glossary of names to help the reader keep the main cast of characters clearly in mind. Ben's letters offer perceptive insights into many different aspects of war, as well as keen observations about some of the key military leaders on both sides of the battle. These letters give a clear sense of the life of a foot soldier on the march, digging trenches, building fortifications, sallying forth to attack, then withdrawing to collect the wounded or to savor the day's successes. Ben candidly expresses his opinions not only on the war at the front but also the conflict at home about the war, criticizing the critics of the campaign. These letters and the accompanying commentary add to the rich heritage of the Van Raaltes.

Robert P. Swierenga brings all his experience and analytical skills to bear on the nature and extent of Rev. A. C. Van Raalte's business dealings. He draws upon his experience with reading land and tax records for his early books on land speculation and tax sales in Iowa. By analyzing land transfers and assessing the shrewdness of Van Raalte's adaptation to the American environment, Swierenga is able to shed new light on Van Raalte's business acumen and the personal cost of some of his miscalculations in land speculation. Van Raalte began his involvement in business dealings during the decade prior to his emigration in 1846, largely for the sake of providing employment to unemployed Separatists. Many of his business dealings and land speculation in Western Michigan were likewise intended for the benefit of those Separatists who had followed him to America. Van Raalte had an "entrepreneurial mindset, capitalistic attitude toward money, and [an] eagerness to take risks." In time, he and his family became very wealthy (but mostly "land rich") because of his constant engagement in business dealings.

History of Hope College

James C. Kennedy's essay on the four presidential eras at Hope College provides an excellent introduction to this section, for he offers a comprehensive overview of the entire history of the college. Kennedy groups the college's presidents under four rubrics: the clerical patrons (Phelps, Mandeville, Scott); immigrant sons (Kollen, Vennema, Dimnent); progressive Protestants (Wichers, Lubbers, Vander Werf); and "defenders of the faith" (Van Wylen, Jacobson, Bultman). In varying degrees, all of the presidents served as mediators of a "middle way" between "more progressive and traditional currents" in society and the church, particularly the Reformed Church in America. Kennedy concisely and perceptively analyzes each of the four eras, summarizing the issues and how the presidents handled them, and prognosticates about the future. He concludes that "the next presidents of Hope College will have to negotiate a new balance, and a new mission. . . ."

Dennis Voskuil provides a long-needed critical history of the development of theological education at Hope College and the creation of a separate theological school, Western Theological Seminary. From early stirrings for secondary education in the West (i.e., the Middle West)—even before Rev. Van Raalte arrived—to the establishment of Hope College, there was an undercurrent of support among churches in this region for theological education. Despite resistance from Eastern churches and New Brunswick Theological Seminary, theological education was approved in 1866; it was suspended, however, in 1877 and not reestablished until 1884. Tensions within Hope College—between President Phelps and his faculty—as well as with the churches in the East, played a major role in these outcomes. Voskuil skillfully tells the story of the developments over the decades, drawing upon the rich resources of the Western Theological Seminary and Hope College Collections at the Joint Archives of Holland. He astutely observes that the two institutions are "separate but not separated."

Larry J. Wagenaar draws upon his experience as the first director of the Joint Archives of Holland to chart the successes and failures of this noble experiment in creating a single community archive. There were two failed attempts—in 1976 and 1980—before the Joint Archives was created in 1988, at the time of the opening of the new Van Wylen Library at Hope College. Wagenaar's pride in the successes at the early stage of this experiment is evident, as is his disappointment in the failure to retain the Holland Historical Trust (the keeper of the City of Holland's official records, as well as of the archives of the Holland Museum) as a partner in this venture. His essay exposes the challenges to cooperation and the difficulties that arise when a new leader of one of the partner organizations does not share the vision that led to the creation of the Joint Archives of Holland, an effort that was inspired and led, to a significant degree, by Elton J. Bruins.

Homage

All fifteen essays are offered in homage to our dear friend and beloved colleague, who has modeled a life of devotion to God, living out among us his calling to the ministry of the Word. With Elton, we acknowledge that we all have a goodly heritage. To him we say: "To you, dear friend, esteemed scholar, beloved colleague, and loyal servant of the church, we offer this festschrift as a token of gratitude to you for enriching our lives, educating us in our rich heritage, and inspiring us in our work and in our walk of faith. God bless you on your eightieth birthday—and always!"

Biography of Elton John Bruins

Elton John Bruins is deeply rooted—in his faith, in the Reformed Church in America, in the Middle West (but especially in Alto, Wisconsin), in his Dutch-American heritage, and in his beloved alma mater, Hope College. To all who know him, it is readily apparent that Elton is a Christian with a deep and abiding faith. His faith is personal, but his ancestors Hendrik and Hendrika Bruins established a pattern of faith that influenced and inspired subsequent generations. Elton says of his great-great-grandparents, who emigrated from the Netherlands to the United States of America in 1847, that they "were very devout Christians. They joined the Separatist movement after it began in 1834."[1] The family farm in the Netherlands was in the Province of Gelderland, near the towns of Twello and Wilp, where the Dutch Reformed Church met in a sanctuary dating back to 1595.[2]

1 *Into the Third Millennium: The Derk and Cynthia Bruins Family, 1865-2002*, ed. Elton J. Bruins (Holland, Mich.: A. C. Van Raalte Institute, Hope College, 2002), 2.

2 Ibid., 1-2; "The church was supposedly founded in 765. The steeple section . . . was constructed about 1000 A.D." Wilp is located east of Apeldoorn, north-northeast of Arnhem. A descendant, Hannah Bruins Vandervelde, says that "Hendrik Bruins built a home for his bride at 'De Vijfhook by Wilp,' a third of a mile from the church at Twelle [*sic*], and three miles from the town of Deventer" (*Bruins' Genealogy and Early History. Heusinkveld*

This ancestral example of Christian devotion passed from generation to generation. The line passes to Elton through Derk Bruins, "the sixth of the eight children born to Hendrik and Hendrika Bruins. He was eight years old when the family emigrated to America."[3] The eldest son of Derk and Cynthia Heusinkveld Bruins, William Henry Bruins (1865-1933), graduated from McCormick Theological Seminary in 1893. He subsequently "served Reformed Church pastorates from 1893 to 1910, when he transferred his credentials to the Presbyterian Church"; his last pastorate was at the Scotland Presbyterian Church in Voorheesville, New York.[4] His younger brother, Henry M. Bruins, also became a minister. Elton therefore had two of his grandfather's brothers as models to inspire him to go into the ministry, although there were undoubtedly other influences upon that decision.

Elton has compiled the last four of the six family histories published between 1941 and 2002.[5] Each of the last five histories has been prepared in conjunction with a Bruins family reunion. With the assistance of his father, Clarence R. Bruins, Elton published the third history in 1980, assembling genealogical data for the family and descendants of Hendrik and Hendrika Wechel Bruins: the genealogy covers a span of 230 years, from 1750 to 1980.[6]

In 1997, Elton produced a special fifth edition for the family's celebration of the sesquicentennial of the arrival of Hendrik and Hendrika and their children in America in 1847, the same year that Rev. Albertus C. Van Raalte and his followers settled in Holland, Michigan.[7] Although this family reunion was held at Central College, in Pella,

---

Genealogy, ed. Hannah Bruins Vandervelde [Waupun, Wisc.: privately printed, 1941; 2nd printing, 2002]), 7.

3 *Into the Third Millennium*, 3.

4 Ibid., 3, 9, 21.

5 The first two were: *Bruins' Genealogy and Early History. Heusinkveld Genealogy*, ed. Hannah Bruins Vandervelde (1941); and *Derk Bruins – Geziena Heusinkveld Genealogy and Early History*, 2nd ed., rev. and enlarged, ed. Paul F. Bruins (privately printed, July 1961).

6 *The Bruins Family of Alto, Wisconsin: Historical and Genealogical Data Relating to the Family of Hendrik and Hendrika Van Wechel Bruins, 1750 to 1980*, ed. Elton J. Bruins (1980; 2nd ed., Van Raalte Institute, Hope College, 2004). Ten years later, he published *Unto the Sixth Generation: The Descendants of Derk and Cynthia Bruins, 1865-1990*, ed. Elton J. Bruins (Holland, Mich.: Hope College, 1990).

7 *The Hendrik and Hendrika Bruins Family in America, 1847-1997*, ed. Elton J. Bruins (Holland, Mich.: A. C. Van Raalte Institute, Hope College, 1997).

Iowa, three of the reunions have been held on the farm acquired in 1880 by Derk and Cynthia Bruins. This farm, which they purchased from the William Smithers family, has remained in the family for five generations.[8]

Elton was born 29 July 1927 to Clarence Raymond Bruins and Angeline Theodora Kemink Bruins, the second of five children. He attended the public school in Alto, Wisconsin. He enlisted in the U.S. Navy in April 1945, shortly before his high school graduation, although he did not enter military service until the end of July. He was in basic training when the atomic bomb was dropped on Hiroshima and Nagasaki, so his military career lasted only slightly over a year. He was discharged from the Navy in August 1946, just in time to enroll in Hope College. He says that he enlisted in the Navy rather than accept a farmer's deferment, since he wanted to attend college.[9] Elton was one of about thirty members of the Bruins family to attend Hope College, beginning with William Henry Bruins, who had enrolled in 1882.[10] At Hope College he earned faculty honors and a B.A. degree, *magna cum laude*, in 1950. He joined the newly-established Arcadian Fraternity in spring semester 1947: he proudly reports that the "Arkies" won the All College Sing three out of the four years that he was a student at Hope.[11]

He entered Western Theological Seminary the following fall, and earned the B.D. degree in 1953; he was honored with the Pietenpol Award for Excellence, which is now described as follows:

> The Henry J. Pietenpol Senior Excellence Award is given to the graduating student in the M.Div. program who demonstrates unusual promise for ministry. The decision is made by the faculty.[12]

He continued his graduate education in 1953-54 at Union Theological Seminary in New York, where his faculty advisors were Dr. Wilhelm Pauck and Dr. Robert Handy. The following year he

8 *Into the Third Millennium*, vii and 3.

9 Notes on a conversation, 12 February 2007.

10 *Into the Third Millennium*, viii.

11 Notes on a conversation, 14 February 2007. The Arcadian Fraternity was founded in fall semester 1946.

12 Description provided by Rayetta Perez, Western Theological Seminary. The M.Div. degree has taken the place of the B.D. degree that was awarded to Elton and his classmates in 1953.

Family home on Bruins farm in Alto, Wisconsin.

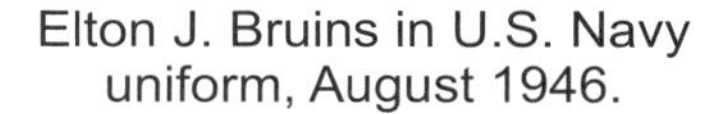

Elton J. Bruins in U.S. Navy uniform, August 1946.

undertook studies in American Christianity at Princeton Theological Seminary, with Dr. Lefferts Loetscher as faculty advisor, but earned an S.T.M. degree from Union in 1957. Over the course of the next five years, he pursued doctoral studies at New York University, receiving a Ph.D. in the history of education in 1962; his faculty advisors were Dr. Lee A. Belford and Dr. William P. Sears.

While engaged in graduate studies, Elton began his ministerial career, first as Assistant to the Minister of the Reformed Church at Hastings-on-the-Hudson, New York, in 1953-54, then as Minister of the Elmsford (New York) Reformed Church (1955-61), and next at the Reformed Church of Flushing, New York (1961-66). His extensive involvement in the Reformed Church in America includes membership on the Board of Trustees of New Brunswick Theological Seminary

Elton J. Bruins with Hope College Science Center in background, September 1946.

(1956-61), the Historical Commission of the Reformed Church in America (1966-72, 1976-82, and 1989-95; chair, 1967-72), and member of the Classis of Westchester, New York (1955-61; president, ca. 1960), the Classis of Queens, New York (1961-66), and the Classis of Holland, Michigan (since 1966; vice president - 1993, president - 1994, and chair of two committees, 1994-98). He has also been a very active member of Third Reformed Church, Holland, Michigan, with service as Moderator of the Consistory (1970-71), Chair of the 125th Anniversary Committee (1991-93), chair of two other committees, and congregational historian (since 1966).

Elton joined the faculty of the Department of Religion at Hope College in 1966 as Assistant Professor of Religion, was promoted to Associate Professor in 1970, and to Professor in 1973. In 1981 he was honored with appointment to an endowed chair as the Evert J. and Hattie E. Blekkink Professor of Religion, a position which he held until his retirement in 1992, at which time he was named the Blekkink Professor of Religion Emeritus. He served as chair of the Department of Religion (1977-84), as Dean for Arts and Humanities (1984-89), and Acting Provost (fall semester, 1989). In 1994 he came out of retirement to become the founding Director of the A. C. Van Raalte Institute at Hope College, a post which he held until 2002, when he was named Senior Research Fellow of the Institute; in January 2004, on the occasion of the tenth anniversary celebration of the Van Raalte Institute, he was appointed as the Philip Phelps Jr. Research Professor.

This brief *cursus honorum* does not do justice to Elton's career at Hope College, nor does the Bibliography in the next chapter complete the story, but together they reveal him as a highly-respected, hard-working teacher, scholar, and administrator. His *curriculum vitae* reveals him also as a trusted colleague and dedicated servant of the college, the church, and the community. A highly selective list of his service on college committees and task forces includes the following: Religious Life Committee (chair), Academic Affairs Board, Campus Life Board, President's Advisory Committee, Status Committee, Archives Council (chair), Library Committee, Van Wylen Library Planning Committee (chair), South Africa Task Force (secretary), and faculty representative on the Board of Trustees.

He served the community of Holland as member of both the 125th Anniversary Committee and the Sesquicentennial Committee; as chair of the Holland Historical/Cultural Relations Committee; as a member and officer of the Board of Trustees of the Holland Historical Trust (1978-93) and member of the Cappon House Task Force; and more recently, on the Windmill Island Study Committee. He also organized the Holland Area Historical Society and served two terms on its board (1980-86 and 1990-93).

This kind of dedication to service was modeled for Elton by his grandfather, Edward Bruins, as can be seen in the following reminiscence by Elton's father, Clarence R. Bruins, written before his death in 1986:

> Father was elected to the [Alto] township board and he was a member of the [Fond du Lac] county board for 12 years. Each year he spent four weeks in Fond du Lac to attend the county board meetings. He helped to plan several important roads in the Township of Alto such as County Trunk E which ran a half mile west of the farm. He also served as deacon in the consistory of Alto Reformed Church, taught in the Sunday School, and served as a trustee of the [Alto] Cemetery Board for eight years. He served as clerk of our local county school, District #6, the Roosevelt School.[13]

Elton's keen interest in archival preservation and research dates back to his years in college and seminary. In an essay elsewhere in this festschrift, Eugene Heideman tells us that "Elton Bruins worked in the

[13] *Into the Third Millennium*, 34.

seminary library for five years during his student years at Hope and Western. . . ." His interest in research was nurtured in graduate school, but it came to full bloom during his years on the faculty of Hope College. Not long after he came to Hope, he became involved in archival work for both the seminary and the city. He was Assistant to the Librarian for historical materials at Western Theological Seminary from 1967 to 1978 and Assistant to the Director for historical materials at the Netherlands Museum from 1968 to 1980. He served for thirty-six years on the Dutch-American Historical Commission, nineteen as treasurer, and as an officer of the Association for the Advancement of Dutch-American Studies for eight years (Vice President, 1977-83; President, 1983-85). He has also been at various times a member of the American Society for Church History, the Michigan Archival Association, the Midwest Archives Conference, the New York Genealogical and Biographical Society, the Presbyterian Historical Society, and the Wisconsin Historical Society.

In recognition of his outstanding professional service, he was given the "Friend of Holland History" award by the Holland Historical Trust (1998), the Heritage Award by the Dutch-American Heritage Committee in recognition of his achievements in Dutch-American Studies (18 November 1998), and the President's Award by the Midwest Archives Conference (1999). He has also been honored by inclusion in *Who's Who in the Midwest*, *Who's Who in Religion*, *Men of Achievement*, and *Michigan Authors*.

Elton's first sabbatical, in spring 1973, was spent in the Hague, the Netherlands, where he studied nineteenth-century Dutch emigration documents, including genealogical materials concerning his family. His second sabbatical was divided between Western Theological Seminary and the University of California, Riverside, and a third one was spent in Holland, Michigan, conducting research on Albertus C. Van Raalte. The fruit of his scholarship is detailed in the Bibliography in the next chapter. Elton's involvement in gathering historical materials for Hope College, Western Theological Seminary and the Netherlands Museum laid the foundation for the establishment of the Joint Archives of Holland in 1988 and of the Van Raalte Institute in 1994. The story of his role in the founding of the Joint Archives of Holland is told by Larry J. Wagenaar in an essay in the last section of this festschrift.

Elton's personal life includes a marriage that has lasted for over fifty years: he and Elaine Ann Redeker were married on 24 June 1954. Their children are Mary Elaine Bruins (b. 18 April 1956) and David

With admiration and appreciation,
the West Michigan Committee of the
Dutch-American Heritage Day
presents the 1998 Heritage Award to

Dr. Elton J. Bruins
OF HOPE COLLEGE

We honor you for exemplary service in preserving the story of Dutch-Americans in "the Colony" and beyond; for keen scholarship and groundbreaking research helping others discover the rich contributions of the Dutch-American pioneer-preacher Albertus Christian Van Raalte; and for a lifetime of dedication to the church, the academy, and the community.

The Heritage Award is granted this day, November 18, in the year of our Lord, 1998, in grateful recognition of your efforts to extend and deepen the cultural, civic, and religious bonds linking West Michigan with the Kingdom of the Netherlands, for the advancement of Dutch-American Heritage.

Dutch-American Heritage Award conferred upon Elton J. Bruins, November 1998.

Lewis Bruins (b. 1 July 1958). Mary Bruins was married to Daniel Plasman on 3 June 1978; their three children are James Daniel (b. 26 May 1981), Katherine Rose (b. 23 August 1983), and Thomas Edward (b. 14 April 1987). David Bruins was married to Elizabeth Ann Lawson on 23 May 1992; their children are Christopher John (b. 10 May 1999), Matthew David (b. 10 September 2001), and Dylan M. (b. 29 September 2003).

Over the past eighty years, Elton J. Bruins has lived a full and productive life. His dedication to his Lord and Savior shines through every endeavor. The writer of Ecclesiastes declares: "I know that there is nothing better for men than to be happy and do good while they live. That everyone may eat and drink, and find satisfaction in all his toil—this is the gift of God" (Eccl. 3:12-13 NIV). To all who know him, Elton has been transparent not only in his love for the Lord, but also in his joy in the work that he was called to do. His choice of Psalm 16:6 as the basis for summarizing his career up to the age of sixty-five is just as valid fifteen years later. The lines have indeed fallen to him in pleasant places and his life lived in gratitude for his goodly heritage bears witness to his faith, his calling, and his hope for life eternal.

Bibliography of Publications of Elton J. Bruins

Books

2004

Albertus and Christina: The Van Raalte Family, Home and Roots (with Karen G. Schakel, Sara Fredrickson Simmons, and Marie N. Zingle). Grand Rapids: Eerdmans, 2004.

1999

Family Quarrels in the Dutch Reformed Churches in the Nineteenth Century (with Robert P. Swierenga). Historical Series of the Reformed Church in America, no. 32. Grand Rapids: Eerdmans, 1999.

1996

Albertus C. Van Raalte, Dutch Leader and American Patriot (with Jeanne M. Jacobson and Larry J. Wagenaar). Holland, Mich.: Hope College, 1996.

1995

The Americanization of a Congregation. Second ed. Historical Series of the Reformed Church in America, no. 26. Grand Rapids: Eerdmans, 1995.

1987

Isaac Cappon: Holland's "Foremost Citizen." Holland, Mich.: Hope College, 1987.

1970

The Americanization of a Congregation. Historical Series of the Reformed Church in America, no. 2. Grand Rapids: Eerdmans, 1970.

BOOK IN PROGRESS

Correspondence of Albertus C. Van Raalte to Philip Phelps Jr., 1857-75.

EDITED BOOKS

2002

Into the Third Millenium: The Derk and Cynthia Bruins Family, 1865-2002. Holland, Mich.: Van Raalte Institute/Hope College, 2002.

1997

The Hendrik and Hendrika Bruins Family in America, 1847-1997. Holland, Mich.: Hope College, 1997.

1995

Daily Jottings: Selected Entries from the Diary of Mrs. Angeline T. Bruins, January 1, 1958–December 31, 1962. Holland, Mich.: Hope College, 1995.

1990

Unto the Sixth Generation: The Descendants of Derk and Cynthia Bruins, 1865-1900. Holland, Mich.: Hope College, 1990.

1987

The Netherlands Museum, Holland, Michigan, 1937-1987: A Brief History of Its Foundation and Development; and an Account of the Special Recognition Given to the First Director, Dr. Willard C. Wichers, on February 7, 1987. Holland, Mich.: Netherlands Museum, 1987.

1986

A Legacy of Memories: Personal Reminiescences of Clarence R. Bruins of Alto, Wisconsin, 1977-1985. Holland, Mich.: Hope College, 1986.

1984

The Dutch in America: Papers Presented at the Fourth Biennial Conference of the Association for the Advancement of Dutch-American Studies, 1983. Holland, Mich.: Hope College, 1984.

1980

The Bruins Family of Alto, Wisconsin: Historical and Genealogical Data Relating to the Family of Hendrik and Hendrika Van Wechel Bruins and Their Descendants, 1750-1980. Holland, Mich.: Hope College, 1980. Second edition, 2004.

Pamphlets

2004

A Step Forward for Hope College: The Building of Graves Hall and Winants Chapel. Holland, Mich.: Hope College, 2004.

1999

Campus Alive: A Walking Tour of Hope College (with Larry J. Wagenaar). Holland, Mich.: Hope College, 1999.

1995

Historic Hope College: A Guide for a Walking Tour of the Campus. Holland, Mich.: Hope College, 1995.

1992

A Self-Guided Tour of the Historic Third Reformed Church, Holland, Michigan: Prepared for the Church's 125th Anniversary Celebration, 1992-93. Holland, Mich.: Third Reformed Church, 1992.

1990

An Immigrant Church in a New Land: A Brief Survey of the History of the Reformed Church in America, 1628-1990 (in outline). Holland, Mich.: Hope College, 1990.

1985

John Calvin, the Genevan Reformer: A Bibliographical Guide for Students. Holland, Mich.: Hope College, 1985 and 1991.

1975

The Dutch in America: A Bibliographical Guide for Students. Holland, Mich.: Hope College, 1975.

1968

A Guide to the Archives of the Netherlands Museum. Holland, Mich.: Netherlands Museum, 1968. Second edition, 1971; third edition (with Barbara Lampen), 1978.

1967

The Manuscript and Archival Holdings of Beardslee Library. Holland, Mich.: Western Theological Seminary, 1967. Second edition, 1970; third edition, 1978.

Articles

2006

"The Americanization of a Congregation." Parts 1 and 2. *Family Ties: Holland Genealogical Society Newsletter* 31, no. 2 (January 2006): 14-17; no. 3 (April 2006): 5-7.

"The Educational Endeavors of the Reformed Dutch Church 1628-1866." *Reformed Review* 59, no. 2 (winter 2005-06): 165-83.

2005

"Biographical Notes on Selected Figures in Hope College's History." In *Can Hope Endure?: A Historical Case Study in Christian Higher Education* by James C. Kennedy and Caroline J. Simon, 240-50. Historical Series of the Reformed Church in America, no. 47. Grand Rapids: Eerdmans, 2005.

2003

"Coming into Genealogy by the Back Door." *Family Ties: Holland Genealogical Society Newsletter* 28, no. 3 (January 2003): 3-5.

2001

"Albertus C. Van Raalte: Leader of the Dutch Emigration to the United States, 1847-1867." *Origins* 19, no. 2 (2001): 4-11.

"Early Hope College History as Reflected in the Correspondence of Rev. Albertus C. Van Raalte to Rev. Philip Phelps Jr., 1857-1875." In *The Dutch Adapting in North America: Papers Presented at the Thirteenth Conference for the Association for the Advancement of Dutch-American Studies, 2001*, ed. Richard H. Harms, 1-8. Grand Rapids: Calvin College, 2001.

"Hope College: Its Origin and Development, 1851-2001." *Origins* 19, no. 1 (2001): 4-13.

1999

"Is a 'Joyful Death' an Oxymoron?" (with Karsten Rumohr-Voskuil). In *Patterns and Portraits: Women in the History of the Reformed Church in America*, ed. Renee S. House and John W. Coakley, 87-94. Historical Series of the Reformed Church in America, no. 31. Grand Rapids: Eerdmans, 1999.

"Donald J. Bruggink's Contribution to Reformed Church in America Historiography." *Reformed Review* 52, no. 3 (spring 1999): 213-24.

"Reformed Church in America." In *Dictionary of the Presbyterian and Reformed Tradition in America*, gen. ed. D. G. Hart, consulting ed. Mark A. Noll, 207-8. Downers Grove, Ill.: InterVarsity, 1999.

1998

"Albertus C. Van Raalte: Leader of the Emigration, 1844-1867." In *The Sesquicentennial of Dutch Immigration: 150 Years of Ethnic Heritage. Proceedings of the Eleventh Biennial Conference of the Association for the Advancement of Dutch-American Studies*, ed. Larry J. Wagenaar and Robert

P. Swierenga, 13-28. Holland, Mich.: Joint Archives of Holland-Hope College, 1998.

1997

"The Classis of Holland: A Brief History" and "Third Reformed Church." In *In Christ's Service: The Classis of Holland and Its Congregations, 1847-1997,* 2-5, 16-18. Holland, Mich.: Classis of Holland Reformed Church in America, 1997.

"One Person's Vision." *Church Herald* 54, no. 2 (February 1997): 8-10.

1996

"A.A.D.A.S.: Hence? Whence?" In *A Century of Midwestern Dutch-American Manners and Mores—and More. Papers Given at the Tenth Biennial Conference of the Association for the Advancement of Dutch-American Studies, 1995.* Orange City, Iowa: Northwestern College, 1996.

"'An American Moses': Albertus C. Van Raalte as Immigrant Leader." In *Sharing the Reformed Tradition: The Dutch—North American Exchange, 1846-1996,* ed. George Harinck and Hans Krabbendam, 19-34. Amsterdam: VU, 1996.

"Third Reformed Church of Holland, Michigan: A Brief History, 1867-1995." In *Third Reformed Church, 1996, "There's a Place for You"* (church pictorial directory).

1995

"Nell V. H. Wichers: Emissary of Goodwill." *D.I.S. Magazine* 27, no. 2 (September 1995): 12.

"A New Organ for Mulder Chapel of Western Theological Seminary." In *Celebrating the Dedication of the van Daalen Organ, Mulder Chapel, Western Theological Seminary* (March 1995), 5.

1991

"Van Raalte: Funding a Christian Community." In *The Dutch and Their Faith: Immigrant Religious Experiences in the Nineteenth and Twentieth Centuries. Proceedings of the Eighth Biennial Conference of the Association for the Advancement of Dutch-American Studies, 1991,* 53-63. Holland, Mich.: Hope College, 1991.

1990

"Reformed Church in America." In *Dictionary of Christianity in America,* ed. Daniel G. Reid et al., 985-86. Downers Grove, Ill.: InterVarsity, 1990.

1989

"The Dutch-Immigrant Congregations of Alto, Wisconsin, 1845-1990." *Origins* 7, no. 1 (1989): 22-33.

"From Calvin to Van Raalte: The Rise and Development of the Reformed Tradition in the Netherlands, 1560-1900." In *Servant Gladly: Essays in Honor of John W. Beardslee III*, ed. Jack D. Klunder and Russell L. Gasero, 89-103. Historical Series of the Reformed Church in America, no. 19. Grand Rapids: Eerdmans, 1989.

1988

"The Archives of the Holland Historical Trust." *Holland Historical Trust Review* 1, no. 3 (summer 1988): 1.

"Gordon J. Van Wylen and Hope College" (with Harry Boonstra). In *Vision for a Christian College: Essays by Gordon J. Van Wylen, President of Hope College, 1972-87*, ed. Harry Boonstra, xiii-xxx. Historical Series of the Reformed Church in America, no. 18. Grand Rapids: Eerdmans, 1988.

1985

"Americanization in Reformed Religious Life." In *The Dutch in America: Immigration, Settlement, and Cultural Change*, ed. Robert P. Swierenga, 175-90. New Brunswick, N.J.: Rutgers University Press, 1985.

"The RCA: The Third Oldest Denomination." *Church Herald* 42, no. 11 (7 June 1985): 18-19.

"Scholarship in the Service of Missions." In *Into All the World: Hope College and International Affairs. Essays in Honor of Paul G. Fried*, ed. Robert J. Donia and John M. Mulder, 25-39. Holland, Mich.: Hope College, 1985.

1984

"Servants to the Church." *Church Herald*, 7 September 1984: 6-8.

1983

"The Kolkman Memorial Archives." *Historical Highlights*, winter 1983: 2-3, 12.

"The Masonic Controversy in Holland, Michigan, 1879-1882." In *Perspectives on the Christian Reformed Church Studies in Its History, Theology, and Ecumenicity, Presented in Honor of John Henry Kromminga at His Retirement as President of Calvin Theological Seminary*, ed. Peter de Klerk and Richard R. De Ridder, 53-72. Grand Rapids: Baker, 1983.

1982

"A Historical Note on the Organs of the Third Reformed Church, 1883-1982." *Dedication Brochure of the New Organ of the Third Reformed Church, September 19, 1982*: 2-3.

1978

"Dimnent Memorial Chapel after Fifty Years Still 'A Hymn Turned to Stone.'" *Hope College Magazine* 31, no. 2 (spring 1978): 3-6.

1977

"Albertus C. Van Raalte and His Colony." *Reformed Review* 30, no. 2 (winter 1977): 83-94.

1976

"Alto, Wisconsin: An Early Dutch Settlement in the Middle West." *The Dutch Immigrant Society Magazine* 6, no. 4 (March 1976): 17-19.

"Immigration." In *Piety and Patriotism, 1776-1976*, ed. James W. Van Hoeven, 56-76. Historical Series of the Reformed Church in America, no. 4. Grand Rapids: Eerdmans, 1976.

1974

"What Happened in 1857?" *Reformed Review* 27, no. 2 (winter 1974): 120-26.

"An Introduction to Books: Current Topics in Our Contemporary World." *Church Herald*, 29 November 1974: 20.

1973

"Your Part in the Awakening." *Church Herald*, 16 March 1973: 11, 22-23.

1972

"Anniversary Time." *Dutch Immigrant Society Magazine* 3, no. 1 (June 1972): 12-13.

"Reflections on an Ecumenical Beginning." *Reformed Journal* 22, no. 10 (December 1972): 23-24.

1971

"A Calamity in the Colony." *Dutch Immigrant Society Magazine* 2, no. 3 (December 1971): 18-19.

"Cumberland Presbyterian Church," "Evangelical and Reformed Church," "Samuel Provoost," "Sidney Rigdon," "George Ripley," "Arthur Ritchie," "Homer Rodeheaver," "Charles Taze Russell," "Ira D. Sankey," "Ida Scudder," "Second Awakening," and "Thomas Shepard." In *Westminster Dictionary of Church History*, ed. Jerald C. Brauer, 252, 314, 678, 719-21, 730, 742, 757-58, 766. Philadelphia: Westminster, 1971.

"History." *Dutch Immigrant Society Magazine* 1, no. 4 (spring 1971): 10.

"The Holocaust in Holland: 1871." *Michigan History* 55, no. 4 (winter 1971): 289-304.

"Van Raalte." *Dutch Immigrant Society Magazine* 2, no. 1 (June 1971): 10-11.

"The Visit of Dr. H. J. Prakke." *Dutch Immigrant Society Magazine* 2, no. 2 (September 1971): 18-19.

1970

"Areas of Tension within the Church: Part 2, The Ecumenical Movement." *Reformed Review* 23, no. 2 (winter 1970), 86-91.

1966

"The Church at the West: A Brief Survey of the Origin and Development of the Dutch Reformed Church in the Middle West." *Reformed Review* 20, no. 2 (December 1966): 2-20.

"Western Theological Seminary: The First Century, 1866-1966." *Church Herald*, 20 May 1966: 4-5.

1965

"Have a Heart: A Lenten Devotion." *Church Herald*, 12 March 1965: 6, 22.

1962

"The New Brunswick Theological Seminary, 1884-1959." Unpublished Ph.D. thesis, New York University, 1962.

1961

"A Prayer Meeting for 103 Years: The Fulton Street Prayer Meeting." *Church Herald*, 13 October 1961: 10-11.

"You Share Christ's Suffering: A Lenten Devotion." *Church Herald*, 3 March 1961: 10, 23.

1960

"The History of the Elmsford Reformed Church, 1790-1960." In *The Elmsford Reformed Church*. Elmsford, N.Y.: Elmsford Reformed Church, 1960.

"What Do You Know about Sunday School Teaching?" *Church Herald*, 15 January 1960: 10.

1959

"The Contribution of the Theological Seminary in New Brunswick to the Church in the West, 1850-1884." *Reformed Review* 13, no. 2 (December 1959): 42-47.

"The Father of the Reformed Church, John H. Livingston." *Church Herald*, 2 January 1959: 4-5.

1958

"Luther and the Scriptures." *Church Herald*, 24 October 1958: 4-5.

1957

"John Henry Livingston, a Reinterpretation." Unpublished Master's thesis, Union Theological Seminary, New York, 1957.

1956

"Revive Us Again: The Story of Revivals in the Reformed Church in America." *Church Herald*, 13 July 1956: 8, 14-15.

REVIEWS

2005

Review of *By Grace Alone: Stories of the Reformed Church in America,* by Donald J. Bruggink and Kim N. Baker. Historical Series of the Reformed Church in America, no. 44. Grand Rapids: Eerdmans, 2004. In *Reformed Review* 58, no. 2 (winter 2004-05): 146-47.

2002

Review of *Equipping the Saints: The Synod of New York, 1800-2000*, ed. James Hart Brumm. Historical Series of the Reformed Church in America, no. 35. Grand Rapids: Eerdmans, 2002. In *Reformed Review* 55, no. 3 (spring 2002): 250.

2001

Review of *More Money, More Ministry: Money and Evangelicals in Recent North American History*, ed. Larry Eskridge and Mark A. Noll. Grand Rapids: Eerdmans, 2000. In *Reformed Review* 55, no. 1 (autumn 2001): 81.

Review of *Zion on the Hudson: Dutch in New York and New Jersey in the Age of Revivals*, by Firth Haring Fabend. New Brunswick, N.J.: Rutgers University Press, 2000. In *Reformed Review* 54, no. 2 (winter 2000-01): 145-46.

2000

Review of *Dictionary of the Presbyterian and Reformed Tradition in America*, gen. ed. D. G. Hart, consulting ed. Mark A. Noll. Downers Grove, Ill.: InterVarsity, 1999. In *Reformed Review* 54, no. 1 (autumn 2000): 61-62.

Review of *Faith and Family: Dutch Immigration and Settlement in the United States, 1820-1920*, by Robert P. Swierenga. New York/London: Holmes and Meier, 2000. In *AADAS News* 1, no. 2 (summer 2000): 5.

Review of *Patterns and Portraits: Women in the History of the Reformed Church in America*, ed. Renee S. House and John W. Coakley. Historical Series of the Reformed Church in America, no. 31. Grand Rapids: Eerdmans, 1999. In *Reformed Review* 54, no. 1 (autumn 2000): 66.

1999

Review of *The Arabian Mission's Story: In Search of Abraham's Other Son*, by Lewis R. Scudder III. Historical Series of the Reformed Church in America, no. 30. Grand Rapids: Eerdmans, 1998. In *Reformed Review* 52, no. 2 (winter 1998-99): 162-63.

1997

Review of *Cosmos in the Chaos: Philip Schaff's Interpretation of Nineteenth-Century American Religion*, by Stephen R. Graham. Grand Rapids: Eerdmans, 1995. In *Reformed Review* 50, no. 2 (winter 1997): 134-35.

1996

Review of *Calvinus Sacrae Scripturae Professor: Calvin as Confessor of Holy Scripture*, ed. Wilhelm H. Neuser. Grand Rapids: Eerdmans, 1994. In *Perspectives* 11, no. 1 (January 1996): 20-21.

Review of *Ever a Frontier: The Bicentennial History of the Pittsburgh Theological Seminary*, ed. James Walther. Grand Rapids: Eerdmans, 1994. In *Reformed Review* 49, no. 3 (spring 1996): 212-13.

1995

Review of *The Impact of the Reformation: Essays*, by Heiko Oberman. Grand Rapids: Eerdmans, 1994. In *Reformed Review* 49, no. 1 (autumn 1995): 61.

Review of *Neither King nor Prelate: Religion and the New Nation,* by Edwin S. Gaustad. Grand Rapids: Eerdmans, 1993. In *Reformed Review* 49, no. 1 (autumn 1995): 65.

1994

Review of *Gathered at the River: Grand Rapids, Michigan, and Its People of Faith*, by James D. Bratt and Christopher H. Meehan. Grand Rapids: Eerdmans, 1993. In *Reformed Review* 47, no. 2 (winter 1993-94): 153-54.

Review of *Classical Beginnings, 1519-1799*, vol. 1 of *Reformed Reader: A Sourcebook in Christian Theology*, ed. William Stacy Johnson and John H. Leith. Louisville, Ky.: Westminster/John Knox, Press, 1993. In *Reformed Review* 47, no. 2 (winter 1993-94): 165.

1992

Review of *Grace and Glory Days,* by Thomas D. Boslooper. Clearwater, Fl.: Woodswalker Books, 1990. In *Historical Highlights* 34 (February 1992): 15-16.

1988

Review of *Sources of Secession: The Netherlands Hervormde Kerk on the Eve of Dutch Immigration to the Midwest,* by Gerrit J. TenZythoff. Historical Series of the Reformed Church in America, no. 17. Grand Rapids: Eerdmans, 1987. In *Church History* 57, no. 3 (September 1988): 384-85.

1987

Review of *The Church Speaks: Papers of the Commission on Theology, Reformed Church in America, 1959-1984,* ed. James I. Cook. Historical Series of Reformed Church in America, no. 15. Grand Rapids: Eerdmans, 1985. In *Reformed Review* 40, no. 2 (winter 1987): 154-55.

Review of *Word and World: Reformed Theology in America,* ed. James W. Van Hoeven. Historical Series of the Reformed Church in America, no. 16. Grand Rapids: Eerdmans, 1986. In *Reformed Review* 40, no. 2 (winter 1987): 180-81.

1986

Review of *Reformed Theology in America: A History of Its Modern Development,* ed. David F. Wells. Grand Rapids: Eerdmans, 1985. In *Church History* 55, no. 4 (December 1986): 558-59.

1985

Review of *Drenthe in Michigan,* by H. J. Prakke. Grand Rapids: Eerdmans, 1983. In *Reformed Review* 38, no. 2 (winter 1985): 167.

Review of *Netherlanders in America: A Study of Emigration and Settlement in the Nineteenth and Twentieth Centuries in the United States of America,* by Jacob Van Hinte. Grand Rapids: Baker, 1985. In *Holland Sentinel,* "Waves of West Michigan," 21-28 September 1985, 8.

Review of *The Reformation of 1834: Essays in Commemoration of the Act of Secession and Return,* ed. Peter Y. DeJong and Nelson D. Kloosterman. Orange City, Ia.: Pluim, 1984. In *Reformed Review* 39, no. 1 (autumn 1985): 73-74.

Review of *Two Centuries Plus: The Story of New Brunswick Seminary,* by Howard G. Hageman (with chapter thirteen by Benjamin Alicea). Historical Series of the Reformed Church in America, no. 13. Grand Rapids: Eerdmans, 1985. In *Reformed Review* 39, no. 1 (autumn 1985): 77-78.

1984

Review of *Dutch Immigration to North America*, ed. Herman Ganzevoort and Mark Boekelman. Toronto: Multicultural History Society of Ontario, 1983. In *Journal of American Ethnic History* 4, no. 1 (fall 1984): 104-6.

Review of *Kentucky Presbyterians*, by Louis B. Weeks. Atlanta: John Knox, 1983. In *Church History* 53, no. 4 (December 1984): 560.

Review of *The Role of Religion in American Life: An Interpretative Historical Anthology*, ed. Robert R. Mathisen. Washington D. C.: University Press of America, 1982. In *Fides et Historia* 17, no. 1 (fall-winter 1984): 91-92.

1983

Review of *A Digest and Index of the Minutes of the General Synod of the Reformed Church in America, 1906-1957*, by Mildred W. Schuppert. Historical Series of the Reformed Church in America, no. 8. Grand Rapids: Eerdmans, 1982. In *Reformed Review* 36, no. 3 (spring 1983): 153.

Review of *Three Centuries: The History of the First Reformed Church of Schenectady, 1680-1980*, vol. 1 by Jonathan Pearson, vol. 2 by Kathryn Sharp Pontius, Gerald F. DeJong, and J. Dean Dykstra. Schenectady, N.Y.: First Reformed Church, 1980. In *Church History* 52, no. 1 (March 1983): 114.

1981

Review of *Three Centuries: The History of the First Reformed Church of Schenectady, 1680-1980*, vol. 1 by Jonathan Pearson, vol. 2 by Kathryn Sharp Pontius, Gerald F. De Jong, and J. Dean Dykstra. Schenectady, N.Y.: First Reformed Church, 1980. In *Reformed Review* 34, no. 3 (spring 1981): 216-18.

1980

Review of *The Roots of Fundamentalism: British and American Millenarianism, 1800-1930*, by Ernest Sandeen. Grand Rapids: Baker, 1978. In *Reformed Review* 33, no. 2 (winter 1980): 119-20.

1978

Review of *The Lord's Free Land: Essays in Baptist History in Honor of Robert A. Baker*. Fort Worth: Southwestern Baptist Theological Seminary, 1976. *The Lutherans in North America*, ed. E. Clifford Nelson. Philadelphia: Fortress, 1975. In *Christian Scholars Review* 8, no. 3 (1978): 270-71.

Review of *Pioneer Preacher: Albertus Christian Van Raalte—A Study of His Sermon Notes,* by Gordon J. Spykman. Heritage Hall Publications, no. 2.

Grand Rapids: Calvin College and Seminary, 1976. In *Reformed Review* 31, no. 2 (winter 1978): 106-7.

1976

Review of *Christ and the Meaning of Life: A Book of Sermons and Meditations*; *Encounter with Spurgeon: The Ethics of Sex*; and *The Freedom of the Christian Man: Christian Confrontations with the Secular Gods*, by Helmut Thielicke. Grand Rapids: Baker, 1975. In *Reformed Review* 29, no. 2 (winter 1976): 89.

Review of *The Day of the Lion: The Message of Amos*, by J. A. Motyer. Downers Grove, Ill.: InterVarsity, 1974. In *Reformed Review* 29, no. 2 (winter 1976): 89.

Review of *The Dutch in America, 1609-1974*, by Gerald F. DeJong. Boston: Twayne, 1975. In *Reformed Review* 29, no. 2 (winter 1976): 87-88.

Review of *De Kolonie, the Church That God Transplanted: A Story about a Small Branch of the Church Universal Called the Christian Reformed Denomination*, by Marion M. Schoolland. Grand Rapids: Board of Publications of the Christian Reformed Church, 1973-74. In *Reformed Review* 29, no. 2 (winter 1976): 88-89.

1975

Review of *Gautama the Buddha*, by Richard H. Drummond. Grand Rapids: Eerdmans, 1974. In *Reformed Review* 28, no. 2 (winter 1975): 104.

Review of *The History of the Revolution in Its First Phase: The Preparation (till 1789)*, by G. Groen van Prinsterer, lecture eleven, from *Unbelief and Revolution*, ed. and trans. Harry Van Dyke with Donald Morton. Amsterdam: Groen van Prinsterer Fund, 1973. In *Reformed Review* 28, no. 2 (winter 1975): 101.

1971

Review of *The Cure of Souls: An Anthology of P. T. Forsyth's Practical Writings*, ed. Harry Escott. Grand Rapids: Eerdmans, 1971. In *Reformed Review* 24, no. 3 (spring, 1971): 135.

Review of *Handbook of Denominations in the United States: Their History, Doctrines, Organization, Present Status*, 5th ed., by Frank S. Mead. Nashville: Abingdon, 1970. In *Reformed Review* 24, no. 2 (winter 1971): 80.

Review of *A History of Christianity in Japan*, by Richard H. Drummond. Grand Rapids: Eerdmans, 1971. In *Reformed Review* 24, no. 3 (spring 1971): 135-36.

1970

Review of *Evolution and the Christian Faith*, by Bolton Davidheiser. Nutley,

N.J.: Presbyterian and Reformed, 1969. In *Reformed Review* 23, no. 4 (summer 1970): 222-23.

Review of *Well, What Is Teaching: Perspectives on the Teaching-Learning Process; The Subject Is Persons: Psychological Perspectives in Christian Education; What Has God Done Lately: Christian Perspectives for the Church School Teacher;* and *New Ways to Learn: Practical Methods for Christian Teaching*, ed. Dale E. Griffin. St. Louis: Concordia, n.d. In *Reformed Review* 24, no. 1 (autumn 1970): 31.

1969

Review of *Jesus and the Historian*, ed. F. Thomas Trotter. Philadelphia: Westminster, 1968. In *Reformed Review* 22, no. 3 (March 1969): 27.

Review of *A Short Life of Christ*, by Everett F. Harrison. Grand Rapids: Eerdmans, 1968. In *Reformed Review* 22, no. 4 (May 1969): 30.

1967

Review of *Luther's Works*, vol. 30, *The Catholic Epistles*, ed. Jaroslav Pelikan and Walter A. Hansen. St. Louis: Concordia, 1967. In *Reformed Review* 21, no. 1 (September 1967): 45-46.

1966

Review of *Luther's Works*, vol. 8, *Lectures on Genesis*, chapts. 45-50, ed. Jaroslav Pelikan. St. Louis: Concordia, 1966. In *Reformed Review* 20, no. 2 (December 1966): 35-36.

Review of *A Study Guide to Genesis*, by J. Henry Coffer. Durham: Family Life, 1966. In *Reformed Review* 20, no. 2 (December 1966): 36.

1965

Review of *Vocabulary of Communism*, by Lester De Koster. Grand Rapids: Eerdmans, 1964. In *Reformed Review* 18, no. 3 (March 1965): 64.

1964

Review of *Reformation Studies: Essays in Honor of Roland H. Bainton*, ed. Franklin H. Littel. Richmond: John Knox, 1962. In *Reformed Review* 17, no. 4 (June 1964): 55-56.

1963

Review of *The Church and Faith in Mid-America*, by Victor Obenhaus. Philadelphia: Westminster, 1963. In *Reformed Review* 17, no. 2 (December 1963): 52-53.

Review of *Chytraeus on Sacrifice: A Reformation Treatise in Biblical Theology*, by John Warwick Montgomery. St. Louis: Concordia, 1962. In *Reformed Review* 16, no. 3 (March 1963): 43-44.

Review of *Great Moments in Church History*, by Frederick A. Norwood. New York: Abingdon, 1962. In *Reformed Review* 17, no. 1 (September 1963): 53.

Review of *The Reformation and Its Significance for Today*, by Joseph C. McLelland. Philadelphia: Westminster Press, 1962. In *Reformed Review* 17, no. 1 (September 1963): 53-54.

Review of *The Structure of Lutheranism*, vol. 1, by Werner Elert. St. Louis: Concordia, 1962. In *Reformed Review* 17, no. 2 (December 1963): 54-55.

1962

Review of *Even Unto Death: The Heroic Witness of the Sixteenth-Century Anabaptists*, by John C. Wenger. Richmond: John Knox, 1961. In *Reformed Review* 16, no. 1 (September 1962): 61.

Review of *The New Essence of Christianity*, by William Hamilton. New York: Association Press, 1961. In *Reformed Review* 16, no. 1 (September 1962): 54-55.

Review of *The Robe and the Sword: The Methodist Church and the Rise of American Imperialism*, by Kenneth M. MacKenzie. Washington, D.C.: Public Affairs Press, 1961. In *Reformed Review* 16, no. 1 (September 1962): 59.

1961

Review of *Calvin on Scripture and Divine Sovereignty*, by John Murray. Grand Rapids: Baker, 1960. In *Reformed Review* 14, no. 4 (May 1961): 49-50.

Review of *The Calvinistic Concept of Culture*, by Henry R. Van Til. Grand Rapids: Baker, 1959. In *Reformed Review* 14, no. 3 (March 1961): 58.

Review of *The Coming Reformation*, by Geddes MacGregor. Philadelphia: Westminster, 1960. In *Reformed Review* 15, no. 1 (September 1961): 55.

Review of *The Inextinguishable Blaze: Spiritual Renewal and Advance in the Eighteenth Century*, by A. Skevington Wood. Grand Rapids: Eerdmans, 1960. In *Reformed Review* 15, no. 1 (September 1961): 54-55.

1960

Review of *Calvin's Doctrine of the Christian Life*, by Ronald S. Wallace. Grand Rapids: Eerdmans, 1959. In *Reformed Review* 14, no. 1 (September 1960): 56-57.

Review of *Children of the Reformation: The Story of the Christian Reformed Church—Its Origin and Growth*, by Marian M. Schoolland. Grand Rapids: Eerdmans, 1958. In *Reformed Review* 13, no. 3 (March 1960): 51-52.

Review of *Engagement and Marriage: A Sociological, Historical, and Theological Investigation of Engagement and Marriage.* St. Louis: Concordia, 1959. In *Reformed Review* 13, no. 3 (March 1960): 60.

Review of *The Story of the Reformation*, by William Stevenson. Richmond: John Knox, 1959. In *Reformed Review* 13, no. 3 (March 1960): 51.

1958

Review of *A Brief History of the Reformed Church in America*, by Elton M. Eenigenburg. Grand Rapids: Douma, 1958. In *Reformed Review* 12, no. 2 (December 1958): 58-59.

Review of *Jonathan Edwards on Evangelism*, ed. Carl J. C. Wolf. Grand Rapids: Eerdmans, 1958. *Jonathan Edwards, the Preacher*, by Ralph G. Turnbull. Grand Rapids: Baker, 1958. *Jonathan Edwards' Sermon Outlines*, ed. Sheldon B. Quincer. Grand Rapids: Eerdmans, 1958. In *Reformed Review* 12, no. 2 (December 1958): 56-57.

Review of *Man in Nature and in Grace*, by Stuart Barton Babbage. Grand Rapids: Eerdmans, 1957. In *Reformed Review* 11, no. 4 (June 1958): 53.

1957

Review of *Netherlanders in America,* by Henry Lucas. Ann Arbor: University of Michigan Press, 1955. In *Reformed Review* 10, no. 3 (April 1957): 60-63.

1956

Review of *Protestant Christianity Interpreted through Its Development*, by John Dillinger and Claude Welch. New York: Charles Scribner, 1954. In *Reformed Review* 9, no. 3 (April 1956): 50-52.

Notes on Contributors

Harry Boonstra is a 1951 emigrant from Oldehove, the Netherlands. A graduate of Calvin College, he earned an M.A. in English from Northwestern University, an M.L.S. from the University of Chicago, a Ph.D. in English from Loyola University, Chicago, and an M.Div. from Western Theological Seminary. He began his career as Library Director and English Instructor at Trinity Christian College (1964-71), served for two years with Wycliffe Bible Translators as editor and teacher, was Associate Professor of English at Covenant College (1975-77), Director of Libraries at Hope College (1977-84), and concluded as Theological Librarian at Calvin College and Seminary (1989-99). He was Associate Editor of *Reformed Worship* for ten years and, since 2002, Associate Editor of *Origins*. He is the author of *Our School: Calvin College and the Christian Reformed Church* (2001) and co-author of *Pillar Church in the Van Raalte Era* (2003). He has also published articles on a wide variety of topics and has translated books by Abraham Kuyper and Herman Bavinck (forthcoming, 2007).

Timothy L. Brown is the Henry Bast Professor of Preaching at Western Theological Seminary, in Holland, Michigan. A graduate of Hope College, he earned both the M.Div. and D.Min. degrees from WTS. To the task of teaching preaching he brings twenty years of pastoral leadership, most of which was spent at Christ Memorial Church in Holland. During his tenure at Western Theological Seminary, he also jointly held a position at Hope College as the Hinga-Boersma Dean of the Chapel from 2001 to 2003. He is a frequent speaker at pastors' conferences, on college and seminary campuses, and at church renewal events. He also is a frequent contributor to a range of periodicals and publications in pastoral theology, including the newly released "Renovare Spiritual Formation Bible" and "Preaching Today," a preaching resource of *Christianity Today*. He is also the author of a soon-to-be-released book on reading the Bible.

Donald J. Bruggink is a Senior Research Fellow of the Van Raalte Institute and the James A. H. Cornell Professor of Historical Theology Emeritus at Western Theological Seminary, where he taught for thirty-seven years. He holds a Ph.D. from the University of Edinburgh and a D.D. from Central College, his alma mater. Since 1968 he has been the founding General Editor of the Historical Series of the Reformed Church in America, which has now published fifty-six volumes. A minister of the Reformed Church in America, he served the Fordham Manor Reformed Church in the Bronx, and has served the denomination on its Board of Education and Commissions on Theology, Worship, and History. He co-authored, with Carl H. Droppers, *Christ and Architecture* (1965) and *When Faith Takes Form* (1971). The above authorship resulted in honorary membership in the Michigan chapter of the American Institute of Architects and of the Interfaith Forum on Religion, Art, and Architecture.

Eugene Heideman is a graduate of Central College (Philosophy). He earned a B.D. degree from Western Theological Seminary (1954) and a Ph.D. from the National University of Utrecht (1959). A minister of the Reformed Church in America, he began in 1957 as pastor of First Reformed Church of Edmonton, Alberta, then spent ten years as an RCA missionary in the Diocese of Madras, Church of South India (1960-70), six years as Professor of Religion and Bible (five concurrently as Chaplain) at Central College, and six years on the faculty of WTS (five as Academic Dean). He concluded his career on the RCA denominational staff in New York City (1982-94), serving variously as Director of Reformed Church World Service, Secretary for World Mission, Secretary for Program, Secretary for Middle East and Africa, and Stewardship Development, New York City and New Jersey. He is the author of five books, including *Revelation and Reason in Herman Bavinck and Emil Brunner* (1959), *The Reluctant Worker Priest* (1967), *Reformed Bishops and Catholic Elders* (1970), *Our Song of Hope* (with commentary, 1975), and *From Church to Mission: The History of the Arcot Mission, 1851-1987* (2001).

I. John Hesselink is a minister in the Reformed Church in America and the Albertus C. Van Raalte Professor of Systematic Theology Emeritus at Western Theological Seminary (WTS), Holland, Michigan. A *magna cum laude* graduate of Central College (Iowa), he earned a B.D. from WTS, with honors in Greek, preaching, and church history, and a Dr.Theol. degree from the University of Basel, Switzerland, *magna cum laude*. He studied with Emil Brunner in Japan, and Karl Barth was his doctoral advisor. He and his wife, Etta, served as missionaries in Japan under the auspices of the RCA for twenty years, including twelve years teaching historical theology and ecclesiastical Latin at Tokyo Union Seminary. He then returned to WTS as President (twelve years) and Professor of Theology. In 1994 he was elected vice president of General Synod of the RCA and the following year as president (moderator). He is the author of, among others, *On Being Reformed* (1983/88), *Calvin's Concept of the Law* (1992), *Calvin's First Catechism: A Commentary* (1997), and *Calvin on Prayer* (2004), as well as twenty-five book chapters and numerous articles and reviews in over thirty journals and periodicals.

Jeanne M. Jacobson earned a Bachelor's degree in English Literature from Swarthmore College, a Master's degree in Reading Education from SUNY Brockport, and a Ph.D. in Educational Psychology and Statistics from SUNY Albany. After college she taught kindergarten and then became head teacher of three-year-olds at the Yale Child Study Center, under Dr. Milton Senn. Subsequently she ran her own nursery school, worked as a reading teacher in the public schools, and served as a private school principal. When she moved to Michigan in 1987 with her husband, John H. Jacobson Jr., the tenth president of Hope College, she joined the faculty of Western Michigan University in the Department of Educational and Professional Development. In 1996, she became a Senior Research Fellow at the A. C. Van Raalte Institute. Widowed in retirement, she runs an online bookselling business, Palm and Pine Books, Inc. <palmandpinebooks.com>. The author of several books, including an educational textbook, she serves on the board of *The Reading Professor*, and reviews books and articles for several publications.

Lynn Winkels Japinga is Associate Professor of Religion at Hope College, where she teaches American Religious History, Feminist Theology, and Introduction to the Bible. Prior to joining the Hope faculty in 1992, she served for four years as Visiting Professor at Western Theological Seminary. An ordained minister in the RCA, she has held interim pastorates at RCA churches in Union City and North Bergen, New Jersey. A Phi Beta Kappa graduate of Hope College, she earned an M.Div. at Princeton Theological Seminary and a Ph.D. from Union Theological Seminary. She was one of the first two Visiting Research Fellows of the Van Raalte Institute, of which she is currently Scholar-in-Residence. She is the author of *Feminism and Christianity* (1999) and many articles and book chapters. She has served on both the Commission on History and the Commission on Theology of the RCA, was a member of the Board of Trustees of New Brunswick Theological Seminary, and has served on various committees of the denomination.

Earl Wm. Kennedy is a native of Los Angeles, Calif., and a 1953 Phi Beta Kappa graduate of Occidental College (History). He earned a B.D. degree at Fuller Theological Seminary and both a Th.M. degree in New Testament and a Th.D. in Church History from Princeton Theological Seminary. He completed further studies at Georg-August Universität, Göttingen, Free University of Amsterdam, University of Cambridge, Indiana University, and University of Iowa. An ordained minister in the RCA, he taught religion at Northwestern College (Iowa) for thirty-five years, the last few of which he held the Marvin and Jerene DeWitt Professorship in Religion. Currently he is a Senior Research Fellow at the Van Raalte Institute, where he has been engaged in the monumental task of annotating the Minutes of the Classis of Holland of the RCA, 1848-76. He is the author of various scholarly articles, largely in the area of church history, and numerous book reviews. His hobbies include genealogy, coin and stamp collecting, and travel. He and his wife, Cornelia Breugem Kennedy, usually spend three months a year in the Netherlands, her native country.

James C. Kennedy has been Professor of Contemporary History at Vrije Universiteit Amsterdam, the Netherlands, since 2003, but will join the University of Amsterdam on 1 September 2007 as Professor of Dutch History. Previously he was Associate Professor of History and Research Fellow of the Van Raalte Institute at Hope College, a Lilly Postdoctoral Fellow and Lecturer in History at Valparaiso University (1995-97), and an Instructor at Northwestern College (Iowa). A graduate of Georgetown University, he earned an M.A. at Calvin College and a Ph.D. at the University of Iowa. He received a Fulbright Fellowship to the Netherlands in 1991. He is the author of *Nieuw Babylon in aanbouw: Nederland in de jaren* zestig (1995/1997/1999), *Een weloverwogen dood: De opkomst van euthanasie in Nederland* (2002), *The Future of Conservative Protestantism in the Netherlands* (2007), and *A Concise History of the Netherlands* (Cambridge University Press, forthcoming). He is co-author of *Can Hope Endure?: A Religious History of Hope College* (Eerdmans, 2005), and editor-translator of *History of the Low Countries* (Berghahn, 1999/2006). He also is the author of numerous articles in both professional journals and the popular press. His papers, presentations, and media interviews exceed one hundred.

Gregg Mast is President of New Brunswick Theological Seminary (NBTS). A graduate of Hope College, he received an M.Div. degree from NBTS, and both M.Phil. and Ph.D. degrees in Liturgical Studies from Drew University. A minister of the Reformed Church in America, he served as pastor of Second Reformed Church in Irvington, New Jersey, and as senior minister of First Church in Albany, New York; he also has served the RCA as Minister of Social Witness and Worship, as Director of Ministry Services, and as President of General Synod (1999-2000). He has at various times been an adjunct faculty member at NBTS, Westminster Choir College, Siena College, and St. Bernard's

Institute, as well as a guest lecturer at Nkhoma Theological Seminary, Malawi. He is the author or editor of seven books, including *Christian Baptism* (1990), *Our Reformed Church* (1995), *And Grace Shines Through—A Journey of Faith Through the Ordinary Stories of Our Lives* (1997), and *The Eucharistic Service of the Catholic Apostolic Church and Its Influence on Reformed Liturgical Renewals of the Nineteenth Century* (1999).

Jacob E. Nyenhuis is Director of the Van Raalte Institute, Professor of Classics and Provost Emeritus of Hope College, where he earlier served as Dean for the Humanities (1975-78), Dean for Arts and Humanities (1978-84), and Provost (1984-2001). After earning a Ph.D. in Classics at Stanford, he spent thirteen years at Wayne State University, ten as both Director of the Liberal Arts Honors Program and Chair of the Department of Greek and Latin Languages and Literature. He has held visiting professorships at the University of California, Santa Barbara, Ohio State University, and the American School of Classical Studies at Athens, Greece, and was a visiting scholar at Green College, Oxford. He is the editor of two intermediate Latin texts, co-author of *Latin Via Ovid: A First Course* (1977/1982) and *A Dream Fulfilled: The Van Raalte Sculpture in Centennial Park* (1997), and author of *Centennial History of Fourteenth Street Christian Reformed Church, Holland, Michigan, 1902-2002* (2002) and *Myth and the Creative Process: Michael Ayrton and the Myth of Daedalus, the Maze Maker* (2003). He is currently working on an architectural history of Hope College and a family history.

Robert P. Swierenga grew up in a Reformed Dutch enclave in Chicago, which shaped his passion for chronicling the Dutch-American experience in such books as *Dutch Chicago: A History of the Hollanders in the Windy City* (2002). It is no coincidence that his former students and friends entitled the festschrift for his sixty-fifth birthday *The Dutch-American Immigrant Experience* (2000). A 1957 graduate of Calvin College, he received an M.A. in History from Northwestern University (1958) and a Ph.D. in History from the University of Iowa (1965). He taught at Pella Christian High School and Calvin College prior to joining the faculty of Kent State University in 1970. Upon retiring in 1996, he came to Hope College as the Albertus C. Van Raalte Research Professor and Adjunct Professor of History. Among his books are *Pioneers and Profits: Land Speculation on the Iowa Frontier* (1968), *The Forerunners: Dutch Jewry in the North American Diaspora* (1994), *Family Quarrels in the Dutch Reformed Churches in the Nineteenth Century* (with Elton J. Bruins, 1999), *Faith and Family: Dutch Immigration and Settlement in the United States, 1820-1920* (2000), and *Elim: Chicago's Christian School and Life Training Center for the Disabled* (2005), as well as numerous others that he edited.

J. Jeffery Tyler is Associate Professor of Religion and Director of Senior Seminar Program at Hope College. Jeff offers courses at Hope on early, medieval, and Reformation Christianity. He earned an A.B. degree from Hope College, a Master of Divinity degree from Western Theological Seminary, and a Ph.D. in History from the University of Arizona. Jeff has served three terms on the Commission on History of the Reformed Church in America and is a sitting member of the board of the North-American Society for Reformation Research. He was the second person to be named a Towsley Research Scholar at Hope College, is a two-time Fulbright Fellowship winner, and was chosen by the senior class in 2001 to receive the H.O.P.E. Award (Hope's Outstanding Professor-Educator). He is the author of *Lord of the Sacred City: the Episcopus exclusus in Late Medieval and Early Modern Germany*. He is currently working on a book on exile and banishment in the Reformation period.

Dennis N. Voskuil is President and Marvin and Jerene DeWitt Professor of Church History at Western Theological Seminary. An honors graduate of the University of Wisconsin (History), he earned a B.D. at WTS and a Ph.D. in the Study of Religion from Harvard University. A minister of the Reformed Church in America, he served as pastor of Trinity Reformed Church, Kalamazoo (1974-77), and interim senior pastor of Third Reformed Church, Holland (1990-92). He was on the faculty of Hope College (1977-94), the last two as the Evert J. and Hattie E. Blekkink Professor of Religion, succeeding Elton Bruins in this position. He received the H.O.P.E. Award (Hope's Outstanding Professor-Educator) from the senior class in 1981, his first year of eligibility for it. He has served the RCA on the Commission on History and the Theological Commission, as well as various committees and as co-author (with Betty Trahms Voskuil) of study guides for both the History and Theology cycle and the Worship cycle of the "Heritage and Hope" curriculum. He is the author of *Mountains into Goldmines: Robert Schuller and the Gospel of Success* (1983) and numerous articles and reviews.

Larry J. Wagenaar was the founding director of the Joint Archives of Holland, from its inception in 1988 until 2001, with the rank of Associate Professor at Hope College. In 2001 he became the Executive Director of the Historical Society of Michigan, the state's official historical society and oldest cultural organization (1828). A graduate of Hope College, he earned a Master of Arts degree from Kent State University. He is the author of numerous articles in newspapers, professional society newsletters, and professional journals. His publications include *The Historic Michigan Travel Guide* (2007), *Michigan History Directory* (2004, 2006), *Albertus C. Van Raalte: Dutch Leader and American Patriot* (with Jeanne Jacobson and Elton Bruins) and *Sites of Dutch Influence in Western Michigan* (1996). He was co-editor of *The Dutch-American Immigrant Experience: Essays in Honor of Robert P. Swierenga* (2000), *Dutch Enterprise: Alive and Well in North America* (2000), and *The Sesquicentennial of Dutch Immigration: 150 Years of Ethnic Heritage* (1998). He revitalized the Holland Area Historical Society and has held leadership positions in professional organizations at the local, state, and national levels.

CHAPTER 1

Singing God's Songs in a New Land: Congregational Song in the RCA and the CRC[1]

Harry Boonstra

The ancient Hebrews in Babylon asked, "How shall we sing the Lord's song in a strange land?" In a very different context the Reformed folks who emigrated from the Netherlands to America asked a similar question. Once they no longer used their familiar *Psalmboek*, how and what should they sing?

In his book *Singing the Lord's Song,* James Brumm[2] comments in passing that it would be desirable to have a comparative study of congregational song in the Reformed Church in America (RCA) and the Christian Reformed Church (CRC). This essay is a first attempt to engage in such a comparison. When discussing the various song books, I will consider the selection of songs and the texts used, as well as briefly

1 Various names were used for the two denominations. For the early part of the history of the RCA I will use Reformed Protestant Dutch Church (RPDC); in the history after 1867 I will use Reformed Church in America (RCA). The CRC was at one time called the True Dutch Reformed Church, but after 1894 it was the Christian Reformed Church. Since most of my discussion deals with the history after 1900, that is the name I will use.

2 James L. H. Brumm, *Singing the Lord's Song: A History of the English Language Hymnals of the Reformed Church in America* (New Brunswick, N.J.: Historical Society of the Reformed Church in America, 1990). Brumm's study is a very fine source in its own right and also valuable for further research. I often cover the same territory as he does, but with a different intent and focus.

noting the musical styles. I will pay special attention to the reasons for and the process of compiling the various song books, including the role of synodical supervision.[3] The confines of this essay will not allow me to explore fully the history or the social milieu of the churches, nor to explore the psalter-hymnals in full detail. However, the juxtaposition of the history of congregational song in each denomination will reveal both commonality and some striking differences.

The Netherlands Background[4]

One cannot understand the origin of the Reformed Church in America and of the Christian Reformed Church without some basic knowledge about the Reformed Churches in the Netherlands. These churches were born out of the religious controversy and persecution of the Protestant Reformation, and that struggle for theological reform and religious freedom marked much of their subsequent history. Although beginning as a persecuted minority, the Dutch church later grew into a dominant, national church, with many of the attributes of a state church.

It was also a church that underwent numerous theological controversies. The most important among these was the dispute between the strict Calvinists and the Remonstrants (Arminians), which culminated in the famous Synod of Dordrecht in 1618-19 and the publication of the Canons and Church Order of Dort. Later, the church suffered both from orthodox rigidity and from the spiritual virus of the Enlightenment. The reaction of the faithful believers was often to find spiritual nourishment outside the church in various streams of pietism.

A related issue in the church struggle was the singing of hymns. The Reformed churches had largely been exclusively psalm singers. In 1807 the Reformed Church in the Netherlands had officially adopted the introduction of hymns (*Evangelische Gezangen*), even though hymns were considered suspect in various parts of the church as usurpers of the Psalms of David.

3 Since we are dealing with psalters, psalter hymnals, and hymnals, I will be using the designation song books when discussing those various types collectively.

4 There are countless sources in Dutch on the Netherlands Reformed Churches, including multi-volume studies. A brief but reliable book in English translation has been published recently: Karel Blei, *The Netherlands Reformed Church, 1571-2005,* trans. Allan J. Janssen (Grand Rapids: Eerdmans, 2006).

The modernist versus conservative controversies came to a head in 1834. Hendrik de Cock, a pastor in the town of Ulrum in the province of Groningen, had taken the side of those protesting the trends in the church, and was suspended from his ministerial office. His consistory, however, supported his stance, and the congregation separated itself from the national church on 13 October 1834. This date is usually cited as the beginning of the Secession (*Afscheiding*). A number of other pastors and congregations also seceded soon after this date. Two secessionist ministers who need to be noted particularly are Albertus C. Van Raalte and Hendrik P. Scholte, who later became prominent leaders of the emigration to America.

The Story of the Reformed Church in America

The story of the immigration of the Dutch to North America in 1626, the founding of New Amsterdam as a settlement under the control of the mercantile Dutch West Indies Company, and the beginning of the Dutch Reformed Church in 1628 has often been told.[5] Rather than trying to recapture that colorful history here, let me briefly trace a few major facts and issues about the Reformed Protestant Dutch Church (RPDC) that helped to shape the story of congregational song.

The beginning of the first congregation in 1628 was followed by the founding of more congregations in the East—mostly small and struggling. The addition of congregations in the Midwest after the beginning of a new wave of Dutch immigrants in 1846 contributed to the numerical growth and also changed the character of the denomination significantly. Later the denomination continued to spread westward.[6]

The first issue of significance for this study is the long-lasting relationship to the Reformed Church in the Netherlands. By 1628 the dominant "denomination" in the Netherlands was the Reformed Church, and it therefore seemed natural that the congregation formed

[5] There is no full-fledged current history of the RCA. Charles Edward Corwin, *A Manual of the Reformed Church in America, 1628-1922* (New York: Board of Publications of the RCA, 1922) is still worthwhile reading, and Firth Haring Fabend is an excellent recent guide in *Zion on the Hudson: Dutch New York and New Jersey in the Age of Revivals* (New Brunswick, N.J.: Rutgers University Press, 2000). There are many histories of local congregations and other specialized studies.

[6] The number of congregations grew as follows: 1700—25; 1750—68; 1800—120; 1850—296; 1900—654; 1950—763; 2000—939.

in New Amsterdam should be a Reformed congregation and come under the supervision of Classis Amsterdam. The problem was that this natural assumption continued for 163 years. Virtually all the decisions for the RPDC were made in Amsterdam, nearly all the ministers were Dutch, and even when they were not, they had to receive their theological training in the Netherlands.

The most significant Dutch connection for our study was the theological and liturgical connection. The immigrants came to New York and New Jersey with their Dutch Bibles (first published in 1637) and their *Psalmboek*, which also contained the Calvinist creeds of the church and the liturgical forms. These documents thoroughly shaped the life of the RPDC. The heavy hand of the Amsterdam classis, the sermons in Dutch, the adherence to the predestination theology of the Canons of Dort, the practice of singing psalms instead of hymns—these factors were the glue that kept the RPDC together, but also became major sources of controversy and division.

Related to the strong connection with the Dutch church was the issue experienced by all immigrants and immigrant churches—acculturation. Acculturation involves every aspect of an immigrant's life, from the minute to the momentous. A major aspect of acculturation is language, which often becomes a burning issue in the church, sometimes lasting for several generations.[7] *Tercentenary of the City of New York, 1626-1926* mentions somewhat in passing how the "Middle Church" changed to worship in English: "Here it was that preaching in the English language was first introduced in the Dutch Church. During the Colonial days the services were conducted in the language of the Netherlands, but in April 1764, a change was made in response to the request of a large number of those who worshipped in this church. The first sermon in English was preached by the Rev. Dr. Laidlie, a graduate of the University of Edinburgh, who had just been installed as one of the Collegiate Ministers."[8]

This notice does not do justice to the struggle that usually accompanied language change. In Schenectady, for example, the controversy lasted for several decades. The initial motive for the change was to keep (young) people from transferring to the Episcopal church,

7 Still the best study on the language issue is John P. Luidens, "The Americanization of the Dutch Reformed Church" (Ph. D. diss., University of Oklahoma, 1969).

8 *Tercentenary of the City of New York, 1626-1926: A Tribute to the Settlement of Manhattan Island* (New York: Collegiate Reformed Church, 1926), 67.

and resulted in a formal resolution: "To wit . . . that for all coming time so long as there are twenty families in the church, who attend Divine Service in the church of the village, who contribute from time to time with others their just proportion for the maintenance of Divine Service, and who declare that they can be better instructed in the Dutch than in any other tongue, so long, either the forenoon or afternoon service in the church of the village shall be delivered in the Dutch and the other in the English." The percentages for either language changed several times, including a period in which one-half of the service was to be in Dutch and one-half in English! The chapter closes as follows: "When Domine Romeyn's long and honored ministry terminated in 1804, stated Dutch preaching ended in the church of Schenectady."[9]

Another issue that impinges on congregational song is the rise of pietism. The RPDC was very much involved in the Great Awakening. Several years of revival meetings in many congregations occurred in the late 1720s, and this influence made a lasting impression on the church as a whole. As we will see later, there were many reasons for wanting to sing hymns besides psalms, but certainly this desire was strongly stimulated by the singing of revival hymns.

Psalmody and Hymnody

Discussions about congregational singing in Reformed churches usually start with John Calvin. Let me summarize these discussions in one (long) sentence.[10] Calvin taught that Reformed congregations should sing only the 150 Psalms of David (and a few other biblically based texts, such as the Ten Commandments and the Song of Simeon), and he was largely responsible for having these psalms translated into French versified form, and to have tunes (125 for the 150 psalms) composed for these versifications; since most of this work was accomplished in Geneva, this began to be called the Genevan Psalter, with the final and complete edition published in 1562.

Reformed folk in other countries (such as the Netherlands and Hungary) followed suit—they also translated and versified the biblical

9 Jonathan Pearson, *Three Centuries: The History of the First Reformed Church of Schenectady, 1680-1980* (Schenectady, N.Y.: First Reformed Church, 1980), 126, 128.

10 One of the most accessible brief treatments is found in an essay by Emily R. Brink, "The Genevan Psalter," in *Psalter Hymnal Handbook*, eds. Emily R. Brink and Bert Polman (Grand Rapids: CRC Publications, 1998), 28-39.

texts into their language and borrowed the tunes from the Genevan Psalter. In the Dutch Reformed congregations the version that became the most favored (although not the best) was by Peter Datheen, who translated from the French Psalter. There continued, however, to be considerable diversity in the choice of songs among these congregations, until the 1618-19 Synod of Dordrecht (which preferred to limit theological and liturgical options) declared in its Church Order: "Only the 150 Psalms of David, the Ten Commandments, the Lord's Prayer, the Apostles' Creed, the songs of Zacharius, Mary, and Simeon, as versified, shall be sung in the churches. Freedom is given concerning the hymn, 'O Thou Who Art Our Father God' [Ambrose], whether to use it or not. All other hymns are to be excluded from the churches, and in those places where some have already been introduced, they are to be removed by the most suitable means."[11] Thus Datheen's venerable *De CL Psalmen Davids* reigned supreme (with countless reprints) in the next two centuries. The Datheen Psalter is the version that the first RPDC minister, the Reverend Jonas Michaelius, and his parishioners took with them from the Netherlands, and which was used as long as the services were conducted in Dutch.[12]

The Eighteenth Century

The first substitution for the Datheen Psalter came from the New York congregation. Along with preaching in English, they needed to sing the psalms in English as well. In 1763 the Collegiate consistory proposed the publication of an English version of the Dutch Psalter, with the stipulation that the Genevan tunes would be retained. Mr. Francis Hopkinson was hired to do the translation, but the consistory bought the proverbial pig in a poke, since Hopkinson was not proficient in Dutch. Instead of translating from the Dutch, he made imaginative use of the English *New Version of the Psalms of David* by William Tate and Nicholas Brady. Hopkinson simply took Tate and Brady's text and added a word here and there to make the lines fit the Genevan tunes. "As for the music, it consisted mainly of fewer than a dozen of Bourgeois's Genevan tunes, used over and over again, and modified here and there."[13] The book was published in 1767 as *The Psalms of David*

11 Dort Church Order, Art. 69.

12 It was not until 1773 that the Reformed Church in the Netherlands published a new Psalter. This was the Psalter that the emigrants to the Midwest (1846 and after) carried with them.

13 Brumm, 9; see Brumm, 7-10, for further details on this skullduggery.

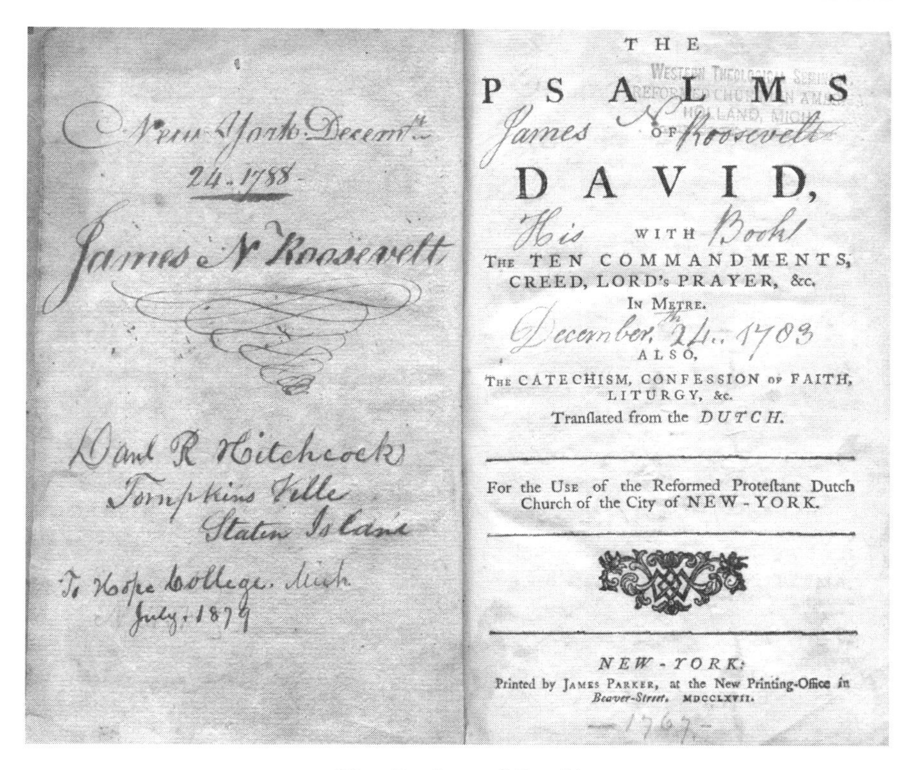
New York Decem^r 24. 1788

James N Roosevelt

Danl R Hitchcock
Tompkins Ville
Staten Island

To Hope College. Mich.
July. 1879

THE

PSALMS

OF

DAVID,

WITH

THE TEN COMMANDMENTS,
CREED, LORD's PRAYER, &c.
IN METRE.

ALSO,

THE CATECHISM, CONFESSION OF FAITH,
LITURGY, &c.
Tranflated from the DUTCH.

For the USE of the Reformed Proteftant Dutch
Church of the City of NEW-YORK.

NEW-YORK:
Printed by JAMES PARKER, at the New Printing-Office in
Beaver-Street. MDCCLXVII.

The Psalms of David

with the Ten Commandments, Creed, Lord's Prayer, &c. In Metre. The preface acknowledges that the book "is greatly indebted to Dr. Brady and Mr. Tate."[14] Sad to say, this first attempt at a combination of an English text with a Genevan-Dutch musical heritage was largely a failure, and another substitution was called for within twenty years.

At the RPDC "provisional" Synod of 1787 a committee was appointed to prepare "another and better version of the Psalms of David, than the congregations as yet possesses in the English language."[15] The committee was fortunate to have as chairman the Reverend John H. Livingston, one of the most illustrious ministers in RPDC history, and the driving force and a major contributor to the new

14 The copy in the Western Theological Seminary Library belonged to James N. Roosevelt.

15 *Acts and Proceedings of the General Synod of the Reformed Protestant Dutch Church in North America*, 1787, 167.

song book. In 1788 the committee was further instructed to choose its psalms from existing psalters, specifically from the Collegiate 1767 *Psalms of David*, Tate and Brady's *New Version*, and Isaac Watts's *The Psalms of David Imitated.*[16]

This borrowing from existing psalters is clearly a departure from the 1767 Collegiate (half-baked) attempt to translate from the Dutch Psalter: there is no reference to either the Datheen Dutch versification or to the Genevan tunes. (*Psalms and Hymns* was published without musical notation, as were the later editions.) One way of telling the difference is the numbering of the psalms. Whereas the Genevan Psalter had 150 numbers (one versification for each psalm), the Livingston psalms were distributed in the English and Scottish mode—Psalm 119, for example, has twenty-two separate versifications. Thus in various ways the RPDC had sloughed off much of its tradition and become "English."[17]

The departure from its tradition went further, however. The synodical mandate continued: "Since it is regarded necessary that some well-composed spiritual hymns be connected as a supplement with this new Psalm-Book, it is ordained that the committee have care over this matter, and print such hymns in connection with the Psalms."[18] Perhaps the fathers of the Dort Church Order did a double take in their celestial home: "What happened to our edict about singing 'only the 150 Psalms of David'?" A similar disapproval was voiced some two hundred years later. When Howard G. Hageman, dean of liturgical studies in the RCA, reviewed the history of RPDC psalmody and hymnody, he was less than enthusiastic when he came to 1787. The clause about adding "well-composed spiritual hymns" made Hageman sigh, "So far as can be determined, this abandonment of the historical Reformed principle of using only the Psalter in worship was carried without a single dissenting vote."[19]

Even though Hageman intimates that the introduction of hymns was done suddenly and cavalierly, certainly the singing of hymns had

16 Brumm (12) notes that 51% of the psalm settings are from Watts. Also see Brumm (12-15) for the implications of borrowing from Watts, who often obscured the distinction between versified psalms and hymns.

17 The collection does recognize and continue its theological heritage by printing the Confessions and Creeds.

18 *Acts and Proceedings*, 1788, 182.

19 Howard G. Hageman, "Three Lectures," in *Remembrance and Hope*, ed. Gregg A. Mast (Grand Rapids: Eerdmans, 1998), 138.

often been contemplated and defended.[20] The arguments for singing hymns are familiar ones that have been raised whenever a church began to turn from exclusive psalm singing to the inclusion of hymns. Let me briefly review them. The most persuasive argument was that congregational singing of only Psalms limits the expression of the Christian faith. Certainly the Psalms are rich and full, and span both the measure of God's dealing with his people and the believers' faith experience as found in the Old Testament. Of course, that final phrase is the crucial one. Why limit our song to Old Testament revelation and experience? Our *theology* is deficient if it does not include revelation about the life, death, and resurrection of Jesus Christ, the pouring out of the Spirit, the life of the early church, the riches of the Epistles, or the visions of Revelation. Our *preaching* and our *prayers* would be flawed without the wealth of grace and the particulars of God's plan displayed in Matthew through Revelation. In the same way, our congregational *singing* will be deficient and flawed if we do not sing "Christ the Lord is risen today."

The committee did its work very promptly. The 1790 General Synod declared that "the Rev. Synod perceive with much satisfaction that the English Psalms, together with the selection of Hymns formerly approved by Synodical decrees, have been happily committed to the press, and are printed and already in use in many congregations."[21] The collection was published as *The Psalms and Hymns . . . of the Reformed Protestant Church in North America*; it contained 272 Psalm versifications and, depending how one counts the various hymns and "hymn sets," 100 or 128 hymn texts. One notable feature of *Psalms and Hymns* is a collection of fifty-two sets ("parts") of hymns to match the fifty-two Lord's Days of the Heidelberg Catechism; for example, for Lord's Day 1 there really are four hymns, one of which has six stanzas, all under "Hymn 1."

It became immediately popular and was adopted by many congregations, especially since the first *Constitution* of the RPDC (1793) specifically limited (English) singing to the "Psalms and Hymns compiled by Professor Livingston." In retrospect one can judge that the book compared well to psalter-hymnals of that time.

[20] The most notable defense was probably Isaac Watts's "Towards the Improvement of Christian Psalmody, by Use of Evangelical Hymns . . .," the essay appended to his 1707 *Hymns and Spiritual Songs*.

[21] *Acts and Proceedings*, 1790, 212.

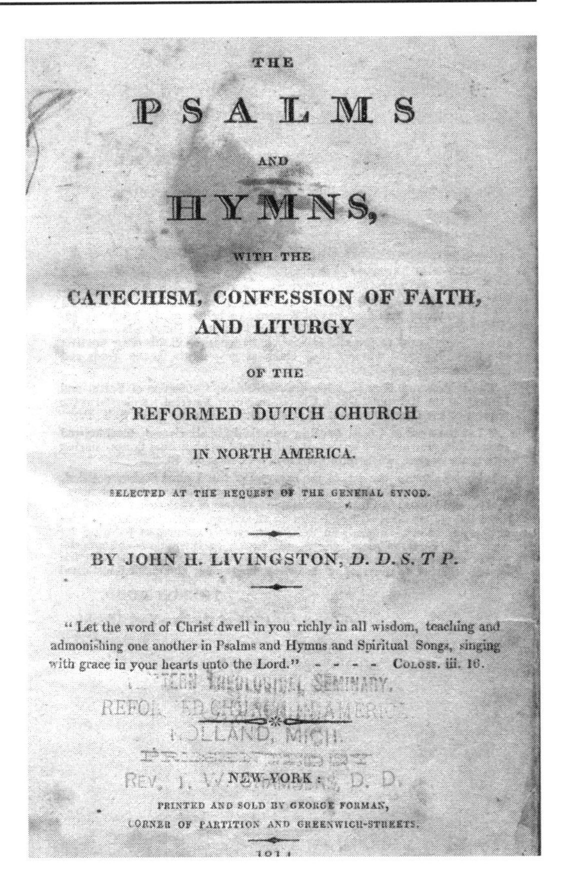

THE

PSALMS

AND

HYMNS,

WITH THE

CATECHISM, CONFESSION OF FAITH,

AND LITURGY

OF THE

REFORMED DUTCH CHURCH

IN NORTH AMERICA.

SELECTED AT THE REQUEST OF THE GENERAL SYNOD.

BY JOHN H. LIVINGSTON, *D. D. S. T P.*

"Let the word of Christ dwell in you richly in all wisdom, teaching and admonishing one another in Psalms and Hymns and Spiritual Songs, singing with grace in your hearts unto the Lord." - - - - COLOSS. iii. 16.

NEW-YORK:

PRINTED AND SOLD BY GEORGE FORMAN,

CORNER OF PARTITION AND GREENWICH-STREETS.

The Psalms and Hymns of 1789

The Nineteenth Century

Livingston is probably one of the few psalter-hymnal editors who was asked to improve and enlarge his collection. This time Synod specified carefully that "it is resolved, that after it is adopted by the committee, it shall be reported to the General Synod and obtain their ultimate approbation before it is published."[22] The book was published in 1814 with the same title, and the new edition contained even more of Watts's psalms than before, and a total of 173 more hymns were added with their own numbering.[23]

22 *Acts and Proceedings*, 1812, 424.

23 A bibliographic trivia item: The clerk of the New York District, in a burst of patriotism, noted that the book was received for deposit in his office, *not* in 1814 A.D., but in "the thirty-eighth year of the Independence of the United States of America."

A similar procedure was followed in 1831, when 150 additional hymns were added. These were published in two formats—one as an addition to the 1814 edition and the other as a separate book. The committee had requested that they mix all the psalms and hymns into one series, divided into categories by subject, but Synod did not acquiesce. In 1848 *Psalms and Hymns* again became heavier as another 150 hymns were added, totaling 788 hymns and twenty-one doxologies. Now the committee finally merged all the songs into one numerical sequence, although the Psalms remained as a separate collection.

The final edition of *Psalms and Hymns* appeared in 1866, with music, but the tunes were added in a novel arrangement—Dutch door style. The top half of the book, titled *The Book of Praise,* was a collection of 416 tunes, arranged arbitrarily, with the bottom half of the book containing the psalms and hymns texts. As the preface boasts, "the musical page is wholly independent of the poetic, although both are bound in the same cover. This secures the advantage of bringing *any* tunes and words together before the eye."

Synod 1868 had commissioned Professor John B. Thompson (a very knowledgeable hymnologist) to chair a committee to judge the quality of various song books, and in 1869 they presented an unusually fine collection, *Hymns of the Church*. The preface credits Dr. Zachary Eddy for his unstinted help; according to Hageman, he presented the committee with a nearly finished product. The hymnal has an Anglican slant, both in the choice and the arrangement of hymns. Although Hageman has some reservations about the *process* of publishing *Hymns of the Church*, he gives the book very high praise.[24] Brumm also appreciates the hymnal, but finds it much too dependent on the British *Hymns, Ancient and Modern*, and he concludes that it "approaches plagiarism."[25]

Before continuing with the history of song books intended and approved mainly for Sunday worship, we must note several other

[24] Hageman, 139-40.

[25] See Brumm, 22-25. It is true that the book has some unusual overlaps with *Hymns, Ancient and Modern*, ones not usually found in Reformed song books. These include a hymn on the circumcision of Christ (121), "a prayer for those at sea" (397), and a Whitsuntide borrowing (228). There are, however, countless hymns *not* found in *Hymns, Ancient and Modern*. Since in the nineteenth century hymns were borrowed willy-nilly from existing hymnals, without worrying about permission and copyright issues, it seems to me that *Hymns for the Church* is not particularly guilty here. (Ethicists would call this the everybody-does-it defense!)

hymnals. In 1843 General Synod approved the publication of *Sabbath Schools and Social Hymns*, a brand new collection of some three hundred hymns. Charles Wesley was strongly represented in this hymnal, which did not differ substantially from other popular hymnals of the time. The *Fulton Street Hymn Book* was adopted in 1862, with yet another origin. One of the New York Collegiate churches conducted the Fulton Street prayer meetings and produced its own collection of hymns. General Synod 1868 received a request by the South Classis of Long Island to publish "two hundred and fifty new hymns and chants"; Synod approved these, apparently sight unseen. Brumm titles his fourth chapter "Rubber-Stamping Hymnals and Failure of Control." One example of such a rubber-stamping was *Hymns of Worship and Service* (1910), and that process continued with more song books than need to be listed here. This is not to say that Synods were happy with the situation. When appraising the hymnals used in Sunday Schools, Synod declared that "the diversity of usage is deplorable."[26] They were especially concerned because many of these Sunday School hymnals were adopted for congregational worship. Hageman no doubt agreed with this assessment, when some seventy years later he complained about the "hymnological chaos, from which, more than a century later, we still suffer."[27] Brumm also notes that the RCA "seems to have lost its way somewhere. . . . This sort of incorrect response to the denominational situation would have dire consequences for the church's hymnody over the next century."[28]

The waves of new hymnals continued, however.[29] In 1890 the last book of the century that was proposed and accepted by Synod was *The Church Hymnary*. Edited by Edwin A. Bedell, an elder in the RCA, the book received high praise ("superior to any collection now extant") and was approved. Perhaps the fact that this collection of 994 hymns was "prepared and published without asking the General Synod to assume any pecuniary responsibility" helped to sway Synod's mind. The book

26 *Acts and Proceedings*, 1899, 424.

27 Hageman, 139.

28 Brumm, 25.

29 In 1888 a synodical discussion took place which acknowledged that "our Holland brethren [the Western churches] are looking anxiously for a book adapted to the peculiar emergencies of their people in passing over from the Dutch Psalmody to the English service . . ." (*Acts and Proceedings*, 1888, 600). It is doubtful if one of the hymnals proposed by the Publications Committee that year, *The Carmina Sanctorum*, would be what the Holland brethren were looking for!

also contains an increasingly popular collection of biblical psalms for responsive reading. Although Synod lamented the presence of too many hymn books in the denomination, and acknowledged the lack of denominational involvement in producing their own song books, the practice continued. As late as 1938 the Synod approved four additional "outside" hymnals.

The Twentieth Century

A very different approach was used in connection with two potential church unions. The RCA and the Reformed Church in the United States (German Reformed) had had an on-and-off courtship for many years.[30] A new rapprochement was begun in 1913, but was completely called off in 1927. A joint committee was formed to explore the creation of a joint hymnal, and the finished product was approved by the Synods of both denominations in 1917, and finally published as *The Reformed Church Hymnal* in 1920.

The range of authors and composers was considerably wider than that found in hymnals in RCA congregations in previous years. The German tradition was now represented by authors such as Rinkart, Meinhold, and von Zinzendorff. Watts and Wesley were still the most numerous, with a rather small selection of Gospel songs. The hymns are arranged partly in a Trinitarian sequence, and partly by miscellaneous subject, including two Temperance songs (for example, no. 613, "Bondage and Death the Cup Contains"). The creedal and liturgical material is very limited, although one certainly would have expected a German and Dutch Reformed joint effort to include the Heidelberg Catechism.

The Hymnbook arose partly from the discussions about union between the RCA and the United Presbyterian Church in the late 1940s. Again, this union did not take place. However, the two denominations had also begun a discussion about producing a joint hymnal. Soon three other Presbyterians denominations joined and *The Hymnbook* was published in 1955. The book's preface (as all hymn book prefaces are wont to) extols the uniqueness and timeliness of the hymn selection: "Nor has the process been merely the sifting of the old and accepted. A

[30] See Gregg Mast, "A Decade of Hope and Despair" (below, pp. 163-80), for a more complete history of efforts to unite the RCA and the German Reformed Church in the nineteenth century, as well as an analysis of the causes for their failure. *Ed.*

number of new hymns and tunes have been included, wrought out of the Christian faith and devotion of our own time." Norman Kansfield notes that "this collection . . . made a serious attempt to reintroduce the psalm tradition of Geneva, both words and music. Six different Genevan tunes are employed with ten texts."[31] Others, no doubt, would have wished for a more serious attempt. Although Brumm acknowledges that the effort on the part of the RCA to be genuinely involved in the production of a new hymn book was laudatory, and that the book was rather well accepted in the RCA, he is not sanguine about its merits. "Was it a great hymnal? The answer, alas, is probably not." He finds that the selections are traditional and safe, with hardly any Reformed-Presbyterian distinctiveness. Moreover, "there are no tunes, and only one hymn in the book written within the 35 years preceding its publication."[32]

The latest venture of the RCA to produce an independent song book began in 1979.[33] Synod appointed a study committee to explore the feasibility of a new hymnal. Part of the motivation for a new hymnal arose from the dissatisfaction with *The Hymnbook* of 1955, which was considered completely outdated. Moreover, the RCA had not produced an independent hymnal for over one hundred years. Although the initial committee had no illusions that Synod could or would *require* use of a denominational hymnal, it did believe that such a book could serve as a unifying factor in the RCA.

One of the first actions was the appointment of an outside editor, the eminent British authority in hymnology, Erik Routley, who had a wide experience in the production of hymn books. He was able to direct and guide the project and be its major compiler until his death in 1982. The book was published in 1985, under the title *Rejoice in the Lord: A Hymn Companion to the Scriptures*.

The subtitle is significant, since it hints at the order and sequence of the hymns (and psalms). The sequence roughly follows the canonical Scriptures, with a Trinitarian sequence superimposed on the canonical: songs of creation and nature come in part one, "The God of Abraham

31 Norman Kansfield, "The Pastoral Hymnologist: The Contribution of Howard G. Hageman to the Hymnology of the Reformed Church in America," in *Pulpit, Table and Song: Essays in Honor of Howard Hageman*, ed. Heather Murray Elkins (Lanham, Md.: Scarecrow Press, 1996), 247.

32 Brumm, 39.

33 Brumm's treatment is again very helpful for many more details than I cover here.

Praise"; about Jesus Christ in part two, "Behold the Lamb of God"; about the work of the Holy Spirit in part three, "The Spirit of Truth, the Spirit of Power"; and songs of the parousia and of the new heaven and earth in part four, "The Hope of Glory." This order (perhaps unique?) is meaningful, although the committee had to do some stretching and squeezing to make it all work. For example, hymns of "Marriage, Family, and Friends" are wedged into the "Hope of Glory" section. The Psalms are represented with fifty-four selections (some with more than one versification; some partial psalms), "with more than twenty-five tunes from the Genevan Psalter."[34]

Rejoice in the Lord exhibits careful choosing from several ecclesiastical and musical traditions; in some ways one can judge it as an example of the "Best of Christian Hymns," which should appeal to the denomination and beyond. The fact that the committee was sensitive to the problem of exclusive language also merits approbation. It is a fine hymnal that filled a need in the RCA, which had been subject for too many years to lowest common denominator hymnals, with virtually no Reformed distinctiveness.

The dream of the committee, however, that the new hymnal would serve as a unifying ingredient in the RCA[35] was not reached—mainly because of what was *not* in the book. Although many in the RCA were very fond of nineteenth-century gospel hymns, hardly any of these are represented in *Rejoice*. Moreover, in the 1980s the RCA was intent on becoming a more culturally and racially diverse denomination, but the annual reports to Synod make no mention of the hymnal trying to contribute to this effort. The hymnal contains one African American spiritual, and the emerging Praise and Worship movement (which, incidentally, produced many Scripture songs) was ignored.

Since *Rejoice* did not capture the interest of most RCA congregations, the diversity and multiplicity of hymnals continued. In the past several decades this has proliferated even more with the explosion of the Praise and Worship tradition and with computerized access and computerized projection (called off-the-wall ditties by its detractors) of virtually any hymn (and psalm).

The conclusion of the RCA song book story comes with the 2001 publication of *Sing! A New Creation*. That story is told in the coda at the end of this essay.

[34] Erik Routley, ed., introduction to *Rejoice in the Lord: A Hymn Companion to the Scriptures* (Grand Rapids: Eerdmans, 1985).

[35] *Acts and Proceedings*, 1978, 165.

A CHRONOLOGY OF RCA APPROVED SONG BOOKS

1628 Dutch (Genevan) *Psalmen Davids*, Datheen versification; also contains several canticles (and liturgy); taken to New Amsterdam by Rev. Michaelius and his congregation

1767 *The Psalms of David*... (with liturgy), published by the Collegiate Church in New York; most of the tunes were Genevan

1789 *The Psalms and Hymns of the Reformed Protestant Dutch Church in North America*; edited by John H. Livingston; psalms chosen from existing English psalters; also one hundred hymns

1814 Revision by Livingston of 1789 *Psalms and Hymns* . . .; more psalms *à la* Watts; added 172 hymns as separate collection

1831 Added 150 hymns to 1789 and 1814 *Psalms and Hymns*, as separate collection

1843 *Sabbath School and Social Hymns*; contained 331 hymns; to control use of unauthorized hymns in the denomination

1848 Added 150 hymns to the 1789, 1814, and 1831 *Psalms and Hymns*; new hymns not a separate collection, but integrated with the previous collections, arranged by subject

1862 *Fulton Street Hymn Book*; published by an independent committee; endorsed by General Synod; 326 hymns

1866 *Book of Praise: Psalms and Hymns of the Church*; same as 1848, but with divided page, music on top, text below

1869 *Hymns of the Church*; about 350 hymns and some psalms; edited by Zachary Eddy

1880 *Christian Praise*; to include "at least the Catechism and the Sacramental forms"

1889 *Christian Church Hymnary*, an existing hymnal endorsed by General Synod

1910 *Hymns of Worship and Service*; an existing hymnal provisionally endorsed by General Synod

1919 *Hymnal of the Reformed Church*; published in conjunction with the RCUS; 646 hymns; no Standards

1938 *The Hymnal; Hymns for the Living Age; The Interchurch Hymnal; The New Church Hymnal*—all existing hymnals

1939 *Christian Worship and Praise*, an existing hymnal endorsed by Synod

1955 *The Hymnbook*; published jointly with four Presbyterian denominations

1985 *Rejoice in the Lord*; arranged in biblical sequence

2001 *Sing! A New Creation*; published jointly with the CRC

The Story of the Christian Reformed Church

The CRC story begins with the Reverend Albertus Christiaan Van Raalte and his followers coming to America in 1846. In 1849 the RCA invited the immigrants to join their fellowship, and the following year the immigrant congregations joined the RCA as a separate Classis of Holland. The union of 1850, however, was soon challenged. Critics among the new immigrants charged that the RCA was not sufficiently known, and that the immigrant congregations had not been consulted about joining the denomination.[36] Moreover, these critics also found practices and teachings in the RCA that could not pass theological muster. The criticism that concerns us most here was the accusation that the RCA had published "a collection of eight hundred hymns, introduced contrary to the church order"[37]—no doubt a reference to the Church Order of Dort. This was not merely an "alleged" abuse, but probably a reference to the *Psalms and Hymns* of 1848.

In 1857 the issue came to a head. At its 8 April 1857 meeting, the RCA Classis of Holland received seven letters of separation, and soon a new denomination was formed.[38] The early years of the new denomination were extremely difficult. The Reverend Koene Van Den Bosch was the only ordained minister until 1863. Later, several other ministers also joined but then left the CRC. Some congregations followed the same pattern. Internal dissension within several congregations, as well as disagreements about doctrine and church polity further weakened the church. The language controversy was also strong, especially since new immigrants continued to join the denomination. Under the Latin saying *Luctor et Emergo* (I struggle and escape), historian Henry Beets considered the years 1857-79 as the period of struggle (chapter 6), followed by a period of emergence and stability from 1880 to 1890 (chapter 7).[39]

[36] For a recent, detailed study of this period, see Robert P. Swierenga and Elton J. Bruins, *Family Quarrels in the Dutch Reformed Churches of the Nineteenth Century* (Grand Rapids: Eerdmans, 1999).

[37] "Documents of Secession of the Graafschap Church, 7 April 1857," in *Classis Holland Minutes, 1848-1858* (Grand Rapids: Eerdmans, 1950), 242.

[38] "Documents of Secession," in *Classis Holland Minutes, 1848-1858* (Grand Rapids: Eerdmans, 1950), 240-43.

[39] Henry Beets, *De Christelijke Gereformeerde Kerk in Noord Amerika: Zestig Jaren van Strijd en Zegen* (Grand Rapids: Grand Rapids Printing, 1918), 121 and 171.

After 1900 the church continued to expand, both geographically and numerically,[40] and founded and supported many educational institutions, although it continued in various ways to be isolated from the larger American church world. In the 1920s it especially experienced great theological disagreement. Since 1950 the CRC has flourished in numerous ways, and also has begun to scrutinize and change many worship patterns.

The English Psalter 1912, 1914

We now turn to the psalter-hymnals of the CRC, which are not nearly as numerous and diverse as in the RCA. The CRC began its musical repertoire with its heritage of the Dutch *Psalmboek* of 1773, and as long as worship services were held in Dutch, this Psalter was used and loved. However, as English became more prominent in the worship services, the singing of English-language psalms also became essential. The most promising direction for providing psalms in English was the invitation from eight other Reformed and Presbyterian denominations to participate in the "Joint Committee on a Uniform Version of the Psalms in Meter." Joining in 1905, the CRC was represented most frequently by the Reverend Henry Beets.[41] The *Psalter* was published in 1912 by the United Presbyterian Church of North America and adopted by the CRC in 1914.[42]

Joining these denominations was not only a major linguistic and ecumenical step for the CRC, but also a crucial step and a major departure in congregational singing. Two related issues come to the fore here. First, the psalm tunes were derived largely from English, Scottish, and American traditions, many of which were not familiar to the CRC. This change also meant that the long tradition of singing Genevan tunes (usually known as "the Dutch Psalms") was virtually lost, since the new Psalter contained only four Genevan tunes.

The other major change was that the numbering of the metrical psalms no longer corresponded to the numbering of the Psalms in

40 The number of congregations was as follows: 1857–4; 1900–145; 1950–341; 2000–826.

41 The Calvin Heritage Hall Archives has several volumes of the committee's proposed versifications ("Confidential Proofs"), with handwritten notes by Beets.

42 The CRC edition was published by Eerdmans, complete with the "Doctrinal Standards and Liturgy." The *Psalter* is still in print today, since it continues to be used by the Netherlands Reformed Church and the Protestant Reformed Churches.

Scripture; Psalm 119, for example, was distributed over numbers 322-42, each with a different tune (and perhaps a different author; one cannot be sure of the latter, since the versifiers' names are not listed). The number of versifications for each Psalm is often puzzling. Obviously the length of the original Psalm is a major reason for multiple renditions, but not the only reason; the two verses of Psalm 117 received four renditions, whereas the ten verses of Psalm 75 had only one. And why nine versifications for the twenty-two verses of Psalm 25? No doubt the more popular psalms tended to receive more versifications and the less read ones (such as the many imprecatory psalms) fewer. The imprecatory versifications also tended to soften the sometimes harsh judgments to be meted out to the "enemies." The King James translation of Psalm 137:7 reads, "Happy shall he be that taketh and dasheth thy little ones against the stones." The Psalter version (no. 379) reads, "How happy he who shall repay / The bitter hatred of her foe."

This is not the place to critique the versifications in detail. Anyone who has attempted to transform a biblical psalm (even from an English translation) into a poem with rhyme and meter realizes the tremendous challenge, and no versification or collection of versifications is completely satisfactory. In the 1912 *Psalter* this challenge is highlighted when one compares the different versifications of the same Psalm.

Let me briefly comment on Psalm 22 as one example that exhibits some of these issues. Number 47 covers verses 1-23 in eleven stanzas, and has the title, "The Cross of Calvary." The versification is satisfactory, although the bulls of Bashan, the dogs, lions, and wild oxen of Scripture have been lumped together as "beasts of prey." Number 48 covers verses 22-31 in eight stanzas, of which stanzas 5-8 are repeated in number 49, but with a different tune. The designation "the Lord of lords and King of kings" is imported from the New Testament. Number 50, titled "The Dominion of Jesus Christ," paraphrases selected verses from verses 22-31, including the line "A faithful Church shall serve Him." Number 51, "Witness-Bearing and Grateful Praise," is better known in (older) CRC circles as "Amid the Thronging Worshipers," as it was carried over into the 1934, 1959, and 1987 *Psalter Hymnals*. Here "Jehovah" and "the Lord" are not (obviously) identified with Jesus Christ.

Hymns: Threat or Blessing?

Soon after 1857 there were occasional voices for the singing of hymns, and these voices became even louder in the twentieth century. Positing these arguments only once, however, was hardly sufficient. In true CRC style the matter was argued, thrashed out, disputed time and again; it was discussed in the denominational magazines, *De Wachter* and the *Banner;* it was submitted to several committees; it was thoroughly reviewed at various Synods.[43]

The question of singing hymns came to Synod early in the history of the denomination, because a number of German Reformed congregations had joined the CRC as Classis Ost Friesland. The German Reformed regularly sang hymns (in German) and had been promised that they could continue to do so "for the time being." Synod 1884 agreed that "one cannot make Germans into Dutchmen, especially when it comes to singing," but there was a concern that this freedom would be used by the Dutch-speaking congregations to lobby for hymns.[44] In addition, the congregations from Hackensack, New Jersey (which had separated from the RCA), joined the CRC in 1890. These churches had continued to use an edition of the *Psalms and Hymns* of the RCA when they were independent, and also when they joined the CRC.

The issue remained unresolved, and in 1908 and 1918 the question arose again, as Classis Hackensack and Classis Ost Friesland again requested continued hymn singing, while others warned that such permission represented a Trojan horse of danger for the CRC. A committee was appointed and reported in 1922 that since these groups had been promised that they could retain their hymn singing, this promise was to be retained—although the rest of the denomination was forbidden to sing hymns.

The Psalter Hymnal 1934

The development of the hymn issue in the next few years is worth discussing in some detail, since it constitutes a major shift in the church's musical tradition and habits. In 1926 Synod tried to reassert the psalms-only tradition by ordering explicitly that the reprinting of the Psalter be without hymns. Nonetheless, the issue would not go away. Synod 1928 faced various overtures—three favoring hymns, three opposing them, and four asking for a study committee. The Committee on Liturgics favored the pro-hymns voices and recommended that work should be begun immediately in the choosing of hymns. "After lengthy

43 Henry Beets (editor of the *Banner* for many years) wrote four articles that fairly represented the spectrum of views; see *Banner*, Oct. 14–Nov. 4, 1927.

44 *Acts of Synod of the Christian Reformed Church*, 1884, art. 12.

discussion of this matter, a *substitute motion* is offered." This motion agreed that "Synod does, from the point of view of principle, not object to the introduction of hymns," but did favor a study committee; this committee was also instructed "that should a sufficient number of suitable hymns be found, the Committee shall not only submit the same to the Synod of 1930, but shall also publish its report six months in advance of that Synod, together with the text of the hymns. . . ."[45] This committee obviously worked hard and came to the following Synod with their task completed. The rationale and arguments for hymn singing were written in Dutch in Synod's *Agenda*, but a separate English translation, "Report on the Hymn Question and the Text of [197] Approved Hymns," was distributed at Synod in June 1930.[46]

The 1930 *Agenda* still presented one overture to reject any hymns by "social Gospel" authors, and two overtures that made a last-ditch attempt to halt the introduction of hymns, but the tide had turned. Synod accepted the Committee's report and the selected hymns, but then charged the committee to reduce the number of hymns, without citing a reason.

The committee complied and reduced the number to 138. Synod eliminated thirteen more hymns (understandably, a hymn for the nation with the title "God, the All-Terrible," and less understandably, "Now Thank We All Our God"). The authors of the hymns were generally those represented in most standard hymn books of the time. Represented by three or more titles are: Horatius Bonar, William Cowper, Fannie Crosby, Frances Havergal, James Montgomery, John Newton, Isaac Watts, and Charles Wesley. Among the composers/arrangers, Lowell Thomas tops everyone with thirty-five tunes.[47] The final step in the process was a change in the Church Order, article 69, which now reads in part, "In the churches . . . the collection of Hymns for Church use, approved and adopted by Synod, shall also be sung. However, while

[45] *Acts of Synod*, 1928, 46-48.

[46] The report assures Synod that the committee has not allowed anything "trashy and thin" or anything "containing pernicious doctrine" into the list of hymns ("Report on the Hymn Question," 4, 26).

[47] For extensive discussion of the music, see Bert Polman, "Church Music and Liturgy in the Christian Reformed Church" (Ph. D. diss., University of Minnesota, 1980, 125-36). Polman especially laments the tradition of singing the Dutch Psalms "in a very slow tempo and in iso-rhythm," and the *Psalter Hymnal*'s perpetuation of that tradition.

the singing of the Psalms in divine services is a requirement, the use of the approved Hymns is left to the freedom of the Churches."[48]

Another issue that needs at least brief discussion is the treatment of the Psalms. Synod 1930 had expressed some dissatisfaction with the versifications of the 1912/14 Psalter and instructed the committee to substitute "new metrical versions of not fewer than twenty-five and not more than fifty Psalms which can be sung to the best tunes of our Dutch Psalter."[49] The Committee chose thirty-five psalms to be rendered in new versifications and to be accompanied by Genevan tunes (called "chorales"). It is not clear what determined the choice of psalms, but certainly many of these psalms were the more favored ones from the Dutch *Psalmboek*, such as Psalms 42, 65, 68, 84, 121, and 150. Psalm 119 was represented by ten selected stanzas. Again, the task of rhyming and metering the biblical text was thorny, and made even more complex in that often the paraphrasers also tried to integrate a versification from the 1912/14 *Psalter*. The texts therefore left much to be desired. The second edition of the *Psalter Hymnal* (1959) retained virtually all of these paraphrases, but the 1987 edition eliminated most. Apart from the substitutions of these Genevan Psalms, changes were minimal, since nearly all of the Psalms were taken over from the 1912/14 *Psalter*.

The official publication date of the CRC's first *Psalter Hymnal* is 1934, although the first edition did not come off the press until January 1935, with the Psalms assigned to 327 versifications, followed by 141 hymns. This edition of twenty thousand copies was sold by the end of February, and a second printing of twenty thousand was nearly sold by the end of the year.

This "red *Psalter*" was eventually used in all CRC congregations and was a major influence in weaning the churches from the Dutch psalms, and introducing them to American church music. Many members also would have been happy to continue using them for the rest of their lives (and their children's lives), but such is not the destiny of psalters and hymnals. Succeeding printings made a number of minor changes, but the church was ready for a major change.

The Centennial Psalter Hymnal 1959

The 1951 Synod adopted an overture to improve the 1934 *Psalter Hymnal*. The committee appointed was given two tasks: "to set forth

48 *Acts of Synod*, 1932, 135.
49 *Acts of Synod*, 1930, 59.

concretely the principles of good music for our churches, and in harmony therewith to revise and improve our Psalter-Hymnal."[50]

In its 1953 Report to Synod the committee provided "principles of good music"; a tentative listing of which psalms and hymns were to be retained, deleted, or changed; and the fond hope that their task would be completed by 1955. Much in the "Principles and Its Implications" statement is beyond dispute and praiseworthy. Implications 6-9, however, suppose that worship music can always be clearly separated from secular music, and number 8 now seems Eurocentric: "Such devices as extreme syncopation and extreme chromatics (although on occasion these may be of value for special text settings) should generally be avoided."

One of the most difficult issues facing the committee was the question of the Genevan tunes.[51] The committee was cognizant of the fact that in its Dutch guise the tunes (especially the rhythms) had changed drastically from the original French version. However, the committee chose to be conservative. "We must avoid the sort of sophistication which would deny that the Dutch version of these tunes is in itself a worthy art form." They also maintained the texts of many of the "Genevan" Psalms produced for 1934.[52]

In terms of selection and changes the intent was certainly not to produce a brand new *Psalter Hymnal*—rather the intent was to produce a revision. In some cases, however, the revision was thorough: for example, Psalm 4 (all eleven stanzas) was completely rewritten by Henry Zylstra, as were a number of other Psalms. One feature of the Psalms that was maintained is the multiple versifications for the Psalms; the 150 Psalms have 310 versifications.

Also remarkable is the reporting to the church. Each year the committee sent copies of its report to each congregation and to Synod, and the reports were thorough. For example, in 1954 a tabulation of nearly thirty pages covers the proposed changes for each psalm;[53] many of the same psalms were listed again the next year to reflect the changes recommended by Synod, church members, or by the committee itself.[54] So also with the hymns. The complete texts of all new hymns were

50 *Acts of Synod*, 1951, 47.

51 *Acts of Synod*, 1954, 278-81.

52 For this question and other musical analysis, see Bert Polman, "Church Music and Liturgy," 142-53.

53 *Acts of Synod*, 1954, 282-309.

54 *Acts of Synod*, 1955, 205-14.

included in the report. Notable among these are three patriotic hymns (none in 1934), five children's hymns, and a wedding hymn.

The number of hymn authors is relatively small, and most of them are represented by only one hymn. Those who have more than two hymns are Horatius Bonar, Francis Havergal, Reginald Heber, James Montgomery, John Mason Neale, John Newton, Isaac Watts, Charles Wesley, and Christopher Wordsworth.

Synod continued its scrutiny until the end. Although final approval to all the material was granted in 1956, Synod still did some more tinkering, such as changing "are" to "art," and "He suffered all for thee" to "He offers all to thee."[55] The final approval included the mandate to prepare the *Psalter Hymnal* for publication, and to have it finished by 1957. That year was the centennial for the CRC, and the book was therefore to be called the "Centennial Edition." (It was familiarly called the "blue *Psalter Hymnal*.") Perhaps even the committee did not fully realize the impossibility of this deadline; the book did not roll off the presses until 1959.

The Psalter Hymnal 1987

At one time the expectation was that any major hymnbook needed revision about every twenty years. The CRC's Psalter Hymnals fit that time line rather closely. The 1977 Synod appointed a new committee to "revise and improve" the 1959 version. In addition to the usual reasons for such a revision (new hymns available, shortcomings and lacunae in the old version, updating of language), Synod added another reason: "the proliferation of hymnals containing songs which are un-Reformed in doctrine, lacking in musical quality now being used in many of our churches."[56] The charge to the committee included revision of the 1959 "Principles," and it is noteworthy how seriously the committee took this task, producing many drafts in successive years. The complete book contained the Psalms, eighty-six Bible songs, and 405 hymns.

The committee made many changes, especially in the Psalms section. The most significant change was a return to the Genevan Psalter method of one complete versification for each psalm (giving Psalm 119 twenty-two stanzas—much shorter than the eighty-eight stanzas in the 1773 Dutch version). Since this policy would mean the loss of many favorite psalm versifications and tunes, the committee mitigated this decision by reprinting a number of old versifications (as

[55] *Acts of Synod*, 1956, 49.
[56] *Acts of Synod*, 1977, 139.

well as other alternate ones) in the "Bible Songs" and "Hymns" sections. The question of the continued use of the Genevan tunes arose again as well. Whereas the 1959 edition had included thirty-nine, the new Psalter used thirty-five, again with new versifications. Perhaps even more important, the tunes were restored to their original rhythms—a change that was especially bothersome to many older church members.

A new feature introduced by the committee was the planning of workshops for both music and texts, giving opportunity to musicians and poets to work intensively on new psalm versifications and hymns and to benefit from mutual criticism. The committee was also very aware of the need to educate congregations about the new book, *while it was being prepared.* Booklets with sample songs were presented for congregational use, the committee offered lectures and demonstrations to congregations, and the *Banner*, the denominational magazine, regularly carried articles. The official reporting to successive Synods was also carried out diligently; Synod actually sang through many of the new songs. Such planning and reporting was greatly facilitated by the appointment of one of the committee members, Emily Brink, as full-time editor.

The feature of the new hymnal that was in some ways the most noteworthy (and controversial) was the change in the language of existing hymns. One change concerned archaic language. The *thee*s, *thou*s, and *thine*s referring to both God and persons were virtually all eliminated. More contemporary language and modern sensibilities were substituted for obsolete words and expressions. A few examples will demonstrate this feature. In "At the Name of Jesus" there is a change from "your captain" to "your Savior," and Jesus' return is not "With his angel train" but "o'er the earth to reign." "O for a Thousand Tongues" changes "Hear Him, ye deaf; His praise ye dumb" to "Hear him, you deaf; you voiceless ones." In "Not What My Hands Have Done" the line "Thy grace alone O God/To me can pardon speak" becomes "Your voice alone, O Lord/can speak to me of grace," and "Can this sore bondage break" now reads "can all my sins erase." The other change concerned exclusive language, that is, the use of masculine nouns and pronouns when both genders are intended. Beginning with the very first line in the *Psalter Hymnal*, "That man is blest" becomes "How blest are they." The telltale *alt.* at the bottom of the page is a signal that indicates changes in the text, and there are many such pages.[57]

[57] Of course, making changes in existing hymns is a respected (if not honorable) tradition, seen in virtually all hymnals. The *Psalter Hymnal* is more open about it by signaling the changes with *alt.*

The committee was also sensitive to the ethnic change in the denomination. Instead of being nearly all Dutch-American and Dutch-Canadian, the church was beginning to enfold those of other ethnic extractions, including Native-American, African-American, Spanish-speaking, Korean, and others. The committee invited representatives from these groups to consult with the committee, and a number of hymns from these traditions were chosen, composed, or translated. A number of songs from Taizé and the Praise and Worship tradition were also included. Thus the new song book served as a unifying force in the denomination.

Others in the church, however, were far from pleased. The language changes in existing hymns were especially offensive to them as yet another attack on tradition. From the rightist wing of the church, the Canadian magazine *Christian Renewal* sniped that in the new *Psalter Hymnal* "the feminist view has prevailed."[58] Classis Chicago sent an overture to Synod 1986 to "reconsider the policy of almost total contemporization of the traditional hymns and Bible songs," especially for poetic reasons.[59] For some the whole hymnal project was a sign of unwanted changes in the CRC—along with the controversies about women in office and the teaching of evolution.[60]

For the CRC generally, the new *Psalter Hymnal* (the "grey *Psalter Hymnal*")[61] was a grand success. The sales were beyond expectation. The *Banner* reported that the first printing of fifty-six thousand copies sold out quickly, and that there was a waiting list for an additional twenty thousand copies. A modified edition was published without the CRC creeds and liturgical forms to entice non-CRC churches to adopt the *Psalter Hymnal*.[62]

58 *Christian Renewal*, 5 May 1986, 4.

59 *Acts of Synod*, 1986, 484-86.

60 The criticism from traditionalists ironically gave new life to the blue Psalter Hymnal. Many of the conservatives left the CRC in the 1990s and established independent congregations and/or joined the new denomination, the United Reformed Church; the songbook of nearly all these congregations is the 1959 Psalter Hymnal.

61 Editor Emily Brink occasionally insists that the color is silver.

62 For additional information on this history of the CRC, see Bert Polman and Jack Reiffer, "Christian Reformed Psalters and Hymnals," in *The Psalter Hymnal Handbook*, 97-108.

Conclusion

As I have noted several times, both denominations and all of the hymnals deserve a longer discussion than I have given them here to provide full understanding of congregational song in the two church bodies. The stories told here, however, and especially the juxtaposition of the two histories, provide a fascinating comparison.

On the one hand, the churches have much in common. The ethnic background, the common heritage of its theology, the serious attempt to continue that heritage on a new continent, the language problem, the struggle of discovering an identity of its own—these were shared by the two denominations.

Seeing the two stories side by side, however, also allows us to see the contrasts. The main contrast concerns two related issues. The RCA has used multiple hymnals throughout its history, and the General Synods often have had minimal involvement in the choices. The CRC had a very restricted number of Psalters and Psalter hymnals, and its Synods controlled the choices and the process rigorously—at times nit-pickingly so. Let me briefly suggest several reasons for these differences.

The control of the RCA by Classis Amsterdam was often heavy-handed and out of touch with the American situation. This 164-year domination also hampered the new church from developing a healthy system of more centralized, synodical government. Both because of this lack of proper jurisdiction and the geographic isolation of many congregations, their consistories, and classes often made decisions as needed for their local issues, including the use of hymnals. Various General Synods bemoaned the proliferation of hymnals and the lack of control over the situation, but the habits of semi-congregationalism had been established.

Related to this congregationalism was the lack of genuine contact on the part of the congregations (apart from their ministers) with the Netherlands Reformed Church. The tradition of the Genevan Psalter, for example, was no longer in the people's blood by the time the 1789 *Psalms and Hymns* was introduced, but they knew the Tate and Brady psalms from contact with other denominations. This was even more true of the hymns. The only hymns known to the members of the RPDC were English and American hymns, many of which they had learned in Sunday School. As the years went by, this Americanization process continued, and the Dutch-Americans became non-hyphenated

Americans with many contacts and joint ventures with other American denominations, including an acquaintance with their hymnals.

The CRC picture is very different. They began their work on an English *Psalter Hymnal* only seventy-seven years after their beginning as a denomination, and in these decades they had often been very isolationist and their numbers small. Thus their church life was more cohesive, with more centralized control.

Also, the memory of the 1834 Secession in the Netherlands, and the ongoing influx of new immigrants continued to provide an ecclesiastical and spiritual climate closely tied to the churches in the Netherlands. Even though the 1934 *Psalter Hymnal* was English and American, many of the parishioners still knew Dutch better than English. Moreover, the process of creating the *Psalter Hymnal* was much more tightly controlled and often accompanied by great suspicion toward non-Reformed American sources. This orientation lingered for a long time and is noticeable even in the 1987 treatment of the Psalms; the decision to return to one versification for each psalm is a deliberate return to the Dutch-Genevan Psalter.

These comparisons are, I think, generally valid, but one has to add a qualification. The RCA certainly had a great number of outside hymnals in use, but the CRC was not free from such importation. One of the reasons for the 1959 *Psalter Hymnal* cited above was "the proliferation of hymnals containing songs which are un-Reformed in doctrine, lacking in musical quality now being used in many of our churches." But neither the 1959 nor the 1987 *Psalter Hymnals* stopped this use; instead the importation continued and, as noted in my final paragraph on the RCA, this trend has increased with computerized projection.

Coda

So far I have treated each denomination separately and have tended to emphasize the differences between the two churches. But the publication of a new hymnal supplement, *Sing! A New Creation*, signals a wonderful rapprochement of the two bodies. Although the hymnal was not officially approved by the two denominations, five committee members from the RCA and five from the CRC compiled this hymnal as a supplement to the song books in use in the denominations. Two important considerations guided the choices: all the songs would be from the last half of the twentieth century and there would be a strong emphasis on songs from other continents and countries. The organization was to follow a combination of the order of worship and the liturgical year, followed by a number of other subjects. *Sing! A New Creation* has been warmly received in both churches.[63]

If I may conclude on a personal note, let me give a testimony. Our congregation, Neland Avenue CRC in Grand Rapids, uses *Sing! A New Creation* every Sunday (along with the 1987 *Psalter Hymnal*, of course). Even though nearly all the songs were unfamiliar to our congregation, the acceptance of *Sing!* has been enthusiastic and has brought an additional blessing to our congregational song.

[63] For a more complete summary of this hymnal, see Emily R. Brink, "Introducing *Sing! A New Creation*," *Reformed Worship* 60 (June 2001): 10-15.

CHAPTER 2

Ancient Wisdom for Post-Modern Preaching: The Preacher as Pastor, Theologian, and Evangelist

Timothy L. Brown

I am grateful to be asked to contribute an essay in honor of Elton Bruins. When I came to Hope College in the late 60s, I was an outsider to the Reformed tradition in general, and to the history of the Dutch founders of the Reformed Church in West Michigan in particular. I knew nothing of Albertus C. Van Raalte, or any of the other venerable names that loom large in the history of the early colony, until, in a classroom in the basement of Dimnent Chapel, I sat enthralled as Elton Bruins spoke of them all as though they were on his family tree.

On the twentieth anniversary of Holland's founding, I learned from Elton, Van Raalte addressed the colony's rising generation with this stirring challenge:

> Beloved, who follow us in this inheritance, we give it over to you with joy. But do not forget, we received it from God as a training school for eternity; a workplace for God's Kingdom. This shall prosper in your hands provided God and His Kingdom remains your precious portion in life.[1]

As a teacher, scholar, and administrator at Hope College, Elton Bruins met Van Raalte's challenge nobly. I bless the Lord often for having been

[1] Memorial placard standing at the grave site of Albertus C. Van Raalte in Pilgrim Home Cemetery in Holland, Michigan.

one of his students and now one of his colleagues in the Kingdom work Van Raalte envisioned a century and a half ago.

The title of this contribution to his *festschrift* requires further definition. Pastor, theologian, and evangelist are essential characteristics of the preaching life, and they are precisely the ones that I would long to see fulfilled by my students who are waiting to take their turn "in the company of preachers"[2] upon graduation from seminary. By "ancient wisdom" I am referring largely to the wisdom of the Bible, and in this instance, one particular scene from the Bible, the preaching of Philip to the Ethiopian eunuch described in Acts 8:26-40. The Bible is a much overlooked resource in defining and shaping our vocational lives as preachers. We still use the Bible's glossary of terms but strangely jettison it when we come to the all-important task of defining them. We are much more likely to turn to the social sciences for definitions of the preaching life, preferring terms like therapist, manager, visionary leader, or motivational speaker. Something significant is lost when we do this. The Bible ought to be used both to define the terms of ministry and to describe its shape and form. I am echoing here what Eugene Peterson so beautifully describes in one of his most recent books, suggestively titled, *Eat This Book*: "I want to attend to the way that the form of Scripture is also the form of our lives."[3] The Bible ought to be considered in such ways that the patterns found there are reproduced when we stash lunch buckets under our arms and head off to the factory floors of our ordinary lives.

This instinct is deeply embedded in the Reformed tradition in which Hope College and Western Theological Seminary are firmly situated. Although each school may have something of a lover's quarrel with it, neither can deny the influence of their spiritual forbear, the sixteenth-century reformer John Calvin. Calvin's most notable contribution to the theology of the Reformation is contained in the large two-volume set, *The Institutes of the Christian Religion*. In our early explorations of Calvin, I invite my students to review the indices in the back of the book. There they discover the deep artesian wells from which the great reformer regularly drank. One of the indices, the index of scriptural references, contains no less than six thousand Bible

2 This phrase is taken from the title of Richard Lischer's wonderful anthology of preaching throughout the ages, *The Company of Preachers* (Grand Rapids: Eerdmans, 2002).

3 Eugene H. Peterson, *Eat This Book: A Conversation in the Art of Spiritual Reading* (Grand Rapids: Eerdmans, 2006), 38.

references. There is hardly a book of the Bible which Calvin does not consider as he pieces his *magnum opus* together. Since the *Institutes* cover more than 1,500 pages, simple math will tell you that there are nearly four biblical references on every page. Calvin's passion was to recover the truth of God's Word for the strenuous work of reformation. He borrowed heavily from the ancient wisdom of the Bible; I want to follow his example in shaping young men and women for the strenuous task of preaching in the post-modern context into which they have been born.

By the phrase "post-modernity" I mean the intellectual climate in which Christians live every day and in which preachers must preach Sunday after Sunday. Simply put, I take post-modernity to refer to the way that the great bastions of modernity—intellectual certainty, national sovereignty, autonomous individualism, and the hope of unending progress and prosperity brought about by ever-increasing knowledge—have all been hung in the balance and found wanting. David Wells summarizes our dilemma adroitly, "The Enlightenment had its eschatology, that of inevitable progress, and now that has died. It is not, however, only the belief in progress that died but, along with it, something that is even larger, which is the belief that there is purpose which has been written into the creation."[4] We now find ourselves paralyzed by the antipathy between East and West, shocked by the economic disparity between North and South, and seemingly helpless to do anything about it. We are left mumbling all together the lines of an old nursery rhyme:

> Humpty Dumpty sat on a wall
> Humpty Dumpty had a great fall.
> All of the king's horses and all of the king's men
> Couldn't put Humpty together again.

The inability of modernity to put our "Humpty-Dumpty world" back together has ushered in post-modernity and has in turn created a crisis for all those called to preach the gospel of Jesus Christ, a crisis that holds within it both danger and opportunity. I would like to explore that opportunity by looking closely at the first occasion of preaching recorded outside the walls of Jerusalem. The preacher is the evangelist Philip, and the congregation to whom he preaches is

[4] David Wells, *Above All Earthly Powers: Christ in a Postmodern World* (Grand Rapids: Eerdmans, 2005), 88.

an unnamed eunuch from Ethiopia. The contours of this pre-modern preaching event, showing us a person living into the preacher's life as pastor, theologian, and evangelist, offers significant suggestions about preaching in our post-modern context.

Here is how the Book of Acts records that remarkable preaching moment:

> Then an angel of the Lord said to Philip, "Get up and go toward the south to the road that goes down from Jerusalem to Gaza." (This is a wilderness road.) So he got up and went. Now there was an Ethiopian eunuch, a court official of the Candace, queen of the Ethiopians, in charge of her entire treasury. He had come to Jerusalem to worship and was returning home; seated in his chariot, he was reading the prophet Isaiah. Then the Spirit said to Philip, "Go over to this chariot and join it." So Philip ran up to it and heard him reading the prophet Isaiah. He asked, "Do you understand what you are reading?" He replied, "How can I, unless someone guides me?" And he invited Philip to get in and sit beside him. Now the passage of the scripture that he was reading was this: "Like a sheep he was led to the slaughter, and like a lamb silent before its shearer, so he does not open his mouth. In his humiliation justice was denied him. Who can describe his generation? For his life is taken away from the earth." The eunuch asked Philip, "About whom, may I ask you, does the prophet say this, about himself or about someone else?" Then Philip began to speak, and starting with this scripture, he proclaimed to him the good news about Jesus. As they were going along the road, they came to some water; and the eunuch said, "Look, here is water! What is to prevent me from being baptized?" He commanded the chariot to stop, and both of them, Philip and the eunuch, went down into the water, and Philip baptized him. When they came up out of the water, the Spirit of the Lord snatched Philip away; the eunuch saw him no more, and went on his way rejoicing. But Philip found himself at Azotus, and as he was passing through the region, he proclaimed the good news to all the towns until he came to Caesarea.[5]

The Preacher as Pastor

I once heard Fred Craddock, formerly Professor of Homiletics

5 Acts 8:26-40 NRSV.

at Candler School of Theology and a recognized leader in the field of homiletics, answer tongue-in-cheek the question he is often asked, "Who is the greatest preacher in America?" by saying, "The local pastor." He is right and bears witness to Philip as a preacher-pastor. Pastors are those people in our lives who remind us to pay attention to God. The ancient word for pastor, ποιμην, locates the work of the pastor in the field and on the hillside of ordinary life. Literally the pastor is a shepherd; if you have ever seen shepherds doing their work, you know that it is hard, lonely, and very demanding. Shepherds lead, protect, watch, and then they lead, protect, and watch some more. And this watching is critical to the life and well-being of each sheep or goat in the flock, and to the flock as a whole. Without the shepherd, the flock is endangered by predators, thieves, and the severe extremities of climate and terrain. Surely Jesus had all of this in mind when he said:

> Very truly, I tell you, I am the gate for the sheep. All who came before me are thieves and bandits; but the sheep did not listen to them. I am the gate. Whoever enters by me will be saved, and will come in and go out and find pasture. The thief comes only to steal and kill and destroy. I came that they may have life, and have it abundantly. I am the good shepherd. The good shepherd lays down his life for the sheep.[6]

Preachers are pastors, and pastors are shepherds, and shepherds take care of the flock!

Preachers who function like pastor-shepherds, in the tradition of Philip, are characterized by many traits; two of them are beautifully embodied by Philip: the first of them is a capacity for reminding people that they belong to God. Everything about our existence is charged with the presence of God, but few of us ever really see it that way. Events in our lives seem as random as dandelion spores blowing in the wind. Pastors are the ones assigned by God to change that perception, but it is not easy to do. So many things conspire to tell us that God has nothing to do with our ordinariness, and the loudest dissenting voice is likely to be an internal one. In a moving poem written in prison, Dietrich Bonhoeffer gives us a picture of just how dogged that internal voice is and how important the awareness of our "God belongingness" is to our survival:

[6] John 10:7-11 NRSV.

Who am I? They often tell me
I stepped from my cell's confinement
Calmly, cheerfully, firmly,
like a Squire from his country house.

Who am I? They often tell me
I used to speak to my warders
freely, and friendly and clearly,
as though it were mine to command.

Who am I? They also tell me
I bore the days of misfortune
equably, smilingly, proudly,
like one accustomed to win.

Am I then really that which other men tell of?
Or am I only what I myself know of myself?
Restless and longing and sick, like a bird in a cage,
struggling for breath, as though hands were compressing
my throat,
yearning for colours, for flowers, for the voices of birds,
thirsting for words of kindness, for neighborliness,
tossing in expectation of great events,
powerlessly trembling for friends at an infinite distance,
weary and empty at praying, at thinking, at making,
faint, and ready to say farewell to it all.

Who am I? This or the Other?
Am I one person to-day and to-morrow another?
Am I both at once? A hypocrite before others,
and before myself a contemptible woebegone weakling?
Or is something within me still like a beaten army
fleeing in disorder from victory already achieved?

Who am I? They mock me, these lonely questions of mine.
Whoever I am, Thou knowest, O God, I am thine![7]

Some time ago, while working in my office preparing a lecture on the role of memory in spiritual formation, I was prompted to

[7] Dietrich Bonhoeffer, *The Cost of Discipleship* (New York: Macmillan, 1961), 18-20. Reprinted with the permission of Scribner, an imprint of Simon and Schuster Adult Publishing Group, from *Letters and Papers from Prison*, rev. and enl. ed. by Dietrich Bonhoeffer, trans. (from German) R. H. Fuller, Frank Clark, et al.

call a local nursing care facility known for its large unit dedicated to the care and well-being of persons with Alzheimer's disease. Having identified myself as a teacher in the local seminary, I inquired about the possibility of asking someone on the unit a few questions. They graciously forwarded my call to a floor nurse named Elaine, a middle-aged woman with a distinct southern accent. I asked her what folks who worked with Alzheimer's patients were called. She said, "We call them MLAs." I responded by asking, "And what are MLAs?" She apologized for the verbal shorthand and filled in the blanks, "MLAs are 'Memory Loss Assistants.'"

Now savvy to her lingo I asked her what MLAs do. She said, "They talk to the patients and read them books. Once a day they work through a series of patterning exercises." She added, "Generally we help them with basic life functions so they retain as much activity as possible." I followed up with this question, "When MLAs talk to them what do they say?"

Her response was profoundly theological. "We tell them their names. We remind them of the names of their family members, and, if possible, we show them pictures. And then we rehearse, as far as we are able, over and over again, significant events that have happened in their past. We do whatever we can to give them a measure of confidence and hope."

It would be difficult to find a more theologically precise definition of a pastor than this one. Pastors assigned to live and work among the flock of God, which is our charge, are "Memory Loss Assistants." With grace offerings of hymn and prayer, table, font, scroll and blessing, we remind the people of God who they are, whose they are, and what great things have happened in their wilderness wanderings past, so that they might have confidence and hope in a promised-land future.

A second trait of Philip as pastor-shepherd is his personal interest in the eunuch. An entire course in pastoral theology could be taught from two striking images in this scene: Philip sitting beside the eunuch in the chariot and Philip going into the waters of baptism with the eunuch. Philip chose to be beside and with, not above and beyond, and that made all the difference in the life of the Ethiopian eunuch. Living as we do in a fractured world where relationships are superficial and commitments are temporary, pastors who live into this image of Philip will make a world of difference in the lives of those whom they are called to serve.

The third century preacher-theologian, Ambrose of Milan, provides us with a great example. Ambrose was the spiritual mentor to Augustine of Hippo, the most influential early theologian in the West. In his pre-Christian days Augustine, as a young rhetorician, aspired to the lofty goal of becoming the greatest orator in the world. Augustine's mother, Monica, who was always vigilant for her son's spiritual welfare, told him that he could never attain that goal so long as Bishop Ambrose of Milan was living. She had challenged her son and he accepted the challenge. He and some friends sailed from their Northern African home to Milan, Italy, with the sole, and ignoble, intent of seeing whether or not Ambrose was as good as his reputation. Monica suspected that God might do something with her son through the life and witness of Ambrose. And she was right. Listen to Augustine's account of his meeting with Ambrose as it is recorded in his *Confessions*:

> So I came to Milan and to Bishop Ambrose, who was known throughout the world as one of the best of men. He was a devout worshiper of you, Lord, and at that time his energetic preaching provided your people with choicest wheat. . . . Unknowingly I was led by you to him, so that through him I might be led, knowingly, to you.[8]

Now listen to the way that Augustine speaks of Ambrose's pastoral instincts:

> This man of God welcomed me with fatherly kindness and showed the charitable concern for my pilgrimage that befitted a bishop. I began to feel affection for him, not at first as a teacher of truth, for that I had given up hope of finding in your Church, but simply as a man who was kind to me. . . . I hung keenly upon his words, but cared little for their content. . . . Yet little by little, without knowing it, I was drawing near. I was taking no trouble to learn from what Ambrose was saying, but interested only in listening to how he said it. . . . Nonetheless as his words, which I enjoyed, penetrated my mind, the substance, which I overlooked, seeped in with them, for I could not separate the two. As I opened my heart to appreciate how skillfully he spoke, the recognition that he was speaking truth crept in at the same time.[9]

8 St. Augustine, *Confessions*, trans. Maria Boulding (New York: Random House, 1998), 93.

9 Ibid., 93.

Augustine's eternity, and our best theology, turned on the willingness of Ambrose to care for another person. Worlds change when pastors position themselves beside and with the congregation. Philip was a preacher-shepherd and he compels us to join him.

The Preacher as Theologian

Preachers are theologians. Anxious for acceptance in the congregation and a measure of respect in the culture, pastors are often duped into thinking of themselves differently: therapists, managers, fundraisers, and politicians. But in sum and at heart preachers are theologians. They think deeply and complexly about God. They reflect thoughtfully and speak winsomely on behalf of God. And they do what they can to draw their people into the artesian life of God. If anyone ever had the right to call himself one, it is Philip. Interestingly, we have no record of any of Philip's theological writings, but we do have a record of his theological method, which may be more important to us now. As a preacher-theologian Philip attended to the spiritual concerns of his congregation by asking and answering questions ("Do you understand what you are reading?"), and he gave careful attention to the reading and exposition of Scripture ("And beginning with this Scripture he told him everything about Jesus"). These are the things that pastors do when they conceive of themselves primarily as theologians.

Spiritual theologian Eugene Peterson has done more than anyone I know to provide a corrective lens for the faulty vision of preachers in the West. Through one of his earliest works, he virtually saved my pastoral soul. I was serving a large and rapidly growing congregation in the Midwest. I was concerned every day with budgets, and personnel policies, and just how our growth projections might be affected by land use decisions made by the City Council of Holland week by week. Peterson's introduction to *Working the Angles* rescued me and pulled me from one pastoral world to another:

> American pastors are abandoning their posts, left and right, and at an alarming rate. They are not leaving their churches and getting other jobs. Congregations still pay their salaries. Their names remain on the church stationery and they continue to appear in pulpits on Sundays. But they are abandoning their posts, their calling. They have gone whoring after other gods. What they do with their time under the guise of pastoral ministry hasn't the remotest connection with what the church's pastors have done for most of twenty centuries.

> A few of us are angry about it. We are angry because we have been deserted. Most of my colleagues who defined ministry for me, examined, ordained, and then installed me as a pastor in a congregation, a short while later walked off and left me, having they said, more urgent things to do. . . . They talk of images and statistics. They drop names. They discuss influences and status. Matters of God and the soul and Scriptures are not grist for their mills.[10]

Peterson and Philip are singing in two-part harmony the song of pastor as theologian. And just think about it, if we refuse to join them, who will sing the song? I mean, where will people be challenged and trained to read the Bible, say their prayers, become instruments of righteousness in the world, if not by the pastor-theologian?

Two aspects of Philip's theological method should be highlighted here. The first is its peculiar relationship to the Bible as its source. Scripture is the beginning point of his theological consideration. Could he have started in a better place? In his recent monograph, *Holy Scripture: A Dogmatic Sketch*, Aberdeen theologian John Webster underscores this conviction in telling fashion. In a very interesting section, he describes a treatise on the nature of Scripture written by Zacharius Ursinus, the reformer and probable co-author of the Heidelberg Catechism, robustly titled, *A Hortatory Oration to the Study of Divinity*. As a systematic theologian, Webster is particularly interested in the way that Ursinus argues for "the primacy of Holy Scripture, both for the whole of theology and the life of the theological school."[11] Webster goes on to make a provocative claim that ought to make anyone who teaches theology in any of its four branches (systematic, historical, biblical, or pastoral) sit up and pay close attention:

> What is clear is that the kind of theology whose defining activity is exegetical reason needs to be ready to take its share of the embarrassment and censure which accompany exile. Survival under the afflictions of exile involves many practices, of which two are primary. One is fellowship under the Word—that is, common life led by delight in the common reality of the communicative

[10] Eugene H. Peterson, *Working the Angles: The Shape of Pastoral Integrity* (Grand Rapids: Eerdmans, 1987), 1, 2.

[11] John Webster, *Holy Scripture: A Dogmatic Sketch* (Cambridge: Cambridge University Press, 2003), 109.

> presence of God. Reason requires koinonia. The second is that fundamental act by which the common life of reason appeals for its cleansing, protection and truthfulness, name prayer: "May the Lord grant that we may study the heavenly mysteries of his wisdom, making true progress in religion to his glory and our upbuilding" (Calvin).[12]

Webster's description of the relationship between theology and the Bible as one of referral is precisely true of the relationship between preaching and the Bible. The Bible ought to tell the preacher both what to say and how to say it. It is the faithful preacher and not the creative one who is closest to this vision. One of the ways that I have sought to accomplish this in my own preaching life, and correspondingly in the preaching lives of my students, is by entering into the centuries-old practice of Scripture memorization. It was the practice of every great preacher from the Apostles to the Reformers to meditate long and hard on the biblical texts from which they preached until they could be reproduced from rote memory. The fourth-century desert mystic John Cassian, an associate of St. John Chrysostom and one of the great preachers of the ancient world, bears interesting testimony to this practice:

> Hence the successive books of the Holy Scripture must be diligently committed to memory and ceaselessly reviewed. This continual meditation will bestow on us double fruit. First, inasmuch as the mind's attention is occupied with reading and with preparing to read, it cannot be taken captive in the entrapments of harmful thoughts. Then, the things that we have not been able to understand because our mind was busy at the time, things that we have gone through repeatedly and are laboring to memorize, we shall see more clearly afterward when we are free from every seductive deed and sight, and especially when we are silently meditating at night.[13]

The second aspect of Philip's theological method that we overlook at our own peril is his bias toward action. Hearing the eunuch reading aloud from the prophecy of Isaiah, Philip asks him, "Do you

12 Ibid., 135.

13 Quoted in Richard Lischer's *The Company of Preachers* (Grand Rapids: Eerdmans, 2002), 187.

understand what you are reading?" The eunuch responds with stunning and refreshing candor, "How can I, unless someone guides me?" The Greek word associated with the explaining of texts is normally *exegesis*, which of course means "to lead out." In this instance, however, the word used by the eunuch is *hodegesis* which means "to lead along the way." The eunuch was not asking Philip to fill his mind with ideas but rather to fill his life with practices. He did not simply want to know about God but he wanted to live the life of God. To do that the eunuch needed a mentor, someone to guide him along the way. The guide is the *hodegete*. Pastoral theologians must concern themselves with the living out of the life of faith and setting in motion the possibility of others doing the same.

Jewish theology speaks in this regard of a distinction between *halacha* (to walk in the truth) and *agada* (to meditate on the truth). Neither is privileged over the other but each is necessary to give life to the other. A Jewish theologian, Abraham Heschel, spells out this distinction and its striking implications in graphic detail:

> Halacha deals with the law; agada with the meaning of the law. Halacha deals with subjects that can be expressed literally; agada introduces us to a realm which lies beyond the range of expression. Halacha teaches us how to perform common acts; agada tells us how to participate in the eternal drama. Halacha gives us knowledge; agada gives us aspiration. . . . The interrelationship of halacha and agada is the very heart of Judaism. Halacha without agada is dead.[14]

Philip astutely asks, "Do you understand what you are reading?" And the eunuch wisely responds, "How can I, unless someone guides me?" Preachers are theologians and as theologians they do what they believe and they mentor people to do the same.

The Preacher as Evangelist

The last image of the preacher given us in this passage is the preacher as an evangelist. No sooner do Philip and the eunuch come up out of the waters of baptism than the Spirit of the Lord grabs Philip by the nape of his neck and does not release him until he arrives in Azotus, about sixty miles southeast of Jerusalem in the present day Gaza strip:

14 Abraham Heschel, *God in Search of Man* (New York: Farrar, Straus and Giroux, 1955), 336.

> When they came up out of the water, the Spirit of the Lord snatched Philip away; the eunuch saw him no more, and went on his way rejoicing. But Philip found himself at Azotus, and as he was passing through the region, he proclaimed the good news to all the towns until he came to Caesarea.[15]

This was not the kind of neighborhood a young Jewish boy wanted to be found in after dark. Historically, the fertile plain along the coast of the Mediterranean on Israel's coast line was pagan territory, Philistine territory, to be more precise. No one here rose early in the morning to say their prayers and no one here lived under the law. Philip was at risk even being found there. But then again it was not his idea—he had been Spirit-placed to preach the gospel in an exceedingly hostile context. And he would do this because he was an evangelist!

Philip's life as an evangelist is marked by at least three characteristics: an awareness of the heart's deepest longing, a keen sense of the relationship between the Word of God written and the Word of God made manifest by the Risen Christ, and an irrepressible desire to tell the good news of Jesus Christ to everyone, everywhere.

Sensitive to the Spirit's leading, Philip runs up to the Eunuch's chariot and immediately engages him in conversation around the deeper meaning of the Isaiah scroll. Why would Philip do such a thing unless he possessed an awareness that the deepest reason for the Eunuch's travel, unknown even to the traveler, was to encounter the living God in the person of the Risen Christ? The story of the Ethiopian eunuch's encounter with the Risen Christ is a kind of Midrash on another conviction of the New Testament. "Long ago God spoke to our ancestors in many and various ways," wrote the author of the Letter to the Hebrews, and the eunuch seems to know this much, as evidenced by his eager reading of Isaiah. However, and this is a sizable however, he knew nothing of God's latest and best move, "but in these last days he has spoken to us by a Son, whom he appointed the heir of all things, through whom he also created the world."[16] Philip knew deeply what John Calvin would write explicitly centuries later:

> Since we see that our whole salvation is comprehended in [Jesus Christ] we are not to seek the least portion of it from anywhere else. If we seek salvation, we are taught by the very name of Jesus

15 Acts 8:39-40 NRSV.
16 Hebrews 1:2 NRSV.

> that it is of him. If we seek any other gifts of the Spirit, they will be found in his anointing. . . . Seeing so great a store of every good thing is found in him let us drink our fill from this fountain and no other.[17]

Philip as an evangelist also possessed a keen sense of the relationship between the Bible and the presence of the Risen Christ. When the Eunuch had finished reading the Isaiah scroll he asked Philip "about whom may I ask does the prophet speak, himself or another?" With this as his starting point, Philip began to tell the eunuch everything about Jesus in the Scriptures. What is curious to me is the eunuch's sense that the prophet might be speaking of someone other than himself. And he had this sense because of the curious relationship between the Word of God written and the Word of God incarnate in Jesus and made manifest by the Risen Christ. Luther describes something of this relationship in his almost quaint way of thinking of the Scriptures as "the garment which our Lord has put on and in which He lets Himself be seen and found. This garment is woven throughout and so wrought together into one that it cannot be cut or parted."[18] For Luther the former is like a doorway to the other. The great German theologian Karl Barth saw this too and he echoes the eunuch's experience in the first volume of his *Dogmatics* with this mysterious conviction: "God's faithfulness to His Church consists in Him making use of His freedom to come to us in His Word, and in reserving to himself the freedom to do this again and again."[19]

Preachers as evangelists recognize that when the Word is read aloud, Jesus Christ is present to do his redeeming work. A few years ago I traveled with a friend at the request of an international missionary agency to Istanbul, Turkey, where we met with twenty-one Iranian house church leaders who had smuggled themselves into the country under the false pretense of visiting the great Islamic shrines of that Near Eastern land. They had actually come to receive training in Christian practices. All but a few of them were Muslim converts to the Christian faith within the last decade.

It was as moving and wonderful experience as I have ever had in my life. I wondered all week where and how, in an environment as

17 *Institutes of the Christian Religion,* 2.16.19.

18 Quoted by Eugene Peterson in *Working the Angles*, 89, 90.

19 Karl Barth, *Church Dogmatics: The Doctrine of the Word of God* (Edinburgh: T&T Clark, 1936),158.

hostile to the Christian faith as Iran, people like these would become Christian believers. I asked that very question throughout the course of the week, and over and over again they bore moving witness to the way that Jesus Christ had simply revealed himself to them. Let me tell you about Anna and Mehmet, whose names I have changed to protect them from certain recrimination. They live in a city in central Iran and each was raised as a devout Muslim. Mehmet drove daily from his home to his place of employment on the other side of the city and every day would pass by an abandoned Armenian church, closed sometime after the fall of the Shah. The government, however, made a tactical error by leaving the church sign in the front yard, a billboard, on which was actually written in Farsi, the language of the people, this verse from the Bible: "Behold! I stand at the door and knock. If you hear my voice and open the door, I will come in to you and eat with you, and you with me."[20]

Mehmet bore witness to the way that the message on the billboard haunted him. It haunted him so much that he finally altered his route so he that he would not have to drive past it each day. One night, while he and Anna slept, as she reported to me in her testimony, Jesus Christ entered their room and spoke to Mehmet saying, "Mehmet, I am he who speaks to you from the billboard." Through a vision, Mehmet was in the presence of the Risen Christ and it flooded him with enormous joy. He had gone to bed a Muslim and awoke the next morning an eager follower of the risen Christ. When he finally muscled up the courage to tell his wife about his experience, he was stunned by her response. "Mehmet," she said through her tears, "He appeared to me in the same way." Now, a few years later, they are learning Christian practices about the Scriptures so that they can be effective witnesses where they live. And as they do, they are testimony to the curious and living relationship between the Bible and the Risen Christ. Preachers who are evangelists know this and they preach in its confidence.

Preachers who are evangelists also have an irrepressible desire to tell the good news of Jesus Christ to everyone, everywhere. As soon as Philip gets his bearings in Azotus, he returns to his passion for preaching the gospel: "And as he was passing through the region, he proclaimed the good news to all the towns until he came to Caesarea." Philip is not alone in this passion. He is preceded by Peter, who stood tall on the Temple Mount on that first Pentecost, boldly echoing the prophets,

[20] Revelation 3:20 NRSV (alt.).

"Everyone who calls on the name of the Lord shall be saved."[21] And he anticipates the Apostle Paul, who, even on trial for his life preaches the gospel to Herod Agrippa. Herod queries, "In such a short period of time do you think to make me a Christian?" To which Paul reveals the heart of the apostolic passion for evangelism by saying, "Whether quickly or not, I pray to God that not only you but also all who are listening to me today might become such as I am—except for these chains."[22] Like Philip before him, Paul wanted all people to become followers of Jesus.

Given the pressure of pluralism under which most of us do our theological training, and the ministries for which we train, this passion seems primitive. But Philip, and every other New Testament witness, seems unable to speak otherwise. Philip preached the way he did because of what he had been given to believe about Jesus Christ. In a recent conversation, David Bast, President and Broadcast Minister of *Words of Hope*, a worldwide radio ministry of the Reformed Church in America, shared with me support that he had discovered for this conviction from the most unlikely source. Liberal theologian John Hick, editor of the controversial book *The Myth of God Incarnate*, once scandalously wrote in an essay concerning Jesus, "That Jesus was the Son of God incarnate is not literally true, since it has no literal meaning." Later in that same essay he wrote, "If Jesus was literally God incarnate, and if it is by his death alone that men can be saved, and by their response to him alone that they can appropriate that salvation, then the only doorway to eternal life is Christian faith. It would follow from this that a large majority of the human race has not been saved."[23] Curiously, Hick bears witness to the heart of the New Testament witness. If Jesus Christ is God in the flesh then, everyone everywhere ought to know about it. The apostles believed this and preached accordingly. And when preachers today do the same, they are never closer to their New Testament ancestors!

As I sat in a classroom in the basement of Dimnent Chapel decades ago under the tutelage of Elton Bruins, a desire arose within me to become a preacher with a heart to "say the big nouns: joy, glory, peace; and live the best verbs: love, forgive, save." These suggestive words come from a poem by Eugene Peterson that provides pre-modern advice for post-modern preachers who are willing to become pastors, theologians, and evangelists:

21 Acts 2:21 NRSV.
22 Acts 26:29 NRSV.
23 Quoted in D. A. Carson, *The Gagging of God: Christianity Confronts Pluralism* (Grand Rapids: Zondervan, 1996), 321.

For us who have only known approximate fathers
And mother manqué, this child is a surprise:
A sudden coming true of all we hoped
Might happen. Hoarded hopes fed by prophecies,

Old sermons and song fragments, now cry
Coo and gurgle in the cradle, a babbling
Proto-language which as soon as it gets
A tongue (and we, of course, grow open ears)

Will say the big nouns: joy, glory, peace;
And live the best verbs: love, forgive, save.
Along with the swaddling clothes the words are washed

Of every soiling sentiment, scrubbed clean of
All failed promises, then hung in the world's
Backyard dazzling white, billowing gospel.[24]

How grateful I am that under the tutelage of Elton Bruins, there was birthed within me a desire to become just this kind of preacher!

[24] Eugene H. Peterson, *The Contemplative Pastor* (Carol Stream, Ill.: Word, 1989), 169. Reprinted by permission of the author and publisher. All rights reserved.

CHAPTER 3

Extra-Canonical Tests for Church Membership and Ministry

Donald J. Bruggink

Among the many contributions of the Reverend Doctor Elton J. Bruins to academia and to the church has been his participation in and support of the Historical Series of the Reformed Church in America. The purpose of this series was early described as "encouraging historical research and providing a medium wherein this knowledge may be shared with the academic community and with the members of the denomination in order that a knowledge of the past may contribute to right action in the present."[1] A historian could receive no greater honor than to actually have his work "contribute to right action in the present." Elton's work in the Historical Series of the Reformed Church in America, no. 32, *Family Quarrels in the Dutch Reformed Churches in the 19th Century*, provides historical precedent for the church today.[2] It should be understood, however, that Elton is in no way responsible for my use of his material for what I perceive as right action in the present.

1 Herman Harmelink III, *Ecumenism and the Reformed Church*, Historical Series of the Reformed Church in America, no. 1 (Grand Rapids: Eerdmans, 1968), v. This statement continued for the first thirty-nine volumes of the series.

2 Elton J. Bruins, "1882–Secession Yet Again, the Masonic Controversy," chap. 4 in *Family Quarrels in the Dutch Reformed Churches in the 19th Century*, Robert P. Swierenga and Elton J. Bruins (Grand Rapids: Eerdmans, 1999), 108-35.

Precedent in the Reformed Church in America (RCA) is against the establishment of extra-canonical tests for individual church membership or ministerial office.

For clarification, extra-canonical is here used to describe any tests beyond those required in the Liturgy of the Reformed Church in America, and because the Liturgy is a part of the Constitution of the RCA, thus the Constitution as well. It should be noted that for church membership the requirements are stated in the broadest possible terms, the most specific of which are the acceptance "of the Scriptures of the Old and New Testaments as the only rule for faith and life."[3] One is also asked to accept the "spiritual guidance of the Church."[4] The attached phrase, "obeying its doctrines and teachings" found in the previous liturgy[5] is omitted. Similarly, for ministers of Word and sacrament, the most specific request is, "Do you believe the books of the Old and New Testaments to be the Word of God and the perfect doctrine of salvation; rejecting all contrary beliefs?"[6] In signing the "Form of Declaration" the candidate also subscribes to the doctrinal standards of the church, the Belgic Confession, the Heidelberg Catechism, and the Canons of the Synod of Dort. The genius of these broad affirmations is that any perceived failure to live up to these commitments must be adjudicated on a case by case basis by the appropriate body: the consistory for church members, the classis for ministers of Word and sacrament.

The most crucial test of this principle occurred in the mid-nineteenth century in the controversy over Freemasonry which pitted the recently arrived immigrant church in the Midwest against the older, largely Americanized RCA in the East.

Modern Freemasonry began in England *circa* 1717, and in 1723 the London Grand Lodge adopted a constitution written by the Reverend James Anderson. Its religious outlook was essentially Deistic, the constitution requiring members only to hold "to that religion in which all men agree, leaving their particular opinions to themselves."[7] In Europe, Freemasonry was widely regarded as an anti-church secret society dedicated to the ideals of the Enlightenment. Pope Clement XII

3 *Worship the Lord: The Liturgy of the Reformed Church in America* (New York: Reformed Church Press, 2005), 34.

4 Ibid., 35.

5 *Worship the Lord*, ed. James R. Esther and Donald J. Bruggink (Grand Rapids: Eerdmans, 1987), 20.

6 *Worship the Lord* (2005), 149.

7 *Encyclopaedia Judaica*, vol. 7, 122.

issued a bull of excommunication against Freemasons in 1738 on the basis that they "are men of all sects and religions, bound together by a natural morality; this bond is secret with an oath enforced by exaggerated penalties."[8] Among nineteenth-century European immigrants to the United States, Reformed, Lutheran, Roman Catholics, and Orthodox alike were against Freemasonry.

In America, many of the late-eighteenth-century Founding Fathers had been Freemasons—and church members. It is widely believed that it was the Freemasons of St. Andrews Lodge in Boston who participated in the Boston Tea Party. Paul Revere was also a Mason. Of the fourteen presidents of the United States that have been Freemasons, George Washington was the first (Gerald Ford the most recent). Nine signers of the Declaration of Independence and thirteen of the Constitution were Masons.[9] Although still a secret society, it was not anti-clerical, and its members did not find being Christians and Lodge members antithetical. Members of the RCA in the East, having experienced the euphoria of the birth of a new nation in the late eighteenth century, embraced the institutions of the Founding Fathers, including Freemasonry, as a positive component of the new nation. Thus the stage was set for conflict within the church, with two opposing views of the same institution.

Perceiving Freemasonry as anti-biblical and anti-Christian, Reformed Christians in the Midwest wished the General Synod to condemn Freemasonry and ban membership in the Order. Perceiving Freemasonry as a respectable American institution with respect for the Bible and having biblical components, many Reformed Christians in the East saw no conflict between their very conservative, mission-minded, orthodox Reformed theology and membership in the Masonic Order.[10]

The issue of Freemasonry first appeared in the *Minutes of the Classis Holland* in 1853 when the classis declared that it was unlawful for a

8 *New Catholic Encyclopedia*, vol. 3 (2003), 790.

9 *Encyclopedia Americana*, vol. 18 (1994), 432.

10 Turretin (1623-87; defender of orthodox Calvinism and co-author of the Helvetic Consensus Formula [1675]) was still being taught at New Brunswick even as John Henry Livingston proclaimed world mission in expectation of Christ's imminent return. John Henry Livingston, "The Everlasting Gospel," in *Vision from the Hill*, ed. John W. Beardslee III, Historical Series of the Reformed Church in America, no. 12 (Grand Rapids: Eerdmans, 1984), 1-26.

church member to belong to a Masonic Lodge.[11] This was the accepted European Reformed position and it was not thought necessary to codify the opinion of classis as an extra-canonical test.[12] Freemasonry became a matter of controversy in 1867 when the fledgling Christian Reformed Church (CRC), having begun its separation in 1857, now established an extra-canonical test for membership by banning lodge membership by synodical order.[13] Since the cause of the CRC secession could be broadly described as dissatisfaction with practices of the RCA which were not in conformity with the secessionist outlook of the Netherlands, the Midwestern members of the RCA, being of the same mind on the Masonic issue, felt constrained to ask their General Synod to "discountenance" Freemasonry and "deliver a distinct utterance of its disapprobation of the connection of the Lord's people with the Order of Freemasons. . . ." The General Synod voted to take no action by a vote of eighty-nine to nineteen.[14] It should be noted that the overture had stopped short of requesting an extra-canonical test which would bar church membership to Masons, although that was probably the intent.

In the following year, Classis Wisconsin again joined Holland in overturing General Synod "with reference to Freemasonry,"[15] "which was referred to a special committee."[16] The following year, the committee of six, which included Philip Phelps of Holland, reported. In the elegant language of the period, they concluded that "the path of prudence and safety lies outside of all oath bound secret societies . . ." and that "the Christian Church possesses, in its holy teachings, and its pledges of mutual love, a far higher capacity for the development of practical benevolence than can be found in the moral lessons of any mere human organization." The committee also stated, "We cannot think, however, that they expect from Synod such a deliverance as would authorize Consistories to exclude Free Masons from church fellowship, *for this would be to establish a new and unauthorized test of membership in the Christian Church, and would interfere with consistorial prerogatives*" (italics mine).[17]

11 Bruins, 114.
12 *Classis Holland: Minutes 1848-1858* (Grand Rapids: Eerdmans, 1943), 144.
13 Bruins, 114.
14 *Acts and Proceedings of the General Synod of the Reformed Church in America*, 1868, 461, 463.
15 *Acts and Proceedings*, 1869, 551-52.
16 *Acts and Proceedings*, 1869, 622.
17 *Acts and Proceedings*, 1870, 96-97.

With reference to the first point, the establishment of "a new and unauthorized test for membership," the formal, canonical requirements for church membership are found in the Liturgy's "Office for the Reception into Communicant Membership," and are essentially limited to belief in the Old and New Testaments. Christians in the Midwest saw Freemasonry as anti-biblical. Many Christians in the East saw no biblical impediment to membership. To have added a test for church membership would have contradicted the biblical interpretation and conscience of other Christians.

The Synod wisely refused a "new test of church membership" respecting the biblical understanding of both groups. Secondly, it is the elders of the church who are to decide on whether the profession of faith of the applicant is satisfactory. Neither the Classis nor the Synod is to usurp this function.[18]

When all of the Midwestern classes again overtured Synod in 1880, Synod sought to satisfy the Midwest by a more severe statement against secret societies, but it did not back down on its refusal to add extra-canonical tests for church membership or ministerial office. "No communicant member, and no minister of the Reformed Church in America ought to unite with or to remain in any society or institution, whether secret or open, whose principles and practices are anti-Christian, or contrary to the faith and practice of the Church to which he belongs. . . . That this Synod also advises Consistories and Classes of the Church to be very kind and forbearing, and strictly constitutional in their dealings with individuals on this subject, and that they be and are hereby affectionately cautioned *against setting up any new or unauthorized tests of communion in the Christian Church*" (italics mine).[19] And that was the last synodical word on extra-canonical tests for over a century.

The next major theological dispute in the nineteenth century concerned the Mercersburg Theology of the German Reformed Church with which the RCA was considering a form of union. In brief, the conflict was over incorrectly perceived Romanizing tendencies in the German Reformed Church. Although the result was to terminate all discussion with the German Reformed Church concerning any further

[18] Allan J. Janssen, *Constitutional Theology: Notes on the Book of Church Order of the Reformed Church in America,* Historical Series of the Reformed Church in America, no. 33 (Grand Rapids: Eerdmans, 2000), 46-49, 80-83.

[19] *Acts and Proceedings*, 1880, 536.

cooperation, at no time did it result in even the suggestion of any extra-canonical test for membership or ministry.[20]

In the major dispute of the twentieth century, the ordination of women, the two principles enunciated in 1870 and 1880 continued to be observed. Sincere Christians in the Reformed Church were divided as to whether the biblical evidence allowed for or denied the ordination of women to the offices of the church. At no time did Synod even consider this issue as requiring an extra-canonical test for church membership. Even when Synod voted that the *Book of Church Order* allowed the ordination of women, it established a conscience clause that allowed those who believed the Bible to be against such ordination to be able to refrain from participating in such ordinations without being subject to any censure.[21] Despite the extreme differences of opinion, at no time were these differences seen as a reason for an extra-canonical test which would deny church membership or ministerial status to opposing ministers.

The Synod of 2004, however, moved precipitously to insert an extra-canonical test into the *Book of Church Order* which in turn opened the door to denying membership and ministerial status to any person not conforming to this new and unauthorized test of membership. The circumstances surrounding this change in longstanding precedent took place on the floor of Synod with little if any consideration of far-reaching consequences. An overture was sent to Synod by the Classis of the Canadian Prairies asking Synod "to affirm that marriage is properly defined as the union of one man and one woman, to the exclusion of all others."[22] The overture was recommended by the advisory committee.[23] From the floor of Synod a motion was made to amend the motion by adding "to direct the Commission on Church Order to consider an

[20] Harmelink, *Ecumenism and the Reformed Church*, 32-35, 38-52. For a history of the conflict between the RCA and the German Reformed Church over the Mercersburg Theology, see Gregg Mast's essay, "A Decade of Hope and Despair," included elsewhere in this festschrift. *Ed.*

[21] *Acts and Proceedings*, 1980, 275; Book of Church Order, 2005 (New York: Reformed Church Press, 2005), 1.II.2.8, p. 30. Cf. Janssen, *Constitutional Theology*, 109.

[22] *Acts and Proceedings*, 2004, 332.

[23] The first reason given cited the "time-honored biblical mandate" which seemingly ignored, in terms of biblical literalism, such notables as Isaac, David, and Solomon, all of whom combined one man with more than one woman. The next three reasons were reflections of the political "cultural values" campaign which of late comes to the fore every two years.

amendment to the *Book of Church Order* which places this affirmation into our church order, for report to the 2005 General Synod."[24] The Synod voted for this extra-canonical test seemingly unaware of overturning a longstanding precedent.

Fortunately, its referral to the Commission on Church Order allowed a more careful consideration of the matter. Reporting to the Synod of 2005, the commission noted that the prior action of the Synod of 2004 did "not carry the weight of definitive church teaching. The General Synod does not have among its powers the determination of what, finally, is the 'teaching of the church.' In Reformed church order, the teaching of the church is determined by the creeds and confessions of the church."[25] In brief, the commission affirmed the traditional stand of the church against extra-canonical tests.

But the Commission on Church Order also reaffirmed the polity of the church in noting that "the conduct of ministers has been and remains under the purview of the classis. Inserting a regulation that affects the conduct of the minister in one matter opens the question of what should be added to such a list. This commission deems it wiser to leave the matter to the classes."[26] The position of the Synods of 1870 and 1880 was again upheld.

The threat of homosexuality, however, continued to distress the Canadian classes, this time that of British Columbia,[27] which sent an overture to Synod requesting to amend the *Book of Church Order* as follows: "No minister of Word and sacrament may endorse a practicing homosexual lifestyle by teaching, blessing a same-sex union, or officiating at a same-sex marriage ceremony. A minister of Word and sacrament found guilty of endorsing a homosexual lifestyle in the manner described will be put under discipline."[28] This went far beyond anything requested by the Midwestern classes in the dispute concerning Freemasonry. Obviously, the contemporary fear of homosexuals far outweighs the nineteenth-century fear of Freemasons. The depth of this fear was evident from a second overture from the same classis which would insert into the *Book of Church Order* an extra-canonical test affecting "elders, deacons, teachers, local church staff, and synod

24 *Acts and Proceedings*, 2004, 333.

25 *Acts and Proceedings*, 2005, 91.

26 Ibid.

27 For several decades this classis has regularly sent overtures to Synod which are concerned with homosexuality.

28 *Acts and Proceedings*, 2005, 98.

or denominational staff" who might "publicly endorse a practicing homosexual lifestyle."[29] In response to both overtures, the advisory committee recommended the denial of the overture, albeit not entirely for the right reasons. In the end, both overtures were denied.

One would have thought that by this time the Classis of British Columbia would have exhausted its antipathy toward homosexuality, but the classis, if nothing else, was thorough and all-encompassing in its hostility. In a third overture, another extra-canonical test was requested for insertion into the *Book of Church Order* to whit: "No RCA classis may knowingly ordain a practicing homosexual licensed candidate or install a practicing homosexual minister of Word and sacrament within the bounds of its classis. A classis found guilty in this matter will be put under discipline and will not be allowed to participate in the business of the regional synod involved nor of the General Synod, as long as it breaks covenant with the church at large."[30] Again, the overture was denied, but again, as in the two prior overtures, one of the reasons was "The judicial precedent of the recent trial replaces the need for constitutional action."[31] The recent trial was that of the Reverend Doctor Norman J. Kansfield, president of New Brunswick Theological Seminary until 27 March 2005.

The rush to impose extra-canonical tests, however, had not been exhausted by the Classis of British Columbia. Similar overtures to add extra-canonical tests to the *Book of Church Order* were also received from the classes of Central Plains, Pleasant Prairie, and West Sioux. Since these classes had previously not exercised themselves on issues of homosexuality, one wonders whether their concern was stimulated by the political landscape which had put the marriage amendment on many state ballots, or whether it was a marriage of like minds—or perhaps both. In any case, the classes of South Grand Rapids and Zeeland were to be commended insofar as their overtures for extra-canonical tests extended to heterosexual fidelity as well as banning homosexuals.[32]

That the RCA was not of one mind on the issue of homosexuality was apparent from the overtures of the classes of Rochester and Schenectady, both requesting the tabling of any requests for changes

[29] *Acts and Proceedings*, 2005, 99.
[30] *Acts and Proceedings*, 2005, 100.
[31] *Acts and Proceedings*, 2005, 101.
[32] *Acts and Proceedings*, 2005, 101-6.

in the *Book of Church Order* or Liturgy, and calling for studies by the Commissions on Theology and Christian Action regarding homosexuals and their place in the life and ministry of the church.[33] These overtures were also denied. Overtures having been considered, it is necessary to return to the "judicial precedent" cited as one of the reasons for the denial of requests to add extra-canonical tests.

The Reverend Dr. Norman J. Kansfield, as well as having been the president of New Brunswick Theological Seminary (NBTS), also held the office of Professor of Theology, the "fourth office" in the RCA, elected and installed thereto by the General Synod, and under the *Book of Church Order* amenable to the discipline of the General Synod. The occasion which resulted in a disciplinary trial before the 2005 General Synod was that Kansfield officiated at the marriage of his daughter Ann to Jennifer, in the Commonwealth of Massachusetts, with a valid marriage license granted by the Commonwealth of Massachusetts.

Kansfield's action, done with neither the advice nor the consent of the NBTS Board of Trustees, clearly left the trustees unsure of what their next step ought to be. During their October 2004 meeting they voted to offer Kansfield a new appointment, extending to June 2007. Following the conclusion of that meeting and the distribution of the minutes, it was determined that this vote had technically failed, since it was passed by a majority of trustees present and voting, rather than the required majority of *all* trustees. In January 2005, the board voted to allow the president's appointment to lapse on 30 June 2005. A teleconference board meeting held near the beginning of March, moved President Kansfield's last day in office to Easter, 27 March 2005. The reason for this action was possibly twofold: it gave the seminary board the appearance of virtue in taking prompt and forceful action against Kansfield; and secondly, that by terminating his office as president, a case could be made that Kansfield was no longer a professor of theology, and therefore not under the discipline of Synod.

Kansfield, convinced of the biblical rightness of his position, desirous of opening the discussion of the issue, and perhaps hopeful that Holy Scripture together with scientific evidence[34] would allow the Synod to vindicate him, exercised his right of appeal, and therefore was entitled to a trial before Synod on the charges brought against him. It is not the purpose of this essay to rehearse the trial and the evidence

[33] *Acts and Proceedings*, 2005, 106-7.

[34] Cf. David G. Myers and Letha Dawson Scanzoni, *What God Has Joined Together: A Christian Case for Gay Marriage* (San Francisco: Harper, 2005).

submitted, but rather to examine the question of extra-canonical tests for membership and office. A description of the documents submitted as evidence is printed in *Acts and Proceedings*, 2005, 43-52. The records of the judicial procedure are stored in the RCA Archives with restricted access.[35]

Summarized, the charges were: 1) that Kansfield, having performed the marriage ceremony between his daughter Ann Margaret and another woman, acted contrary to Holy Scripture and the

[35] While the chair had ruled that the "Report on Sufficiency of Charges" (henceforth Report) by Synod's Investigative Committee would be distributed to delegates prior to trial (*Acts and Proceedings*, 43), the charges as described in *Acts and Proceedings*, 43-44, are at considerable variance from those in the Report, which were the charges to be voted upon. With reference to Accusations 1 and 2 (that Kansfield "violated his declaration to 'accept the Scriptures as the only rule of faith and life,'" and the second, "that he violated his declaration to 'believe the gospel of the grace of God in Jesus Christ as revealed in the Holy Scriptures . . .'"), the Investigative Committee reported, "We have determined that both of these accusations lack sufficient merit to warrant further consideration by the General Synod" (Report, 15-16). Accusation 3, that Kansfield "violated his declaration to 'walk in the Spirit of Christ, in love and fellowship within the church, seeking the things that make for unity, purity, and peace.' We have determined that this accusation has sufficient merit, and we submit this accusation to the General Synod for further consideration" (17-18). Accusations 4 and 5, that "Kansfield violated his declaration to submit to 'the counsel and admonition of the General Synod, always ready, with gentleness and reverence, to give an account of [his] understanding of the Christian faith' was also judged to have 'sufficient merit.'" In a note of clarification the Investigative Committee declared that it did not consider Kansfield to have violated the phrase "always ready, with gentleness and reverence, to give an account of my understanding of the Christian faith" (21). The "Six Accuser Charge," that "Kansfield's actions were 'contrary to our faith and beliefs as affirmed by the Holy Scriptures and the decisions of the General Synod concerning the relationships of active homosexuality,'" was also seen to "have sufficient merit to warrant further consideration . . ." (19-20). Further clarification was also given with reference to his actions as having been contrary to Holy Scripture. The Investigative Committee emphasized that it was "neither equipped nor empowered to interpret Scripture" but relied on "the authoritative statements and decisions of the General Synod" (22). It should be noted that the "Six Accuser Charge" became Charge One in the *Acts and Proceedings*, the third Accusation became Charge Two, and Accusations 4 and 5 became Charge Three (*Acts and Proceedings*, 43-44).

authoritative statements of General Synod;[36] 2) his actions contradicted his affirmations for Licensure, as Minister, and as Professor of Theology; and 3) that he violated his promise to submit himself to the counsel of the Synod.[37] The Synod by a roughly two-to-one margin voted that the charges were proven with a "high degree of probability" (a considerably lower bar for conviction than the "beyond reasonable doubt" of a criminal court). The Synod then voted "to exercise discipline of the Rev. Dr. Norman Kansfield by deposing him from office of General Synod Professor of Theology and suspending him from the Office of Minister of Word and Sacrament."[38] The numbers voting were not published. The magnitude of this disciplinary action must be seen in the fact that never before had a Professor of Theology been disciplined for any cause, let alone been deposed from office or suspended from ministry.

36 The charge as defined by the Investigative Committee and to be voted upon by Synod was that "in officiating at a same-sex marriage ceremony, Rev. Dr. Kansfield's actions were 'contrary to our faith and beliefs as affirmed by the Holy Scriptures and the decisions of the General Synod concerning relationships of active homosexuality.'" The committee found the accusations "of sufficient merit to warrant further consideration." However, as recorded in the *Acts and Proceedings*, the charges voted upon were, "In a letter, dated November 2004, Rev. Kansfield disclosed that during 2004 he had 'presided at the marriage of his daughter to another woman' to quote his own words. This action allegedly took place in June of 2004 according to a letter addressed to the General Synod by the Classis of Illiana in March of 2004 [*sic*]. The Reformed Church in America has reaffirmed its stand against the marriage of same-sex partners several times in the past few decades. Rev. Kansfield's actions were contrary to our faith and beliefs as affirmed by the Holy Scriptures and the decisions of General Synod concerning the relationships of active homosexuality" (*Acts and Proceedings*, 2005, 43). Since a court stenographer was present, is it fair to assume that someone in presenting the charge to the Synod increased the rhetoric in the direction of conviction? Most blatantly, the assertion was made that the RCA reaffirmed its stand against same-sex partners several times in the past few decades. Although a fair inference, as stated it is false.

37 *Acts and Proceedings*, 2005, 43-44. Charge Three was presented to Synod with the following editorial addition to that of the Investigative Committee: "If there was ever a situation where this statement could and should have been applied it would have been the June 3-9, 2004 meeting of General synod [*sic*], before the 'marriage' in Massachusetts later in June." Is it a fair inference that Synod delegates were asked to vote on an altered and highly charged accusation?

38 *Acts and Proceedings*, 2005, 44.

Comparatively, in the all too many cases of ministerial adultery, it is rare that a classis either deposes or suspends the adulterer.

In view of the harshness of the discipline, it is necessary to examine the charges more closely and ask if it sets a precedent for extra-canonical tests. The Synod determined that "the stipulated facts submitted by the parties at the commencement of the proceedings would constitute the reasons for the judicatory's decisions."[39] Charge One, that "Kansfield's actions were contrary to . . . Holy Scripture and the decisions of General Synod" leaned heavily in the direction of judicially attempting an extra-canonical test. That his actions were contrary to Holy Scripture was based upon the affirmation of the 2004 General Synod regarding marriage, which were never made extra-canonical tests for ministers or members by a two-thirds vote of the classes for inclusion in the *Book of Church Order.* In fact, the "contrary to Holy Scripture" phrase was an assumption made on the basis of reports by the Theological Commission to the General Synods of 1978 and 1979 and which were not declared to be the position of Synod but were merely made "available . . . for study."[40] Again, no biblical evidence was cited. Similarly, in Charge Two, citing the affirmations, it is again the assumption that Kansfield's actions violated these broad promises, albeit nowhere in Scripture or the Standard*s* is anything said about lesbianism, let alone performing a marriage for such. For the prosecution, guilt was by extrapolation of the 1978 and 1979 papers made "available . . . for study."[41] Only in Charge Three was there a

[39] Ibid., cf. 43-52.

[40] 1978, 240; 1979, 135. In 1990 the Classis of Cascades overtured General Synod to "adopt" the report of 1978 (but not of 1979) as "the official position of the RCA" (460). The advisory committee softened the language to "adopt" without explicit reference to either 1978 or 1979 (461). It further recommended a new study and referred both 1978 and 1979 to the churches as "pastoral advice" (461). The 1994 General Synod "adopted" a lengthy statement, the core of which was a call "to a process of repentance, prayer, learning, and growth in ministry [to the homosexual]" (376). In 1995 this position was reaffirmed, with an instruction to provide resources to that end (388).

[41] Seemingly neither the Investigative Committee nor many of the members of the Synod had taken seriously the entirety of the 1978 paper on "Homosexuality, a Biblical and Theological Approach," which can be found in *The Church Speaks, Papers of the Commission on Theology, Reformed Church in America,* ed. James I. Cook, Historical Series of the Reformed Church in America, no. 15 (Grand Rapids: Eerdmans, 1985), 243-57. A close reading reveals two strains of thought, one which saw all homosexual activity as a

degree of specificity, i.e., that he violated his promise to submit himself to the General Synod, insofar as on 7 June 2004 Synod in response to an overture voted, "To affirm that marriage is properly defined as the union of one man and one woman to the exclusion of all others. . . ." Despite the fact that Kansfield stated that he was not aware of this action when on 19 June 2004 he officiated at his daughter's wedding, the Synod obviously held that ignorance of even recently-enacted synodical, but non-constitutional, affirmation was no excuse.

The Synod, however, evidently failed to take seriously the report of its Committee on Church Order and Governance which held, with specific reference to the above resolution, that, "The General Synod does not have among its powers the determination of what, finally, is the 'teaching of the church.' In Reformed church order, the teaching of the church is determined by the creeds and confessions of the church."[42] The basis for discipline by Synod repeatedly referred to the overture of 2004, and to the "decisions of General Synod."[43] Even the Investigative

---

sin, and another which makes an important distinction between those for whom homosexuality is a matter of choice and those for whom as a result of genetic or other reasons the person has no choice [the paper speaks of this as homosexual *inversion* in distinction from *perversion*]. The 1978 paper goes on to observe that "the church must learn to deal differently with persons who are homosexual by constitution and not by choice" (255). "As Jesus remained silent on the entire subject, so the biblical writers did not address the human condition now [1978] known as homosexual inversion" (255). "A person cannot be blamed for a situation over which he/she has neither control nor choice. There is firm biblical support and every humane reason to understand the invert's predicament as evidence of the problem of evil, *rather than sin*" (italics mine) (256).

42 *Acts and Proceedings*, 2005, 91.

43 The Investigative Committee cited Synod's actions in 1977 (204), 1978 (229-40), 1979 (128-35), and R-11 (*Acts and Proceedings*, 1990, 460-62) and R-92 (*Acts and Proceedings*, 2004, 333). This was proper in terms of the charges, and really focused on the Theological Commission's report of 1978. However, another side of Synod can be seen in the initial overture of 1977, which arose as a result of "greater oppression of homosexuals and lesbians" and asked Synod to: "affirm the human and civil rights of homosexuals and lesbians" (*Acts and Proceedings*, 1977, 204). In response to the 1978 paper came the 1979 paper of the Theological Commission on the "Christian Pastoral Care for the Homosexual." In 1990, R-11 was bracketed by R-12 and R-13 calling for another study paper [a regular tactic by those wishing to update the thinking of the church]. Similarly, in 2004, R-92 was followed by R-93 calling for a study paper on "human sexuality and marriage." All of this is cited to emphasize the fact that the church is not

Committee cited the "authoritative statements and decisions of synod,"[44] that is, the papers by the Commissions on Theology, as if they represented definitive church teaching. However, Synod has made "authoritative statements" on everything from being against SUVs to being against the elimination of the capital gains tax. If one were to extrapolate the "judicial precedent" of the Kansfield case, i.e., that the statements of Synod are binding on the church, then a classis, or a consistory, could discipline someone for driving an SUV or being for the elimination of the capital gains tax.

The *Book of Church Order*, however, already has some very specific requirements which ministers have promised to uphold in their vows upon licensure and ordination but for which discipline is not exercised. For example, "'The Office for the Administration of Baptism' *shall be read*," and "'The Office for the Administration of the Lord's Supper' *shall be read*" (italics mine).[45] Were we to suspend from the ministry every violator of that section of the *Book of Church Order* we would be hard pressed to fill our pulpits. Obviously, for some, homosexuality is far more important to the church than its sacraments. Nevertheless, the authority of the *Book of Church Order* is of such magnitude that only a two-thirds vote of the classes can change it. As such, the fulfillment of vows should weigh far more heavily as they are defined by the *Book of Church Order* than by the reports to Synod, or even its resolutions. Was Kansfield's deposition from office and suspension from ministry on the basis of assumption and assertion the *de facto* equivalent of an extra-canonical test?

The General Synod of 2005 was not "very kind and forbearing" as the Synod of 1880 admonished. It is also open to question as to whether its harsh judgment of Kansfield resulted in Synod's forbearance in denying the overtures seeking to impose extra-canonical tests upon the church, or whether its perceived "judicial precedent" will only encourage further attempts to add such tests. In our presbyterial church order, the ultimate power to change any part of our constitution must receive approval by two-thirds of the classes. Thus it is patently obvious that papers that General Synod "makes available to the church for study" do

---

of one mind on this issue, and to engage in an extra-canonical test, or even an appeal to "judicial precedent," is to ignore the scriptural convictions of other Christians—and without a conscience clause.

44 "Report on Sufficiency of Charges," pp. 9-14.

45 Book of Church Order (2005), 1.I.2.11b and c, p. 15; Janssen, *Constitutional Theology*, 59-61.

not in themselves have binding, constitutional authority for the church. For that they would need the approval of two-thirds of the classes. Even then, it is up to the classis to impose discipline on its ministers, and up to the elders to discipline its members. Even with constitutional authority, it has been a long time since any classis disciplined any of its ministers for failing to have an order of worship "in accordance with the *Liturgy* of the Reformed Church in America," or not singing hymns "in harmony with the Standards of the Reformed Church in America," or of failure "to explain the points of doctrine of the Heidelberg Catechism every four years,"[46] despite their constitutional mandate. In any case, the Synod of 2006 rejected further attempts to add extra-canonical tests.[47]

The genius of the refusal to establish extra-canonical tests is that it allows the church to live with serious differences of opinion until a consensus is reached. When the Synods of 1870 and 1880 refused an extra-canonical test denying membership to Freemasons, it allowed Christians of varying convictions to live in one church and at the same time live out their convictions. In the Midwest, many RCA churches denied membership to Masons, and ministers who were members of the Masonic order were unknown. In the East, members of the RCA lived out their Christian convictions, with many members, and some ministers, as Masons. But they continued in the unity of the body of Christ.

One can only hope that the church will continue to reject "new and unauthorized tests" for membership and leadership, especially when proposed hurriedly and/or in hostility. Classes and consistories should be allowed to fulfill their historic Reformed roles to exercise discipline within their proper spheres. The church should avoid the use of extra-canonical tests to address issues of disputed biblical interpretation and complex social issues. It is sincerely hoped that the precedent set by the Synods of 1870 and 1880 will continue to provide a guide to right action in the present.

[46] Janssen, *Constitutional Theology*, 58, 62, 64.

[47] Specific references cannot be given as the *Acts and Proceedings*, 2006, was not yet published at the time of writing.

CHAPTER 4

Dr. Albertus Pieters, V.D.M.: Biblical Theologian

Eugene Heideman

Publication of a book in honor of Dr. Elton Bruins provides an opportunity to also remember the ministry of Dr. Albertus Pieters (1869-1955). Albertus Pieters and Elton Bruins both were born in Alto, Wisconsin, and graduated from Hope College and Western Theological Seminary. Albertus Pieters almost single-handedly built up the small Beardslee Library at the seminary, fighting for budget, selecting the books to be purchased, and then cataloging, pasting in the pockets for the check-out cards, and even shelving the books. Elton Bruins worked in the seminary library for five years during his student years at Hope and Western, meticulously opening the books, pasting in the pockets, and shelving the books while serving the students and faculty who came to the library.

Both of them have made major contributions to our understanding of the origins of the community of Holland, Michigan, and the role of Rev. Albertus Van Raalte in the founding of the colony of Holland and the union of the Classis of Holland with the Reformed Church in America. Both have written about the history of Hope College and Western Theological Seminary.[1] They have also traced the

[1] See, for example, Albertus Pieters, "Remembering the Lord's Leading" (sermon on Deut. 8:2 given on 18 October 1925); "Remembering the Ways of the Lord" (address at Centennial Celebration of First Reformed Church,

history of the conflict concerning admission of Freemasons as members of the church.[2] Above all they have been loyal and active members in the congregations to which they have belonged in Holland and in the denomination that they have loved.[3]

Although Albertus Pieters spent much of his career in academic teaching,[4] he took little satisfaction in academic degrees. He preferred the letters V. D. M. (*Verbi Dei Minister),* "Minister of the Divine Word." While he rejected the idea that as a faithful minister of the Word it was necessary to take a "prophetic" stance against the great evils of his day, he was often engaged in writing polemical or controversial articles. Reformed Church classes called him to account for his contention that the Fourth Commandment is not the basis for the observance of Sunday as a day of rest.[5] He wrote against the Scofield Bible and dispensational theology that was coming to be accepted by many within the denomination.[6] In 1925, at the time of the Scopes trial about teaching evolution in the public schools, he wrote that laws

---

Holland, 27 April 1947) (Western Theological Seminary Collection, Joint Archives of Holland; hereafter cited WTS/JAH). All Pieters's articles and manuscripts are located in Pieters Papers, WTS/JAH. See also Elton Bruins, "Albertus C. Van Raalte and His Colony," *Reformed Review* 30, no. 2 (winter 1977): 83-94.

2 See, for example, Albertus Pieters, "Problems of Christian Membership in Secret Societies" (sermon on I Cor. 5:14-15) and "Freemasonry and Church Membership" (WTS/JAH), and Elton J. Bruins, "The Masonic Controversy in Holland, Michigan, 1879-1882" in *Perspectives on the Christian Reformed Church Studies in Its History, Theology and Ecumenicity*, ed. Peter de Klerk and Richard R. De Ridder (Grand Rapids: Baker, 1983), 523-74.

3 Pieters was a lifelong member of the First Reformed Church in Holland; see his sermon "The Help of God for Sixty Years" (on Acts 26:1-22), preached on the sixtieth anniversary of having made confession of faith in that church. See also Elton J. Bruins, *The Americanization of a Congregation*, 2nd ed. (Grand Rapids: Eerdmans, 1995).

4 He taught at Steele Academy, Nagasaki, Japan, 1891-99 and 1905-10, and he was Professor of Bible, Hope College, 1923-26, and Dosker-Hulswit Professor of Bible and Missions at Western Theological Seminary, 1926-39. As emeritus professor, he continued to teach as needed for a number of years.

5 Albertus Pieters, "The Value of Sunday" (address given at Community Betterment League, Ellsworth, Mich., 23 November 1936); "Calvin's View of the Fourth Commandment" (WTS/JAH, n.d.); and "Correspondence with Classis of East Sioux" (WTS/JAH, 1944).

6 Albertus Pieters, *The Lamb, the Woman and the Dragon* (Grand Rapids: Zondervan, 1937), 57-63, and in many other writings.

should not be passed prohibiting teaching about evolution. He taught that Genesis 1 must be interpreted in terms of six long ages rather than six twenty-four hour days.[7]

Albertus Pieters was the son of Rev. Roelof Pieters. Shortly after Albertus was born, Roelof Pieters accepted a call to follow Rev. Albertus Van Raalte as pastor of the First Reformed Church (Pillar Church) in Holland, Michigan. At the time of Roelof Pieters's death in 1880, there was a conflict in the Reformed Church in America about the admission of members of the Masonic Order into the membership of the church. On 27 February 1882 the congregation voted to secede from the denomination and in 1884 joined the Christian Reformed Church. The seceders gained possession of the Pillar Church building. Three months after the vote to secede, the thirteen-year-old Albertus Pieters made his public confession of faith in the presence of the remaining forty families and eighty communicant members of the First Reformed Church that had "no parsonage, no church, and no minister."[8] Later in life, after missionary service in Japan, he wrote and lectured often about the breach between the Reformed Church and the Christian Reformed Church. Although his stance was often polemical, he never ceased to reaffirm his friendship with those in the Christian Reformed Church and his hopes for reunion.[9]

A Missionary Family in Japan

Albertus Pieters graduated from Hope College in 1887 and Western Theological Seminary in 1891. He married Emma Kollen, also a member of the Hope College class of 1887. Following their marriage they went to Japan. The Pieters family experienced tragedies that tested and refined their faith. Five children were born to them. Their long-awaited son Henry Kollen Pieters was born in 1907 but died at the age of fifteen months. In their grief they did not forget to share their faith with the Japanese. They printed an announcement folder with his picture and the question, "Is it well with the child?" on the one side, and the words, "It is well," on the other.[10] Their oldest daughter, Ruth Wilhelmina, died in 1915, a few weeks after graduating from Hope

[7] Albertus Pieters, *Notes on Genesis* (Grand Rapids: Eerdmans, 1943), 29-33.

[8] Pieters, "The Help of God for Sixty Years."

[9] See, for example, "The Reasons Assigned to the Secession of 1857" (address given to the Adelphic Society, Western Theological Seminary, 6 April 1937) and Letter to Editor, *Banner*, 20 September 1947.

[10] *Leader*, 27 July 1951, 15.

College. Their daughter, Elizabeth, became an invalid with tuberculosis for many years. Another daughter, Dorothy Henrietta, suffered a mental breakdown but eventually recovered. After their daughter Mary married John Keohane, she became a teacher and writer of textbooks.[11]

During his thirty-two years of service as a missionary in Japan, Albertus Pieters pioneered the ministry of newspaper evangelism. He wrote several series of articles explaining the Christian faith and printed them in daily newspapers.[12] He called upon the leaders of Japan to follow their own laws regarding freedom of speech and civil rights. In 1913 he went to Korea to observe and report in the newspapers about the "Korean Conspiracy Case" in which several Koreans, including Christians, were falsely accused of conspiring against the Japanese occupation of their country.[13] In 1921-22 when Japanese militarism and State Shintoism were becoming dominant, he wrote a series of articles attacking the emperor system and the growing militarism of Japan. This was a criminal offense and brought him to the attention of the authorities.[14] Even if the health of his daughters had been such as to allow them to return to Japan, it is questionable that the Japanese Government would have permitted them to do so.

Albertus Pieters, Professor of Theology

After returning to the United States in 1923, Pieters was asked to teach Bible and religion at Hope College. In 1926 he was called to Western Theological Seminary to serve as Professor of English Bible and Missions. As a member of the Seminary's small faculty, he taught other subjects as necessary from year to year. These included

[11] *Leader,* 12 September 1951, 4, 8.

[12] Albertus Pieters, *Seven Years of Newspaper Evangelism in Japan* (Kyobunkwan, Japan: Association for the Promotion of Newspaper Evangelization, 1919); "Newspaper Evangelism: Present Status and Prospects" (paper read at Evangelical Committee, 28 January 1921); and "The Daily Paper as an Evangelist" (report for *CMS Quarterly*).

[13] Albertus Pieters, "The Korean Conspiracy Case," *Japan Advertiser,* 13 November 1913. Pieters had gone to Korea to report on the trial of Koreans, including several Christians, accused of conspiring to kill the Japanese Governor General, but the facts of the case did not support the charges.

[14] Pieters wrote, "that such an attitude as this towards the Emperor is genuine deification, demanding for him that which can be yielded only to God, and that it is therefore utterly inconsistent with Christianity, is too evident to call for discussion" (*Japan Advertiser,* 16 April 1921).

Systematic Theology, Biblical Theology, Ethics, Old Testament History, New Testament History, Church History, and Non-Christian Religions. In each of these fields he prepared voluminous class notes for his students.[15] His real love was for biblical theology and history. This is clear not only in his class notes but also in the books that he published and notes for Bible classes he taught in the Grand Rapids YMCA, in a Berean Bible Class, and in local churches. His careful and extensive notes for these classes and his seminary courses are on file at the Joint Archives of Holland, Western Theological Seminary Collection, in Holland, Michigan.

Albertus Pieters: Bridging Two Theological Eras

The First Era: The Stability of Reformed Systematic Theology

From our vantage point today, we can understand that Pieters served as a bridge between two theological eras at the seminary. In the first era that lasted from its origin in 1866 through World War II, classical Reformed systematic theology was dominant in the curriculum. Throughout that era the interpretation of the Bible was carried out from the perspective of systematic theology. Systematic theology moved in a straight line, beginning with epistemology and the doctrine of Scripture. It then went through the doctrines of God, anthropology, Christology, and the Holy Spirit. After that, it set forth the *Ordo Salutis* (Order of Salvation) in steps from election through regeneration, conversion, justification, sanctification, and eventual glorification. It proceeded through the doctrine of the church and sacraments and concluded with eschatology or the doctrine of the Last Things. In that era, the technical vocabulary of systematic theology often governed the definitions of the biblical words.[16] Systematic theology propounded the Bible as the divinely inspired book to be mined for propositional

---

15 Eerdmans, Grand Rapids, published his *Notes on Genesis* in 1943 and *Notes on Old Testament History* in 1950.

16 All of the professors of systematic theology at WTS followed this line of development through the three-year course of study. Class notes of Gerrit Dubbink, Egbert Winter, Albertus Pieters, and John R. Mulder are available in the WTS/JAH. There is also ample evidence in the archives that the other professors, Cornelius E. Crispell, Nicholas Steffens, Henry E. Dosker, and Evert Blekkink, followed what is known as the *Loci* course of instruction. The *Loci* method of teaching systematically led students through the study of the doctrines of Scripture, God and the Trinity, Creation, Anthropology,

truth in each of the areas of theology. The great strength of systematic theology is that it is comprehensive, timeless, and efficient. It provides clear definitions that can serve as a guide for preaching and teaching throughout the whole ministry of theological students.

The curriculum of the era from 1866 through World War II served well to meet the needs of the Midwestern Reformed Church. In an era when Dutch immigrants were integrating into American life, and when the acids of modernity and theological Modernism were threatening from many sides, it provided a solid, stable theology that enabled the church to hold to the orthodox Reformed confessions (the Belgic Confession, the Heidelberg Catechism, and the Canons of Dort) and the church order handed down by the National Synod of Dort in the Netherlands in 1618-19. Reformed Church believers could trust the seminary to hold to the old paths and not to give way to the latest theological fad.

Albertus Pieters was the last professor at Western Theological Seminary who had learned the Dutch language before English. In his doctrine of the church and sacraments as well as the other *Loci* he was influenced by Nicholas Steffens, one of the two full professors at the seminary during his student days. Dr. D. Ivan Dykstra wrote an article, "His Theological Contribution," in the *Western Seminary Bulletin* issue in honor of Pieters's eightieth birthday. He observed that Pieters's work was constantly in the service of conservatism, opposing church union and membership in the Federal Council of Churches. Pieters also remained conservative in matters such as infant baptism, biblical inspiration and interpretation, opposition to revision of the Reformed Church confessional statements, and defense of miracles in the Bible.[17] Thus Pieters remained a man of the old era in his basic orientation to theology. It was this conservatism that made it possible for the church to continue to trust him even when some of the positions he took were upsetting to them.

Christology, Soteriology, Ecclesiology, and Eschatology. Students were required to learn precise definitions of the various terms. Biblical words often acquired academic technical definition that was far more precise and more narrow than was the biblical usage of the words.

17 D. Ivan Dykstra, "His Theological Contribution," *Western Seminary Bulletin,* December 1948, 2-4.

Opening a Way to a New Era

As will become more apparent below, while remaining basically in the old era, he opened the way to the new era that the seminary began to enter during World War II. In the old era, truth was basically understood as the objective knowledge of things as they really are in themselves and in their relationships with each other.[18] Truth rested on observable, empirical "facts" rather than the ideas spun out by ancient philosophers. Theological truth was the inductive system of doctrine that could be known from the facts collected from Scripture.[19]

In 1948, Dr. John E. Kuizenga, a professor at Princeton Theological Seminary who had taught at Western Theological Seminary from 1915 to 1930, placed an article in the *Western Seminary Bulletin* entitled "Truth as Encounter." It was a discussion of the theology of the Swiss theologian Emil Brunner, who made a sharp distinction between "I-It" objective truth and "I-Thou" truth encounter between two subjects, God and the living human being.[20] "I-Thou" truth is the truth that happened to Abraham when he was called out of Ur, to Moses when he stood before the burning bush, and to the disciples when they heard Jesus' words, "Follow me." Truth as encounter between God and human beings gives higher priority to commitment and faithful relationships than to abstract, objective propositions.[21] Eschatology replaced providence as the dominant perspective.

Dr. Richard Oudersluys agreed with John Kuizenga. He too was not ready to accept the radical disjunction between "I-It" and "I-Thou" truth or between "supra-history" (*Geschichte / Heilsgeschichte*)

[18] Theodore Dwight Bozeman, *Protestants in an Age of Science: The Baconian Ideal and Antebellum American Religious Thought* (Chapel Hill, N.C.: University of North Carolina Press, 1977), 57.

[19] Charles Hodge, *Systematic Theology* (London: Thomas Nelson and Sons, 1883), 9-13.

[20] John E. Kuizenga, "Truth as Encounter," *Western Seminary Bulletin,* October 1948, 4-9.

[21] The emphasis on truth as faithful "I-Thou" relationships, or as being encountered by God, was not foreign to what had been taught to previous generations at the seminary. The Reformed pietists of the seventeenth century also knew what it was to be encountered by God (M. Eugene Osterhaven, "The Experiential Theology of Early Dutch Calvinism," *Reformed Review* 27 [1973-74]: 180-89). Nicholas Steffens in the nineteenth century already had written that truth is found in the faithfulness of God; truth is not only objective truth ("Waarheid en Heiliging," *De Hope,* 28 August 1889, 41).

and ordinary history (*"Historie"*) that some of the "neo-orthodox" theologians were proclaiming after Karl Barth wrote his *Römerbrief* in 1919.[22] Nevertheless, influenced by Oscar Cullmann's "Salvation-history theme" and Geerhardus Vos, *Pauline Eschatology,* Oudersluys concluded that eschatology was the perspective and organizing theme from which the New Testament can best be taught.[23] In a lecture on "Eschatology and the New Testament" delivered at Calvin Theological Seminary, he argued that eschatology "has established a whole new perspective from which we now read and study the New Testament."[24]

> If we had to put to former generations the question, "what is the New Testament all about?" they would have replied, "the fatherhood of God,"[25] "the Sermon on the Mount," or "Jesus Christ." In our own Reformed Church circles, the framework within which we read and studied the Scriptures were either the *ordo salutis* or the various *loci dogmata* such as anthropology, theology, Christology, soteriology, ecclesiology, and finally eschatology. If you put this same question to Christians the world around today, "what is the New Testament all about?"—the answer will be eschatology. Not only has the doctrine of last things moved from the periphery to the center of biblical studies, it has become the perspective from which all is read and interpreted.[26]

Other Western Seminary faculty members recognized the centrality of eschatology for the life of the church and God's mission in the world. Elton E. Eenigenberg was pleased that the World Council of Churches meeting in 1954 had focused on the theme of Jesus Christ, the hope of the world, in response to the secularism and disorder in the post World War II world.[27] Eugene Osterhaven used Emil Brunner's

22 Richard C. Oudersluys, "Biblical History and Faith," *Western Seminary Bulletin,"* September 1953, 1-4. Richard Oudersluys taught New Testament at Western Theological Seminary from 1942 to 1988, including ten years as adjunct professor following his retirement in 1977.

23 Oudersluys, introductory note to "Eschatology Lectures" (Oudersluys Papers, WTS/JAH, n.d., typed).

24 Oudersluys, "Eschatology and the New Testament" (WTS/JAH, n.d., manuscript).

25 Dr. Evert Blekkink, Emeritus Professor at the seminary, published *The Fatherhood of God* in an attempt to provide a more orthodox understanding of this favorite liberal theme (Grand Rapids: Eerdmans, 1942).

26 Oudersluys, "Eschatology," 2-3.

27 Elton M. Eenigenberg, "The Christian Hope," *Western Seminary Bulletin,* March 1953, 1-4.

books, *The Mediator* and *Man in Revolt,* as textbooks for a time. Lester Kuyper spoke of truth as the faithfulness of God in Jesus Christ. The intent of John the Evangelist was

> to place Jesus, the fullness of truth, vis-à-vis Pilate, who represented truth in the Greek world. Salvation-truth is not to be found in Greek or Roman systems of culture or law, not in truth as they understood it. Rather salvation-truth is incarnated in Jesus; and it is through him that salvation-truth becomes redemption for the world.[28]

Pieters as Apologist for the Faith

The Facts and Mysteries of the Christian Faith

It now remains for us to explore how Albertus Pieters, who always remained a man of the first era, served as a bridge to the new era and generation of teachers at the seminary after World War II. In what may be his most widely read book, *The Facts and Mysteries of the Christian Faith,* first published in 1926, he remained clearly positioned in the first era. He wrote that the Christian religion is a "revealed religion, but there is an element in it that is not revealed."[29] It is "rooted first of all in the soil of facts, by which we mean externally observable and historically provable events, things that really happened, and can be shown to have happened."[30] Among such facts are the crucifixion and the empty tomb on Easter morning, the existence of the people of Israel in the days of the Old Testament, the existence of the temple of Solomon, the carrying off of the people of Israel into Assyria and Babylon, and the facts that John the Baptist, Jesus, and Paul lived in the first century A. D. There are also facts that cannot be proven by the strictest criteria of modern historiography, but can be accepted on the basis of the

28 Lester J. Kuyper, "Grace and Truth," *Reformed Review,* September 1962, 15. Kuyper, Oudersluys, Osterhaven, and Eenigenberg all studied at Western Theological Seminary while Pieters was on the faculty.

29 Albertus Pieters, *The Facts and Mysteries of the Christian Faith* (Grand Rapids: Eerdmans, 1926), 8. The wide use of the book in the church was probably due to its simple and clear exposition in non-technical language, its defense of the orthodox Reformed faith against "modernism," and because its emphasis on "facts" had a close fit with its readers' common sense empiricism.

30 Ibid.

testimony of credible witnesses, such as the miracles that Jesus did and the missionary activities of the Apostles.

The "mysteries" are all those teachings of Scripture that can be known only by revelation. These would include such matters as the creation of the world out of nothing, the coming of the Son of God in the flesh, the atonement, the new birth in Christ, the resurrection of the body, and the teaching that Jesus will come at the end of the world to judge the living and the dead. The mysteries must be accepted on faith, but they are not mere speculation. They come from "well-accredited organs of revelation, but that can not, independently of such revelation, be supported by sufficient proof—many of them by any kind of proof."[31]

The mysteries can be known to us through God's revelation in the Bible. Pieters was influenced by the common sense realism philosophy that had been brought to Princeton from Scotland by its president, John Witherspoon. Princeton's outstanding theologian, Charles Hodge, emphasized that the principles of theology must be built on the facts in the Bible. "As the facts of nature are all related and determined by the nature of God and by physical laws, so the facts of the Bible are all related and determined by the nature of God and of his creatures."[32] *The Facts and Mysteries of the Christian Faith* was written in the style Pieters had used for his newspaper evangelism articles in Japan. Pieters had newspaper readers in mind as he wrote its forty-four chapters, each the length of a newspaper article. Pieters's purpose was not only to strengthen the faith of Christians, but also that those outside the faith would "learn to accept the gospel."[33] Therefore he could not begin with the assumption that his readers accepted the Bible as the Word of God, but he could assume that they accepted the empirical or "Baconian" inductive scientific method with its assumption that knowledge must be based on facts.[34] He also believed that objective scientific facts were common ground, valid for believers and non-believers alike.

[31] Ibid., 9.

[32] Charles Hodge, *Systematic Theology,* quoted in Bozeman, *Protestants in an Age of Science,* 155.

[33] Pieters, *Facts and Mysteries,* 7.

[34] Bozeman, *Protestants in an Age of Science,* gives a full exposition of the impact of "Baconianism" on Presbyterian theology in the nineteenth and early twentieth century; see especially 101-158.

The Historicity and Inspiration of the Bible

Because he could not count on immediate acceptance by his readers that the Bible is the Word of God, he set out to provide evidence that the four gospels tell the truth about Jesus Christ. He observed that "we need the facts related in the gospel documents to explain the course of history."[35] We can check at numerous points to see whether they stand the test of historical accuracy. We find that "they are reliable at all points that can be checked" and so can conclude that they are equally reliable where they cannot be checked.[36] Acknowledging then the reliability of the gospel records about facts, we must also be open to their testimony that Jesus came as the Son of God in fulfillment of prophecy,[37] that he was crucified to make atonement for the sin of humankind,[38] and that there is clear evidence that when he rose from the dead on Easter, the tomb was empty.[39]

Pieters taught that the acceptance of the biblical canon of the Old Testament depends on our answer to the question, "What think ye of Christ?"

> [If] we regard Jesus as God manifest in the flesh, and look upon the apostles as men guided in their utterances and activities as founders of the Christian Church, then we shall receive the Old Testament with all reverence; for an essential part of their work was to guarantee to the Church these books as coming from God.[40]
>
> To sum up: the primary ground, and the strongest ground we have for confidence in the Holy Scriptures is the confidence we have in Jesus Christ. Believing Him, and receiving from Him the Scriptures, we believe them.[41]

Pieters taught that alongside the confidence we have in the words of Jesus as the objective grounds for believing that the Scriptures are inspired and authoritative, we have also received in our hearts the

35 Ibid., 30.
36 Ibid., 32.
37 Ibid., 40-43.
38 Ibid., 107-113, 142-51.
39 Ibid., 122-41.
40 Pieters, *Can We Trust Bible History?* (Grand Rapids: Society for Reformed Publications, 1954), 19.
41 Albertus Pieters, *The Inspiration of the Holy Scriptures* (Grand Rapids: Church Press, 1933), 14.

testimony of the Holy Spirit that God is speaking to us through these words. This forms the subjective grounds for our recognizing biblical authority: "as they read it grips them. It speaks to them in accents of authority to which their hearts respond. . . ."[42]

He wrote that we can trust Jesus' words about the Old Testament to guide our study of it. Since Jesus spoke of Moses as the author of the first five books, we must hold to Mosaic authorship. Because Jesus said that Jonah's three days and nights in the belly of the sea monster was also a sign of Jesus' resurrection from death, it must follow that the Book of Jonah is a historical record, not just a legend.[43] Yet Pieters was not dogmatic on the historicity of Jonah.

> If any one thinks that he has reason to interpret the story of the prophet Jonah as a parable, on general literary grounds, we shall not quarrel with him. Let him follow his literary judgment, provided he is not led to do so by any desire to get rid of the supernatural. . . . If so interpreted, the question of historicity does not arise.[44]

Pieters often wrote in opposition to "Modernists" in the church who either (1) "have overthrown everything distinctive of Christianity as a historical religious system" or (2) "others, who do not think clearly, and do not know where they are going . . . and are intellectual tight-rope walkers," who claim to hold to the faith but actually are not far from the first group.[45] He rejected the conclusions of Modernists who considered much of the Old Testament history to be forged, who hold that its moral teachings have been outgrown, and who outlaw the supernatural on purely *a priori* grounds.[46] In contrast to the Modernists, we "have excellent reasons for looking upon them as bona fide reliable history. Accepting this, the utterances reported in them from the Savior and the apostles certainly are inspired utterances in the strict sense;

42 Ibid., 13.
43 Ibid., 70-73.
44 Ibid., 70. During the first half of the twentieth century the question about the historicity of Jonah was often understood in conservative circles to be a test of whether one really believed in the inspiration and authority of the Bible.
45 Albertus Pieters, *The Inspiration of the Holy Scripture* (Grand Rapids: Church Press, 1933), 5.
46 Ibid., 13.

and for the rest we have good reasons to believe the gospel record true, whether inspired or not."[47]

Pieters did not hold to a doctrine of verbal inspiration or dictation theory of inspiration. The contents of Holy Scripture conform to the substance of God's message, without requiring that God chose every word. He held the belief in the "Plenary inspiration" of the Holy Scriptures.[48] Belief in plenary inspiration holds that the Bible in all its parts is the word of God. It is incorrect to say that the Bible *contains* the word of God; it *is* the word of God. It is not primarily a record of the spiritual experiences of the human race; it is "above all a record of progressive *revelation*, something that came *into* human life from God."[49]

In contrast to the teachings of the Princeton Theological Seminary faculty, especially Charles Hodge and Benjamin Warfield, Pieters rejected the idea that it is necessary to hold to the doctrine of the inerrancy of the original manuscripts of the Bible in all matters, including historical or geological details and in being totally internally non-contradictory.[50] Pieters objected that there can be no appeal to the original manuscripts regarding inerrancy since those manuscripts do not exist. He insisted that

> When it comes to statistics, dates, and similar matters, there are certainly errors in the Bible as we now have it. It is probable that many, perhaps most, of these errors are errors in transmission, and did not exist in the original documents; but no one can be sure that this is true of them all. . . . A document can be a trustworthy source of information even though minor errors exist in it. . . .[51]

Pieters always remained within the framework of the older pre-World War II perspective. Nevertheless, in *Can We Trust Bible History?* (1954), he looked with favor upon the "*Heilsgeschichte*" (History of Redemption) perspective of the new era.

47 Ibid., 15. It should be noted here that for Pieters truth refers to the objective accuracy and faithfulness of the Bible in recording historical events.

48 Pieters, *Notes on Genesis* (Grand Rapids: Eerdmans, 1943), 1.

49 Pieters, *The Inspiration of the Holy Scriptures,* 18-19.

50 See Benjamin Warfield, *Revelation and Inspiration* (Grand Rapids: Baker, 2000), 214-26. In 1976, the issue of the inerrancy of the Bible again became a matter of great public controversy when Harold Lindsell's *The Battle for the Bible* (Grand Rapids: Zondervan, 1976) became a bestseller.

51 Pieters, *Notes on Genesis,* 12.

> The Old Testament contains history, but it is not merely history, as the early history of Greece and Rome is history; it is history and religious revelation combined. Nor is it merely that history provides a certain setting and that then the religious revelation is something else, independent of it, existing within that setting. No, the history itself is a revelation of the nature, will and saving work of God.[52]

In his 1938 course on Old Testament Biblical Theology, Pieters taught that biblical theology does not deal with revelation as the finished product of the divine activity or the setting forth of ideas about God. It is the study of the actual self-disclosures of God that lie behind the facts committed to writing.[53] He further taught that revelation as a divine activity is not a smooth process, but is "epochal," focused on events such as God's call of Abraham, leading the people from Egypt to the Promised Land, the anointing of David, the Exile, etc. The process of revelation became incarnate in history. God's act-revelation must be placed alongside word-revelation. Act-revelations are never left to speak for themselves; they are preceded by and followed by word-revelation. Thus we have the messianic words of the Old Testament prophets, the testimonies to the incarnation of Christ in the gospels, and the witness of the apostles in the other New Testament writings.[54]

In his lecture notes on Old Testament biblical theology, as well as in his favorable comments in favor of a theology of "*Heilsgeschichte,*" we see how Pieters served as a bridge between the pre-World War II era of teaching at Western Theological Seminary and the post-war era. The "facts" reported in the Old Testament are not simply the objective, bare facts of history upon which all can agree, whether or not they are

52 Pieters, *Can We Trust Bible History?*, 31.

53 Pieters, Course Notes on Old Testament Biblical Theology (WTS/JAH).

54 Ibid., 3-4. It is interesting to compare Pieters's comments to what G. Ernest Wright wrote in *God Who Acts: Biblical Theology as Recital* (London: SCM Press, 1952), 38: "In considering Biblical faith, it seems to me that the point at which we must begin is not with the history of its evolving ideas but with history in another sense. It is history as the arena of God's activity. Biblical theology is first and foremost a theology of recital, in which Biblical man confesses his faith by reciting the formative events of his history as the redemptive handiwork of God. The realism of the Bible consists in its close attention to the facts of history and of tradition because these facts are the facts of God."

believers. The events are recited again and again by the people of Israel, the true descendants of the seed of Abraham.[55]

The Bible, Science, and Evolution

In his exposition of the Old Testament, however, Pieters seems always to have thought of the books from Genesis through 1 and 2 Kings as being essentially historical in nature, in spite of the fact that the New Testament and the Jews refer to them as to "the Law and the Prophets." It was important to show how the facts reported in the Bible were not contradicted by the facts as they were known through historical, archeological, or scientific research. In the years when he was teaching his Old Testament survey courses, one of the burning issues in the church and the country was that of the relation of the six days of creation reported in Genesis 1 to the long evolutionary ages becoming accepted in the fields of geology and biology.

In his belief that the truth in God's book of nature was consistent with the truth in the Bible, Pieters was ready to listen to what science was saying about the origins of the universe and life on earth. In 1925, the year of the notorious Scopes trial about teaching evolution in the public schools, he gave an address in which he advocated teaching of religion in the schools. In that same address he stated his opposition to laws that forbade the teaching of evolution in schools.[56]

With regard to the interpretation of Genesis 1, we must regard its language as "phenomenal" or popular language. Its facts are stated in the language of a "phenomenal observer," as they appear to the naked eye. Thus we read about the sun rising and setting, and about the sky above like a dome or "firmament." In Leviticus 11:6 we read that the hare chews the cud, and in Genesis that the waters covered "all the high mountains that were under the whole heaven." These things are reported in terms of how they appear to the naked eye rather than being an attempt to give us precise scientific language.[57]

55 Albertus Pieters, *The Seed of Abraham* (Grand Rapids: Eerdmans, 1950), 11.

56 Albertus Pieters, "Christian Education: The Gateway to a Splendid Opportunity for World-wide Influence for our Reformed Churches" (address delivered before the Classis of Wisconsin, Alto, Wisconsin, 8 September 1925), 2. Pieters spoke against laws prohibiting the teaching of evolution in public schools in the year of the notorious Scopes trial in Dayton, Ohio.

57 Pieters, *Notes on Genesis,* 23.

Pieters taught that the six days of creation refer to long ages rather than six twenty-four-hour days.[58] He did not identify them with the various geological and biological ages laid down in textbooks, because in the field of science the division of time into geological and biological ages was still undergoing changes. He agreed that the fossil record makes a strong case for processes that took a very long time.[59] He rejected the concept of "instantaneous creation" and favored "the co-operation of natural forces and processes in the creative work."[60] The creation of living things "after their kind" does not rule out variation and evolution of the various species.[61] He did not believe that all of the animals, fish, and birds were vegetarians before the fall.[62] Humankind's bodies may or may not have evolved from lower mammals, but in any case human beings were a special act of creation when God gave them souls and made them in His own image.[63]

Pieters's *Notes on Genesis* found wide acceptance among the ministers and people of the Reformed Church, with the result that the denomination has not gone through some of the bitter divisions over the theory of evolution that has split some other churches. It also prepared the way for the General Synod of the Reformed Church in America to come to a resolution of the controversy about the historicity of Adam that erupted when Dr. Lester Kuyper published two articles on "Interpretation of Genesis Two-Three" in the *Reformed Review* in December 1959 and March 1960. Kuyper had followed Pieters in stating that Genesis 2-3 was written in language common to the ancient world and was not intended to write history in the modern sense of the word.[64]

58 Ibid., 26-46.
59 Ibid., 32-33.
60 Ibid., 42-43.
61 Ibid., 45-46.
62 Ibid., 55-61.
63 Ibid., 52.
64 Lester Kuyper, "Interpretation of Genesis Two-Three," *Reformed Review*, December 1959, 5. Albertus Pieters insisted that the fall of mankind had to have taken place within human history rather than as a mythical event. Therefore he insisted upon the historicity of an actual Adam and Eve. He was less certain of the historicity of the some of the details of the account, such as whether the serpent actually talked and the change in the shape of the serpent. He pointed out that Satan or the Devil is not mentioned (*Notes on Genesis,* 92-101).

The Bible, the Standards of Unity, and Christian Liberty

The Midwestern Reformed Church had always maintained that the Scriptures are their only norm for faith and practice, with the three Standards of Unity being subordinate to the Scriptures. In practice, however, because the three Confessions provide a short and convenient summary of doctrine, they functioned as a theological screen through which the Scriptures were read and interpreted. At the seminary, the theological chairs were more prominent than the biblical chairs. Albertus Pieters through his ability as a teacher, speaker, and writer changed that equation. When controversies arose in the life of the church, he was quick to speak or write on the issue, calling upon the church to hear what the Bible had to say on the subject. The theological and local practices had to conform to the Bible, not the other way around.

He challenged the church's legalism on the matter of Sunday observance by insisting repeatedly that the Fourth Commandment was the only command not repeated in the New Testament. It was time to stop quibbling about what was not to be permitted on the Day of Rest and follow the New Testament law of liberty. There are just two principles to guide us in the use of the day: "That the public worship requires a day free from secular occupations, and that man requires for his welfare a regular and stated period of rest from toil."[65]

When the question arose about whether a man or woman should be allowed to remarry after a divorce, he agreed with a decision of the Christian Reformed Synod that marriage created a permanent bond between a man and a woman, but after reviewing the scriptural evidence he disagreed with its decision that a man who remarried after a divorce should be kept from the Lord's Table until his first wife died, and that the man should always seek to return to his first wife. He maintained that a marriage *ought* not to be broken, but that it *can* be broken.[66]

Pieters's Covenantal Theology

Albertus Pieters also contributed to a shift of emphasis in covenantal theology at the seminary. In the decades prior to his coming

[65] Albertus Pieters, *The Christian Comfort* (self-published, 1944), 40; see especially Questions 137-144.

[66] Pieters, "Marriage and Divorce" (lecture presented to the Consistorial Conference of the Classis of Zeeland, 20 October 1947).

to the seminary, the "Federal Theology" of the Westminster Assembly tradition had been dominant in systematic theology. In classical Presbyterian and Reformed thought, the "Covenant of Works" had been established with Adam as the representative of the whole human race. According to that Covenant, Adam had to choose whether to be obedient or disobedient to God. When Adam sinned, his guilt was not only his own but was "imputed" to all his descendants.[67] Pieters objected to this teaching on the grounds that there was no formal covenant instituted in Genesis 2, that it is inconsistent with justice in naming Adam as the representative when his descendants had no possibility of naming him their representative, and because the doctrine of "imputation" neglects the doctrine of the union of Christ with the believer.[68]

Pieters's covenantal theology had its focus on the covenant of God with Abraham and his seed (Gen. 12:1-30; 17:14).[69] "Federal Theology" had usually proceeded directly from exposition of the Covenant of Works to consideration of the Covenant of Grace, without taking time to deal with God's covenant with Abraham or God's covenant with Israel (Exod. 19),[70] with the result that theology had a very logical structure without regard to biblical narrative. Pieters's covenantal theology placed God's actions in history at the center of theological reflection. Although he never used the word, *"Heilsgeschichte"* (History of Redemption) in *The Seed of Abraham,* it was at the center of his theology. He wrote:

> With the call of Abraham begins the record of the great redemptive enterprise by which God sought, and is still seeking, to win back to Himself a lost world. All that the world has known since that time of true religion and divine salvation, including the Old Testament history, the law, the prophets, the psalms, the coming

[67] See William G. T. Shedd, *Dogmatic Theology,* vol. 2 (New York: Charles Scribner's Sons, 1888), 184-200. See also Westminster Confession, Articles 6-7.

[68] Pieters, "Objections to Federal Theology" (address to the Adelphic Society, WTS, 16 October 1951). See also "Sinful and Guilty," *Church Herald,* 25 February 1944: 17, where he objects to inclusion of the words in the baptismal liturgy that says that children are "guilty before God." Pieters objected that it is difficult to explain to parents why the baby is guilty. The phrase is due to Federal Theology with its doctrine of imputation of Adam's guilt.

[69] Pieters, *The Seed of Abraham,* 11-23.

[70] Westminster Confession, Articles 6-9; see also Shedd, *Dogmatic Theology,* iii-v, 257-61.

of Christ, the writing of the New Testament, the founding of the Christian Church and its long development to this very day—nay, even beyond that, all that at the present time offers any well grounded expectation of future good for a suffering world stems scripturally, logically and historically from the call of Abraham and the promise made to him: "In thee shall all the families of the earth be blessed."[71]

During the decades when Dr. M. Eugene Osterhaven served as Professor of Systematic Theology at Western Theological Seminary (1950-86), the theological legacy of Albertus Pieters remained strong. Dr. Osterhaven had read all of the major writings of Pieters and often expressed his great appreciation for the contribution Pieters had made.[72] Federal Theology faded into the background. Like Pieters, however, Osterhaven feared that the "God who acts" could replace the "God who speaks" and therefore remained cautious about an overemphasis on "*Heilsgeschichte*" to the neglect of an emphasis on creation. Osterhaven and his successor, I. John Hesselink, turned toward the writings of John Calvin, not only to his *Institutes of the Christian Religion,* but also to his many biblical commentaries and other writings. In doing so, it was the covenantal tradition represented by Pieters rather than that of Federal Theology that was followed at Western Theological Seminary. The language of the Bible and the language of systematic theology were therefore brought close together again.

Pieters's Opposition to Pre-Millennial Dispensationalism

Finally we would be remiss if we did not briefly note Pieters's great contribution to the understanding of the Book of Revelation in opposition to Dispensationalism. Relying on his covenantal theology, Pieters combined his careful attention to biblical detail with his loyalty to the church in his constant attacks on the Scofield Bible and the dispensationalists. The dispensationalists taught that the unfulfilled Old Testament prophecies were to be fulfilled in the millennial age after the Jews had returned to Jerusalem and Jesus reigned as king. In their eyes, the church is not the recipient of the blessings of the prophecies. The church is a mixed multitude with many unfaithful members in it.

71 Ibid., 11-12.

72 From time to time, Dr. Osterhaven would tell the story about how he had offered to take Dr. Pieters to the airport just so that he could talk with him without interruption.

At the beginning of the millennial age those who are still faithful on earth will be raptured before the Anti-Christ will rule for a short time and the Mark of the Beast will oppress believers. Pieters attacked their understanding repeatedly in his writings that included many articles and speeches, his lengthy exposition on the Book of Revelation, *The Ten Tribes in History and Prophecy*, and *The Seed of Abraham*. As a biblical theologian, he assisted the church to understand the Book of Revelation rather than to avoid it because of its complicated and vivid imagery.

His Spirit as Minister of the Word, V. D. M.

In his loyalty to the biblical message and to the church, Pieters often found himself in the middle of controversy. He came under attack and did not fear to respond in kind. Yet he was never mean spirited or unfair to his opponent. The spirit of his ministry was summed up in his prayer written for a "Devotional Guide":

> O Thou who lovest all men, teach us to love Thee first, that we may be able to love them also. Help us to be so confident of Thy keeping and provision that all anxiety for ourselves shall pass away. Enable us to be open handed in helping to provide for others because Thou providest for us: to be forgiving, because we are forgiven, to do unto others as we have been done by, and always are done by, of Thee. Amen.[73]

The question once was asked of Jesus, "Can any good thing come out of Nazareth?" (John 1:46). We close not with a question, but with an exclamation, "What good, gifted, and faithful men have come out of Alto!"

[73] Pieters, "Meditations for the Devotional Guide" (WTS/JAH, undated manuscript).

CHAPTER 5

Scripture and Tradition—A Reformed Perspective: Unity in Diversity—Continuity, Conflict, and Development

I. John Hesselink

Preface

It is an honor and a joy to be able to contribute to this special volume in honor of my good friend Elton Bruins. Since we went to different colleges, our first encounter was as classmates at Western Seminary. We hit it off immediately, sensing that we were kindred spirits. That friendship continued during the years when the Bruinses were in New York and we were in Japan. For the past thirty-three years we have shared in many ventures, not least of which has been our membership at Third Reformed Church here in Holland. I am proud of Elton's many accomplishments and know that they will continue as he retires once more.

Introduction. Historical Background: Diversity

Christians in the Reformed tradition, while holding to their various confessions with varying degrees of loyalty, have always affirmed at the same time the Reformation principle *sola scriptura*. However, as Jaroslav Pelikan astutely observes, "Despite their protestations of 'sola scriptura,' the Reformers showed that 'Scriptura' has never been 'sola.'"[1] Pelikan is quite correct. Even the so-called Free churches in

1 *The Christian Tradition: A History of the Development of Doctrine*, vol. 4, *Reformation of Church and Dogma, 1300-1700* (Chicago: University of Chicago Press, 1983), vii.

Protestantism, which claim to have no creeds or confessions but the Bible, are influenced more than they realize by traditions, both oral and written, which tend to undercut their insistence that the Bible and the Bible alone is their only authority for faith and practice. All religious bodies are susceptible to the same danger, i.e., that their official tenets and beliefs may not be their actual beliefs due to a variety of influences. These may be local, cultural, the current *Zeitgeist*, or an alien ideology.

At the time of the Reformation the magisterial reformers were convinced that in the Roman Catholic Church of their day, the Word of God (Scripture) had become so encrusted with traditions alien to the Scriptures and the catholic faith of the first four centuries that they felt it necessary to enunciate the *sola scriptura* principle. Thereby they may have appeared to reject the importance of tradition, but this was not the case, either in theory or in practice.

In the Lutheran reformation, for example, specifically Lutheran confessions were not long in coming. The Augsburg Confession was composed and presented to Charles V at the Diet of Augsburg in 1530. A revised version, largely the work of Philipp Melanchthon, was issued in 1540 (the *Variata*, accepted by Calvin and many Reformed churches in Germany). In the meantime, Luther drew up the Schmalkald Articles for presentation to a general council summoned by Pope Paul III. This was only the beginning! Eventually a large collection of Lutheran confessions–including Luther's two catechisms–were published in a volume called *The Book of Concord* (1580).[2]

In contrast to the Lutherans, most of whom acknowledge this whole collection as authoritative, Reformed churches have never agreed on one common confession. "There is no such thing as a Reformed *corpus doctrinae*."[3] In the first half of the sixteenth century, confessions or series of doctrinal articles were drawn up by Zwingli (1523), by the church leaders in Bern (1528), Basel (1534), Lausanne (1536), and in Geneva by Calvin and Farel (1536), all within less than fifteen years of the beginning of the Swiss Reformation. With typical Swiss independence, none of these cities accepted their counterparts' confessions as their own.[4] One might cite the First Helvetic Confession

2 The English edition, edited and translated by Theodore G. Tappert, was published by Fortress Press, Philadelphia, in 1959.

3 Arthur Cochrane, introduction to *Reformed Confessions of the Sixteenth Century*, ed. Arthur Cochrane (London: SCM Press, 1966), 15.

4 Eventually, however, Calvin was able to work out a common confession of sorts for all the Swiss Reformed churches, both French and German

of Faith as an exception since it was accepted by almost all the German Swiss Protestant cities. It was drawn up in Basel in February 1536 by a small group of reformers including Bullinger, Grynaeus, Myconius, and Leo Jud. It was, however, eventually superseded by the Second Helvetic Confession of 1566.

Not even the preeminence of Zwingli during the early years of the reform movement in Switzerland, or the generally acknowledged leadership of Calvin from 1536 until his death in 1564, resulted in their respective confessional statements being accepted in other Reformed domains, although Calvin's influence in France, southwest Germany, and other European Reformed centers was considerable in the 1540s and 1550s. Even so, Calvin's two catechisms (1537 and 1542), originally written in French, were translated into Latin in order that they might be used in ecumenical exchanges; but they never gained the universal acceptance that Luther's catechisms have enjoyed in the larger Lutheran world until this day.

The one Reformed catechism which has had an influence far beyond the borders of its origin is the Heidelberg Catechism, written in 1563 in an attempt to resolve a dispute over the Lord's Supper between Lutheran and Reformed factions in the Heiliggeist Kirche in Heidelberg. Today it is still the most widely used catechism in Reformed churches around the world, e.g., in Hungary, Germany, and the Netherlands in Europe, and Reformed churches of Dutch, German, and Hungarian background in this country—as well as the United Presbyterian Church, U.S.A., since 1967—and in several countries in Asia such as Japan and Indonesia. The only Reformed confession to have comparable influence is the Westminster Confession of Faith (1647), which has been the standard (along with the Westminster Catechism) of English-speaking Presbyterian churches throughout the world for over three centuries.[5]

The point I want to make here is that churches in the Reformed tradition, though generally confessional churches—with the notable

---

speaking, with Heinrich Bullinger, Zwingli's successor in Zurich. The result was the Consensus Tigurinus, known in English as the Zurich Consensus (1549).

5 Reformation scholars regard the Second Helvetic Confession (1566) as the finest of the sixteenth-century Reformed confessions. Ironically, it has no official status in Switzerland, the land of its origin, but it is one of the confessions of the Reformed Church in Hungary and was adopted by the United Presbyterian Church in the U.S.A. in 1967, along with its new Confession of 1967, the Heidelberg Catechism, and the Barmen Confession (1934) of the Confessing Church in Germany.

exception of the Swiss Reformed Church—have no one common, binding confession. Reformed leaders and scholars have occasionally deplored this diversity, feeling that this is one of the reasons why the Reformed family of churches lacks the cohesion and loyalty of similar confessional groups such as the Lutheran World Federation and worldwide Anglican Churches which meet once every ten years in the Lambeth Palace in England (although the resolutions of these Lambeth Conferences are not binding on the member churches). Such diversity within the Reformed tradition is accentuated by the inclusion of several United Churches (e.g., the United Church of Christ in Japan) and churches of Congregational background that are members of the World Alliance of Reformed Churches.

One of the few things the churches of the Reformed Alliance once held in common was the Presbyterian system of church government, although even here there were exceptions, such as the Reformed Church in Hungary, which has always had bishops. However, in order to include churches with a Congregational polity, the phrase "holding a Presbyterian System of Church Government" was dropped by the World Alliance of Reformed Churches in 1954.

There have been attempts in the past to make a collection of Reformed confessions. In 1581, and again in 1612, collections of Reformed confessions were published,[6] but neither one was ever recognized as authoritative by an ecclesiastical body. The closest we come to a canon of Reformed confessions in our time is the collection approved by the Presbyterian Church U.S.A.[7] Hence, when one speaks of *the* Reformed tradition, it cannot be assumed that even those within this tradition will agree on what its fundamental tenets are. Or, if

6 In Geneva, a *Harmonia Confessionum* was published in 1581 and later a *Corpus et Syntagma* in 1612. Cf. Cochrane, *Reformed Confessions of the Sixteenth Century*, 15.

7 See the Constitution of the Presbyterian Church U.S.A., part 1, *Book of Confessions*, published by the Office of the General Assembly, New York, N.Y., in 1983. In addition to the Catechism and Confessions listed in note 5, it contains the Apostles' and Nicene Creeds, the Scots Confession (1560), and the Shorter and Larger Westminster Catechisms (1648). The largest collection of Reformed confessions is found in Cochrane, *Reformed Confessions of the Sixteenth Century*. By limiting himself to the sixteenth century, however, Cochrane omits some influential seventeenth century confessions: the Westminster Confession, the two Westminster Catechisms, and the Canons of Dort (1619). The most complete collection of catechisms is found in *The School of Faith: The Catechisms of the Reformed Church*, ed. Thomas F. Torrance (London: James Clarke, 1959).

they agree that election and the covenant are key motifs, they may interpret these concepts so differently that they lose any meaningful commonality. The doctrine of double predestination, for example, as taught in the Canons of Dort and the Westminster Confession, still has its defenders,[8] whereas Karl Barth saw this as the Achilles heel of Reformed theology and proposed instead a radical election in Christ which hardly allows for unbelief.[9] The majority of Reformed theologians and ministers either fall somewhere in between these two positions[10] or are so uncomfortable with the doctrine that they simply avoid it.[11]

Some Characteristic Motifs: Unity

These differences of interpretation and the variety of confessions notwithstanding, it is still possible to speak of *the* Reformed tradition. There are within it, of course, liberals and conservatives, more "spiritual" types, and social activists, but this is true of any tradition and most denominations. Even so, there are certain theological accents, as well as a distinctive ethos, in some cases, and a specific

8 See the essays by the late Professor Fred Klooster (Calvin Seminary) and the late John Murray (Westminster Seminary), in the symposium edited by Peter Y. De Jong, *Crisis in the Reformed Churches: Essays in Commemoration of the Great Synod of Dort, 1618-1619* (Grand Rapids: Reformed Fellowship, 1968). Cf. R. C. Sproul, *Chosen by God* (Wheaton, Ill.: Tyndale House, 1986). He defends double predestination but insists that God is not arbitrary and that the notion of equal ultimacy (in regard to God's decrees of election and reprobation) "is *not* the Reformed or Calvinist view of predestination" (142).

9 Karl Barth has discussed this doctrine in various places, but his fullest treatment is in *Church Dogmatics*, vol. 2, pt. 2 of *The Doctrine of God*, trans. G. W. Bromiley, J. C. Campbell, Iain Wilson, J. Strathearn Mc Nab, Harold Knight, and R. A. Stewart (Edinburgh: T & T Clark, 1957), especially 306ff.

10 Moderate positions are taken by the Dutch Reformed theologian, G. C. Berkouwer, in *Divine Election* (Grand Rapids: Eerdmans, 1960), and by the American Presbyterian theologian who taught at Fuller Seminary, Paul Jewett, in *Election and Predestination* (Grand Rapids: Eerdmans, 1985).

11 See James Daane, *The Freedom of God: A Study of Election and Pulpit* (Grand Rapids: Eerdmans, 1973). In his introduction, Daane asks, "Why is election, which runs like a vertebra through the Scriptures, so rarely preached? This question is especially striking when asked within the Reformed theological tradition in which I stand" (6). Some of the sharpest critics of the doctrine of the reprobation have been Christian Reformed scholars. Daane is one; Harry Boer is another. The case of Harry Boer will be considered later.

Weltanschauung which distinguishes the Reformed tradition from other Protestant traditions, not to mention the Orthodox and Roman Catholic traditions. It would require another paper, or even a book, to try to delineate the distinctive characteristics of the Reformed ethos or *Weltanschauung* (a term particularly popular in Dutch neo-Calvinistic circles). Moreover, to some extent this has already been done by M. Eugene Osterhaven in his book *The Spirit of the Reformed Tradition,*[12] and the Presbyterian theologian, John H. Leith, in a similar work, *An Introduction to the Reformed Tradition.*[13] I have also dealt with this theme in a semi-popular way in *On Being Reformed: Distinctive Characteristics and Common Misunderstandings.*[14]

There are also gaps between what Reformed/Presbyterian denominations and their confessions, ancient or modern, *say* they believe and what is the belief of the person in the pew. A good case in point is the understanding of the Lord's Supper. John Calvin and John Knox had a high view of the sacrament, holding firmly to a real presence of Christ in the celebration of the sacrament, albeit in a spiritual, not a physical manner. Here Calvin was closer to Luther than to Zwingli. This view is represented in the vast majority of Reformed confessions. Yet the popular view held by most laity in Reformed and Presbyterian churches in North America is more akin to the symbolical-memorial view of Ulrich Zwingli.

Such gaps or divergences between the confessional stance of a church or tradition and the commonly held view are not unique to the Reformed family of churches. Consequently, first I shall point out a few of the common characteristics in most Reformed confessions, then note their emphasis on the priority and final authority of Scripture, and close with illustrations of how the *sola scriptura* principle has been honored in one case where a doctrine has been challenged on the basis

12 M. Eugene Osterhaven, *The Spirit of the Reformed Tradition* (Grand Rapids: Eerdmans, 1971).

13 John H. Leith, *An Introduction to the Reformed Tradition* (Richmond, Va.: John Knox Press, 1977).

14 I. John Hesselink, *On Being Reformed: Distinctive Characteristics and Common Misunderstandings*, 2nd ed. (New York: Reformed Church Press, 1988). Cf. a similar work by the Christian Reformed theologian John Bolt, *Christian and Reformed Today* (Jordan Station, Ontario: Paideia Press, 1984). There are also several older books on Calvinism of a semi-popular nature, one of which has recently been re-issued and revised by Paul A. Marshall: H. Henry Meeter, *The Basic Ideas of Calvinism* (1939; rev. ed., Grand Rapids: Baker, 1990).

of Scripture, and maintained in another case where a specific doctrine has been modified in the light of recent exegetical insights.

Some Common Motifs

I have already suggested one of the typical emphases of Reformed confessions: election or predestination. A related motif is the majesty and sovereignty of God.[15] To this extent, Reformed theology is representative of Augustinianism, or at least one strain of it. The same is true of its radical view of sin, often depicted as total depravity (better, total inability), and its corollary, the bondage of the will.[16] Whether explicit or implicit, the twin evils of Pelagianism and Arminianism are being attacked in the typical Reformed confession, the antidote being an emphasis on God's sovereign grace and the work of the Spirit in our salvation.[17]

In common with the Lutheran confessions there is also an emphasis on the sole sufficiency of Christ's once-for-all sacrifice for our salvation, justification by grace through faith, and the necessity of good works according to the law of God, not as a means of gaining merit but as an expression of gratitude. What distinguishes many Reformed confessions from their Lutheran counterparts, however, is the positive role of the state and the civil magistrate as God's instruments not only for maintaining order but also for preserving true religion.[18]

15 First Confession of Basel 1; First Helvetic Confession 9; French Confession 12, 21; Scots Confession 8; Belgic Confession 16; Second Helvetic Confession 10; Canons of Dort 1; Westminster Confession 3. It is noteworthy that neither in the Geneva Confession of 1536 nor in Calvin's Geneva Catechism of 1542/45 is election or predestination mentioned. The same is true of the Heidelberg Catechism. What is curious, however, is that in his first Catechism (1537/38) Calvin has a whole section on election.

16 Basel 2; First Helvetic 8 and 9; Geneva 4; French 9; Belgic 15; Second Helvetic 9; Heidelberg Catechism Q and A 5-9; Dort 3.1-4; Westminster 6. N.B. Nowhere in these documents is the expression "total depravity" found.

17 First Helvetic 12-13; Geneva 8-10; French 12, 21; Scots 12; Belgic 22-23; Second Helvetic 16; Heidelberg Cat. Q and A 8, 21, 60; Dort 3, 4.12-14; Westminster 9.3; 13.1-5; 14.1; 16.1-3; 34.3 (this last article was added by American Presbyterians in 1930).

18 Basel 8; First Helvetic 26; Geneva 21; French 39, 40; Scots 24; Belgic 36; Second Helvetic 30; Westminster 25.

Scripture the Only Rule of Faith and Practice

What particularly distinguishes the Reformed tradition is not so much any set of doctrines as its emphasis on the *sola scriptura* principle. This was first enunciated by Luther, but in Lutheran Confessions and Lutheranism the *material* principle of the Reformation, justification, became its hallmark, whereas in the Reformed tradition the accent falls on the *formal* principle, Scripture. In the Lutheran confessions and in Lutheranism the emphasis is on the *material* principle.[19]

There are a few exceptions, notably the Heidelberg Catechism, but a hallmark of Reformed confessions is their emphasis on the *sola scriptura* principle. Confessions—whether the ancient catholic creeds or later Reformation confessions—are recognized as authoritative, but it is always a relative or secondary authority. It is also important to notice that in many of the Reformed confessions it is not simply Scripture alone but the Word *and* the Spirit which are the court of final appeal.[20] In other words, it is not the letter of Scripture in and of itself, but the Word which is empowered, activated, and accompanied by the Spirit which is the only rule of faith and practice.

Semper reformanda! Contemporary Confessions

I have already pointed out some of the distinctive ways in which the Reformed confessions treat Scripture. There is nothing unusual about their understanding of the relation of Scripture and tradition, at least from a Protestant standpoint. Tradition, as represented by early Christian creeds, is important and merits respect, but it must always be subordinate to "the one infallible rule of faith and life" (a conflation

[19] This is the generally accepted distinction. See, e.g., Emil Brunner, *Truth as Encounter* (Philadelphia: Westminster, 1964), 87: "The 'formal principle,' the Word of God, and the 'material principle,' redemption through Jesus Christ or justification by faith alone, are not two but one and the same principle seen in two aspects."

[20] As noted above, the Heidelberg Catechism has no separate treatment of Scripture; it simply assumes it. But it does appeal several times to the Word and the Spirit. In its explanation of the second petition in the Lord's Prayer, for example, the first part of the answer reads: "So govern us *by thy Word and Spirit* that we may more and more submit ourselves unto thee" (Q and A 123). Cf. the definition of the church in Q and A 54: "I believe that . . . the Son of God, *by his Spirit and his Word*, gathers, protects, and preserves for himself, in the unity of the true faith, a congregation chosen for eternal life" (emphasis in both cases mine).

from several confessions).[21] No tradition has affirmed the *sola scriptura* principle more emphatically and unequivocally than the Reformed tradition.

At the same time, however, the Reformed tradition takes its confessions seriously, although perhaps not as seriously in some cases as the Lutheran tradition. Much depends on how conservative and cohesive a denomination is. For example, the Lutheran Church Missouri Synod and the Orthodox Presbyterian Church take their respective confessions more seriously (i.e., strictly or rigidly) than their main line or ecumenical counterparts.

In contrast to the Lutheran and Anglican traditions, however, churches in the Reformed tradition have not been loath to compose new confessions. They take seriously a venerable and popular Reformed slogan: *Ecclesia reformata semper reformanda est*, or a simpler version, *semper reformanda!*[22] As a result, it is a rare Presbyterian or Reformed denomination which has not commissioned a contemporary statement of faith within the past fifty years. The Presbyterian Church U.S.A. as early as 1903 added two chapters to the Westminster Confession in order to make up for what were perceived as serious omissions in the original (1647) version of the confession, namely, a chapter (34) on the Holy Spirit and a chapter (35) entitled "Of the Gospel of the Love of God and of Missions."[23]

[21] This language, or a variation of it such as "infallible rule of faith and practice," is common to many historic Reformed confessions and is also the language employed today by most American Reformed/Presbyterian denominations in their books of church order/government. In view of the recent "Battle for the Bible" (see Harold Lindsell's book by that title) and the debate in conservative evangelical circles about inerrancy, it should be noted that even a conservative denomination like the Christian Reformed Church in North America interprets "infallible" as meaning not inerrant in every geographical or historical detail, but "infallible in what it [Scripture] intends to teach."

[22] The origin of this phrase is uncertain. Another variant is *ecclesia reformanda quia reformata*. Gyula Barczay, a Hungarian-Swiss pastor, in his doctoral dissertation on the larger theme of the renewal (*Erneuerung*) of the church, concluded that it originated in the seventeenth century, but he could not discover any author. He simply concludes, "Sein Ursprung ist unbekannt" (*Ecclesia semper reformanda* [Zurich: EVZ Verlag, 1961], 19). He concludes with A. Schweizer and W. A. Visser 't Hooft that these phrases probably originated in seventeenth century Reformed Orthodoxy.

[23] See the Presbyterian *Book of Confessions*, Westminster Confession of Faith, chapters 34 and 35.

Generally, however, Reformed-Presbyterian denominations have not followed this route. That is, they have left their historic confessions intact, even when there was opposition to certain tenets, for either historical or doctrinal reasons.[24] Instead, they have been more open than most confessional groups to writing new confessions. In most cases, they have supplemented, not supplanted, the older sixteenth and seventeenth century confessions.

The first of these new confessions within the European-North American sphere was composed by a commission of the Netherlands Reformed Church (*Hervormde Kerk*) in 1946 and was officially adopted by its General Synod in 1950.[25] This was the first attempt to write a new confession since the Canons of Dort in 1619! As the Introduction states, "Our Netherlands Reformed Church desires to become once more a confessing church."[26]

The theme of this confession—the proclamation of the Kingdom of God—is both a response to the totalitarian regimes and their claims during World War II and a fleshing out in contemporary terms of a traditional Reformed motif.[27] It consists of nineteen sections, the first of which is "God, our King," the last being "The Triune God." A unique feature of this confession is its two sections on Israel: "The Election of Israel" (3), and "The Present and Future of Israel" (17).

[24] In the Reformed Church in America, for example, Article 36 of the Belgic Confession has long been ignored or denied. Here one of the functions of civil authorities is "to maintain the holy worship of the Church, to prevent and remove all idolatry and false religion, to destroy the kingdom of the Antichrist. . . ." Those churches which have the Heidelberg Catechism as one of its standards are also generally willing to drop the reference to the Roman Catholic mass as a "cursed" or "condemnable idolatry" (Q and A 80). The original reads *vermaledeite Abgötterei*). This question, however, can be omitted or relegated to a footnote without much difficulty because it was not in the first edition of the Catechism. Probably the most general discontent with, if not downright opposition to, a given doctrine is that of double predestination as taught in the Canons of Dort and the Westminster Confession. Here, however, Reformed Presbyterian theologians can take refuge in the Heidelberg Catechism or the Second Helvetic Confession which either omit the doctrine or state it in a more positive fashion.

[25] Translated by a committee appointed by New Brunswick Theological Seminary, New Brunswick, N. J., and published by the seminary in 1955 with the title *Foundations and Perspectives of Confession*.

[26] Ibid., 4.

[27] It may be a slightly exaggerated claim, but in my book, *On Being Reformed*, I have claimed that "Reformed theology is kingdom theology" (64).

The first attempt of a similar nature in the United States was by the Presbyterian Church in the U.S. (commonly known before the union with the United Presbyterian Church as the Southern Presbyterian Church), which came out with a "Brief Statement of Belief" that was adopted by their 102nd General Assembly in 1962,[28] but it was dropped when they joined the United Presbyterian Church to form the Presbyterian Church U.S.A.

In the meantime, in 1958 a committee was appointed by the United Presbyterian Church in the U.S.A. (UPUSA) to prepare a new confession, but it was not forthcoming until 1965. It was approved by the General Assembly in 1967 and is accordingly known as the Confession of 1967. At that time three other confessions were added to the traditional Westminster documents and the Scots Confession of 1560: the Heidelberg Catechism, the Second Helvetic Confession (1566), and the Barmen Declaration (1934).

The Confession of 1967 was composed in the midst of the troubled 1960s and seeks to speak particularly to the racial conflict, polarization, and social unrest in the United States during that period. Hence the distinctive motif is reconciliation. Part 1 treats "God's Work of Reconciliation," and Part 2 is on "The Ministry of Reconciliation."

During the same period, the Reformed Church in America (RCA) commissioned its theological commission to draft a contemporary confession, but it could not produce anything which elicited general consent. It was then decided to commission one person, Eugene Heideman, then on the faculty of Central College in Iowa, to try his hand at this task. He was remarkably successful and the result, *Our Song of Hope*, was first presented to the General Synod in 1974. It was eventually approved, with revisions, in 1978.[29] Heideman, a doctoral student of the great Dutch theologian A. A. van Ruler, reflects his mentor's influence in the eschatological approach and emphasis on the work of the Spirit in the world as well as in the church.

Our sister denomination, the Christian Reformed Church in North America (CRC), followed suit in 1984 with a new confession modestly called "A Contemporary Testimony" (its subtitle)—its

[28] This is appended to the *Book of Confessions* of the Presbyterian Church U.S.A.

[29] *Our Song of Hope* was first published with a commentary (Grand Rapids: Eerdmans, 1975). A slightly revised version is available in a book of liturgical services, *Worship the Lord*, ed. Donald J. Bruggink and James R. Esther (Grand Rapids: Reformed Church in America/Eerdmans, 1987).

title, *Our World Belongs to God.*[30] This "testimony" seeks to address in particular the current ethos of secularism and practical atheism. "A recurring theme . . . is that because we live in God's world, not our own, we must see ourselves as God's servants, fulfilling our tasks in his kingdom."[31]

The latest and shortest attempt at a contemporary confession by an American Presbyterian denomination is a "Brief Statement of Faith," submitted by the Presbyterian Church U.S.A. to the 202nd General Assembly in 1990.[32] Like the Heidelberg Catechism, it begins with the affirmation that "In life and death we belong to God." Its form is Trinitarian, but instead of beginning with God the Father, the "Statement" begins with Jesus Christ. If a theological point is being made with this reordering, one might characterize these three most recent American confessions as respectively pneumatocentric (*Our Song of Hope*), theocentric (*Our World Belongs to God*), and christocentric ("Brief Statement of Faith").

Here, as in the confessions of the sixteenth and seventeenth centuries, we have considerable variety, but at the same time they have a number of Reformed motifs in common: the sovereignty of God (even if that term as such is rarely used),[33] a Trinitarian way of viewing the world and our place in it, our bond with Israel and the one covenant of grace, concerns which transcend the church and encompass the kingdom, and an ethical thrust stemming from the Reformed emphasis on the third use of the law.

Although the formulations vary, one characteristic Reformed presupposition is still prominent, that the only rule of faith and practice is the Bible. This is assumed in the Dutch *Foundations and Perspective*, but

30 *Our World Belongs to God* (Grand Rapids: Board of Publications of the CRC, 1984). This version also contains a commentary.

31 From the commentary, 37.

32 "Brief Statement of Faith" was adopted by the General Assembly in 1991. I am omitting an earlier contemporary confession of the Presbyterian Church U.S.A., *A Declaration of Faith*. It is not included in the *Book of Confessions* of the Presbyterian Church U.S.A. It was originally drafted by the Presbyterian Church U.S. (the southern church) in 1977 and adopted in 1985 by the union Presbyterian Church (U.S.A.) as "a reliable aid for Christian study, liturgy, and inspiration" (*Minutes*, PCUS, 1977, part 1, 168). It contains nine chapters and is the longest of the postwar American Reformed/Presbyterian contemporary confessions.

33 It is used only once in contemporary confessions, in "Brief Statement of Belief" (Southern Presbyterian), which also speaks of God's "sovereign power" and "sovereign purpose."

that lack is fully remedied by a fifteen-page supplemental statement on the nature, authority, interpretation, and use of the Scriptures. *Our Song of Hope* and *Our World Belongs to God* both have at least one paragraph which treats that theme.[34] The Presbyterian "Brief Statement of Faith" is just that, brief, and hence contains only two lines regarding Scripture. It is the Spirit who "rules our faith and life in Christ through Scripture" and "engages us through the Word proclaimed" (lines 60-61).

Continuity and Development

At the outset I raised the question posed by Jaroslav Pelikan as to whether *scriptura* has ever been *sola*. The answer, of course, is no. Even the most fundamentalist, biblicistic groups which eschew creeds and formal confessions are far more influenced by tradition(s) than they realize. It is not only more honest but also more salutary to acknowledge one's confessions and the relative authority they possess. But there is always the danger for confessional groups, such as the Lutheran and Reformed, to lapse into confessionalism, despite repeated affirmations of *sola scriptura*. When theological debates have raged within these groups, it is sometimes a phrase or an article from one of the confessions, not Scripture, which has been used as a battering ram to demolish opponents.

However, what happens to the authority of a confession when the majority of the members or ministers of a denomination no longer take seriously one or more of the tenets of one of their confessions? In the RCA the vow taken at ordination reads: "I believe the Scriptures to be the Word of God and accept the Standards [i.e., the ancient creeds and three confessional documents] as faithful *historical* witnesses to the Word of God" (emphasis mine). If, on a historical basis, some tenet is generally agreed upon as being no longer relevant, as is the case with Article 36 of the Belgic Confession in Dutch-American circles, the problem is not acute.

Illustration One: Double Predestination

The problem becomes more complex, however, when a number of fundamental doctrinal points are either denied or ignored by the leaders and theologians of a given church. An interesting case in point is the doctrine of reprobation, which is taught in the Canons of Dort

[34] In *Our Song*, stanza 4.6, and in *Our World*, paragraphs 39-41.

and the Westminster Confession. It has been denied in the classroom, more or less quietly rejected by a majority of Reformed and Presbyterian ministers, and quietly left out of all the recent Reformed-Presbyterian Confessions.

Not only that, this doctrine has been challenged officially with a gravamen (a formal complaint or official objection to a church doctrine) against his denomination by the redoubtable Christian Reformed missionary-theologian, Harry Boer. Boer's contention was that this doctrine is unbiblical and therefore should be excised from the Canons of Dort where it is taught.[35] Moreover, since Christian Reformed ministers in the Form of Subscription declare that "we heartily believe and are persuaded that all the articles and points of doctrine [in their three confessions] . . . do fully agree with the Word of God,"[36] and since, Boer maintains, a majority of their ministers do not believe in the doctrine of reprobation, therefore they are guilty of silence, evasion, cowardice, and duplicity.[37]

Boer presented his gravamen to the General Synod of the Christian Reformed Church in 1977. A study committee was appointed at that Synod and charged "to study the gravamen in the light of Scripture, and to advise the Synod of 1980 as to the cogency of the gravamen and how it should be further dealt with by synod."[38] Ironically the committee, with minor reservations, found Boer's exegesis to be correct but it did not agree that the doctrine of the reprobation as taught by Dort had been invalidated by the new interpretation of key texts such as Romans 9:13, 18 and Ephesians 1:11.

The whole affair ended in a virtual stalemate. The Synod did not declare Boer heretical; nor would it exscind the articles Boer found unbiblical. Instead, they concluded: "The Scriptures do teach a doctrine of election and reprobation in that they teach that some but not all have been elected to eternal life."[39]

[35] Boer particularly objected to 1, articles 6 and 15. Article 6 begins with this statement: "That some receive the gift of faith from God, and others do not receive it, proceeds from God's eternal decree." Cf. the Westminster Confession 3.3: "By the decree of God, for the manifestation of his glory, some men and angels are predestinated unto everlasting life, and others foreordained to everlasting death."

[36] Cited in Boer, *The Doctrine of Reprobation in the Christian Reformed Church* (Grand Rapids: Eerdmans, 1983), 72.

[37] Boer, ix, 78-79.

[38] Boer, 18.

[39] Boer, 21.

In view of this dispute, it was extremely interesting to see how the committee appointed by the CRC to write a contemporary confession would handle this hot issue in its "Contemporary Testimony," which came out a few years later. This is the longest of the recent confessions cited in this paper. Yet only a half paragraph is devoted to the subject of election or predestination, and that in its section on Christ, not God and Creation:

> Therefore the Father chose in Jesus
> Those whom he would save.
> And Jesus' love through his Spirit
> Moves us to faith and obedience.[40]

This is a far cry from the doctrine of double predestination or reprobation! And yet the committee apparently felt they had to use the language "election and reprobation" in their commentary for political reasons.[41]

In this case traditionalism has won out over the scriptural principle. Harry Boer challenged his denomination to come clean and be honest with itself, but they failed to respond to his challenge. Even though he failed, however, this is an all-too-rare example of taking one's confession seriously and seeking to be honest about it. The preferred path of most denominations is simply to disavow quietly and individually those parts of a confession with which they have come to disagree. The other path is that of ignoring such embarrassing doctrines in new confessions—or re-working the doctrine in a way deemed more biblical. The Dutch Reformed, for example, in their *Foundations and Perspectives* have a section (3) on the election of Israel, but it is developed from the perspective of *Heilsgeschichte*, not predestination. The only other allusion to election is in the opening sentences of section 10, "The Means of Grace," which begins: "The electing love of God that comes to us in Christ through the Spirit makes use of earthly means to arouse, to sustain and to strengthen our faith."

In the Confession of 1967 (UPUSA) there is no mention of either election or predestination, and the recent "Brief Statement of Faith" of the Presbyterian Church U.S.A. is equally reluctant to use such words,

[40] *Our World Belongs to God*, par. 33.

[41] Ibid., 44. After quoting the lines from "The Testimony," the committee comments: "We gladly testify now why we keep teaching these doctrines," i.e., election and reprobation.

including "choose" or "chosen." In *Our Song of Hope* (RCA) the first sentence in the section on the church (6) reads: "Christ elects his church to proclaim his Word and celebrate the sacraments," but that is the sole reference to election.

It appears that Presbyterian/Reformed denominations today have jettisoned one of the key doctrines in their confessional heritage, if the newer confessions are indicative of the current theological outlook. As far as the doctrine of reprobation is concerned, few will lament this loss, but this writer at least wonders whether they have thrown out the baby with the bath water. Is it not striking that not one of these confessions even allude to the text (Ephesians 1:3-4) that Karl Barth felt was the basis of the most comforting doctrine of all, namely, our election in Christ?[42]

Illustration Two: The Providence of God

The doctrine of the providence of God is a related doctrine which has been highlighted in the older Reformed confessions and has played an important role in Reformed theology and piety. As Benjamin Farley notes in his survey of the doctrine of providence, "The doctrine of providence constitutes a central tenet of Reformed theology and belongs to the essence of the biblical message."[43]

As over against the doctrine of predestination, this doctrine has not been rejected but refined and reformulated. This is not readily apparent in the newer Reformed confessions which pay scant attention to the doctrine.[44]

The post-war confessions do not always have a section on providence, but the idea is often there even when the word is absent. For example, the Dutch Confession, *Foundations and Perspectives*, has near the end a section entitled simply "History." As will become clear from the following quotation, it is virtually a discussion of providence, but from an eschatological rather than a decretal perspective. So the

[42] "The truth of the doctrine of predestination is first and last and in all circumstances the sum of the gospel. . . . It is itself evangel: glad tidings; news which uplifts and comforts and sustains" (Karl Barth, *Church Dogmatics*, vol. 2, pt. 2 of *The Doctrine of God* [Edinburgh: T & T Clark, 1957], 12).

[43] Benjamin Farley, *The Providence of God* (Grand Rapids: Baker, 1988), 229.

[44] Cf. the lengthy treatments given in the Heidelberg Catechism, Q and A 26 and 28; the Belgic Confession, Article 13; and the Westminster Confession, Chapter 5.

tradition is being maintained but is being reformulated in a way that reflects biblical-theological insights of the last half century.

> Because of our faith in the Christ who has come, and in the future consummation in the Kingdom of God, we look upon the events in time, not as the arbitrary play of free force, nor as the unbreakable decree of fate, but as the arena of God's blessed rule, as the history which extends to the destiny determined by Him. God makes all the world events to contribute to the completion of His plan of redemption. In the irresistible progress of the preaching of the gospel, and in the founding and preserving of the church in all the world, our faith discerns the signs of God's sovereign rule. But it also discerns the essential futility of all powers that would seek to establish another rule, the actual frustration of their plans, and the chaos into which, regardless of their purpose, they throw the world. These are the comforting and warning signs of the dominion of God, which is the earth's ineluctable destiny.[45]

The next section, "Personal Living," continues the providence theme but more in terms of the individual believer.

> In reliance upon God's promises, our personal lives are not abandoned to chance or fate but sheltered in the hand of the Father of our Lord Jesus Christ, without whose will not a hair of our heads will fall to the ground. He will keep His own and guide them into His heavenly Kingdom and cause all things to work together to that end.[46]

In the United Presbyterian Confession of 1967 there is no explicit treatment of providence. The same is true of the "Brief Statement of Faith" of the Presbyterian Church U.S.A. The only sentences that reflect the doctrine of the providence of God are the opening one, which echoes the first answer of the Heidelberg Catechism, "In life and death we belong to God," and the affirmation at the end based on Romans 8: 38-39: "With believers in every time and place, we rejoice that nothing can separate us from the love of God in Christ Jesus our Lord" (lines 77-79).

[45] *Foundations and Perspectives*, sec. 14, 24-25. The same motif is expressed briefly in the opening section which states the theme, "God, our King," but here the emphasis is more doxological.

[46] Ibid., sec. 15, 25.

Our Song of Hope does not do much with this doctrine explicitly, but the theme song of *Our Song* affirms general providence within a Trinitarian framework:

Our God loves this World,
God called it into being,
God renews it through Jesus Christ
God governs it by the Spirit

In what follows there is no explicit treatment of providence, although a major motif in this confession—the work of the Spirit in the world—could be considered an indirect way of expressing one aspect of this doctrine. On the other hand, the theme as well as the title of *Our World Belongs to God* (CRC) reflects the theme of providence. It also speaks of the Spirit being "at work, renewing the earth" (par. 3) and of God's "hold[ing] this world in sovereign love" (par. 7). Then, in the context of creation (par. 17) there is a paragraph that gives a fairly complete definition of providence, although the christological accent found in the Heidelberg Catechism and in the Dutch *Foundations and Perspectives* is missing.

God rules and shapes
what he made in the beginning.
The unfolding drama of world events
is under his control.
God is present in our world
by his Word and Spirit.
The faithfulness
of our great Provider
gives sense to our days
and hope to our years.
The future is safe, because
our world belongs to God.

Conclusion

We have seen how difficult it is to amend a traditional confession or excise certain tenets from it that are no longer believed by a majority of the adherents of that particular confessional group. Here the tradition overwhelms the *sola scriptura* principle. In the long run, however, it can still be maintained, I believe, that in the Reformed tradition there is a continuing attempt to be faithful to the biblical witness. *Scriptura* may never be *sola*, but it is ultimately *suprema*.

At the same time, the number of new confessions and their attempts to speak relevantly to new issues and challenges indicates how seriously the Reformed tradition takes its slogan *semper reformanda*! I have not demonstrated this in detail but a perusal of any of the confessions cited in this essay will reveal how they have addressed issues as varied as totalitarianism and social justice, on the one hand, and ecological issues, on the other.[47]

Finally, however, we need to be reminded of the fact that the goal of scriptural, and secondarily, confessional fidelity is not loyalty to a principle or a tradition but to the living God to whom the Bible and all traditions witness. Here, some early words of Karl Barth are still very germane:

> What makes us Reformed churchmen is not the pleasure we find in certain aspects of truth but the recognition of the one truth, the recognition of that word of God which must prevail, if the worst comes to the worst, even against our own ideals—a recognition which is occasioned and caused by the truth itself.[48]

[47] The concern for contemporary issues faced by Reformed/Presbyterian churches in Asia and Africa in particular further substantiates this point. A good illustration is the Belhar Confession of the Uniting Church of South Africa, which deals particularly with racism as experienced in that country.

[48] Karl Barth, *The Word of God and the Word of Man* (1928; New York: Harper, 1957), 235.

CHAPTER 6

"No One Has Ever Asked Me This Before": The Use of Oral History in Denominational History

Lynn Winkels Japinga

Elton Bruins seems to know everybody in the Reformed Church in America. He values connections and relationships. He knows who is related to whom and a woman's maiden name and who served what church and when. Norman and Mary Kansfield, both historians of the RCA and friends of Elton, joke about keeping a copy of the *Historical Directory* in their car. I don't think Elton needs to. He appears to have it memorized.

I have enjoyed many conversations with Elton over the last twenty-five years and my research has benefited from his wide knowledge of the RCA. Elton, along with Mert DeVelder, Richard Oudersluys, and John Beardslee III, spent many hours talking with me about events in the RCA prior to World War II. Elton was just a child during those years, but he had met some of the older ministers when he was a young pastor and heard their stories. These conversations were so informative that I began to wonder what other RCA ministers might say about their lives and careers. I had begun a book project on the post-World War II history of the RCA, and oral history offered an intriguing way to add life and depth to that research. I began an oral history project in November 1999 and have interviewed over eighty RCA ministers, missionaries, and elders.[1] A Hope College student, Jennifer Hill, interviewed about

[1] A grant from the Louisville Institute provided travel money and released time to conduct most of these interviews and related research.

sixty lay and clergy women.[2]

We now have a sample of more than 125 interviews which deal with childhood, college and seminary, life in the RCA, and the recent development of American culture. They provide a resource for future work not only on RCA history, but also on vocation, spiritual development, ministerial formation, and feminism. In this paper I will offer some reflections about the use of oral history for writing denominational history. Oral history has the potential to provide insights and perspectives that might not be found in traditional sources such as denominational magazines and minutes of meetings. I will explore some of the themes that I have observed in the interviews I conducted with retired ministers and missionaries.

Most of these were male and born in the 1920s and 1930s. Most attended Hope or Central College and Western or New Brunswick Seminary. Most were raised within the RCA. Most served within the RCA their entire career. All but one were white. They grew up and worked in all regions of the RCA. They served rural, urban, and suburban churches of varying sizes. One pastor spent his thirty-six years of ministry in the same congregation. Others moved every four years. A number of them were raised in Iowa or Wisconsin but spent their careers in New York and New Jersey. Others moved back and forth between East and Midwest. Some never lived east of Grand Rapids, Michigan. A few taught in colleges, a few were missionaries, but most were parish pastors. Nine were elected President of General Synod. Several served in denominational staff positions. Some were known throughout the denomination; others were not. It was not a random sample, but I think the group is reasonably representative of RCA ministers.[3]

2 In the summer of 2001 my student researcher, Anna Cook, transcribed several of these male minister interviews and wondered what their wives might say if they were being interviewed. Jennifer Hill then conducted about forty interviews with a cohort of women who graduated from Hope in the 1940s and 1950s. Some of these women were married to ministers; many of them were the first to be ordained as elders and deacons in the RCA. She also interviewed about twenty-five younger RCA women who had been ordained as ministers or elders.

3 Ministers who retired to a region less populated by other retirees were less likely to be interviewed. It was more cost effective to interview ten people in Pella, Iowa, than to make ten separate trips to various regions of the country. There are a number of people I intend to interview as time and resources permit.

When someone agrees to an interview, I provide a list of about twenty questions that move chronologically through the subject's life and ministry. I ask about childhood, college and seminary, places and events in their ministry, conflicts within the RCA, events like the assassinations of John F. Kennedy Jr. and Martin Luther King Jr., cultural influences on the church, and changes they have observed over time. The interviews usually take three to four hours and a few have lasted more than five hours. Each generates a transcript of fifty to one-hundred pages.

When I called Edwin Mulder, a former General Secretary of the RCA, to ask for an interview, he was eager to participate. "No one has ever asked me this before," he said, a bit wistfully. One of the most amazing aspects of this project has been the willingness of the subjects not only to agree to talk with a complete stranger, but also to invite me into their homes, feed me, and share their life stories in surprisingly honest ways. That says something about the family quality in the RCA, but perhaps more importantly, it speaks about their eagerness to reflect on their lives and tell their stories. They hear the request to tell their stories as an affirmation of their forty years of ministry. They care about the denomination and have significant things to say about and to the church they served. They have come to a place of wisdom and appreciate the opportunity to share it.

A few subjects wondered why I wanted to talk to them. One noted at the outset of our conversation that he had nothing to say. Three hours later I left his house, running late for my dinner meeting. Given a bit of encouragement, most did not find it difficult to talk about themselves.

The interviews were almost all intelligent, interesting, and insightful. Some were very powerful and moving. At times the subjects were in tears as they recalled a particular event in their lives or the presence of God's grace. At other times I was struck by their courage or by a tragedy they encountered or by the deep affection they had for their parishioners or by the way they articulated the Gospel.

Oral history is not an objective process. It obviously depends on memory, which is not always accurate and usually becomes less sharp and precise as we age. Most subjects found it helpful to think through the questions in advance and perhaps consult old files. I was always impressed by how much they remembered. Oral history constructs a narrative. No one can recall or recite every event in their life, so subjects choose what to talk about. They may leave out some facts that are embarrassing or difficult. For example, no one mentioned being divorced, and I assumed they were all still in their first marriage. But someone had been married and divorced very young, and hadn't mentioned it in the interview. In general, I think the subjects were quite honest about the difficult places in their lives. Many had served one parish that was not a good fit for them. Some spoke quite openly about conflict, difficult parishioners, leaving when they should have stayed, and staying when they should have left. One pastor recounted a painful story of his daughter's abuse by a parishioner. Most could speak about mistakes they had made. At this point in their lives, most of the subjects did not appear to be overly concerned about protecting their egos.

The interviewer also has limits and needs to work at maintaining objectivity. He or she is there to listen, not to talk, debate, or re-educate. There were times I had to bite my tongue when someone made a negative comment about women's ordination or ethnic minorities, but it is essential to avoid judgment or critique. The interviewer has the power to ask the questions and determine the shape of the conversation. This is essential to avoid a vague "tell me what you remember about your past" approach, but it does mean that some important topics may be omitted. For example, I do not ask a specific question about a minister's prayer life. Some choose to mention it; others don't. Finally, while the interviewer does possess a certain power to lead the conversation, it must be held rather lightly. Some subjects wander despite efforts to keep them on track, but there are often profound insights in the wandering.

Regardless of these minor limitations, denominations would be well served if they conducted these interviews with all clergy after they have been retired for a few years. These ministers led interesting lives, and their stories are worth recording and preserving in the denominational archives. An interview would also be a tribute to the ministers and a sign that their lives, memories, and observations are valued. There is an African proverb which says, "When a grandfather dies, a library is burned down." When I see an obituary of someone I intended to interview, I know that an important story has been lost.

In a budget-conscious era, some people might ask what relevant information would be gained from interviewing ministers who began their careers a half century ago. The past seems to hold little value in our rapidly changing culture. "This is not your father's Oldsmobile," sang the commercial jingle, and it appears that most people have even less interest in their father's or mother's church. Clergy who began their careers during World War II or the Cold War might not appear to have anything to say to those living with the war against terrorism.

This generation of ministers actually lived through extraordinary change: World War II, the atomic bomb, suburbanization, rapid church growth, the Cold War, Vietnam, student rebellions, death of God theology, civil rights for ethnic minorities and women, the 1987 stock market crash (which affected many of their pensions), the growth of technology, 9/11, and the war in Iraq. Their insights about how the church has dealt with all these changes are well worth attending to. For example, during the Vietnam War, Harold Schut gave some advice to Carl Kleis: "Let your parishioners speak their minds, and then they will let you speak. Be pastor to them no matter what." That is still fine advice for a pastor who begins ministry during the war in Iraq.

Conducting these interviews has been an extremely rewarding experience. I met interesting people, made friends, and heard fascinating stories. Alice Walker, in her book *The Temple of My Familiar*, includes this speech from a woman who studied the ways of the elders in her African community. "One thing I know . . . learning from one's elders does not permit pessimism. Your day is always easier than theirs. You look at them, so beautiful and so wise, and you cannot help trying to emulate them. It is courage given by osmosis, I think." I am grateful for the opportunity I have had to sit with the elders and soak up their beauty and wisdom. In the remainder of this essay I will reflect on three ways in which oral history has shaped the way I think about and write denominational history.

Multiple Voices

Oral history reminds the historian that there is no single story of the denomination. Histories of the RCA written a century ago told the story as if God had ordained the denomination to come into being and then providentially protected it from harm and heresy. They considered the RCA to be the truest form of the Christian faith. When there was conflict, the side that "won" must be right because God's truth must always triumph. Historians and Christians in general believed that God worked through denominations.[4]

[4] Elton is deeply committed to the study of denominational history, particularly the nineteenth-century Dutch immigration to the Midwest. His scholarly life has been devoted to telling this story thoroughly and accurately. He models the participant-observer approach to writing

Today denominations are likely to be viewed as passé and irrelevant at best. At worst they are rigid, restrictive organizations that take money away from real ministry. A more accurate perception lies somewhere in the middle. Denominations can provide a common identity and sense of mission for otherwise isolated congregations. Some analysts have observed that the only glue holding denominations together is the pension plan. It is true that denominations are often more relevant to ministers than to lay people, since denominations fund pensions and health insurance, as well as provide employment. For both ministers and lay people, however, denominations can be a source of education and friends and professional contacts. Denominations may not be ordained by God, but they still function in significant ways in American religious life. Historians can best communicate that by telling a variety of stories.

One of the most helpful insights of post-modernism is that there are always multiple perspectives. Ten people will tell their story of their relationship with the RCA in ten different ways. This is messy and complicated. The history of the RCA cannot be told simply by recounting what the General Synod or the General Secretary and the staff did. Those actions may form the bulk of the story, but a historian can never presume that they are the whole story. Oral history is a tangible reminder of the many perspectives that must be brought to bear on an analysis of a denomination's history. The pastor who loved committee work and church politics and was elected President of General Synod plays a role in the broader history of the RCA, but so does the pastor deeply committed to social justice and the pastor who faithfully serves a small congregation. Sunday School teachers and choir members and the people who prepare the potlucks are all part of the story as well. Some of the many stories present in the RCA will be evident in the remainder of the paper.

The Greatest Generation

Oral history reminds the historian of the web of relationships that have often connected people in the RCA.

The generation of clergy that began ministry during the 1940s and 1950s shaped and led the RCA until their retirements in the

history. Elton would never be considered dispassionate about Albertus C. Van Raalte and related issues, but he has always written critical assessments rather than hagiographic history which simply praises its subject.

1990s. Despite all the attention that has been paid to the Baby Boom Generation (born between 1945 and 1962), it is this older cohort that exerted far more influence upon the RCA between 1945 and 1995. The first Baby Boomer President of General Synod was elected in 1991, and the first Boomer General Secretary began in 1994. Those who came of age during the war years provided much of the leadership and creative energy. To understand the denomination and the ways it grew and changed after World War II, the historian needs to understand the lives of the clergy who helped to shape it.

The interviews suggest that these clergy were deeply affected by connections and relationships which developed in the church of their childhood, college, seminary, and the denomination. It is a truism within the RCA that the denomination is one big family. People are interrelated and they know each other. The small size, Dutch ethnicity, and the annual General Synod meeting contribute to that family sense.

Most of the ministers had very positive memories about growing up in the church. They were nurtured and educated by church members. The pedagogy may not have been the most innovative or inspiring but they learned the Bible and theology. Pastors took an interest in them, taught their catechism classes, and visited in their homes. Several spoke about the role a particular minister played in their life, often by encouraging them to go to college or to consider the ministry. Almost all the ministers of this generation had a strong connection with the local church.[5]

College was an expansive experience for most of these pastors. They encountered new ideas and different people. Professors were particularly influential. Almost all the Central graduates mentioned Laura Nanes, who taught history. She was a liberal Democrat who had little patience with traditional piety, but she helped them learn how to think and develop a much larger view of the world. John Beardslee III taught the required Bible courses at Central during the 1950s and introduced students to critical biblical scholarship. Neither college

[5] Many of my college students today have a very different experience. They may have attended multiple churches in different denominations, or no church at all. Some begin to think about ministry because of the chapel program or their religion courses. When they consider going to seminary, they have no idea which denomination to pursue ordination in, if they are aware of ordination at all. Or, they might have attended a megachurch, but are not necessarily prepared to serve a small church in a rural area.

offered a religion major during the 1950s,[6] so pre-seminary students usually majored in history, English, or psychology.

Central College produced a number of graduates in the early 50s who would become very influential pastors and leaders in the RCA. Donald Bruggink, Herman Harmelink, Eugene Heideman, John Hesselink, John Hiemstra, Leonard Kalkwarf, Edwin Mulder, and Alvin Poppen grew up in Iowa or Wisconsin and later provided significant leadership in RCA missions, churches, institutions, and denominational staff. Many of them worked as waiters at Central—an elite job at the time. One of the strongest "old boy" networks in the RCA got its start in the kitchen and dining room of Central College.

The seminary experience at Western or New Brunswick was even more essential for these pastors in the development of Reformed identity, loyalty, and community. Students spent a great deal of time with their classmates. Many students had been in the armed services, so they were older and had seen more of the world and its ugliness. There was a strong sense of camaraderie among the veterans and almost all of them recalled that the service had exposed them to many new ideas and people. In seminary, both liberals and conservatives experienced extended conversations and a good-natured tolerance of different perspectives. These clergy built relationships based on trust and respect which endured despite differences. Relationships were more important than complete theological agreement.

Professors shaped them in significant ways. Those who attended New Brunswick in the 1950s identified the most influential professor as Hugh Baillie MacLean, a Scottish Presbyterian who taught Old Testament using the methods and insights of higher criticism. He challenged their sometimes simplistic views of the Bible, but it was clear that he loved the Bible and was a deeply spiritual man. They also spoke highly of Justin VanderKolk, who taught theology, and John Beardslee Jr., who taught New Testament.

At Western Seminary the students respected Lester Kuyper and Richard Oudersluys who taught Old and New Testament. Like MacLean and Beardslee, they combined scholarly perspectives on Scripture with deep Christian faith and pastoral hearts. Students were trained in preaching and practical theology by Henry Bast. Harris VerKaik noted

6 Elton Bruins was instrumental in strengthening the religion department at Hope, bringing in professors with doctoral degrees and developing a religion major.

that Bast helped them to develop their own styles as preachers rather than imitate his.

Graduates of both seminaries complained a bit about a lack of practical training. Some said they did not know how to run a consistory meeting, conduct a funeral, or do pastoral counseling. But they were exposed to solid theological and biblical scholarship, and they developed habits of mind that helped them to think theologically and gave them a solid foundation for preaching and teaching.

Still, the first parish was often a challenge. Herbert Van Wyk said that the mentoring he received after he graduated from seminary consisted of "there's a church . . . be the pastor!" When asked how he learned to be a minister, Leonard Kalkwarf replied, "You flounder!" Connections with other pastors became particularly important when they began ministry. Those who began ministry as associate pastors often received guidance and mentoring from the senior pastor. Many solo pastors established groups (often including spouses) that met weekly or monthly for encouragement and help with ministry issues. These groups were essential to their health and well-being. A few of the groups continued for decades. When ministers experienced conflict, they often turned to other ministers for help. Donner Atwood was ready to resign his first parish, but two RCA pastors advised him that if he ran from this church, he would run for the rest of his career. Others received specific vocational advice from friends or mentors that helped them deal with a crisis. Almost every interview contains multiple examples of similarly strong relationships.

Cultural critics in the 1950s mocked the "Man in the Gray Flannel Suit" for his conformity and willingness to become a "company man." Some clergy were similarly guilty of conformity. The seminaries seemed to produce a small army of men in black polyester preaching robes who looked and sounded the same. RCA ministers in this era could indeed be described as a network of white men with similar ethnic and cultural backgrounds who had been taught by older men with similar backgrounds. Critics might conclude that it was no wonder the RCA found it difficult to expand beyond the Dutch if the ministers simply tried to reproduce the church of their childhoods because they were unable to deal with change.

Oral history suggests that this was definitely not the case for all RCA ministers in this generation. Donner Atwood was the second pastor of a new RCA church in Levittown, New York, which was filled with hundreds of veterans and their families who had never heard of the RCA. Edwin Mulder started a church in Holland that became an oasis for divorced people who were not welcome in other churches. Robert Bedingfield became a Navy Chaplain and later helped the Navy develop an anti-racism program. Alvin Poppen, Isaac Rottenberg, and Arthur Van Eck provided creative leadership to the denominational staff in the 1960s and 70s. Many of these ministers actively supported women's ordination in the 1970s.

Childhood in Oostburg, Wisconsin, or Parkersburg, Iowa, did not necessarily give people a narrow vision of the world. Small town roots gave the ministers a clear sense of personal and denominational identity.[7] They felt little need to impose the RCA upon the rest of the world or defend it as the only way to be Christian, but they believed this small denomination had something to offer to the nation and even the world. Others in this generation took a more defensive approach to Reformed theology and identity, but in general, this group defied stereotypes about being traditional and rigid. They knew the church had to adapt to changing times. They shared a strong loyalty to the denomination that had nurtured and educated them, but they also kept the RCA connected with other mainline Protestant churches.

The RCA may be composed of people of similar backgrounds and ethnicity who were well connected, but like all families, it has its share of dysfunction, sibling rivalry, and competition over resources. Paul Kranendonk grew up in the Presbyterian Church but attended Hope College and Western Seminary and became an RCA minister. He experienced the RCA more as a family, while Presbyterian meetings seemed to be all business. He mentioned this to an older colleague, who laughed and observed that the RCA was indeed like a family, but some people always left their dirty socks on the floor!

The interviews provide many examples of dirty socks. There have been sharp conflicts during the last sixty years over biblical interpretation, ecumenism, and the nature of the church. Conflict did not begin in the post-war period, however. There were serious disagreements in the eighteenth century, and a new set of conflicts which arose with the Dutch immigration in the nineteenth century.

7 Robert Bedingfield grew up in the Bronx in the Union of Highbridge church. He recalled that six hundred people came to his ordination service. There was a solid sense of community here and in many other eastern communities when this generation grew up. Bedingfield also observed that New Brunswick Seminary had prepared him for the church, but Hope College prepared him for the world.

The first impression of a student of RCA history would probably not be admiration at how well its clergy all got along but surprise that the denomination did not self-destruct long ago. Oral history demonstrates the many connections between RCA clergy but also their many differences, particularly in theological perspectives.

Isaac Rottenberg served as a pastor and a denominational executive. He was also a member of the Commission on Theology in the early 1960s, when there were serious disagreements about biblical interpretation. I asked how he understood conflict within the RCA. He said that for him the fundamental issue was not between liberals and conservatives but between lovers and haters. "Lovers" valued relationships and worked at preserving them. They had strong beliefs and expressed them honestly, but they did not impugn the Christianity or commitment of those with whom they disagreed. They often had a sense of humor. As an example he cited Jerome DeJong, a prominent spokesman for the most conservative element of the RCA. He and Isaac had been friends for decades. "Haters," on the other hand, valued rightness more than relationships. They were quick not only to disagree, but to question the motives and faith of others. Those who might be labeled this way probably would protest that they did not hate anybody, but rather they loved the truth and would defend it at all costs. The fact that people disagreed about core issues such as the nature of the church and the meaning of truth suggests these were not merely superficial differences.

All these stories—of liberals and conservatives, lovers and haters—need to be part of the larger story of the RCA.

Nuance/Complexity

Oral history reminds the historian that denominational history is far more nuanced and complex than what one might read in the *Church Herald* and the *Minutes of General Synod* and other official papers. There is always more to the story. This is especially important in conflict situations. The *Minutes of General Synod* includes reports and results of votes, but it is nearly impossible to capture a sense of the nature and tone of debate. The *Church Herald* usually reported disagreement, but rarely with sufficient depth and detail. The letters-to-the-editor page in the *Church Herald* includes diverse opinions, but one cannot be sure how representative they are of RCA opinion.

Oral history can be useful in modifying the historian's bias. For example, based on my reading of the *Church Herald* (especially the letters to the editor) and the *Minutes of General Synod*, I concluded that the RCA had not put much effort into maintaining a presence in Chicago when the neighborhoods began to change in the 1950s. Some churches and pastors seemed guilty of racism and they certainly seemed to promote white flight. As I listened to pastors talk about their experience in Chicago, I heard a very different story. Several of them had worked quite hard to stay in the city and continue a ministry to their new neighbors. Some finally left when they felt they were putting their children at risk. One minister was told by an African-American pastor not to bother trying to integrate an RCA church, because African-Americans would not come anyway. Obviously the issue is complex. Oral history made it clear that there was more to the story that I needed to explore before coming to any conclusions.

Oral history makes the human aspect clearer than is often possible in traditional sources. I read about Hugh Baillie MacLean in the *Church Herald* and *Minutes of General Synod* and in MacLean's personal papers in the archives. Oral history added a completely different perspective.

In 1948 New Brunswick Theological Seminary called MacLean, a Scottish Presbyterian, to teach Old Testament. He began teaching in the midst of a very conflicted time, when the Eastern and Midwestern sections of the RCA were not getting along very well. MacLean preached his inaugural sermon in the fall of 1948 and it was published in the denominational magazine. He wondered whether the destruction of the Canaanites was necessarily the will of God. Several letters to the editor criticized him for an inadequate view of biblical authority. Some classes asked General Synod to censure him, but others supported him and asked Synod to censure his critics. He explained his views before a Synod committee in 1949 and that appeared to end the debate.

Other kinds of evidence suggest that the matter was not resolved so simply. The General Synod Archives contains a letter from MacLean to the Board of Superintendents of New Brunswick Theological Seminary expressing his disappointment that no one had ever contacted him directly to ask about his views. To his critics he was a faceless liberal they did not know, and it was easy to make accusations from a distance. The accusations cost them nothing, but he paid a price. It was a dismal welcome to the denomination.

His students recalled that MacLean was a great teacher who made the Bible come alive for them. He sounded like a prophet when he spoke their words of justice. He introduced people to biblical criticism in a way that helped them understand and appreciate the Bible more. Bob

Hoeksema came from a fairly conservative background and a relatively simplistic Bible course in college. He felt as if MacLean tore his Bible out from under him. The critical issues of two creation stories and multiple authors of Isaiah were new and threatening. The process was so painful that he almost left the seminary. And then Bob said, with tears in his eyes, "I have spent the rest of my life thanking the good Lord that I sat under Hugh Baillie MacLean, who gave me a Bible that I can now live with. He was a very key person in my theological orientation. I am forever grateful to him and for him." When I asked why he stayed, when the ideas were so difficult, Bob said, "I knew the guy loved me. I knew the guy wanted the best for me. I knew the guy prayed for me. He embodied, for me, what it was to be a prophet. He changed my life."

To some of his critics, MacLean was a liberal who needed to be corrected. To his students he was a prophet and pastor and friend who made an extraordinary difference in their lives. He was such a powerful presence that fifty years later they still spoke of him with deep respect and affection. Oral history helped to humanize the story and reminded me that it was not simply a conflict between right and wrong but a story about people.

Another example of the broader perspective that oral history provides is in discussion of the Synod of 1969, which was one of the most difficult in RCA history. The denomination was deeply divided over a failed merger proposal with the Southern Presbyterians, which the Eastern section of the RCA supported and the Midwestern section opposed. The debate had been intense and at times ugly. The conflict continued at the Synod meeting. Delegates tabled indefinitely a motion to become a full participant in Churches of Christ Uniting, which made the Eastern delegates furious. There was also a lengthy debate about membership in the National Council of Churches, and Synod narrowly voted to stay in the NCC, in part because of a late-night speech by the General Secretary who threatened to resign if the RCA could not maintain even this minimal level of ecumenical commitment. Also during this Synod, James Foreman occupied the denominational offices in New York, asking for reparations for slavery, and this led to the formation of the Black Council in the RCA. Several young men tried to deposit their draft cards with the denomination as a sign of their objection to the war in Vietnam. A group of women held a march to protest the church's repeated refusal to ordain women. The mood was extremely tense. Some Eastern clergy and churches talked about leaving the denomination and merging with the Northern Presbyterians. Some

Midwestern churches and clergy would have been happy to see them go.[8]

The most noteworthy element of this Synod occurred when Harold Schut, pastor in Scotia, New York, and a former president of Synod, made a motion asking for the orderly dissolution of the RCA. If the two sections of the church could not agree on their future, he said, it would be better to separate with peace and dignity rather than to continue fighting. The minutes of the meeting and the denominational magazine both report the incident rather matter-of-factly as another piece of business. The oral histories, however, give a better sense of the pain and passion involved. Fred Mold recalled: "I can remember him getting up and making his proposal with tears in his eyes, you know? It was a very emotional moment, and I remember him beginning about how he loved the Church and saying, 'but it's obvious that we are moving in two different directions.'"

Others who were present described the shock they felt. "This can't be happening," they said. The church had fought before, but had never come so close to dividing. Harold Schut recalled in his interview that it seemed wrong to dissolve the church, but it had become difficult to find common ground. The RCA seemed to be spending so much time fighting that it had no idea what its mission was. His proposal helped, he thought, because it forced the church to decide whether it wanted to stay together.

As it did with Hugh Baillie MacLean, oral history about the Synod of 1969 offered some poignant reflections that were not available in traditional sources. Several ministers said that this Synod shaped their professional life in positive and negative ways. But oral history also reminded me that not all clergy were affected in the same way. I talked to one Midwestern minister whose name was on the roster of delegates to this Synod, but when I asked him about it, he couldn't remember being there! Eastern clergy were affected very differently by the event, and oral history makes this clear.

The ordination of women was another controversial issue in the RCA that severely tested the sense of family and connections. The

8 The Reformed Church Studies Center at New Brunswick Theological Seminary organized a conference about this Synod in October 2005. A number of people who had attended the Synod of 1969 offered their reflections and there was extensive group discussion. For an overview essay, personal reflections, and summaries of discussion, see *Reformed Review*, spring 2005, <www.westernsem.edu/Brix?pageID=15056>.

interviews provide significant insights about this period in the church's history. They illustrate why people opposed it, how their minds were changed or not, and why some males chose to mentor women and work for their ordination. The interviews with women illustrate why women felt called, their experience in seminary and later as pastors of congregations, and the role of mentors. The interviews are often painful to read because they report the mean-spirited or bizarre things that were said to them. One parishioner told a female seminary student that she could improve her preaching by losing weight in her legs. Another woman was told by both her father and her consistory that she should have been a boy. The interviews demonstrate how the church has changed its view of women, but also the many ways women continue to be second-class citizens in ministry.

Will There Be Institutions in Postmodernity?

The interviews suggest that these ministers generally felt very connected to ecclesiastical institutions (local and national) and were deeply loyal to the denomination. They preached and taught, they called on every family every year, they went to classis meetings, and they paid their dues. They were rewarded in varying degrees for being good servants of the institution, often by being elected to office, which required still more service to the institution!

Recent developments in American religion (first the megachurches and now the emergent or postmodern churches) suggest that institutions, particularly denominations, are rapidly losing their authority. Critics say that denominations stifle creativity with their rigidity and unreasonable "taxes." Twenty Somethings care little about denominational affiliation and more about a congregation where they can make friends and get their spiritual needs met. Given this trend, is it foolish to think that anything relevant can be learned from these interviews? Is denominational loyalty an admirable but wholly outdated practice? To some degree, perhaps. But Brian McLaren and others who write about the emergent church also discuss the need to recover ancient spiritual practices and Christian virtues. What are the values which shaped the church's identity and helped it function well in the past? If community and connection were important characteristics of these older ministers, might they also be important for younger ones?

In *The Cloister Walk*, Kathleen Norris writes about the monastic community: "In any traditional society, stories are where the life is, where those in the present maintain continuity with the past."[9] The world in which humanity lives has changed dramatically, even in the last fifty years, but what it means to be human remains basically the same. People are broken, they find redemption, they search for a meaningful life and work, they need friends and mentors. Oral history allows us to hear these stories and maintain continuity with the past and provides an opportunity to sit with the elders, learn from their wisdom and courage, and perhaps find some of our own.

[9] Kathleen Norris, *The Cloister Walk* (New York: Riverhead Books, 1996), 340.

CHAPTER 7

Richard Baxter: An English Fox in a Dutch Chicken Coop?

Earl Wm. Kennedy

A Call to the Unconverted, the bestselling little book by the seventeenth-century English Puritan Richard Baxter (1615-91), contributed significantly to the 1857 secession from the Reformed Protestant Dutch Church (RPDC) because it contained views perceived as unorthodox by some of the Michigan immigrants.[1] Its distribution and defense by certain pastors in the RPDC evoked a strong reaction from its detractors.

The Seceders Divide

Those in Michigan who left the RPDC[2] a century and a half ago to form what became the Christian Reformed Church (CRC) intended to return to the doctrine and polity of the Synod of Dort (1618-19), reenacting what they had done in the 1834 *Afscheiding* (Secession) from

[1] Baxter's book was not, however, listed among the official reasons given by the seceders of 1857 (Classis of Holland Minutes [henceforth CM], 8 April 1857, Art. 16, in *Classis Holland Minutes 1848-1858* [Grand Rapids: Eerdmans, 1943], 240-43 [henceforth *CHM*]).

[2] The RPDC changed its name in 1867 to the Reformed Church in America (RCA).

the *Hervormde Kerk* (Reformed Church) in the Netherlands.[3] The few ministers and almost all the elders and deacons who settled in and near Holland, Michigan, beginning in 1847, were *Afgescheidenen* (Seceders). Although those who joined the *Afscheiding* generally agreed on the "Three Formulas of Unity,"[4] they soon quarreled about how to adopt the Church Order of Dort and other matters, some of which would also agitate the early Dutch immigrants in Michigan.[5] One of these issues, to be examined in the present article, was whether the gospel of Jesus' death for sinners should be preached ("offered") to all indiscriminately. These differences helped define at least three parties ("mentalities") among the seceders.

[3] The *Hervormde Kerk* was the Dutch public church, seen by the seceders as having become hopelessly corrupt by its departures from Dort. For a recent brief survey of the *Afscheiding* and its antecedents and consequences, see Robert P. Swierenga and Elton J. Bruins, *Family Quarrels in the Dutch Reformed Churches in the Nineteenth Century* (Grand Rapids: Eerdmans, 1999), 1-42. For a fairly positive (in comparison with the usual) assessment of the state of the *Hervormde Kerk* at the time of the *Afscheiding*, see Gerrit J. tenZythoff, *Sources of Secession: The Netherlands Hervormde Kerk on the Eve of the Dutch Immigration to the Midwest* (Grand Rapids: Eerdmans, 1987); similarly, he is not wholly favorable to the Synod of Dort and the *Afscheiding*. For a short up-to-date overview of the Synod of Dort, see Karel Blei, *The Netherlands Reformed Church, 1571-2005*, trans. Allan J. Janssen (Grand Rapids: Eerdmans, 2006), 28-35.

[4] Heidelberg Catechism, Belgic Confession, and Canons of the Synod of Dort.

[5] Among the issues that were debated during the first years of the "Christian Seceded Church" in the Netherlands were whether elders should "retire" after one term of service, whether the Christian "festival days" should be observed, whether the children of baptized non-confessing members should be baptized, whether the *Afscheiding* was a positive good or a necessary evil, whether there could be any ecclesiastical association with those from other denominations, and whether the authority of synodical decisions was relative or absolute. Much of this discussion was about the nature of the church and how to apply to the contemporary situation the decisions made at Dort over two centuries earlier (Melis te Velde, "The Dutch Background of the American Secession from the RCA in 1857," in *Breaches and Bridges: Reformed Subcultures in the Netherlands, Germany, and the United States*, ed. George Harinck and Hans Krabbendam (Amsterdam: VU, 2000), 87-92; Henry Beets, *De Christelijke Gereformeerde Kerk in Noord Amerika. Zestig Jaren van Strijd en Zegen* (Grand Rapids: Grand Rapids Printing, 1918), 37-48; D. H. Kromminga, *The Christian Reformed Tradition: From the Reformation to the Present* (Grand Rapids: Eerdmans, 1943), 93-97; Swierenga and Bruins, *Family Quarrels*, 27-33).

The "Northern" party of the Revs. Hendrik de Cock and Simon van Velzen, located largely in the provinces of Friesland, Groningen, and Drente, was made up of very traditional, exclusivist Calvinists who emphasized God's sovereignty in election and reprobation, and adhered the most firmly to the doctrine, order, and liturgy of Dort. They should not, however, be confused with the similarly oriented but more heavily introspective, semi-mystical "Drente" mentality, although there was some overlap. This latter group, strongly influenced by the seventeenth-century Dutch *Nadere Reformatie* ("second" or "further" Reformation) and eighteenth-century pietism, stressed predestination combined with regeneration (as something to be felt) and met in "conventicles" for mutual edification by means of the Bible, prayer, and sharing of experiences; it was prevalent not only in Drente but also in parts of Overijssel and Zeeland. The Drente mentality ("strict experientialists") and the Northern mentality ("more lenient experientialists") were often allied.

The centrist "Gelderland" party, mainly located in the province of Gelderland and parts of Overijssel and Zeeland, was led by the Revs. Anthony Brummelkamp and Albertus Christiaan van Raalte, who promoted a moderate experiential piety, the offer of the gospel to all, and some congregational autonomy. It adhered less closely than the Northern/Drente group to the Church Order of Dort. Also, it saw the *Afscheiding* as an unfortunate necessity and recognized that the national church contained a remnant of true Christians with whom cooperation was possible. On the whole, this mentality tempered its firm convictions with a mediating, less exclusive spirit.

The third party, that of the talented and cultured maverick, Rev. Hendrik Pieter Scholte, who in 1847 founded the colony of Pella, Iowa, reflected the pietistic individualism of its leader. He promoted a biblicist, non-confessional, non-denominational, non-clerical, premillennial, disciplined, separatist Christianity, emphasizing an evangelical conversion experience more than doctrine. Scholte freely modified the Church Order of Dort and the Reformed tradition, sought a pure congregation of the regenerate, and championed the separation of church and state.

The second party would be dominant in the early days of the Michigan colony, with the first party soon to make its presence known and contribute to the 1857 secession. The third party had relatively little organized following in Michigan.[6]

6 Scholte's party was at first dominant in Pella, and it wasn't until 1856 that a Reformed church was formed there, aided by Van Raalte, who led it into the

The *Afgescheidenen* were thus already badly divided on their arrival in the U.S.A. Scholte had been suspended from the ministry in 1840 by the seceders' national synod (he was never restored), while the Northern/Drente group and Gelderlanders went their separate ways between 1846 and 1854 over the issues of clerical garb (not covered by Dort) and synodical authority.[7] It has been aptly said, "The immigrants brought their religion in their baggage, so to speak, and church life in America continued the controversies and ways of behavior that had been part of life in the Old Country."[8]

It is conceivable, therefore, that the Michigan secession of 1857 might have happened sooner or later, even if Van Raalte had never taken the Classis of Holland into the fast-Americanizing RPDC in the East in 1850.[9] Recent interpreters have tended to blame the admittedly unattractive personalities of early CRC leaders for the schism and to minimize the role of doctrine, polity, liturgy, and piety.[10] Doubtless

---

Classis of Holland. Scholte's mindset was the most "American" of the three and would reappear in evangelicalism in the RCA and elsewhere (Earl Wm. Kennedy, "Eden in the Heartland," *Church Herald* 54 [March 1997]:8-10, 15; H. Reenders, "Albertus C. van Raalte," in *"Van scheurmakers, onruststokers en geheime opruiers . . .": de Afscheiding in Overijssel*, eds. Freek Peereboom, H. Hille, and H. Reenders [Kampen: IJsselakademie, 1984], 149-59; H. Hille, "Verdeeldheden in de afgescheiden kerken," in *De Afscheiding in Overijssel*, 312-16; Kromminga, *Christian Reformed Tradition*, 94-97, 102, 106; Swierenga and Bruins, *Family Quarrels*, 33-34; Beets, *Christelijke Gereformeerde Kerk*, 79-81; Te Velde, "Dutch Background," 85-92, 98-99).

7 Melis te Velde, *Anthony Brummelkamp (1811-1888)* (Barneveld: De Vuurbaak, 1988), 193-225; Swierenga and Bruins, *Family Quarrels*, 30-33.

8 Robert P. Swierenga, "True Brothers: The Netherlandic Origins of the Christian Reformed Church in North America 1857-1880," in *Breaches and Bridges*, 61.

9 This is especially true when consideration is given to the American environment, to which some Dutch would adapt more rapidly than others. The pace and degree of Americanization was a problem for all immigrants. In any case, the union of 1850 doubtless exacerbated the differences among the Dutch newcomers and hastened a schism.

10 A recent critique of 1857 by an RCA scholar asks: "Why the split? The real reasons were non-theological. They were attitudinal and emotional. . . . They had to do with . . . party spirit . . .; with ignorance and narrowness and accompanying prejudices; with jealousies and pride. . . ." He adds that the schism was mainly due to "the quarrelsome, contentious nature of many of the immigrants" (M. Eugene Osterhaven, "Saints and Sinners: Secession and the Christian Reformed Church," in *Word and World: Reformed Theology in America*, ed. James W. Van Hoeven [Grand Rapids: Eerdmans, 1986], 59; also 49-53).

many factors were involved, but care should be exercised not to impose current ideas of what is important or true upon people of another era, or too facilely to impugn motives or psychoanalyze at a distance.

Dort, Limited Atonement, and the Order of the Divine Decrees

Richard Baxter's denial of the doctrine of "limited atonement" was judged a fatal flaw by some of those involved in the CRC schism. The Canons of Dort teach that although Christ's death was "more than sufficient to atone for the sins of the whole world, . . . it was God's will that . . . Christ . . . should effectively redeem . . . all those and only those who were chosen from eternity for salvation"; i.e., Christ's atoning death was "sufficient" for all but "efficient" only for the elect (designed by God to make their salvation absolutely certain).[11] This doctrine was deemed important because it was an integral part of a theology for which many immigrants had suffered in the Netherlands, and around which they rallied as a part of their identity in an unfamiliar new world.[12] Although

[11] Canons of Dort 2.3 and 8; Fred H. Klooster, "The Doctrinal Deliverances of Dort," in *Crisis in the Reformed Churches: Essays in Commemoration of the Great Synod of Dort, 1618-1619*, ed. Peter Y. De Jong (Grand Rapids: Reformed Fellowship, 1968), 73-78.

[12] Could "Dort" also have been a virtually empty shibboleth, especially among the less well educated? Issues related to the doctrine of limited atonement (and the other Dort canons) included covenant (or federal) theology (which gained momentum just after Dort and could modify Dortian predestinarianism), the assurance of salvation (election) (which could be tied to doing good works and neonomianism; see below), and whether infants (including the children of baptized, non-communicant members) should be baptized (which could be linked to the question of the presumptive election of covenant children). Reformed pietists disliked "covenant optimism," i.e., "the inclination to consider all baptized church members to be born-again Christians" (Fred van Lieburg, "Pietism beyond Patria: A Dutch Religious Heritage in North America," in *Morsels in the Melting Pot: The Persistence of Dutch Immigrant Communities in North America*, ed. George Harinck and Hans Krabbendam [Amsterdam: VU, 2006], 46-47). See also Dewey D. Wallace Jr., "Federal Theology," in *Encyclopedia of the Reformed Faith*, ed. Donald K. McKim (Louisville: Westminster/John Knox, 1992), 136-37; K. L. Sprunger, "Covenant Theology," in *Dictionary of Christianity in America*, ed. Daniel G. Reid et al. (Downers Grove, Ill.: InterVarsity, 1990), 322-24; J. F. Cooper, "Half-Way Covenant," in *Dictionary of Christianity in America*, 505-6; P. A. Lillback, "Covenant," in *New Dictionary of Theology*, ed. Sinclair B. Ferguson, David F. Wright, and James I. Packer (Downers Grove, Ill.: InterVarsity, 1988), 173-76; R. W. A. Letham, "Assurance," in *New Dictionary of Theology*, 51-52.

the common mnemonic device "TULIP" (total depravity, unconditional election, limited atonement, irresistible grace, and perseverance or preservation of the saints) for the doctrines taught in the Canons of Dort does not work in Dutch, the immigrants were quite familiar with the concepts it represents, including the idea that the Father intended that Christ die for no one who would not actually be saved. The teaching of "limited atonement" (properly, "definite atonement" or "particular redemption") has, however, been the Achilles' heel of Dort, since its biblical basis (e.g., John 10:15) has appeared weaker than TULIP's other four points, and since it seems contrary to God's universal love (John 3: 16) and the missionary mandate to offer the gospel to everyone, saying to each unbeliever, "Christ died for you."[13]

The doctrine of limited atonement emerged in post-Reformation Calvinist discussions about the logical (not the temporal) order of the divine decrees or purposes. Just before the Synod of Dort, three views on this obscure topic competed within the Dutch Reformed churches.[14] The first said that the true order of the eternal decrees in God's mind was: (1) elect some to salvation and others to damnation, (2) create, (3) permit the fall, (4) send Christ to die for the elect, (5) send the Holy Spirit to regenerate and give faith to the elect. This idea is called "supralapsarianism" (from Latin, "above," i.e., before, the fall). The second view of the decrees' order was: (1) create, (2) permit the fall, (3) elect some to salvation and bypass others destined for damnation, (4) send Christ to die for the elect, (5) send the Holy Spirit to regenerate and give faith to the elect. This is called "infralapsarianism" (from Latin, "below," i.e., after, the fall). Supralapsarianism has often been regarded as the more consistent of the two positions but with less biblical warrant and bad consequences for the justice and goodness of God, who created some in order to damn them.[15]

The Canons of the Synod of Dort, while not rejecting supralapsarianism, give clear preference to the infralapsarian view and

13 Thus there have been quite a few "four-point Calvinists."

14 The scholarly descriptions of the rival views on the order of God's decrees differ slightly from each other in detail but agree on the essentials. A partial biblical justification for discussing such matters is seen in Romans 8:28-30.

15 A vigorous debate about the relative merits of supralapsarianism and infralapsarianism occurred in the CRC around the turn of the twentieth century, in the wake of a similar controversy in the Netherlands, largely evoked by the supralapsarianism of Abraham Kuyper (James D. Bratt, *Dutch Calvinism in Modern America: A History of a Conservative Subculture* [Grand Rapids: Eerdmans, 1984], 46-50, 244-45).

do condemn a third position, namely that of the "Remonstrants."[16] The Synod had been convened in order to still the disruptive controversy in the Dutch Reformed public church between those holding the first two views of the decrees and the Remonstrants, who, influenced by the Christian humanism indigenous among certain segments of Dutch society, endorsed the ideas of Jacobus Arminius (1560-1609); they were therefore later called "Arminians."[17] Their order of the divine decrees was: (1) create, (2) permit the fall, (3) send Christ to die for all on condition that they believe, (4) send the Holy Spirit with a universal prevenient grace to free the fallen will and to regenerate all whom God foresaw would believe the gospel and persevere in faith. The Canons of Dort rejected this view, because it appeared to make salvation ultimately dependent on human free will rather than on God's free grace.[18]

The Canons, initially endorsed by the Dutch Reformed Church, were often neglected or rejected in the eighteenth and early nineteenth centuries, partly because of growing optimism about human nature. After the French Revolution and the Napoleonic era, there was a reaction against the Enlightenment as well as a spiritual quickening in Western Europe as a whole; this revival led to a fresh appreciation of the Canons of Dort among some of the Dutch Reformed.

One more part of the story of the limited atonement is needed to set the stage for Richard Baxter and the Michigan controversies of the 1850s. The Reformed churches in Roman Catholic France were a barely tolerated minority in the mid-seventeenth century, just after

16 So named because they had signed a "remonstrance" in 1610, setting forth their views over against those of the stricter Calvinists.

17 Kromminga, *Christian Reformed Tradition*, 28-37; Donald Sinnema, "Remonstrants," in *Encyclopedia of the Reformed Faith*, 317; Robert Letham, "Arminianism," in *Encyclopedia of the Reformed Faith*, 11-12; Donald Sinnema, "Dort, Synod of," in *Encyclopedia of the Reformed Faith*, 108-9.

18 Benjamin B. Warfield, *The Plan of Salvation* (1915; rev. ed., Grand Rapids: Eerdmans, 1942), 21-28, 31; William Stacy Johnson and John H. Leith, eds., *Reformed Reader: A Sourcebook in Christian Theology*, vol. 1, *Classical Beginnings, 1519-1799* (Louisville: Westminster/John Knox, 1993), 94-99, 107-15, 221-24; Herman Bavinck, *Reformed Dogmatics*, vol. 2, *God and Creation*, gen. ed. John Bolt, trans. John Vriend (Grand Rapids: Baker, 2003), 361-69, 388-92; L. Berkhof, *Systematic Theology*, 4th ed., rev. and enl. (Grand Rapids: Eerdmans, 1949), 118-25, 393-99, 421-22; Charles Hodge, *Systematic Theology*, vol. 2 (New York, 1871), 316-21, 327-28; Earl William Kennedy, "An Historical Analysis of Charles Hodge's Doctrines of Sin and Particular Grace" (Th.D. diss., Princeton Theological Seminary, 1968), 192-97, 199-200.

the Synod of Dort, to which they had been invited but were unable to attend. Moïse Amyraut (Amyraldus in Latin), the leading theologian at their academy at Saumur, sought a *via media* between the Canons' infralapsarianism and the "heresy" of the Arminians, since he desired good relations with the Roman Catholics in France (potential enemies) and with the Lutherans in Germany (potential friends), both of whom were repelled by Dort's predestinarianism. He therefore proposed in the 1630s yet a fourth order of God's decrees: (1) create, (2) permit the fall, (3) send Christ to die for all, on condition that they believe (for which they have the natural ability), (4) elect some to salvation, to whom the Holy Spirit was sent to give the moral ability to believe.[19] Richard Baxter embraced Amyraldianism, often called "hypothetical universalism," but most Reformed theologians rejected it, because, although it still affirmed divine election, it undercut limited atonement. Amyraut's view was (theo)logically deficient (since it pits universalism against particularism) but admirable in trying to do justice to the well-meant offer of the gospel to all.[20]

It was to oppose the influence of the school of Saumur that the last confessional document of orthodox Calvinism, the Helvetic Consensus Formula, appeared in 1675, co-authored by Francis Turretin (1623-87) of Geneva.[21] It defended Dort's infralapsarianism and attacked a number of the teachings of Amyraut and his colleagues, including his hypothetical universalism and his idea that sinners have natural but not

19 Brian G. Armstrong, *Calvinism and the Amyraut Heresy: Protestant Scholasticism and Humanism in Seventeenth-Century France* (Madison: University of Wisconsin Press, 1969), 58-59, 72-74, 137-38, 169-71, 212; Warfield, *Plan of Salvation*, 23-25, 31; Hodge, *Systematic Theology*, 2:321-22, 547-48, 726-28; Berkhof, *Systematic Theology*, 394; Johnson and Leith, *Reformed Reader*, 99-104. Amyraut affirmed natural ability (sinners *can* believe) but not moral ability (sinners *will* not believe). Most Calvinists rejected this distinction; Jonathan Edwards and the New England theology, however, employed it (Armstrong, *Calvinism and Amyraut*, 65, 215-16).

20 This has been the common opinion, at least (Philip Benedict, *Christ's Churches Purely Reformed: A Social History of Calvinism* [New Haven: Yale University Press, 2002], 316-17; Warfield, *Plan of Salvation*, 89-90, 92-96; A. A. Hodge, *The Atonement* [Philadelphia, 1867], 375-80; Hodge, *Systematic Theology*, 2:323-24; Kennedy, "Hodge's Doctrines," 197-99).

21 James T. Dennison Jr., "The Twilight of Scholasticism: Francis Turretin at the Dawn of the Enlightenment," in *Protestant Scholasticism: Essays in Reassessment*, ed. Carl R. Trueman and R. Scott Clark (Carlisle, Cumbria, U.K.: Paternoster Press, 1999), 244-55.

moral ability to believe.[22] Although this creed soon fell into disuse with the eclipse of Reformed orthodoxy in the eighteenth century, Turretin's three-volume Latin textbook of "didactic and polemic theology" (1679-85) enjoyed a vogue in a few Reformed theological schools (perhaps most notably Princeton Seminary of the Presbyterians) affected by the modest Calvinist upsurge during the early decades of the nineteenth century.[23]

Richard Baxter's Amyraldianism, Abraham Krabshuis, and the Classis of Holland

On Sunday, 31 July 1853, Elder Hessel Ottes Yntema of the pastorless Vriesland Reformed Church, read aloud to his congregation from a Dutch version of Richard Baxter's popular *Call to the Unconverted*, presumably in lieu of the usual published sermon by an orthodox Dutch Reformed clergyman. The next Friday, three Vriesland laymen came to their church's consistory meeting, complaining that Baxter was not Reformed. One of them was Gijsbert Haan Jr., son of the man commonly known as the leader of the 1857 CRC schism. Although the consistory said that "not a single expression" in Baxter's book was unbiblical or contrary to the Three Formulas of Unity, Yntema agreed, for the sake of congregational peace, not to use it in public worship.[24]

Shortly thereafter, at the 26 September 1853 meeting of the Classis of Holland in Zeeland, questions arose about the orthodoxy of both the RPDC and the classis itself.[25] Moreover, during the preceding

[22] The Formula denied both natural and moral ability. See Philip Schaff, *The Creeds of Christendom . . .*, 6th ed., rev. and enl., vol. 1, *The History of Creeds* (New York: Harper, 1919), 477-89; John H. Leith, ed., *Creeds of the Churches: A Reader in Christian Doctrine from the Bible to the Present*, 3rd ed. (Atlanta: John Knox, 1982), 308-23.

[23] Kennedy, "Hodge's Doctrines," 10-17, 205-7, 211-16; Franciscus Turrettinus, *Institutio Theologiae Elencticae*, 3 vols. (Geneva, 1679-85). It was the theological textbook at Princeton Seminary from its beginning in 1812 until the 1870s, when Charles Hodge's *Systematic Theology* replaced it. Turretin's work was also used in Scotland during this time. The decline of students' facility in Latin, besides the emergence of new issues in theology, finally doomed its usefulness in the later nineteenth century.

[24] Consistory Minutes, Vriesland Reformed Church, 5 August 1853 (translation mine).

[25] A man of Van Raalte's flock asked if a Freemason could be a church member, to which classis answered that "all look upon it as works of darkness, and thus unlawful for a [church] member"; this was the first

two years there had already been two mini-secessions from the classis by groups that later joined a small Presbyterian denomination, more conservative than the RPDC.[26] The most contentious issue at the 26 September session was Baxter's *Call.* The minutes do not tell who raised the topic, but a look at the list of the twenty-two delegates suggests that a spokesman for the protesters must have been Elder Gijsbert Haan Sr., of Grand Rapids, the father of the recent Vriesland objector. The complaint was that "some ministers had circulated" this "little work," which taught "a reconciliation of all people with God, or a [doctrine of] universal grace." The objectors had thus spotted Amyraldian hypothetical universalism in Baxter. But the minutes also note that, "Other writings of Baxter are [also] presented, from which passages are read aloud clearly teaching election, etc. However, the ministers declare that there are a few expressions in the little work in view that they themselves do not dare to defend or to employ."[27] As it turned out, the pastors who circulated the *Call* were Van Raalte himself and Rev. Cornelis van der Meulen of Zeeland (and probably Van Raalte's protégé, Rev. Seine Bolks of Grand Haven).

Two years later, at the 5 September 1855 classis session at Vriesland, four Grand Rapids consistory members, including Haan

time that this fateful issue was raised in classis. Also, Van Raalte's report about his attendance at the June meeting of the RPDC General Synod was a bit defensive in tone. He had, he said, had a fine time and "found there a maintaining of the Reformed doctrine, which also everywhere became manifest, as against the unsound German Reformed Church, which was not pure in . . . doctrine . . . as also in the maintaining of discipline" (CM, 26 September 1853, Arts. 6 and 10, in *CHM*, 144-45). The (German) Reformed Church in the U.S. was then embroiled in a debate about Mercersburg Theology, which the RPDC was watching with alarm (Eugene Heideman, "Theology," in *Piety and Patriotism: Bicentennial Studies of the Reformed Church in America, 1776-1976*, ed. James W. Van Hoeven [Grand Rapids: Eerdmans, 1976], 102-4). On the debate over the Mercersburg Theology, see also Gregg Mast, "A Decade of Hope and Despair," elsewhere in this festschrift. *Ed.*

26 Jacob Roelofs Schepers and Roelof Harms Smit led dissident groups into the Associate Reformed (or "Scottish") Church; see n. 74 below. Swierenga and Bruins, *Family Quarrels*, 67-75; Swierenga, "True Brothers," 64-65.

27 CM, 26 September 1853, Art. 9, in *CHM*, 144. The statement in the minutes (composed by Van Raalte, the clerk) that Baxter teaches "election" is, strictly speaking, irrelevant, since the issue was not election (which neither Baxter nor Amyraut denied) but the extent of the atonement.

Sr., by then a high-profile dissident, protested "against the further circulation of Baxter's *Call to the Unconverted.* The assembly receives the said protest for information."[28] Obviously neither the Van Raalte nor the Haan camp had been convinced by the discussions of 1853. Less than two years later, the Grand Rapids four, with others (e.g., two of the August 1853 Vriesland protesters),[29] would exit the RPDC to form what became the CRC.

Discord over Baxter also arose in Van Raalte's own congregation, initiated by one of its members, Abraham Krabshuis (1815-71), the future early leader of the CRC in Holland.[30] Evidently reacting to the September 1853 meeting of classis, Krabshuis wrote a piece for a now missing issue of *De Hollander*, the local Dutch-language weekly, objecting to the *Call*'s use in classis, to which "K. S." of the Zeeland church replied in another missing issue (24 November 1853), to which Krabshuis in turn responded in a sixteen-page pamphlet, since *De Hollander* had

28 CM, 5 September 1855, Art. 13, in *CHM*, 181-82; Van Raalte, the clerk, was absent from this meeting.

29 Hendrik Dam in 1856 and Gijsbert G. Haan in 1857 ("Register van Lidmaten in de Holl. Geref. Gemeente te Vriesland, Mich." [Membership Register, Vriesland Reformed Church], 8-9, 20-21, Joint Archives of Holland).

30 A native of Almelo, Overijssel, and a weaver, Krabshuis had emigrated from there as a seceder deacon in 1847; he had already been involved in a quarrel with an elder in his home church. His first wife, fifteen years his senior, soon died; he was married by Van Raalte in 1849 to a widow, seventeen years older than he and the mother of Isaac Cappon, the future business leader and first mayor of Holland, as well as a Van Raalte supporter. Given the ages of Krabshuis's wives when he married them, it is no surprise that he was himself childless. He settled near Graafschap (just southwest of Holland) but joined the Holland rather than the Graafschap church. He first appeared in the Holland consistory minutes in 1851 when he was urged not to let bitterness about money owed him by a fellow member keep him from communion. By the end of 1853, however, he had found the role for which he was fated, i.e., an outspoken advocate of Dortian orthodoxy (J. Wesseling, *De Afscheiding van 1834 in Overijssel, 1834-69*, vol. 2, *De classes Holten en Ommen* (Barneveld: De Vuurbaak, 1986), 156-58, 164; 1850, 1860, and 1870 federal census, <www.ancestry.com>; Ralph Haan and Richard H. Harms, compilers, "Weddings (1847-1875) Performed by Rev. Albertus C. Van Raalte," from a wedding register in Van Raalte Papers, Archives of Calvin College, Grand Rapids, <www.calvin.edu/hh/family_history_resources/vanraalte_weddings.htm>, accessed 11 Jan. 2007; "Pilgrim Home Cemetery," <http://holland.cemeterydata.com/burial_search>, accessed 11 Jan. 2007; Consistory Minutes, First Reformed Church, Holland, 18 December 1851 [henceforth MFRCH], Joint Archives of Holland).

denied him further publication. The pamphlet was signed by him and nine others, including Elder Jannis van de Luijster, the respected founder of Zeeland.[31] The work argues against K. S.'s Remonstrant views that Jesus died for all and that believers can fall away. While Krabshuis affirms a well-meant offer of the gospel to all, Christ nevertheless died only for the elect, who can never be finally lost. Thus the debate, begun on the subject of Baxter, was continued on the overt Arminianism of K. S. himself (e.g., his denial of the saints' perseverance). The pamphlet relies mostly on biblical texts and cites only in passing the Heidelberg Catechism, the Belgic Confession, and Wilhelmus à Brakel, the main theological guide of the orthodox Reformed laity. The Canons of Dort, implicitly defended here by Krabshuis, are not mentioned at all.[32]

Concern about an additional, perhaps more serious defect in Baxter's *Call*, namely, its "neonomianism" (literally, "new-law-ism"), also arose among the Michigan Dutch at this time, although there is little direct indication of this in the records. Neither Krabshuis nor the consistory or classical minutes refer to his reputed legalism.[33] It needs inclusion here as part of the larger discussion of Baxter, but it is odd that the classis seems to have paid relatively little heed to his widely-noticed tendency to obscure the Reformation doctrine of justification by grace through faith.[34] In 1915, Engbertus van der Veen (1828-1917), an early member of Van Raalte's congregation, recalled that, "The first trouble in our church life began at the time that a supply of Baxter's

31 Other signers included Graafschap Elders Johan Frederik van Anrooij and Mattheus Naeije (Van de Luijster's brother-in-law), both of whom would later join Krabshuis in the CRC.

32 Abraham Krabshuis et al., *Aanmerkingen tegen K. S., in de beantwoording mijner vragen, in No. 52 van De Hollander, van 24 November 1853* [Observations against K. S., in Response to My Questions in No. 52 of *De Hollander* of 24 November 1853], Holland Museum Archives, 1-3, 12-16. In discussing the doctrines of election and reprobation, Brakel includes a full paragraph on Amyraut's hypothetical universalism, which he rejects (Wilhelmus à Brakel, *Redelyke Godsdienst* . . . , 16th ed., vol. 1 [Rotterdam, 1749], 178).

33 The Synod of Dort ante-dated Baxter.

34 Could a partial explanation be that the *Afgescheidenen* in Michigan were so centered on Dort that they sometimes overlooked the larger question of faith and works? Or was it that Van Raalte and Krabshuis and their followers were united in their opposition to Baxter's legalism and differed chiefly on the extent of the atonement? Note Krabshuis's letter to the consistory in January 1856 (below p. 136 and n. 45), saying that it was indifferent to every doctrine except justification, but this was intended as a complaint, not a compliment.

Call was received and the books distributed among the people. It taught that nobody should neglect their duties in Christian work, to lead a consecrated life, and to give freely of their resources for the good cause. Some of the uneasy characters would not tolerate such doctrine, for they would do neither and called this heresy, a confidence in the merit of outward work, their belief being that those who were ordained to eternal life would be saved through grace."[35] Van der Veen's non-technical, lay description of Baxter's supposed deviation from standard Reformed doctrine sounds much like the neonomianism of which he had long been accused. This topic will be addressed later.

In any case, Krabshuis and another signer of the pamphlet next approached the Holland consistory on 5 December 1853 to ask if it had fobidden the publisher Hermanus Doesburg to accept Krabshuis's piece in *De Hollander*.[36] The consistory members said that they did not have such authority, but that they "heartily regretted that Brother Krabshuis involved himself in polemics [*twistgeschrijf*], and that about a disputed matter [*geschilpunt*], namely, the well-meant offer, about which so much has already been said and written." Furthermore, they had "always judged it to be [its] duty to discourage such things to all, including the publisher." This resulted in a "lengthy discussion about the orthodoxy or lack thereof of Baxter, and about one-sided treatment of the truth, about the natural consequences of controversies, etc., etc."[37]

35 "Life's History of Engbertus Van der Veen of Holland, Michigan" ([Holland, Mich., 1915], privately printed), photocopy at A. C. Van Raalte Institute, 16-17. Van der Veen remembered that "a young farmer from Graafschap [most of whose church's members left in 1857] said to me when he saw that I had a book, 'What! Have you also one of those Baxter books? I despise the Armenian [*sic*] doctrine, and use it for scrap paper when I shave myself" (17). There is, of course, a theological connection between K. S.'s denial of the perseverance of the saints and Baxter's neonomianism, if keeping God's law contributes in any way to the believer's retention of salvation. Unfortunately, the version of these remembrances ("rearranged," with "repetitions omitted") published in *Dutch Immigrant Memoirs and Related Writings*, ed. Henry S. Lucas, rev. ed. (Grand Rapids: Eerdmans, 1997), 489, 507-8, eliminates vital elements of the narrative.

36 MFRCH, 5 December 1853, Art. 1. Of course Doesburg at this time would have been reluctant to publish anything unfavorable to Van Raalte, since in 1852 the Holland consistory had placed him temporarily under discipline (he soon repented publicly) for printing articles in *De Hollander* displeasing to it and especially to Van Raalte (Robert P. Swierenga, "Clerical Censorship or Freedom of the Press: The Reverend A. C. Van Raalte and *De Hollander*," unpublished paper, 2006). But the content of Krabshuis's pamphlet was

Just over a year later, the Holland congregation elected Krabshuis for the first time to be an elder.[38] Some of the consistory (and also of the congregation), however, questioned whether he should be allowed to assume that office because of his divisiveness, one-sided stress on election, attacks on Baxter, and attitude toward classis members he deemed insufficiently Calvinistic. In fact, he had reportedly impugned, in *De Hollander*, the orthodoxy of the classis's ministers (e.g., Van Raalte) and had penned an admonitory letter to Rev. Seine Bolks of Grand Haven.[39]

Much consistorial time in several sessions was taken up with discussion of these issues, with the majority agreeing with Van Raalte that Krabshuis and his views should be given the benefit of the doubt and tolerated, but that, to satisfy the minority, the matter should go to classis. Van Raalte, treading carefully, also held that latitude should be given with regard to Baxter, about whom "already in former days the most diverse testimonies were given by the most respectable men," but that, "however much Baxter also may be regarded as an instrument of blessing and outstanding writer," he uses expressions that Van Raalte would not wish to endorse.[40]

---

not directed against Van Raalte or even Baxter, but only against "K. S.," the "Remonstrant." Thus Doesburg declined to publish it probably because of its length, its polemical character, or its being a stale subject (note the consistory's response to Krabshuis).

37 MFRCH, 5 December 1853, Art. 1 (translation mine). Present were only three elders, one deacon, the two visitors, and Van Raalte (who took the minutes).

38 He came in second, with forty votes; the frontrunner had fifty. This shows that Krabshuis had a constituency.

39 The private letter to Bolks was somehow made public in consistory and later at classis. In it, Krabshuis admonishes Bolks for a sermon in which he had put down people of "small faith," i.e., people who said "*Och en mogt*" ("Oh, and could [it be]!") presumably in their intense spiritual struggle. Bolks had rejected this kind of faith and, instead, commended the simple, easy (implied) faith of Eve in Genesis 4:1, who said, after the birth of Cain, "I have gotten a man from the Lord." Krabshuis may here represent those who combined a heavy experientialism with predestination, so that coming to assurance of salvation was a slow process, involving spiritual wrestling, even agony (i.e., the Drente mentality) (MFRCH, 5 March 1855, Art. 3).

40 Congregational Meeting Minutes, First Reformed Church, Holland, 12 February 1855; MFRCH, 5 March 1855, Arts. 2-3 (the main discussion and the Van Raalte quotations); 16 March 1855, Art. 3; 29 March 1855, Art. 3; 9 April 1855, Art. 1; 7 May 1855, Art. 1; and 14 May 1855, Art. 1 (the minutes were recorded by Van Raalte, the regular clerk).

The next meeting of classis (11 April 1855) discussed the Krabshuis case at length, with Van der Meulen, the president, summing up his good and bad sides; by a majority vote it sided with Van Raalte and most of the consistory and agreed to let Krabshuis be installed as elder.[41]

The controversy, however, erupted again within the consistory in the fall of 1855, with Elder Krabshuis making more specific, written accusations of unorthodoxy against both the classis and Van Raalte. With regard to the former, Krabshuis charged that at its last session (5 September 1855) it had asserted that "the Lord's Supper should be held with all denominations," and that it "denied infant baptism, the perseverance of the saints, particular redemption, etc." This was, at best, a series of half-truths.[42] With regard to Van Raalte, Krabshuis protested that he "defended Baxter's errors," that he "threatened to censure, will censure, members and the consistory who stand firmly for truth, and [that he] wished to be separated from them, and he labels them 'Popish Inquisitors,' that he rejects the Secession [of 1834], and that one should not teach the youth about doctrinal distinctives." Van Raalte answered only some of these charges, simply stating that the last two were untrue,

41 CM, 11 April 1855, Art. 15, in *CHM*, 173-74. The voice of Van Raalte, the clerk, can be heard in the minutes. Krabshuis was not the only one in Van Raalte's flock to doubt his orthodoxy. Johannes Hoogesteger (who later went to the CRC) was barred from the Lord's Supper in 1854 for saying that Van Raalte was a Remonstrant, likely in the context of the dispute about Baxter's *Call* (MFRCH, 11 April 1854, Art. 4).

42 Elder Gijsbert Haan of Grand Rapids, reputedly the chief instigator of the 1857 schism, had objected at the September meeting of classis to the June 1855 General Synod's invitation to "all the Christian people" in New Brunswick to join with the Synod in partaking of the Lord's Supper; Rev. Cornelis Van der Meulen, who had been there, gave a defense of this, after which there was much discussion both for and against this practice. Also, at this same session of classis, the letter from Haan and three other Grand Rapids members was read complaining about the continued circulation of Baxter's *Call to the Unconverted*; classis took no action; see above. Krabshuis is presumably referring to this when he speaks of the denial of particular redemption (and perseverance of the saints?) (CM, 5 September 1855, Arts. 9 and 13, in *CHM*, 179-82). The question of whether infants of non-confessing baptized members should be baptized had arisen earlier at classis; Krabshuis may be siding here with the heavily introspective, predestinarian Reformed who hesitated to confess their faith but who wanted their children baptized on the basis of the covenant (CM, 13 September 1854, Art. 11).

and by implication the first charge (about Baxter), too; he detected the bothersome Grand Rapids consistory, led by Gijsbert Haan, behind much of this criticism. Also mentioned at this gathering was Van der Meulen's spreading of Baxter's *Call*.[43]

At the next consistory meeting, Krabshuis admitted that he should have spoken privately to Van Raalte, following Matthew 18: 15-17. Van Raalte, while allowing for diverse opinions about opening communion to all Protestants, declared himself opposed to it. Moreover, in teaching catechism classes, he believed, on the one hand, in teaching the church's doctrines as well as in refuting theological error, but, on the other hand, in being mainly positive and edifying, leading the youth to Christian faith and life. The dispute with Krabshuis seemed to have been settled.[44]

Shortly thereafter, however, in late January 1856, less than a year after his installation as elder, Abraham Krabshuis resigned that office, and he and his wife left the congregation and the denomination to "return to the old path of the Fathers, where one heard of discovery, conviction, affirmation, and edification in the spiritual life."[45] Their secession letter was read at a consistory meeting attended by all three of the pastors then in the classis (Dominies Van Raalte, Van der Meulen of Zeeland, and H. G. Klijn of Grand Rapids). No reason is recorded for their presence, but each of them had some sort of link with Krabshuis, and also his departure could have been seen as ominous for the future of the classis. However this may be, Van Raalte had spoken with him before the meeting and conveyed to the consistory and pastors several of his complaints, one of which was that the consistory was indifferent

43 MFRCH, 22 October 1855, Art. 7. See Adrian Van Koevering, *Legends of the Dutch: The Story of a Mass Movement of Nineteenth Century Pilgrims* (Zeeland, Mich.: Zeeland Record Co., 1960), 524.

44 MFRCH, 2 November 1855, Arts. 9-10.

45 MFRCH, January 1856 (the day is missing in the minutes; the previous consistory meeting was 18 January), Art. 9. Krabshuis was a traditionalist, whose piety was most likely heavily influenced by "the Old Writers" (*de Oude Schrijvers*), such as Wilhelmus à Brakel, whom he cited once in his pamphlet. The words recorded in the minutes, *ontdekking, overtuiging, bevestiging, en opbouw* ("discovery, conviction, affirmation, and edification"), sound as though they may be Van Raalte's version of some of the elements of Krabshuis's introspective spirituality. Van Raalte also said that Krabshuis complained about there always being something lacking in Van Raalte's sermons. For a sketch of the piety and preaching of the *Nadere Reformatie*, see Blei, *Netherlands Reformed Church*, 39-42.

to every doctrine except that of justification.[46] The consistory, in response, lamented Krabshuis's "dishonesty," "slander behind the back," and "faithlessness," which it deemed to be poor return for its patience with him, so it was glad to accept his resignation as elder; the consistory viewed his secession as wrong but recognized his right to follow his conscience before God.[47] Krabshuis spent most of the rest of his troubled, contentious life as an elder in the CRC, dying in 1871, apparently little mellowed by age.[48]

[46] MFRCH, January 1856. The doctrine of justification by grace through faith in Christ was the key doctrine of the Protestant Reformation, and Krabshuis may possibly be reacting to Van Raalte's mention of Protestant intercommunion (i.e., with non-Calvinists) in the minutes of 2 November 1855. In any case, this was the era of the international Evangelical Alliance (organized 1846, partly against Roman Catholicism), to which the RPDC, Van Raalte, and Brummelkamp were committed (Edward Tanjore Corwin, *A Digest of Constitutional and Synodical Legislation of the Reformed Church in America* [New York, 1906], 257-58; Te Velde, *Brummelkamp*, 373-81). Another possible meaning of Krabshuis's remark is that at least the consistory agreed with him on one point, namely, the doctrine of justification, as over against the "neonomianism" of Baxter; see Van der Veen's comment above and the discussion of Baxter and the "Marrow Men" below, p. 146ff.

[47] MFRCH, January 1856, Art. 9.

[48] Krabshuis became a charter elder in the Graafschap CRC, representing it at the Classical Assembly already in October 1857 and often thereafter until the end of 1865, when, having moved to Holland, he became the first elder of its CRC (Central Avenue CRC now), which he led in founding. He continued appearing at CRC assemblies until 1870, but he was suspended as elder in 1862, for neglect of duty and calling his pastor and another elder "troublemakers in Israel," and in 1870 for implacability. While suspended, he took communion at the newly organized Old School Presbyterian Church in Zeeland, defending this by saying (in 1863) that the CRC was not a church ("Early History of Graafschap Christian Reformed Church, Holland, Michigan," in the 100th anniversary book, 1957, <http: //www.rootsweb.com/~miottawa/churches/graafschap.htm>, accessed July 2006, but no longer accessible on 11 January 2007; 7 October 1857 and often thereafter [especially 4 June 1862, 22 July and 7 October 1863, 4 October 1865, and 21 February 1866] until 19-20 February 1870, in "Minutes of the Highest Assembly of the Christian Reformed Church 1857-1880," <www.calvin.edu/library/database/synod>, accessed 11 Jan. 2007; Beets, *Christelijke Gereformeerde Kerk*, 129. H. J. Brinks, "Church History via Kalamazoo 1850-1860," *Origins* 16, no. 1 (1998): 39-40, 42, gives additional insight into Krabshuis, based on an 1859 letter from him to Paulus den Bleijker. Curiously, the name Krabshuis means "crab's house," which is not a pun in Dutch.

Richard Baxter's "Call to the Unconverted": A Neonomian Wolf in Sheep's Clothing?

Rev. Richard Baxter (1615-91) was a mildly Calvinistic, "reluctant" Nonconformist, Puritan theologian and pastor, famous for his remarkably successful ministry at Kidderminster, Worcestershire, where most of the village professed conversion. His lengthy career spanned the English Civil War, the Commonwealth, the Restoration, and the Glorious Revolution, including many years when he paid for his convictions. A deeply devout, ecumenical, irenic advocate of "mere Christianity," Baxter aligned himself with no Puritan party, although he was probably closest to the Presbyterians. His Amyraldianism put him at odds with his stricter Calvinist contemporaries, like John Owen.[49] Among Baxter's many publications were the widely and perennially popular *Saints' Everlasting Rest*, *Reformed Pastor*, and *A Call to the Unconverted*.[50] The last named, published in 1657, bore the full title, *A Call to the Unconverted, to turn and live; and accept of mercy while mercy may be had; as ever they would find mercy in the day of their extremity; from the Living God, when he shall judge the world in righteousness*. "Baxter's *Call* is the first evangelistic pocket book in English which, in its year of publication, sold twenty thousand copies and brought an unending stream of readers to faith during Baxter's lifetime."[51]

Indicative of the widespread influence of Baxter's *Call* is its publication history, a notion of which is given by the Online Computer Library Center, which (as of January 2007) lists 293 editions of it, 267 of them in English, published both in Europe and in the United States, especially during the eighteenth and nineteenth centuries; it is still in print and available in libraries worldwide today.[52] The American Tract

49 Johnson and Leith, *Reformed Reader*, 224-27.

50 J. I. Packer, "Baxter, Richard," in *New Dictionary of Theology*, 82-83; Sidney H. Rooy, *The Theology of Missions in the Puritan Tradition: A Study of Representative Puritans: Richard Sibbes, Richard Baxter, John Eliot, Cotton Mather, and Jonathan Edwards* (Grand Rapids: Eerdmans, 1965), 66-70, 79-81, 148-52; Benedict, *Christ's Churches*, 327.

51 James I. Packer, quoted in Maurice Roberts, "Richard Baxter and His Gospel," *Banner of Truth Magazine* 339, December 1991, <www.puritansermons.com/baxter/baxter19.html>, accessed 11 Jan. 2007.

52 Online Computer Library Center, <www.oclc.org>, 11 Jan. 2007. Most of the ensuing data about the publication history of Baxter's *Call* comes from this source. Over the years, the *Call* has appeared in complete and in abridged versions, sometimes combined with similar works of Baxter or other authors. Before the end of the seventeenth century, there were Dutch,

Society, largely in the hands of those with Calvinist sympathies, issued not only English versions but also German, Danish, Swedish, and Dutch ones. Its Dutch edition of the *Call* was probably a reprint of a version earlier published in the Netherlands and was presumably the troublemaker in Michigan.[53] The little book was no doubt also familiar in English to the Eastern RPDC, since editions were put out in New Brunswick, New Jersey (1797 and 1813), as well as in Albany, New York (1811), both Dutch Reformed centers. The American Methodists (who were "Arminians") issued it often in the early nineteenth century; the Baptists also published an American edition of the *Call*. The work had a big influence on the eighteenth-century Calvinist evangelist George Whitefield and on the renowned nineteenth-century Calvinistic Baptist preacher Charles Haddon Spurgeon.[54] Also, it was highly recommended by Thomas Chalmers, the moderately orthodox Presbyterian founder (1843) of the Free Church of Scotland, as well as by Rev. James Spencer Cannon of New Brunswick Theological Seminary in his posthumously published *Lectures on Pastoral Theology* of 1853, the same year that the dispute about Baxter broke out in the Classis of Holland. Baxter's decorous Puritan approach to evangelism provided an attractive alternative in the RPDC to the more freewheeling techniques of contemporary American revivalists, such as the ardently "free-will" Charles Grandison Finney.[55]

French, and German versions in print. John Eliot, the Massachusetts Puritan missionary to the Indians with whom Baxter corresponded for many years, published it in Algonquin already in 1665 (Rooy, *Theology of Missions*, 69). Dutch editions appeared, e.g., in 1673, 1684, 1711, and 1742; many English Puritan works were published in Dutch in the Netherlands during the seventeenth century. Eventually the *Call* was put into Welsh and Scottish Gaelic.

53 Gift copies from the American Tract Society of Bunyan's *Pilgrim's Progress* (long popular in Dutch translation in the Netherlands) had been distributed at the 29 April 1852 meeting of classis (CM, Art. 4, in *CHM*, 89-90). The fact that Bunyan was a Baptist posed no difficulty for the classis, presumably since his book did not deal with the sacraments.

54 Roberts, "Richard Baxter and His Gospel"; Rooy, *Theology of Missions*, 70.

55 Cannon recommended that "in his efforts in *promoting a revival of religion*, the pastor should recommend strongly, when he cannot be present with a praying society, that such sermons as . . . Baxter's 'Call to the Unconverted,' *should be read*. These works are highly instructive and have been instrumental in enlightening and awakening thousands" (James Spencer Cannon, *Lectures on Pastoral Theology* [New York, 1853], 582-83; Firth Haring Fabend, *Zion on the Hudson: Dutch New York and New Jersey in the Age of Revivals* [New

Baxter's popular works, including his *Call to the Unconverted*, have been acclaimed by the many and sharply criticized by the few. This divergence of opinion can be seen in the Classis of Holland's discussions in the 1850s, as well as in the larger arena of the history of the church over the past three and a half centuries. He was a controversial figure already in his own lifetime. To oversimplify, it might be said that Baxter was a good evangelist but a bad Calvinist. Although he created works accessible to a wide lay readership, he was also an enormously erudite author of a notable body of technical, philosophically-informed, theological literature.[56] Vital for Baxter, the pastor, evangelist, and communicator, was the well-meant offer of the gospel to all, as well as the necessity of combining faith and holy living. His emphasis on calling sinners to immediate, radical repentance resonated more with the Gelderland party of Brummelkamp and Van Raalte than with the Northern party, which had a greater fear of "Arminianism."[57] Of Baxter the heavy academic theologian, the Michigan Dutch had little or no inkling.

A perusal of the American Bible Society's Dutch edition of Baxter's *Call to the Unconverted*[58] (216 small pages) gives the impression of

---

Brunswick: Rutgers University Press, 2000], 53; "Cannon, Jas. Spencer," in Edward Tanjore Corwin, *A Manual of the Reformed Church in America, 1628-1902*, 4th ed. [New York, 1902], 360-61). In his lecture on sermon subjects, Cannon advises "that the pastor should not ring the changes, from Sabbath to Sabbath, upon ancient heresies, which are unknown to those who hear him; nor dwell constantly upon *the Divine decrees* [italics mine], upon Millerism, upon temperance, or upon controversial points which have little connection with a life of faith and godliness" (Cannon, *Lectures*, 134). Although he provides detailed instructions as to the content, preparation, and delivery of sermons, he says nothing about how to prepare messages explaining the doctrinal system of the Heidelberg Catechism (mandated by the RPDC Constitution); this omission would have been disquieting to at least some of the Michigan immigrants in the RPDC, had they known it.

56 Richard A. Muller, *After Calvin: Studies in the Development of a Theological Tradition* (New York: Oxford University Press, 2003), 18; Carl R. Trueman, "A Small Step towards Rationalism: The Impact of the Metaphysics of Tommaso Campanella on the Theology of Richard Baxter," in *Protestant Scholasticism*, 181-95.

57 How the respective parties felt about Baxter's neonomianism is not as clear.

58 Richard Baxter, *Roepstem tot de onbekeerden om zich te bekeeren en te leven* (New York: Amerikaansche Traktaat-Genootschap, n.d.). For a short summary of its contents, see Rooy, *Theology of Missions*, 79-81.

a sustained, terribly earnest, fairly repetitious, and ultimately powerful plea in seven "lessons" (chapters),[59] from "a dying man to dying men," to turn from a worldly ("carnal," "godless") life of nominal Christianity (drinking, amusement, unchastity) to Jesus, to receive forgiveness and a new life of holiness, without which no one can see the Lord.[60] Baxter's style is simple, direct, conversational, personal, and pastoral, with lavish use of Scripture (especially the Old Testament) and reason to support his case and answer questions and objections. God can in no way be blamed for the sinful human condition, which is totally our own fault.[61] He has made us responsible creatures, with enough "freedom" to remain in sin or to turn to him; no one goes to heaven or to hell unwillingly.[62] Christ has died for each and every one (on condition of repentance and faith),[63] and the Holy Spirit is available to enable the elect to repent. Election appears only at this point (in passing) and once again late in the book (as a lame excuse used by the unrepentant).[64] God wants no one to go to hell but, rather, waits patiently for the sinner to choose the way of life.[65] Baxter, in stressing conversion, the "new creation" in Christ (2 Corinthians 5:17), and holy living (but not perfection), puts far more weight on sanctification than on justification.[66] Martin Luther (or even John Calvin) he was not! Baxter also insists that, since salvation is of such great urgency, haste can and should be made to "turn" (i.e., repent, be converted; Ezekiel 33:11) for death can come at any time.[67]

It is clear why this little book, despite its rich biblical citation and devout tone, troubled "high" Calvinists since it first appeared and why it caused unrest in the Classis of Holland. Three issues stand out: (1) its hypothetical universalism, which virtually ignored God's sovereign grace in election; (2) its stress on the radical difference between the holiness of the converted and the worldliness of the unconverted, which could readily lend itself to a Christian moralism that obscured

59 Baxter, *Roepstem tot de onbekeerden*, 31-32.

60 Ibid., 15, 81, 130, 190-91. The devil teaches that sinners can go to heaven without being holy. It is impossible, however, for there to be salvation without sanctification.

61 Ibid., 164, 180, and often.

62 Ibid., 182, 200.

63 Ibid., 8, 10, 20, 25, 49-50, 77, 92-93, 110-12, 165, 168, 177, 204.

64 Ibid., 50, 191.

65 Ibid., 30-31, 165, 169, 178.

66 Ibid., 52-56, 58-63, 135, 143, 176. Christ gives the believer the promise of "the law of grace" (50-51).

67 Ibid., 212.

the Reformation doctrine of justification by grace through faith, apart from works of the law; and (3) its insistence that a sinner can and should be saved instantly, which ran counter to the *Nadere Reformatie*'s experiential predestinarian piety, perhaps shared by Krabshuis, that anticipated an often painfully slow "struggle of faith" to arrive at assurance of salvation (i.e., of election).[68] It is also easy to see, however, that Baxter's call for sinners to repudiate their evil ways and embrace the new life in Christ would attract not only American evangelicals but many of the Michigan Dutch, particularly those in tune with the Gelderland party and Van Raalte.

The Marrow Controversy: Thomas Boston and the Erskines

Baxter's theology had already been controversial two centuries before the debates about the *Call* in the Classis of Holland. The English Puritan Revolution of the 1640s had given birth not only to the Westminster Assembly (1643-49) and its monumental confession of faith and catechisms but also to a wide variety of opinion within Puritanism, much the same as the *Afscheiding* of 1834 exposed differences among those who had opposed the "tyranny" of the *Hervormde Kerk*. For instance, Edward Fisher[69] published *The Marrow of Modern Divinity* (1645) intending to set forth—over against "nomianism" (legalism)—the standard Reformation, Calvinist, and Puritan doctrine, that justification was by grace through faith alone and that justifying faith would normally include an assurance of salvation. Richard Baxter issued a reply in 1649, in which, aiming to foster holy living over against Fisher's supposed "antinomianism" ("anti-lawism," i.e., Christians need not keep the moral law), he maintained that "faith included obedience" and that "the formal cause of justification was not the imputation of Christ's righteousness to the believer but rather the reckoning of the believer's obedient faith as righteous."[70] This debate was revived with a

[68] See note 39 on *och en mogt* regarding Krabshuis vs. Bolks and J. P. Zwemer, *De bevindelijk gereformeerden* (Kampen: Kok, 2001), 20-33, 72-73.

[69] Some have questioned whether the "E. F." who wrote *The Marrow* was actually Edward Fisher.

[70] E. Brooks Holifield, *Theology in America: Christian Thought from the Age of the Puritans to the Civil War* (New Haven: Yale University Press, 2003), 58. There was considerable opposition in the seventeenth century to both Baxter's Amyraldian "hypothetical universalism" and his "neonomianism." His emphasis on the tie between justification and sanctification seemed to make good works contribute to salvation, and this might be linked to

vengeance among Scottish Presbyterians in the early eighteenth century by Thomas Boston (1676-1732), a popular minister and theological author, whose discovery in 1700 of Fisher's simple work had opened his eyes to the Reformation's understanding of grace and justification, so that henceforth he tried to avoid both antinomianism and legalism, i.e., the neonomianism of Baxter and some Presbyterians.[71] Boston's reprinting of *The Marrow* in 1718 precipitated a pamphlet war and an ecclesiastical struggle, with the Presbyterian General Assembly condemning Fisher's book (1720) and rebuking its ministerial supporters (1722), "the Marrow Men," as antinomians; the latter charged the former with being Baxterian neonomians.[72] Moreover,

---

the Remonstrant leanings of his Amyraldianism (e.g., human natural ability); ultimately, Baxter could be seen as subverting free grace. After all, the TULIP "predestinarianism" of the Canons of Dort was consciously intended (whatever its result may have been) to magnify God's sovereign grace, which is not very different from Luther's concerns, as opposed to the Dutch Christian humanist Erasmus. "Baxterianism," regarded by many as simply an extension of Baxter's views, sometimes led to moralism, rationalism, and even Unitarianism among English Presbyterians, with whom he was most closely associated during his later years (Trueman, "A Small Step Towards Rationalism," in *Protestant Scholasticism*, 184-85, 190-95; Benedict, *Christ's Churches*, 323). Rooy holds, against the majority opinion, that Baxter was not a "Baxterian," i.e., someone who held that the gospel was "a new remedial law" that enabled sinners to contribute to their own conversion (*Theology of Missions*, 152).

71 Donald Jay Bruggink, "The Theology of Thomas Boston, 1676-1732" (Ph.D. diss., University of Edinburgh, 1956), 72-77. Fisher's quotations from Luther may have particularly attracted Boston to *The Marrow* (74-75).

72 "The upshot of the controversy was that the Presbyterian Kirk affirmed its leaning toward a legal interpretation of the covenant (God and humans entered into mutual obligations with each other), while 'the Marrow brethren' who sided with Boston affirmed a gracious interpretation of the covenant (God's offer of fellowship with repentant humans rested solely on his mercy in Christ). Later evangelicals would look back on this incident both as a sign of theological weakness in the Scottish state church and as a courageous defense of the gospel by Boston and his colleagues" (Mark A. Noll, *The Rise of Evangelicalism: The Age of Edwards, Whitefield and the Wesleys* [Downers Grove, Ill.: InterVarsity Press, 2003], 59). Against *The Marrow*'s "antinomianism," Baxter distinguishes "between a legal righteousness, which might be had only by keeping the law; and evangelical righteousness, which must be performed by us. Because legal righteousness is impossible for us, Christ fulfills it for us, but we ourselves must perform [by grace] the conditions of this evangelical righteousness" (Bruggink, "Boston,"

Boston, also accused of espousing Amyraut's hypothetical universalism and denying the limited atonement, merely asserted, with Dort and Westminster, albeit in some striking ways, that Christ's death was sufficient for all (Christ was "dead for all") but nevertheless efficient only for the elect (Christ did not die for all). It cannot be denied, however, that he and his allies, although they repudiated hypothetical universalism, were forceful advocates of the free offer of the gospel to all and therefore opponents of "hyper-Calvinism."[73]

After Boston's death, most of the Marrow Men, led by Ebenezer and Ralph Erskine, seceded from the Church of Scotland, beginning in 1733, to begin what would become the Associate Synod, some of whose members emigrated to the United States, where most of them merged in 1782 with a group of Scottish Presbyterian "Covenanters" to form the Associate Reformed Church.[74] A few mid-nineteenth-century Dutch immigrants would affiliate with the last-named body.[75]

---

33). Bruggink says Boston was certainly right "in associating Baxter with Neonomianism" (35; also, 32-39, 343-44). See also D. C. Lachman, "Marrow Controversy," in *Encyclopedia of the Reformed Faith*, 236-37; A. T. B. McGowan, "Boston, Thomas," in *New Dictionary of Theology*, 108-9; Herman Bavinck, *Reformed Dogmatics*, vol. 3, *Sin and Salvation in Christ*, gen. ed. John Bolt, trans. John Vriend (Grand Rapids: Baker, 2006), 531-34.

73 Bruggink notes Boston's support of limited atonement and opposition to Saumur ("Boston," 24, 184-87, 203-4, 273, 276); he is at pains to refute the charges by "hyper-Calvinists" that Boston and the Marrow Men were Arminian/Amyraldian in their views on the universal offer of the gospel ("Boston," 28-31, 271-87, 345, 348). Probably the greatest influence on Boston's theological system as a whole, at least structurally speaking, was the covenant theology of Herman Witsius ("Boston," 74, 105-6; see pp. 153-56, below). But Boston was especially fond of citing Francis Turretin (P. G. Ryken, "Scottish Reformed Scholasticism," in *Protestant Scholasticism*, 200).

74 The Associate Reformed Church, made up of Scots-Irish Presbyterians, was a union of the Associate Presbytery of Pennsylvania (Seceders, followers of the Erskines) and the Reformed (Presbyterian) Presbytery of America (Covenanters). Its northern wing merged in 1858 with the Associate Presbyterian Church (Seceders who had stayed out of the 1782 union) to form the United Presbyterian Church (which merged a century later with the [Northern] Presbyterian Church in the U.S.A.) (M. S. Johnson, "Erskine, Ebenezer [1680-1754] and Ralph [1685-1752]," and W. L. Fisk, "United Presbyterian Church of North America," in *Dictionary of the Presbyterian and Reformed Tradition in America*, ed. D. G. Hart and Mark A. Noll [Downers Grove, Ill.: InterVarsity Press, 1999], 92-93, 264-65).

75 See note 26 above.

Overall, recent scholars have generally concluded that the Marrow Men represented a more evangelical orthodoxy than that of the Church of Scotland's majority, which inclined, on the whole, toward a more rationalistic, moralistic, dead Calvinism, en route to the latitudinarianism of the Presbyterian "Moderates" and, ultimately, to the unbelief of the Enlightenment.[76]

The questions argued in the Marrow Controversy have remained alive in various guises down to the present time. Although opposition to Boston, and even to Baxter, on the extent of the atonement is confined to a few small, conservative Calvinistic circles in the Netherlands and the English-speaking world,[77] the antinomian-neonomian issue, echoing the old Reformation debates about faith and works, continues to elicit discussion in the larger Reformed/evangelical world.[78]

[76] Lachman, "Marrow Controversy," 236-37; McGowan, "Boston, Thomas," 109; Johnson, "Erskine, Ebenezer and Ralph," 93; Noll, *Rise of Evangelicalism*, 59; Bruggink, "Boston," 51-63.

[77] See more on this later. A search of the internet shows that even today, some (e.g., the Protestant Reformed Church, the Evangelical Presbyterian Church of Australia, and the followers of Gordon Haddon Clark) still think that the Marrow Men's well-meant offer of the gospel was a denial of the limited atonement. Of a different standpoint, Archibald Alexander Hodge, professor at Princeton Seminary in the late nineteenth century, made a careful analysis of the theology of the Marrow Men and concluded that it is orthodox on the extent of the atonement and is therefore not Amyraldian, but that its use of universalist language, in its eagerness to offer the gospel to all, was confusing at best (Hodge, *Atonement*, 380-86; note also Berkhof, *Systematic Theology*, 394, 398-99).

[78] Many instances can be found on the internet. Rev. Norman Shepherd had to resign his position as professor of theology at Westminster Theological Seminary in 1982 because he was suspected of neonomianism (similar to that of Baxter). Also, the "Lordship salvation" debate, beginning in the late 1980s, between Rev. John MacArthur Jr. (real faith and repentance go together, as the result of regeneration; one cannot receive Christ as Savior without receiving him as Lord) and the "antinomian" advocates of free grace (e.g., dispensationalists at Dallas Seminary) clearly echoes the issues argued by the Marrow Men and their "neonomian" opponents. Recent discussions between Catholics and Protestants are another evidence of continued interest in the perennial faith/works question, e.g., the unofficial and controversial (in some conservative Protestant circles) 1994 document "Evangelicals and Catholics Together" states, among many other things, that "we are justified by grace through faith because of Christ," and "living faith is active in love" (Charles Colson and Richard J. Neuhaus, eds., *Evangelicals and Catholics Together: Toward a Common Mission* [Nashville: Nelson, 1995]).

The Marrow Men among the Dutch Seceders

Alexander Comrie, a Scot who settled in the Netherlands and became one of the favorite "Old Writers" of the Dutch Reformed pietists, published in 1741 a Dutch translation of Thomas Boston's major work on the covenant of grace. *The Marrow* appeared in Dutch in 1757, while the Erskines' works (especially sermons) in translation came out in the mid-eighteenth and mid-nineteenth centuries (and more are still issued by conservative Dutch Calvinists).[79] Particularly noteworthy is the fact that Höveker, publisher of the Seceders' early synod minutes, issued nine of Ralph Erskine's sermons in 1836-37—at the behest of, and with a foreword by, Hendrik Pieter Scholte[80]—and another twenty-two from 1853 to 1856, as well as nine of Ebenezer Erskine's sermons in 1855-56, including a climactic edition of "all" the Erskines' works. By contrast, Höveker put out only one edition of Baxter's *Call* (*Roepstem*), in 1858.

[79] The Marrow Men's answers to the 1719 General Assembly's questions, as well as the Erskines' 1753 exposition of the Westminster Shorter Catechism, were published in Dutch in 1948 by Rev. Gerrit Hendrik Kersten, founder of the pietist Calvinist *Gereformeerde Gemeenten* (known in the New World as the Netherlands Reformed Congregations) and heavily influenced by Comrie (Willem Westerbeke, ed., "Het verbond der genade en de evangelische voorschriften in de roeping van zondaars . . .," trans. G. H. Kersten [1948; reprint, Middelburg: Stichting de Gihonbron, 2001], <www.theologienet.nl/documenten/1_genadever_kersten_erskine.rtf>, accessed July 2006). Joel R. Beeke, pastor of the Heritage Netherlands Reformed Congregation and president of the Puritan Reformed Seminary, Grand Rapids, promotes the publication and distribution of the Erskines' works in the United States. See Online Computer Library Center, accessed 11 Jan. 2007; Van Lieburg, "Pietism beyond Patria," in *Morsels*, 47-49.

[80] Online Computer Library Center, accessed 11 Jan. 2007. Lubbertus Oostendorp plays down Scholte's admiration of Erskine, assigning it to his "Reformed period" and the reading of works characterized by a "not entirely wholesome," "passive," "pessimistic pietism" that involved "detailed self-analysis," resulting in "hopeful hopelessness" (*H. P. Scholte: Leader of the Secession of 1834 and Founder of Pella* [Franeker: T. Wever, 1964], 84, 86). A partial list of the Erskine sermons, published with a Scholte foreword, appears in *H. P. Scholte*, 195. Scholte advised in 1835 that, in seceded churches lacking regular qualified leaders, the sermons of the Erskines or of several other trustworthy ministers should be read at public worship (Johan Stellingwerff, *Iowa Letters: Dutch Immigrants on the American Frontier*, ed. Robert P. Swierenga, trans. Walter Lagerwey [Grand Rapids: Eerdmans, 2004], 628).

Publication of Baxter's popular works in Dutch had taken place mainly in the late seventeenth and early eighteenth centuries.[81]

At the 1869 triennial Synod of the Christian Seceded Reformed Church, Simon van Velzen, the early leader of the Northern party, in responding to the visiting delegates from the United Presbyterian Church of Scotland (descended in part from the Erskines' Associate Synod), noted that "the works of our Witsius, Marck, the Venemas, and Vitringas are studied [in Scotland], while the writings of your Erskines and others are read everywhere in our families and are nourishment for many."[82] It would seem, then, that the two opposite poles of the *Afscheiding*, represented by Scholte and Van Velzen, were at least united in their appreciation of the Erskines. Moreover, Herman Bavinck, the chief early twentieth-century theologian representing the tradition of the *Afscheiding*, lucidly explained and firmly repudiated both the hypothetical universalism and the neonomianism of Baxter and his ilk.[83] In fact, Bavinck commended warmly the piety of the Erskines in the foreword for a new edition of their selected sermons in 1904.[84]

81 Online Computer Library Center. In January 2007 it yielded the following number of hits for Dutch editions of these authors: Ralph Erskine 191, Ebenezer Erskine 79, Richard Baxter 50, and Thomas Boston 49.

82 "Handelingen van de Synode der Christelijk Afgescheidene Gereformeerde Kerk in Nederland . . . 1869," addendum, in *Handelingen en verslagen van de algemene synoden van de Christelijk Afgescheidene Gereformeerde Kerk (1836-1869)* . . . (Houten/Utrecht: Den Hertog, 1984), 1046 (translation mine). The Erskine name had been invoked, similarly fondly, at each of the three preceding synods (1860, 1863, and 1866) in the course of the ecumenical greetings between the two denominations (*Handelingen en verslagen*, 744, 886, 965). "The mediating systems of Witsius and Marckius . . . obtained a great hold in Scotland. Witsius would be called a follower of Cocceijus while Marckius was reckoned a Voetian; but as far as Scotland was concerned they stood for the same thing" (G. D. Henderson, *Religious Life in Seventeenth-Century Scotland* [Cambridge: Cambridge University Press, 1937], 74). For more on Witsius and Marck, see pp. 153-56 and nn. 106, 109-12, 114-5, and 117, below.

83 Herman Bavinck, *Reformed Dogmatics*, vol. 1, *Prolegomena*, gen. ed. John Bolt, trans. John Vriend (Grand Rapids: Baker, 2003), 182, 186-87, 191-92; Bavinck, *Reformed Dogmatics*, 3:460-70, 531-37.

84 Joh. Jansen, "Erskine," in *Christelijke Encyclopaedie voor het Nederlandsche volk*, ed. F. W. Grosheide et al., vol. 2 (Kampen: Kok, [1925?]), 110-11. From at least as early as the seventeenth century, exchanges were frequent between the Calvinists of Scotland (and England) and those of the Netherlands, aided partly by the use of Latin as a lingua franca in the universities and partly by translations into Dutch or English, as the case might require.

Finally, A. C. Van Raalte himself included Boston's most popular book, *Human Nature in Its Fourfold State* (1720), (along with three works by John Owen, Baxter's chief orthodox Calvinist rival and critic) in his order of nearly thirty English-language books and pamphlets from the East, for "the Holland Church Library" (probably mainly for his own use) in August 1854, just a year after the outbreak of the Baxter controversy; nothing by Baxter was on Van Raalte's reading list.[85] Years later, Rev. Egbert Winter, a Van Raalte protégé, wrote that the latter was "a mild Calvinist" (like Winter himself), who "admired Baxter as well as Erskine."[86]

It thus appears that the distribution by Van Raalte and Van der Meulen of the American Tract Society's Dutch version of Baxter's *Call* may have been due less to an affinity for his theology at every point than to a miscalculation, probably occasioned by the book's relative availability in the West and its popularity in the East, the urge to bring the immigrants to conversion, and the theological tolerance of (at least) Van Raalte. This whole affair may also indicate an incipient Americanization of the immigrant leaders. Unfortunately for the peace of the Michigan church, the American Tract Society seems to have published nothing by the Erskines in Dutch.[87]

[85] Also included in the order were Calvin's *Institutes* and works by Jonathan Edwards, Samuel Rutherford, John Newton, Stephen Charnock, Archibald Alexander, and others (Receipt for books, Robert Carter and Brothers to Holland Church Library, 7 August 1854, Calvin College Archives). Van Raalte ordered the English edition of Boston's work (greatly popular in Scotland), although it had been published in Dutch already in 1742, and reprinted in 1847 (Online Computer Library Center, accessed 11 Jan. 2007; Bruggink, "Boston," 341). Carel G. de Moen (Van Raalte's brother-in-law) and Anthony Brummelkamp (Van Raalte's wife's brother-in-law), Van Raalte's friends and cohorts in the Netherlands, underwent criticism from the Drente party for the reprint in *De Bazuin* in 1856 of a sermon by Ebenezer Erskine opposing passivity and urging obedience to Jesus' command to believe the gospel, even if the faith is only natural, since God promises that the grace acquired in so doing will turn it into a supernatural act of faith. The critics saw Erskine's statement as Remonstrant; after discussion, the seceders reaffirmed the doctrine of limited atonement (Te Velde, *Brummelkamp*, 265-66, 268-69, 274-75, 302).

[86] Beets, *Christelijke Gereformeerde Kerk*, 81, quoting Winter's posthumously published article on Van Raalte in *De Grondwet*, 22 August 1911. Beets also reports that the Erskines viewed Baxter as "heretical" (84, 91).

[87] Online Computer Library Center, accessed 11 Jan. 2007. The Erskines were friends of revival, having invited George Whitefield to come to Scotland as an itinerant evangelist in the early 1740s, although they and he soon

American Instigators of Dutch Immigrant Unrest

Just how knowledgeable the West Michigan Dutch dominies (pastors) and their flocks had been about Baxter or the Marrow Men when they left the Netherlands is not clear. Already in the early days of the *Afscheiding*, differences had emerged about the free offer of the gospel,[88] and those with theological training had presumably run across these issues in their textbooks, while the laity may have been acquainted with Baxter's or the Erskines' popular works. However this may be, in the new American and RPDC contexts, the immigrants were confronted with Baxter's *Call* as an evangelistic tool promoted by Van Raalte and his colleagues. Moreover, there were now two mini-denominations, unavailable in the Netherlands, ready, willing, and able, if not eager, to inform the newcomers about Baxter's and the RPDC's theological shortcomings.[89]

The first was the Associate Reformed Church, the Psalm-singing Presbyterian body that had begun under the Erskines and other Marrow Men. Some of their followers had eventually settled in Michigan, where they were augmented in 1851 and 1853 by two little flocks of Dutch people who had seceded from Van Raalte's "lax" RPDC Classis of Holland; they were precursors of the 1857 schism. The first group was shepherded by Rev. Jacob Roelofs Schepers of South Holland (Graafschap) and the second by Rev. Roelof Harms Smit of Drenthe.[90]

The other, clearer source of unrest was the True Reformed Dutch Church, whose members had seceded from the RPDC in New Jersey and New York around 1822 because of its perceived weak handling of the case of Rev. Conrad Ten Eyck, a minister in Upstate New York who had espoused "Hopkinsianism" (named for Samuel Hopkins, a

---

fell out over the question of church government, presbyterial vs. episcopal (Noll, *Rise of Evangelicalism*, 111).

88 All were agreed on the extent of the atonement, but relatively early differences emerged between the Northern and Drente parties, on the one hand, and the Gelderland and Scholte parties, on the other hand, about the preaching of the free offer of the gospel to all (Te Velde, "Dutch Background," in *Breaches and Bridges*, 88-89). There seems to have been no disagreement about justification or neonomianism.

89 The complaints from these groups, and the issues with the Eastern RPDC, center around the doctrine of the limited atonement. Therefore, the remainder of the present article will focus on that.

90 Swierenga and Bruins, *Family Quarrels*, 67-76; Swierenga, "True Brothers," in *Breaches and Bridges*, 64-65.

New England disciple of Jonathan Edwards), which taught universal atonement and natural ability. This attenuated form of Calvinism, with its advocacy of the free offer of the gospel to everyone, was influential in the RPDC in northern, central, and western New York, where the Congregationalists, Presbyterians, and Reformed cooperated and also competed in trying to evangelize people in the burgeoning frontier settlements.[91] Although the General Synod of 1820 judged Ten Eyck's initial answers to some of its questions to be inadequate, it accepted his subsequent not altogether satisfactory clarification of his views and simultaneously declared its belief that the Bible and the Reformed standards teach that Christ's atoning death was only for those whom the Father had given him.[92] The case of Ten Eyck has been said to show the corrosive effects of American revivalism on the theology of Dort.[93]

[91] Although Edwards and Hopkins, like Amyraut, distinguished between natural and moral ability, Edwards was more "Calvinistic" than Hopkins (George M. Marsden, *The Evangelical Mind and the New School Presbyterian Experience: A Case Study of Thought and Theology in Nineteenth-Century America* [New Haven: Yale University Press, 1970], 33-43). See also James W. Van Hoeven, "Dort and Albany: Reformed Theology Engages a New Culture," in *Word and World*, 19-22; Allan J. Janssen, *Gathered at Albany: A History of a Classis* (Grand Rapids: Eerdmans, 1995), 39-44; Allan Janssen, "A Perfect Agreement? The Theological Context of the Reformed Protestant Dutch Church in the First Half of the Nineteenth Century," in *Breaches and Bridges*, 52-53; Heideman, "Theology," in *Piety and Patriotism*, 99.

[92] The complicated Ten Eyck case involved the General Synod and its seeming inability to enforce its directives in lower judicatories, i.e., the Particular Synod of Albany, the Classis of Montgomery, and the the Owasco consistory.

[93] In 1816 and 1817, Ten Eyck had witnessed a revival in his RPDC congregation in Owasco, Cayuga County, in Western New York. The New School Presbyterians ("Hopkinsians") founded Auburn Theological Seminary in 1819 in this same county, which was part of the area so ravaged by revival fires that it would be called the "Burned-over District" (Marsden, *Evangelical Mind*, 43-45; "Ten Eyck, Conrad," in Corwin, *Manual*, 779-81; *Acts and Proceedings of the General Synod of the Reformed Protestant Dutch Church in North America*, June 1820, 18-20, 66-67, 77; *Acts and Proceedings*, October, 1820, 17-28; *Acts and Proceedings*, 1822, 57; *Acts and Proceedings*, 1823, 48-50; *Acts and Proceedings*, 1824, 43-44, 46, 52. See also "Froeligh, Solomon," in Corwin, *Manual*, 478-81; Classis of Hackensack of the True Reformed Protestant Dutch Church, *Church Manual: Containing the . . . Church Government Adopted by the Synod of Dort . . . Together with the Reasons of Separation from the Reformed Dutch Church . . . in 1822 . . .* (Hackensack, N.J., 1879), 93, 96, 140-41, 148; Adrian C. Leiby, *The United Churches of Hackensack and Schraalenburgh, New Jersey, 1686-1822* (n.p.: Bergen County Historical

Initially, the 1822 schism that resulted from his casual treatment by the RPDC, involving, as it did, twenty-four pastors and twenty-six churches, was much larger and more significant than that of 1857 in Michigan, with only four congregations (or parts thereof).[94] In November 1856 Rev. John Berdan, the energetic True Reformed Dutch Church pastor at Passaic, New Jersey, wrote to the wealthy Kalamazoo Seceder immigrant Paulus den Bleijker, declaring that he believed that Christ died for the elect only and that he could not "unite with those [e.g., the RPDC and Methodists] who preach or hold forth that Christ . . . died as much for the reprobate as for the elect . . . [and] that man has natural ability." This letter was translated into Dutch and circulated in Western Michigan; Schepers even read it to his Associate Reformed congregation. Moreover, the March 1857 minutes of the Graafschap consistory (whose majority would secede the next month) recorded Berdan's opinion, in a letter, that the RPDC was not "the true church." After the secessions of 1857, he initiated relatively fruitless merger talks between his denomination and the nascent CRC, although these groups eventually united, in 1890.[95]

Society, 1976), 277-92; William O. Van Eyck, *Landmarks of the Reformed Fathers or What Dr. van Raalte's People Believed* (Grand Rapids: Reformed Press, 1922), 166-232; Heideman, "Theology," in *Piety and Patriotism*, 99-101. For another view on the theological meaning of 1822, see Swierenga and Bruins, *Family Quarrels*, 46-47. Richard Harms suggests that the roots of the 1822 seceders were in the pietism of the churches in the New Jersey valley between the Hudson River and the Ramapo Mountains, as opposed to the formalism of the New York Dutch; how does this west-east view relate to the south-north theory enunciated below? (Richard Harms, "Piety beyond the Palisades: The True Reformed Dutch Church, 1822-1924," in *Morsels*, 55-58).

94 Janssen, "A Perfect Agreement?" in *Breaches and Bridges*, 53; Fabend, *Zion on the Hudson*, 29-30, 243-44. The figures vary, maybe depending on which year is meant; Harms says at first twelve pastors and thirteen churches left ("Piety beyond the Palisades," in *Morsels*, 55, 58-60, 66).

95 Brinks, "Church History via Kalamazoo," 37-38, 41-42; Beets, *Christelijke Gereformeerde Kerk*, 92, 259-62; Van Eyck, *Landmarks*, 202-6; "Berdan, John," in Corwin, *Manual*, 311; William H. Rauchfuss, "The True Reformed Church of Passaic" (Passaic, N.J.: Passaic County Historical Publication, 1929), <www.lambertcastle.org/TrueRefCh_Passaic.html>, accessed 11 Jan. 2007. Van Eyck dates the letter to Graafschap as March 1857, correcting Beets, who says it was March 1856. Berdan led a revival in True Reformed Dutch Church life (Harms, "Piety beyond the Palisades," in *Morsels*, 62).

How Dortian Was the RPDC in 1857?

Opinions have differed ever since the 1850s as to how loyal to Dort the Eastern RPDC actually was at that time. On the one hand, many CRC and some other observers have pointed to the acquiescence of the General Synod in, if not endorsement of, the anemic Calvinism of Ten Eyck. Additionally, there was a brief commotion in 1831 in the denomination's weekly, the *Christian Intelligencer*, about the ostensibly non-Dortian views of Rev. John F. Schermerhorn, the RPDC's first missionary agent, based in Albany; the General Synod decided unanimously not even to consider the charges.[96] Furthermore, in 1834 the General Synod exonerated Rev. Alexander McClelland, professor at the New Brunswick theological school, although it disliked elements of his published sermon on "Spiritual Renovation, Connected with the Use of Means"; his explanations to the Synod of total depravity, good works, and irresistible grace satisfied it, while it did not comment on his teaching of the "free offer of salvation to all indiscriminately."[97]

On the other hand, most RCA historians have stressed the basic orthodoxy of the Eastern RPDC in 1857. Supporting its doctrinal soundness is the personal testimony of the Classis of Holland's two delegates to the June 1855 General Synod in New Brunswick, namely, Rev. Cornelis Van der Meulen (a disseminator of Baxter) and Jannis Van de Luijster (a perceptive elder and certainly no liberal, judging from his signing of Krabshuis's 1853 anti-Baxter writing), both of Zeeland. The classical minutes (written by Van Raalte, the clerk) report that "Brother Van de Luijster has found complete agreement with the confession of the fathers, and is fully satisfied," although he "found deficiency in the regular preaching of the Catechism, and also some laxity in discipline."[98] Also, "Rev. Van der Meulen praises their firm and close

96 *Acts and Proceedings*, 1831, 10; Heideman, "Theology," in *Piety and Patriotism*, 100, 178; Van Hoeven, "Dort and Albany," in *Word and World*, 22.

97 *Acts and Proceedings*, 1834, 283, 285, 301-19, 333; Howard G. Hageman, *Two Centuries Plus: The Story of New Brunswick Seminary* (Grand Rapids: Eerdmans, 1984), 60-61; Elton M. Eenigenburg, "New York and Holland: Reformed Theology and the Second Dutch Immigration," in *Word and World*, 33-34; "Alexander McClelland, 1794-1864: Spiritual Regeneration Connected with the Use of Means," in *Visions from the Hill: Selections from Works of Faculty and Alumni, . . . on the Bicentennial of the New Brunswick Theological Seminary*, ed. John W. Beardslee III (Grand Rapids: Eerdmans, 1984), 39-48.

98 CM, 5 September 1855, Art. 9, in *CHM*, 179. The following spring Van de Luijster presented to classis a letter, intended for General Synod, expressing these same views and concerns (CM, 3 April 1856, Art. 12, in *CHM*, 202).

adherence to the Reformed doctrine, discipline, and service [liturgy] and says that many ministers and professors use Mar[c]k and Witsius as a hand-book."[99] Van der Meulen himself had almost certainly cut his theological teeth on Marck, since in 1838-39 he had prepared for the ministry under Scholte, who had studied this work at the University of Leiden and who recommended it alone early in 1838 as the ["very good"] compendium for theological study.[100] Moreover, during the first decade of the Christian Seceded Church's theological school at Kampen, which began in 1854 as a joint effort of the Northern and Gelderland parties, Marck was a required textbook in theology.[101] In December 1856, the last classis meeting before the 1857 schism, the Easterner John Van Vleck, a teacher at the Holland Academy and an 1855 graduate of New Brunswick Seminary, was unanimously approved for ordination after a three-hour examination in theology, "especially in the Five Points against the Remonstrants."[102] Finally, at the end of the 1860s, two former members of Van Raalte's church, then RCA ministers, testified in *De Hope*, the organ of Hope College, that each of the seminary's most recent theology professors held solidly to the Canons of Dort.[103] At this

99 CM, 5 September 1855, Art. 9, in *CHM*, 180. Van Raalte, given the increasing tension in classis, would have been pleased with Van de Luijster's and Van der Meulen's endorsement of the orthodoxy of the East. The classis had sent Van Raalte alone to the General Synods of 1853 and 1854 (no one had gone in 1851 or 1852), so it may be assumed that the essentially positive report of two independent witnesses, Van de Luijster and Van der Meulen, gratified him, even though balanced by Van de Luijster's criticism of Eastern laxity about catechism preaching and discipline.

100 C. Smits, *De Afscheiding van 1834*, vol. 5, *Documenten uit het archief ds. H. P. Scholte, bewaard te Pella, Iowa, U. S. A. (vervolg)* (Dordrecht: J. P. van den Tol, 1982), 202, 431, 434, 435. Brummelkamp also studied Marck at Leiden, and it may be assumed that Van Raalte had done the same when he was there (Te Velde, *Brummelkamp*, 43).

101 C. Smits, *De Afscheiding van 1834*, 5:250, 276, 282.

102 CM, 17 December 1856, Art. 10, in *CHM*, 231. Van Vleck was the first New Brunswick graduate to be examined by the classis. Curiously, the unanimous vote included Rev. Koene van den Bosch, who seceded three months later.

103 R. Pieters, "De Ger. Kerk," *De Hope*, 18 November 1868; D. Broek, "De Leer der Gereformeerde Kerk," *De Hope*, 13 January 1869. Pieters (class of 1861) and Broek (class of 1864), answering CRC allegations about the Eastern RCA's unorthodoxy, quote their class notes to show that Professors Samuel Van Vranken (died 1861) and Joseph Berg held to Dort (Earl Wm. Kennedy, "The Summer of Dominie Winter's Discontent: The Americanization of a Dutch Reformed Seceder," in *The Dutch American Experience: Essays in*

juncture, a closer look at the Eastern RPDC's theological orientation will be helpful, particularly in light of Van der Meulen's reference to Marck and Witsius.

Rev. John Henry Livingston (1746-1825), the "father" of the RCA and its seminary's founder and first professor (1784-85), combined a deep piety and an evangelical, missionary heart with a basic acceptance of the doctrines of Dort, although he agreed to dropping the Canons' negative sections, the "Rejection of Errors" of the Arminians, from the Constitution of the RPDC at its organization as a denomination in 1792-93.[104] This omission may suggest a degree of Americanization, i.e., a more "ecumenical" stance amidst the pluralism of the United States and a modest retreat from total commitment to the Canons of Dort.[105] Livingston had studied for four years for the doctorate in theology at the University of Utrecht. His dissertation, "On the Nature of the Sinaitic Covenant," was indebted to the moderate covenant theology of Herman Witsius (1636-1708),[106] a student and admirer of the very influential Gisbertus Voetius (1589-1676) of Utrecht, who had been a delegate to the Synod of Dort and a stalwart Calvinist as well as pietist.[107] Livingston's mentor at Utrecht was Gijsbert Bonnet (1723-

---

Honor of Robert P. Swierenga, ed. Hans Krabbendam and Larry J. Wagenaar [Amsterdam: VU, 2000], 228). See more on Van Vranken and Berg on p. 156 and n. 118.

104 Corwin, *Digest*, 129-30, 618; Janssen, "A Perfect Agreement?" in *Breaches and Bridges*, 51; Heideman, "Theology," in *Piety and Patriotism*, 96-98. By temperament, Livingston was probably more at home in didactic than in polemic theology.

105 Could Livingston's commitment to freedom of conscience (derived from John Locke) have played a role in his seemingly more tolerant attitude toward the Arminians? (John Coakley, "John Henry Livingston and Liberty of Conscience," *Reformed Review* 26, no. 2 [winter 1992]: 119-35). The CRC has retained Dort's Rejection of Errors sections. In 1902, responding to the CRC, the RCA General Synod defended its omission of the Rejection of Errors, arguing that Dort had aimed to exclude elements *within* the Reformed Church, whereas this was not needed in 1792 (*Acts and Proceedings*, 1902), 122-25.

106 *Acts and Proceedings*, 1902, 121-22, 132; J. van Sluis, "Witsius, Herman," in *Biografisch Lexicon voor de Geschiedenis van het Nederlandse Protestantisme*, vol. 4 (Kampen: Kok, 1998), 456-58.

107 D. Nauta, "Voetius, Gisbertus (Gijsbert Voet)," in *Biografisch Lexicon voor de Geschiedenis van het Nederlandse Protestantisme,* vol. 2 (Kampen: Kok, 1983), 443-49; Willem J. van Asselt, "Gisbertus Voetius, gereformeerd scholasticus," in *Vier eeuwen theologie in Utrecht . . .* , ed. Aart de Groot and Otto J. de Jong (Zoetermeer: Meinema, 2001), 99-108; Joel R. Beeke,

1805), a temperate Voetian.[108] Bonnet used as his theological textbook the widely used *Christianae Theologiae Medulla* of Johannes à Marck (Marckius) (1656-1731),[109] whose system owed much to that of his friend and mystical older colleague Witsius.[110] The latter's *magnum opus*, which appeared in Latin in 1677 and in several later editions, firmly espoused, against the Remonstrants, Dort's doctrine of particular atonement and had considerable circulation in English as *The Economy of the Covenants between God and Man*, which came out in London in 1763.[111] This English version was reissued, with corrections, several times, most recently in 1990.[112] Witsius influenced, among many others, Thomas Boston[113] and the Erskines. In 1798, *The Economy* was published in New York, introduced with a warm recommendation by Livingston (whose name appears first) and sixteen other Reformed and Presbyterian (including Associate Reformed) pastors.[114] In sum, Livingston, who was not inclined to theological innovation, inherited and would perpetuate a moderate, evangelical version of the experientially-oriented Dortian orthodoxy of the Dutch theologians Bonnet, Witsius, Marck, and, ultimately, Voetius.

"Gisbertus Voetius: Toward a Reformed Marriage of Knowledge and Piety," in *Protestant Scholasticism*, 227-43.

108 J. H. van de Bank, "Op de grens van twee werelden: G. Bonnet," in *Vier eeuwen theologie in Utrecht*, 162-73; A. de Groot, "Bonnet, Gijsbert," in *Biografisch Lexicon,* 2:78-80.

109 J. H. van de Bank, in *Vier eeuwen theologie in Utrecht*, 165; D. Nauta, "Marck(ius), Johannes à (van)," in *Biografisch Lexicon voor de Geschiedenis van het Nederlandse Protestantisme*, vol. 3 (Kampen: Kok, 1988), 259-61; Kromminga, *Christian Reformed Tradition*, 47, 52, 54.

110 A. de Reuver, "Herman Witsius, een mystiek bevlogen theoloog," in *Vier eeuwen theologie in Utrecht*, 120-30.

111 Herman Witsius, *The Economy of the Covenants between God and Man: Comprehending a Complete Body of Divinity*, trans. William Crookshank, vol. 1 (London, 1822), 255-71. This chapter explains Dort's canon that Jesus died for the elect (but his "satisfaction" was sufficient for all) but does not mention Saumur or Amyraut; it also omits several key theological topics, e.g., Trinity, creation, and providence (and the order of God's decrees), which Witsius deals with elsewhere (D. Patrick Ramsey and Joel R. Beeke, *An Analysis of Herman Witsius's* The Economy of the Covenants . . . [Grand Rapids: Reformation Heritage Books, 2002], xi).

112 Ramsey and Beeke, *Analysis of Witsius's Economy*, vi-vii, xx-xxi.

113 Bruggink, "Boston," 106.

114 Witsius, "The Oeconomy of the Covenants . . . ," <www.angelfire.com/nh/politicalscience/1798witsius.html>, accessed 11 Jan. 2007.

Livingston's successor as professor of didactic and polemic theology at New Brunswick from 1825 to 1841 was Philip Milledoler (1775-1852), who had joined Livingston in recommending Witsius in 1798. At the seminary, he required his students to memorize Marck's textbook[115] (much shorter than that of Witsius) for classroom recitation, until a student revolt brought about an end to this catechetical, rote method of instruction, as well as Milledoler's resignation, after the General Synod told him to prepare his own lectures (although he could continue to assign Marck as a textbook for the students to read). He had presumably "inherited" the use of the *Medulla* from Livingston, under whom he had studied at New Brunswick. In any case, the General Synod of 1828 had prescribed Marck for the course in "didactic and polemic theology" required of the second- and third-year students at New Brunswick, but already in 1833 a question was briefly raised about this requirement.[116] Marck's compendium of "didactic and polemic" theology explicitly stated, against "the Universalists," that Christ's death ("satisfaction") was neither for angels nor for all people but only for the elect.[117] Although it is unknown which textbook(s) were used by Milledoler's successors, Samuel A. Van Vranken (1841-61) and Joseph F. Berg (1861-71),[118] each was declared thoroughly Dortian by two students from the immigrant churches (see above, n. 103). Berg, in particular, championed traditional Calvinism over against the theology of John W. Nevin of the German Reformed seminary at Mercersburg, Pennsylvania.[119]

115 Johannes Marckius, *Christianae Theologiae Medulla Didactico-Elenctica . . . Editio Prima Americana* (Philadelphia, 1824).

116 *Acts and Proceedings,* 1828, 143; *Acts and Proceedings,* 1833, 163, 219-20; Hageman, *Two Centuries Plus*, 54, 64-65.

117 Marckius, *Medulla*, 199-201. The limited atonement comes here, in the section on the "office of Jesus Christ," not in the earlier sections on the divine decrees and predestination. Marck omits the order of the decrees, except to prefer infralapsarianism to supralapsarianism and to reject Arminianism. This handbook for students, first published in 1690, mainly uses biblical citations, not Reformed confessional documents or other theologians, to make its points. A copy of "the first American edition" of 1824, cited in n. 115, is in the Western Seminary library; its original owner was Rev. James A. H. Cornell of the New Brunswick class of 1841. If Livingston actually used the *Medulla* as a textbook, it would have had to have been imported from Europe.

118 This information may be in their manuscript lectures at New Brunswick Seminary (Corwin, *Manual*, 314, 864).

119 Hageman, *Two Centuries Plus*, 80; Van Hoeven, "Dort and Albany," in *Word and World*, 26.

In any case, the 1841 General Synod, in its mandate to Milledoler about his teaching, stated that "there are at least four great controversies coming within the range of the Didactic Professor, where he should not merely act on the defensive, as he does in his general course, but carry the war into the enemies' camp; these are the *Deistical*, the *Socinian* or *Unitarian*, the *Arminian* and the *Universalist* [Amyraldian]. On all these, the theological student should be made perfectly at home, for he has to encounter them . . . as soon as he enters upon his ministerial work."[120] Furthermore, significant time was to be spent on each of these topics. This shows the importance the General Synod gave the doctrine of limited atonement, at least on this particular occasion.

It may be concluded, with James W. Van Hoeven who unwittingly echoed an observation by Van Raalte himself,[121] that, through the 1850s, the RPDC in New Jersey and the New York City area, including the seminary at New Brunswick and the denominational weekly, the *Christian Intelligencer*, remained loyal to Dort[122] but willing to tolerate (at least reluctantly) the less robust Calvinism of its Dutch Reformed kinsmen on the revivalist frontier in Upstate New York, near Albany and westward, where the "universalist" leaven of New England Congregational and New School Presbyterian "Hopkinsianism" (and its offspring) was more prevalent.[123]

120 *Acts and Proceedings*, June 1841, 450-51, 520-23; *Acts and Proceedings*, September 1841, 22; the disposition of the students' complaint is on 10-26.

121 Van Raalte, replying to Gijsbert Haan's citation of an anti-RPDC booklet by the True Reformed Dutch Church at the April 1856 classis meeting, said that he, in probing the 1822 secession, had been "informed that in the southern portion of the Dutch Church there never had been manifested any departure from the Dutch confessional standards, . . . and that this southern portion has constantly exercised a saving influence upon the northern portion, consisting of congregations composed [of people] from all kinds of countries, in which they did not show themselves to be so attached to the Dutch confessional standards. . . ." (CM, 3 April 1856, Art. 12, in *CHM*, 206-7).

122 Like its Old School Presbyterian neighbors at Princeton Seminary in their loyalty to the Westminster Confession.

123 Van Hoeven, "Dort and Albany," in *Word and World*, 21-27; Van Hoeven, "The American Frontier," in *Piety and Patriotism*, 38-42. Fabend, *Zion on the Hudson*, 25-26, tells the story of the slowly increasing influence of evangelical revivalism on the insular Eastern RPDC, as it Americanized, during the nineteenth century.

As damaging as was the RPDC's loss in 1822 of its most anti-Hopkinsian wing, it did not rival the catastrophe that befell the Presbyterian Church in 1837, when the five-ninths Old School majority in the General Assembly excised the four-ninths New School ("Hopkinsian") minority.[124] The break would last until reunion was achieved in 1869. During this Presbyterian schism, Van Raalte, in Detroit at the end of 1846 and start of 1847, on his way to settle farther west, established cordial relations with, and enlisted the support of, among others, the New School Presbyterian minister, George Duffield Jr. (1818-88; later of "Stand Up, Stand Up, for Jesus" fame), ardently evangelical and presumably against limited atonement. Van Raalte attended more than one of Duffield's services and liked his piety. Van Raalte's amity with Duffield may have been partly a case of "any port in a storm," but it was also likely a sign of the ecumenical breadth of the Gelderland party, in general, and of Van Raalte, in particular, who was by no means a "heresy hunter." The two men remained friends long after this initial encounter.[125]

Farewell to "L"?

The doctrine of limited atonement had a particularly hard time surviving the twentieth century's evangelistic, missionary, and democratic mindset, not to mention its distaste for "theological hairsplitting." The northern Presbyterians, led by Princeton Theological Seminary and its chief oracle, Charles Hodge, whom Van Raalte likely admired at a distance,[126] maintained, at least on paper, the Calvinist

[124] Marsden, *Evangelical Mind*, 62-66. There was also a schism ca. 1810 on the Kentucky frontier, where revivalist Presbyterian ministers embraced Arminianism and formed the Cumberland Presbyterian Church (with New School Presbyterian affinities); others went further to begin the non-denominational "Christian" movement (Marsden, 14, 116).

[125] A. C. van Raalte to Anthony Brummelkamp, Detroit, 16 December 1847, *Stemmen uit Noord-Amerika, met begeleidend woord van A. Brummelkamp* (Amsterdam, 1847), translated in *Voices from North America* (Grand Rapids: Heritage Hall Publications, 1992), 24-26, 29; Jeanne M. Jacobson, Elton J. Bruins, and Larry J. Wagenaar, *Albertus C. Van Raalte: Dutch Leader and American Patriot* (Holland, Mich.: Hope College, 1996), 45-47; Albert Hyma, *Albertus C. Van Raalte and His Dutch Settlements in the United States* (Grand Rapids: Eerdmans, 1947), 64, 72, 76, 133. Duffield's father was a New School Presbyterian leader; for him, see Marsden, *Evangelical Mind*, 52-53, 55-56, 122-23, 191, 218-19; for Jr., see Marsden, 182-83, 197-98.

[126] He read the Princetonians' books (A. C. Van Raalte to Philip Phelps, Holland, 4 November 1860, Van Raalte Collection, Joint Archives of

doctrine of limited atonement throughout the nineteenth century; but in 1903, despite Princeton's mild protests, the denomination revised the Westminster Confession of Faith, effectively eviscerating that belief.[127] The CRC, with its deep Dortian roots, continues officially to hold that Jesus died only for the elect, but its handling in the 1960s of the case of Harold Dekker, Calvin Theological Seminary's missiology professor ("God so loves . . . all men"), weakened this tenet, by merely admonishing him for his "ambiguous" and "abstract" statements that

---

Holland). In this note Van Raalte asks Phelps to lend him "Hodge on the Hebrews," but neither Charles Hodge nor anyone else at Princeton Seminary had written a commentary on the Epistle to the Hebrews. Van Raalte owned a copy of Archibald Alexander (Princeton Seminary's first professor), *The Canon of the Old and New Testaments* . . . (Philadelphia, 1851); this volume is in the Joint Archives of Holland, stamped as having belonged to Van Raalte. Also, he ordered Alexander's *Practical Sermons: To Be Read in Families and Social Meetings*, published by the Presbyterian Board of Publication, Philadelphia, 1850 (Receipt for books from Robert Carter and Brothers to Holland Church Library, 7 August 1854).

[127] The Westminster Confession (1647) says: "The Lord Jesus . . . hath . . . purchased . . . reconciliation . . . for all those whom the Father hath given unto him" (8.5); "Neither are any other redeemed by Christ, . . . but the elect only" (3.6). It does not decide between supra- and infralapsarianism. The 1903 revision adds chapter 35 ("Of the Gospel of the Love of God and Missions"), stating that "God, . . . having provided . . . through the . . . sacrifice of . . . Christ, a way of life and salvation, sufficient for and adapted to the whole lost race of men, doth freely offer this salvation to all men in the gospel," and that "God declares his love for the world and his desire that all men should be saved." A Declaratory Statement was also added, that God's eternal decree (chap. 3) "is held in harmony with . . . his love to all mankind, his gift of his Son to be the propitiation for the sins of the whole world," and so on. When the United Presbyterian Church (formed in 1858 by the Associate Reformed Church and other groups) joined the Presbyterian Church in the U.S.A. in 1958, it too, in effect, deserted its Calvinist roots and accepted the 1903 revisions, which, as Lefferts Loetscher, a friend of the changes, admitted many years later, represented open acceptance in American Presbyterianism of the Remonstrant views repudiated by Dort (*Constitution of the United Presbyterian Church in the United States of America* [Philadelphia: Office of the General Assembly of the United Presbyterian Church in the USA, 1960], 7-9, 42-44; D. G. Hart and John R. Muether, "Turning Points in American Presbyterian History. Part 8: Confessional Revision in 1903," in *New Horizons*, August/September 2005, <www.opc.org/new_horizons/NH05/08c.html>, accessed 11 Jan. 2007; Lefferts A. Loetscher, *The Broadening Church: A Study of Theological Issues in the Presbyterian Church since 1869* [Philadelphia: University of Pennsylvania Press, 1954], 83-89, 95-97; Kennedy, "Hodge's Doctrines," 219-20, 247-55, 343, 352).

many saw as inconsistent with the limited atonement as taught by Dort.[128] The RCA, uneasy with the Canons of Dort in particular, in 1971 took another route than the CRC, when it decided no longer to require its ministers, as it had since 1792, to believe that "all the articles and points of doctrine" of the Three Formulas of Unity "fully agree" with the Bible; henceforth candidates needed simply to accept the standards as "historic and faithful witnesses to the Word of God."[129]

[128] Its treatment of Rev. Herman Hoeksema in 1924 on common grace foreshadowed its handling of Dekker, which, in turn, is reminiscent of the RPDC's treatment of Ten Eyck a century and a half earlier. Dekker's language was more universalist than the Marrow Men's (Bratt, *Dutch Calvinism*, 206-7, 298; James C. Schaap, *Our Family Album: The Unfinished Story of the Christian Reformed Church* [Grand Rapids: CRC Publications, 1998], 155, 244-46, 250-52; *Acts of Synod of the Christian Reformed Church, . . . 1966* [Grand Rapids: Christian Reformed Publishing House, 1966], 436-507). The report links the Hoeksema and Dekker cases, rejects Amyraldianism, and backs "particular" ("definite") and dislikes "limited" atonement (*Acts of Synod*, 1966, 439-45, 506; *Acts of Synod*, 1967, 486-607, 727-37).

[129] Corwin, *Digest*, xv. The RCA's Theological Commission proposed the change because the Three Formulas were dated. "We find this particularly true of the Canons of the Synod of Dort. The scholastic form of their polemic, while understandable in their time, render them relatively ineffective today for teaching and witness. We find the Heidelberg Catechism and the Belgic Confession more useful" (*Acts and Proceedings*, 1971, 215; also 211-16). The new wording is reminiscent of the loose subscription introduced by the 1816 *Hervormde Kerk*'s national Synod (handpicked by King William I) that was one of the irritants that led to the *Afscheiding* of 1834. "The new oath [of subscription, 1816] allowed candidates to accept the doctrines of the three official creeds 'in so far as' (rather than 'because') they agreed with Scripture" (Swierenga and Bruins, *Family Quarrels*, 10-11). The CRC still requires not only its ministers, but also its elders and deacons to subscribe to "all the articles and points of doctrine," at their ordination and/or installation. Will this affect the "orderly exchange of clergy" with the RCA approved by the 2006 CRC Synod? Meanwhile, the *Hervormde Kerk* adopted a new church order in 1951 and realized that "the confessional writings do not have an unshakably valid authority anymore"; Dort's doctrine of election was viewed by the majority as unbiblical, deterministic, and too logical, while the Remonstrants were seen as partly right in supporting "human responsibility and the universality of God's grace." In 1961 the Synod issued a "pastoral document," stating that "doctrinal discipline is an extreme means which must be practiced as little as possible." In fact, it doubted that "the Reformed Church in its current condition was either authorized or capable to practice doctrinal discipline" (Blei, *Netherlands Reformed Church*, 114-17). No new *Afscheiding* occurred.

Dort's doctrine of limited atonement, however, had not been indigenous to, and never fully at home in, the nineteenth century. While Van Raalte, the Michigan immigrants, and the Eastern RPDC pledged their allegiance *ex animo* to the Canons, including the limited atonement, it can at least be asked whether this commitment was not attenuated, willy-nilly, by post-Dortian tides, such as *Nadere Reformatie* pietism in the Netherlands and revivalism in the USA. Thus, although "the hands were the hands of Esau" [Dort], "the voice is Jacob's voice" [pietism and revivalism].[130]

In any event, Richard Baxter's *Call to the Unconverted*, whatever it may have done to convert West Michigan immigrants, helped crystallize differences in attitude toward the Canons of Dort and prepared the way for the division in 1857 between the professedly more zealous adherents of "the faith of the fathers" and those who, like Van Raalte and the Eastern RPDC, could tolerate a greater degree of diversity and inclusiveness, as well as accommodation to the American evangelical environment.

130 Genesis 27:22.

CHAPTER 8

A Decade of Hope and Despair: Mercersburg Theology's Impact on Two Reformed Denominations

Gregg Mast

It was August of 1844 when delegations from the Reformed Protestant Dutch Church and the German Reformed Church made their way to Harrisburg, Pennsylvania, in what they hoped would be the first of many Triennial Conventions. Indeed, the whispered rumor was that the denominations, both American children of the Reformed Church in the Netherlands, hoped that the Triennials would lead to closer relationships, which in turn would culminate in organic union. Three years later, the second Triennial was held in Reading, Pennsylvania, where most of the agenda time was spent arguing about whether they ought to make the second convention the last. A majority vote sent the dissolution of the Triennial Conventions back to the denominations, which quickly confirmed their demise. Six years later, in 1853, the Dutch Church voted to suspend all communication with the German Church, a decision that was not lifted for a decade. What happened? How did two churches, so close to serious conversation about union, stop talking with each other? The story of a decade of hope and despair (1844-53) is one that not only changed the course of these two small denominations, but in a sense altered some significant ecumenical relationships and theology to this very day.[1]

[1] This topic was briefly addressed by Eugene Heideman, "Theology," in *Piety and Patriotism*, ed. James W. Van Hoeven (Grand Rapids: Eerdmans, 1976), 102-4, 179-80, notes 32-41.

The handwritten minutes of the Triennial Conventions of 1844 and 1847 provide a number of clues as to the reasons the two denominations moved so quickly from a hopeful and growing intimacy to a decade-long divorce characterized by acrimony and distrust. Both churches had realized their independence from the Reformed Church in the Netherlands in the 1790s when the Dutch Church acted at its first Synod in 1794 to enact the following resolution:

> As a friendly correspondence with sister Churches will doubtless conduce to strengthen and establish the cause of religion, the General Synod sincerely wishes to open such a correspondence, and prosecute it to a union with the Reformed German Church in Pennsylvania. For which purpose they shall be to take the earliest opportunity, and, if possible, the most effectual measures, to bring so desirable a thing into effect. [2]

In pursuit of such a union, the Dutch Reformed Church began to send three delegates to the annual synodical meeting of the German Church in 1812, a commitment the church fulfilled until 1853 when it suspended all communication. The German Church followed a similar pattern, albeit with fewer delegates and more frequent exceptions. Dr. John Henry Livingston, in many ways the father of the Dutch Reformed Church, suggested in 1819 that the German Church share in the benefits of New Brunswick Theological Seminary, an overture that appears to have fallen on deaf ears. In the following year, 1820, the Dutch Church was eager to explicitly explore union and appointed a committee to meet with any group designated by the Germans. Because no committee was forthcoming, the courtship needed to wait until 1842 when two pastors, Drs. Berg and Heiner, of the German Church, suggested the time was right to nurture serious conversations. John Knox, the chair of the committee responsible for considering the overture, reported to the June 1842 Synod of the Dutch Church:

> The two churches of common origin, closely connected in their history and in their sympathies, adhere, in part at least, to the same standards, are identical in their form of government. Their actual present condition and circumstances are such that were a union affected upon sound principles and with mutual cordiality,

2 *Acts and Proceedings of the General Synod of the Reformed Protestant Dutch Church in North America*, 1794, 258.

> both would be benefited, and the result of their united effort upon the welfare of the community, would far exceed the sum of their separate efforts. . . . For these and other reasons, it is obvious therefore that a carefully and cordially arranged union would be beneficial, and greatly subserve the cause of the Redeemer in our beloved land.[3]

A joint committee from both the German and Dutch Churches was appointed to lay the ground work for the first Triennial and a plan was submitted to each of the synods and their classes for approval. Quite remarkably the plan called for two-thirds of the delegates to come from the two synods of the German Church, one located almost exclusively in Pennsylvania and the other mostly in Ohio. The balance of the convention would obviously come from the Dutch Church. While the actions of the Triennial would be only advisory, it was clear to all that this was the first step toward the altar.

As the delegates appeared in Harrisburg, they were met at the German Church by Professor John Williamson Nevin, who had been invited to preach the opening sermon. The Dutch Reformed weekly, the *Intelligencer*, had not only warmly welcomed Nevin to his new post as Professor at the German seminary in Mercersburg in 1840, but had favorably reviewed a book he had published in 1843, entitled *The Anxious Bench*. In the book Nevin had roundly criticized a revivalism that had begun to negatively transform American church life through ignoring the covenantal, catechetical nurture of each parishioner, pastor, and congregation. The publication of *The Anxious Bench* revealed that the mainline denominations not only had grave concerns about what they called "Finneyite revivalism," but that they had also begun to experience the loss of members to the passionate revivalists on the one hand and to the rich liturgical life of the Anglican and Roman Church on the other.

Nevin had come to the German seminary at Mercersburg having been educated at Union College in upstate New York, which was a product of the Dutch Reformed and Presbyterian Churches. He proceeded to Princeton Seminary and then on to a career as a professor at Western Theological Seminary in Allegheny City, Pennsylvania. His arrival in Mercersburg came as a great boon to the school, which was attempting to find its moorings after the resignation of one of its two professors in 1839 and would struggle with the death of

3 *Acts and Proceedings*, June 1842, 72.

the other in 1841. It would be Nevin, and Philip Schaff, who would arrive from Germany just in time for the 1844 Triennial Convention, who would sow the theological seeds of discord that would cause the denominations to move from altar to divorce in a decade.

Philip Schaff had been called to become the other professor at Mercersburg after his mentor, Dr. F. W. Krummacher, pastor of the largest Reformed Church in Germany, had declined to accept the invitation. Krummacher, however, had commended Schaff to the committee of two that had traveled to Germany from Pennsylvania. With his acceptance, Schaff traveled to America as a newly ordained twenty-five-year-old minister and scholar. Schaff, of course, would become one of the best known and often cited church historians of the nineteenth century. When he arrived in the United States in the summer of 1844, he preached the first Sunday in German in a Dutch Reformed Church in New York City, and then was escorted by rail and coach to the Triennial Convention in Harrisburg.[4] Few would have guessed that the young German theologian, Philip Schaff, and the old school Presbyterian, John Williamson Nevin, would so quickly find each other to be kindred spirits. Within a couple of years their writings would become the foundation of what was to be known as Mercersburg Theology, and the two would be called to defend their views in front of the General Synod of the German Reformed Church. They also would so enrage the leaders of the Dutch Reformed Church that the old, distinguished denomination could not abide them or what was branded as their "Romanizing tendencies."

Perhaps a hint of problems to come could have been seen in the title of Nevin's opening sermon at the Triennial in Harrisburg, "Catholic Unity." He chose as his text the familiar passage from Ephesians which called for the church to remember it has come from "one God and Father of us all." While Nevin did refer to the Pope as the antichrist, an almost obligatory attack considering his background, he also encouraged the church to remember its catholic roots. Nevin confessed that the Dutch and German churches were one in faith, and lauded the role the Reformed Church in the Netherlands had played in the birth of both denominations. A few years later, however, Nevin revised both of these positions, and began to identify the spirit of sectarianism as the antichrist, and the German Church as owing far more to Melanchthon than to the Dutch or to the Palatinate.

4 David S. Schaff, *The Life of Philip Schaff* (New York: Charles Scribner's Sons, 1897), 92.

Reading the reports presented at the Triennial following Nevin's sermon, one can detect some important differences between the churches. The Dutch Church claimed 279 congregations within its bounds and 271 ministers. The number of congregations without a pastor was reported as 43 and the number of ministers without a charge, 53. This landscape was dramatically different from the one found within the German Church. In the Eastern German Synod, there were 123 ministers actively engaged in ministry, with 487 congregations, whereas the Western Synod claimed 58 pastors serving 208 congregations. It is apparent that although the Dutch Church was more than adequately supplied with pastors, the Germans had almost double the number of congregations with far fewer pastors. From the earliest days, the German church had moved quickly toward the West and founded congregations wherever they discovered German families and neighborhoods. The Dutch, on the other hand, had remained relatively comfortable and contained in the states of New York and New Jersey. They had anticipated their need for pastors with the founding of the seminary in New Brunswick, which traced its birth to 1784, a decade before the American Dutch Church declared its independence. Buried in the midst of the reports of both delegations was the news that the Dutch had eight foreign missionaries, whereas the Germans had been able to underwrite only one. Although the Germans felt that they should make their own way in the New World, there remained a nagging sense that their Dutch sibling was richer, better served by its seminary, and certainly far more connected to the power elite of the East Coast.

By the end of the first Triennial, a small committee had hammered out a set of five proposals that would move the denominations toward its goal of closer relations and possible union: (1) The licentiates of either of the theological schools of the three denominations (the Eastern and Western Synods were perceived as independent from each other) would be considered as candidates in either Church. Each seminary was then directed to send the names of their most recent graduates to the other seminary; (2) The students were encouraged to keep up an active correspondence with their colleagues in the other bodies in order to cultivate affection and awaken a mutual interest in each other's ministry; (3) It was decided that the system of instruction in the seminaries should be as similar as possible, and that the same text books in didactic theology should be used;[5] (4) The liturgies of each

5 It should be noted that this last provision was the only one of the five that did not claim the approval of the sending bodies. Perhaps it was a case in

body should be conformed to each other as nearly as possible; (5) The domestic missionary operations should be blended together as much as possible.[6] It may be helpful to pause at this point and review the tone of the fifth proposal that had come from the General Synod of the Dutch Church to the Triennial:

> That the General Synod of the Protestant Dutch Church do regard the great lack of ministerial help in their sister church as presenting strong claims upon their Christian sympathy, and do cordially recommend to the youth who may be educated in their Theological Seminary to direct their attention to said church, as affording in their judgment one of the most promising and inviting fields of ministerial usefulness.[7]

The German Synod approved this plan at their meeting in October 1844 and the Dutch at their synod in June 1845 (with the exception of the provision of common textbooks). At the Dutch Synod, an action was also taken to provide a generous gift of $1,000 toward the domestic mission field of the Germans with promises that more would be sought and subsequently sent. While the gift was undoubtedly appreciated, it may also have reminded the Germans of their dramatic needs, their lack of resources to address them, and the great wealth of both personnel and money of their sister denomination.

At the meeting of the Eastern Synod of the German Church, held in Allentown in October 1844, Schaff was invited to present his inaugural address. It should be noted that before he did so, Dr. Joseph Berg offered a traditional defense of Protestantism as an outgrowth of the purest intent of the apostolic age. Indeed, he went one step further and suggested that the Protestant movements of the sixteenth century had accessed the riches of the past not through the soiled and defective tradition of the Roman Church, but through the unusual faithfulness of the Waldensians. It is apparent that Protestant scholars and pastors of the age were going to remarkable and questionable lengths to distance themselves from Rome and the papacy. It should come as no surprise that when Schaff delivered his address entitled "The Principle of Protestantism," there was great interest to ascertain the "purity" of

---

which professors would not yield their freedom to choose texts and/or that the texts in each seminary favored the mother tongue of each.

6 *Acts and Proceedings*, 1845, 424-30.

7 *Acts and Proceedings*, 1843, 180.

his views. Whereas American Protestant scholars argued against the corruption of the Roman Church of the Middle Ages and for a return of the church to the first-century model, those of the Anglican perspective proposed that it was the first four or five centuries that needed to form the church, a position which clearly allowed for the apostolic offices. Schaff, following in the footsteps of his German professors, suggested a third alternative, that of historical development.

A century later, Bard Thompson and George Bricker published Schaff's address with an introduction which included this dramatic paragraph:

> Against the background of Berg's sermon, the inaugural address of Philip Schaff is seen to be one of the most significant events in the history of the American church. The young professor who stood in the pulpit of the Reformed Church in Reading also stood against the inadequacies of American Christianity, its unhistorical character, its provincialism, its subjectivism and sectarianism. Schaff rejected Berg's "desperate" history as preposterous. The Reformation, he argued, far from being a revolutionary disjuncture with Medieval Christianity, could only be understood as "the legitimate offspring" and "greatest act" of the Catholic Church—the unfolding of "the true catholic nature itself." With that astonishing piece of intelligence, he introduced his colleagues to his theory of the historical development of the church.[8]

Schaff proposed that the church was developing in an organic way, like the development of any living organism. Thus, it was apparent that within each and every age the church was moving forward toward God's intention. Indeed, Schaff suggested that the development would continue until the day when Protestantism and Catholicism would finally unite again. Schaff's son David, who wrote his biography some years later, noted that his father often observed that he had no idea that his "harmless" remarks would cause such a furor. Indeed, fifty years later (1893), Philip Schaff stood in the same Allentown pulpit and after pronouncing the benediction exclaimed: "Here I stood fifty years ago and flung out a firebrand. However, I did it unintentionally."[9] In

8 Bard Thompson and George Bricker, eds., *The Principle of Protestantism* (Philadelphia: United Church Press, 1964), 14.

9 Schaff, 114.

1845, both Schaff's "Principle of Protestantism" and Nevin's "Catholic Unity," although not delivered at the same venue or written in consultation with each other, were published together. It was in 1845, less than a year after the first Triennial, that the church began to notice that there was a new message coming out of Mercersburg.

Schaff's address was being affirmed by some and criticized by others as being far too irenic in its view of Rome and thus totally out of step with the views of the Reformed Churches in America. Dr. James I. Good, historian of the German Reformed Church, decades later reminded his readers of an incident in the Philadelphia area that was illustrative of the "bad blood" between the Roman Catholics and the Protestants of the day:

> For it is to be remembered that the address was delivered just at the time of the bitterest feelings against Catholics. On May 3, 1844, the Irish Catholics of Kensington, Philadelphia, had attacked a meeting of the American party at which a number were killed and wounded. The American party afterward paraded with the American flag, which they had taken from the Catholics in the riot and on it they placed the inscription, "This is the flag trampled upon by Irish papists." This feeling was so bitter that a fire broke out which consumed thirty-nine houses and the militia were called out. Two Catholic churches in Philadelphia were burned.[10]

It was Good's contention, albeit posited more than sixty years after the events, that Schaff had touched upon a tinder box of emotions that he had little idea existed. The young German scholar had begun his first American appointment thinking that he was simply sharing the cutting edge of German historical thought, whereas he was actually taking on a culture saturated with tension and hatred.

The Classis of Philadelphia took an official action against Schaff's contentions in September of 1845, a position which was not sustained a month later at the meeting of the Eastern Synod. In the debate around the complaint from Philadelphia, Good reports that Joseph Berg, Schaff's major and most articulate opponent, spoke for

[10] James I. Good, *History of the Reformed Church in the U.S. in the Nineteenth Century* (New York: Board of Publications of the Reformed Church in America, 1911), 219.

[11] Good, 227.

two hours, Nevin for two, and Schaff for three, mostly in German.[11] In the end, by a vote of 37 to 3, the complaint was rejected. In spite of this clear action, the Classis of Philadelphia, meeting a year later (1846), adopted a platform that it believed to be faithful to the Protestant cause and in opposition to what it was hearing from the Mercersburg professors. Philadelphia affirmed that scripture, not tradition, was the only rule of faith and practice; that the sacraments had no inherent efficacy; and that the humanity of Christ was not to be found on earth, but only in his divine presence. It also challenged Schaff about an article he had written while still a student, in which it appeared he made some allowance for conversation about a "middle state" between life and death, in which the souls of the living awaited the final judgment. The Synod of 1846 took seriously the concerns of the Classis of Philadelphia, but in the end decided that Schaff had distanced himself from his earlier writings and had no intent of teaching a "middle state" at Mercersburg.

The gauntlet, however, had been laid; the battle had begun. The denominational papers of the Dutch and the Lutherans especially began to weigh in on the side of the "orthodox" positions espoused by those who wondered if Mercersburg was becoming an outpost of Rome and Canterbury. While charges flew back and forth, Nevin published *The Mystical Presence: A Vindication of the Reformed and Calvinistic Doctrine of the Holy Eucharist.* Although Nevin had clearly arrived at Mercersburg with a very predictable old school theology, it appears that early on in his career he had embraced a Calvinistic rather than Zwinglian view of the presence of Christ in the Eucharist. Indeed, it was Nevin's intent not only to remind the church of the long-forgotten theology of Calvin and the Supper, but to use his theology to reform the church regarding its view of itself, its history, and its worship. Nevin believed that Calvin's richly developed understanding of the mystical union between Christ and his church meant that the church was finally founded on the objective and gracious presence of the resurrected Christ, rather than on the often sentimental faith of his followers.

At the heart of the developing controversy was Joseph Berg, who would less than a decade later desert the Germans as well as the Mercersburg professors, Schaff and Nevin, to join the Dutch and finally teach at New Brunswick Seminary. In the spring of 1846, Nevin publicly challenged Berg to respond to the following four questions: 1) Has the humanity of Christ no organic part in his personality as Mediator? 2) Is not the sin of Adam organically imputed to his offspring? 3) In justification, is the sinner viewed by God in justifying him as in Christ or out of Christ? 4) Is the active obedience of Christ imputed to us or only his passive obedience? Good records Berg's response as following:

> Berg replies to the first question that if the natures were so closely united, as Nevin suggests, he would ask how could the divine nature suffer. The divine nature was not made finite or the human nature made infinite according to the Heidelberg Catechism (Answer 48). In regard to the second question, imputation was not only imputed but inherent because of the covenant with Adam. As to the third question, justification must be sundered from sanctification. It is a forensic act. But every justified person must be regenerated, although regeneration is not the ground of justification. As to the fourth, both active and passive righteousness is imputed to us.[12]

In response to the increasing debate within and around the German Church, the Classis of Bergen in the Dutch Reformed Church began to raise questions about the wisdom of continuing the Triennials with the Germans. At the General Synod of 1846, Bergen overtured the Synod to discontinue the Triennials and to ask the German Church to provide an accounting of the theology being written by the professors at Mercersburg. The Synod was addressed not only by its own delegates who had been in attendance when the Germans had voted not to "convict" Schaff and Nevin, but by the Rev. B. C. Wolff, who pleaded with the Synod that both Schaff and Nevin were not being understood because of the use of German terms that did not translate well into English or Dutch. It would be most helpful at this point to share a portion of the minutes of the General Synod of the German Church meeting at Carlisle, Pennsylvania, in October 1846.

> By some in the Sister Church (Dutch), the Convention appears to be regarded as constituting, in effect, an alliance, or union of the Churches "intimate and controlling." In this aspect, it is thought, no one has regarded it in the German Church. By us, it is considered an arrangement for mutual counsel and cooperation, in promoting the general interest of religion of the Churches respectively, without giving to either the right, or privilege, to interfere in any way with order, organization, or peculiar domestic concerns of the others.
>
> Some unpleasant feeling, it is believed, has also arisen in the minds of Brethren of the Sister Church, in consequence

[12] Good, 252.

> of mistaken impressions of the extent and character of the destitution of the German Church.[13]

A year later, in August 1847, the next Triennial Convention was held at Reading, Pennsylvania. But by then, the positive and hopeful mood of the first convention had turned. The Dutch Synod had unanimously voted to discontinue the conventions, which prompted a conversation that lasted almost until midnight. It appears that the Dutch were resolute in their decision to dissolve the Triennials, while the Germans wanted the conversation and partnership to continue. In the end, the two denominations, so close to serious talks about merger, left Reading farther apart than at any time in their brief histories. It was clear that the common and inspiring vision that brought them to the Triennial of 1844 had turned to acrimony and name calling just three years later.

There is little doubt that the writings of Schaff and Nevin were very much responsible for this turn. Whereas the two professors sought to open up the American Reformed churches to a more "enlightened" view of the church, its history, and its sacraments, their opponents could only see the face of the pope and the presence of the Anglo-Catholic movement in the Church of England behind their positions. It is also possible that feelings of German inferiority and Dutch superiority played a role in the demise of the relationship. Although the Triennials were abandoned, the denominations continued to exchange delegates until 1853 when the Dutch proclaimed that they were suspending all communication, a position that prevailed until it was lifted a decade later in 1863.

In 1849, perhaps tired of always being in a reactive stance, Nevin and Schaff blessed the beginning of the *Mercersburg Review* by the alumni of Marshall College. Its pages provided ample opportunity for the professors and their supporters to explain the tenets of the Mercersburg theology. The initial publication included long articles by Nevin on the Apostles' Creed, in which he explicated his ecclesiology and called the church to stand in historic and organic unity with the apostolic soul of the church. Whereas many nineteenth-century theologians and historians wrote about the visible and invisible church, both Nevin and Schaff embraced a view that described a community growing from a kernel to fruition. This organic model allowed them to find the essence of the faith in every age and in every church.

[13] *Acts and Proceedings*, 1846, 18.

As the *Mercersburg Review* was beginning, the German Church was also eager to look more closely at its liturgical life. With all of the charges of "Romanizing," the direction that was finally embraced by the church a decade later could only add fuel to an already roaring fire. The dramatic story of the renewal of worship in the German Reformed Church began with a momentous resignation. Because Nevin held out little hope that the synod would do more than approve a new translation of the Palatinate liturgy, he resigned in 1851 from his role as chair of the liturgical committee. He was replaced by Schaff, who promptly created a whole new and creative direction for the committee. In 1852, the committee met regularly, imagining "a general plan, also four forms for the regular service on the Lord's Day, two baptismal services, a form for the solemnization of matrimony, and a plan of the Scripture lessons and collects for the ecclesiastical year."[14] This brief quotation, from an article published in the *Mercersburg Review* six years later, hints at the remarkable changes the committee envisioned. The committee hoped to move the church from a sermon/preacher dominated service of free prayer to one which included a book of forms and prayers for the whole congregation. It imagined a service that would be attentive to the church year and would include many opportunities for all worshippers to verbally participate. It also committed itself to a liturgical life where the Eucharist was at the center, a place Nevin had long advocated. In 1852, the committee's report included the following first principle:

> The liturgical worship of the Primitive Church, as far as it can be ascertained from the Holy Scriptures, the oldest ecclesiastical writers, and the Liturgies of the Greek and Latin Churches of the third and fourth centuries, ought to be made, as much as possible, the general base of the proposed Liturgy; the more so, as they are in fact also the source from which the best portions of the various Liturgies of the 16th century were derived, such as the form of confession and absolution, the litanies, the creeds, the Te Deum, the Gloria in Excelsis, the collects, the doxologies, etc.[15]

There is little doubt that Schaff and the committee had moved the liturgical vision and thus the practice of the German Church in directions that few had ever imagined. Sources that were understood

[14] James Hastings Nichols, *Romanticism in American Theology* (Chicago: University of Chicago Press, 1961), 295.

[15] Nichols, 296.

to be outside the realm of "orthodox" Reformed use were suddenly on the table for the committee to review and appreciate. While it is evident that the *Book of Common Prayer* and the Roman mass were simply far too controversial to play a role in the liturgical process, Schaff discovered, on a trip to England in 1853, a sect that would allow him and the committee to move the German Church toward the main current of Western liturgical life while remaining "unstained" by Rome or Canterbury. His son David records, in his father's biography, a portion of a remarkable letter Schaff wrote one day from London:

> Sunday I spent the greater part of the day with the Irvingites. In the morning I found their beautiful Gothic church in Gordon Square, the first of the seven churches of London, thronged with devout worshippers. The Lord's Supper was administered with great solemnity, an imposing ceremonial, many hundreds communing. . . . The liturgy is very beautiful. I dined with the angel of the church, Mr. Heath, meeting his large and amiable family. . . . Then at four I attended the service designed for the congregations; at seven the service of the evangelists for outsiders. The service this morning, I believe, was the most beautiful and perfect liturgical service I have yet attended. . . . The real body and brawn of the English nation is radically Protestant and will certainly never submit to the yoke of an Italian church ruler or permit itself to be despoiled of the Bible, the pulpit and other forms of the Reformation.[16]

The Irvingites, who are more properly identified as the Catholic and Apostolic Church, were an outgrowth of a strange charismatic movement in the 1830s. Edward Irving, a Scot by birth and the founder of one of the first "mega" churches in England, had affirmed an outbreak of glossalalia in his London congregation and had also accepted the stories of miraculous healings. In response to these views, as well as a theology that had turned toward a more millennial and incarnational bent, Irving had been deposed by the Church of Scotland, but not before a majority of his congregation followed him. It is here that the story turns even stranger, for it appears that a group of lay leaders took control of the renegade congregation and nurtured a movement that was charismatic, millennial, and yet strangely liturgical. Following the untimely death of Irving, the London congregation began a passionate

[16] Schaff, 178.

search for the best liturgical material in the world in order to construct its own worship. The only reason this is important is that it is clear that Schaff and the American German church, as well as the Church of Scotland, both discover the Catholic and Apostolic Church and utilize it in their own liturgical renewals.[17] These renewals clearly nudged both denominations toward worship that was eucharistically centered, radically participatory in nature, responsive to the church year, and clearly consistent with the main current of Western liturgical tradition. At the same time, the renewals place both churches out of step with the sermon-dominated and often liturgically impoverished life of most Protestant denominations.

While this liturgical development was taking place, both Schaff and Nevin had intimated to the Synod of 1851 that they should leave their posts at Mercersburg. There was no doubt that Nevin had lost considerable heart in the increasingly personal battles for the very soul of his adopted denomination. The fact that a number of the critiques had been launched at him and Schaff from the pages of the *Intelligencer*, the newspaper of the Dutch Reformed Church, and the *Lutheran Observer*, as well as from his teachers and supporters at Princeton, had undoubtedly added greater pain to the controversy. Schaff had apparently received a call to a congregation in Philadelphia at the same time that Nevin tendered his resignation to the Synod. Both Nevin and Schaff were encouraged to remain at Mercersburg, a fact that caused the Dutch church to believe that the Synod had endorsed the theology of the two professors. The Dutch Synod took immediate action in 1852 and voted to send but one delegate instead of three in order to express its dismay at the actions of the Germans. There was considerable debate about whether the retention of the professors simply expressed a general support and affection for them, or if the German Synod had intended by its vote to signal its full acceptance of all of Nevin and Schaff's views. The following year witnessed the move of Joseph Berg, the main antagonist of the Mercersburg professors, to the Dutch Reformed Church. This was followed in 1853 by the following action by the Dutch Synod:

17 My doctoral dissertation traces the influence of the Eucharistic liturgy of the Catholic Apostolic Church on the renewals in the German, Scot, and Dutch Churches in the nineteenth century: Gregg Alan Mast, *The Eucharistic Service of the Catholic Apostolic Church and Its Influence on Reformed Liturgical Renewals of the Nineteenth Century* (Lanham, Md.: Scarecrow Press, 1999).

> That this Synod do hereby express, in the most decided and unequivocal manner, their protest against all those sentiments of a Romanizing character and tendency which are technically known as the "Mercersburg Theology," as being essential departures from the faith as calculated to lead yet farther astray from the old landmarks of truth, and to undermine the great principles of the Reformation from Popery.[18]

This action culminated in the suspension of all correspondence with the German Church until it was restored a decade later, in 1863. In these same years, the Classis of North Carolina, of the German Church, made overtures to be accepted into the Dutch Church. It appears that the request was finally withdrawn because the Dutch could not abide the pro-slavery stance of the classis.

The response to the action of the Dutch Church could not have been swifter or more scathing. Casting aside the normal courtesy that characterized synodical reports, the German Synod meeting in Philadelphia in October 1853 adopted a report that consumed three full pages of its minutes. While it is not salutary to quote the report in its entirety, its tone of outrage cannot be missed. After complaining that the Dutch had not properly communicated their decision just months before (undoubtedly an interesting conundrum for the Dutch since they had suspended all communication), the report lauded the German commitment to dialogue since the independence of the two churches some sixty years before. While the Germans had followed a course of expected courtesy, the Germans clearly felt the Dutch had not.

> On the contrary, there has been an evident attempt, in many instances, on the part of the brethren of the Reformed Dutch Church, during the last ten years, to interfere in matters that concerned us alone. In some cases, no doubt, our movements have been modified by influence, and in those instances in which Synod has shown herself unwilling to yield her rights, we have been made, in a private way at least, to feel that we have by far too much independence to meet with the approbation of those who have so long condescended to evince towards us a patronizing air. . . .
>
> In their late Synod in this city they gravely charge us with having done what "amounts to a tacit connivance with, if not a

18 *Acts and Proceedings*, 1853, 319.

> virtual approval of views which strike at the vitality of the truth as maintained by the Protestant Church." This your committee regard as an unqualified slander, and one which has already rebounded to the merited disgrace of the source whence it sprang. The doctrines and sentiments charged upon our Professors and others, but which they disclaim *in toto*, are doctrines and sentiments in regard to which this Synod has never felt itself called upon to sit in Judgment, and to which it has never given "a virtual approval." The genius of our Church allows diversity in nonessentials. And that there is some difference among us on points not affecting the great plan of salvation is not to be denied. The absence of such diversity would argue the want of manly and independent thought. Diversity in unity is a privilege enjoyed by the ministers and membership of our Church, and we never contracted to barter our birth-right for a mess of pottage, nor could our brethren of the Dutch Church have reasonably expected it. . . .[19]

This remarkable diatribe concludes with a poetic, biblical, and long-suffering resolution which reads:

> That, feeling, with "the father of the faithful," the disgrace caused by the existence of strife between his herdsmen and the herdsmen of Lot in the presence of the Canaanite and Perizzite, we acquiesce in the discontinuance of correspondence with the Reformed Protestant Dutch Church and that notwithstanding the grievances inflicted upon us by that body, we still cherish towards them the spirit of love and forbearance enjoined by our blessed Saviour.[20]

There can be little doubt that the relationship between the two churches had been deeply affected by the theological writings of Nevin and Schaff. In Mercersburg's attempt to develop a third way in which the Protestant church could relate to Rome and, more importantly, to the Western tradition of the church that had been increasingly ignored by American denominations, Nevin and Schaff had ventured into territory that the Dutch and the Lutherans, to say nothing of the American revivalists, were unprepared to consider. This fact was

[19] *Acts and Proceedings of the German Reformed Church in the United States,* 1853, 16-18.

[20] Ibid., 18.

exacerbated by the utilization of the denominational magazines to attack the positions of Mercersburg. Finally, one cannot help but glean from the German minutes a sense that the Synod felt a certain arrogance in the Dutch denomination. Indeed, it may be argued that the Dutch were both shocked and exasperated that the Germans had deigned to enter into complex theological conversations that had not followed their lead.

It is also interesting to note that New Brunswick Theological Seminary initiated in 1854 the *New Brunswick Review*, which published as its first article a long and critical review of Schaff's works on church history. The *Review* produced only two issues, which are found in one volume. One of the articles concluded with a paragraph that can only be characterized as the point of the battle: "Our examination has extended only to a little beyond the middle of Dr. Schaff's work. But the positions he has already advanced, are such as to lay the whole truth and grace of God, and the whole liberty, hope, and salvation of the human race, at the feet of the Roman Papacy."[21]

What can we learn from this sad and dramatic footnote in the ecumenical annals of the German and Dutch Churches of the nineteenth century? After the resumption of communication in 1863, the two churches attempted, on a couple of occasions, to reconsider union. Although such a union was not to be, the German Church did unite with the Evangelical Church to create the Evangelical and Reformed Church, which in turn united with the Congregational Church in 1957 to create the United Church of Christ. It should be noted that in the late 1990s, the Reformed Church in America and the United Church of Christ had another conflict that almost led to a second suspension of communication. The United Church of Christ has been one of the few historic American denominations that has allowed the service of duly-ordained gay and lesbian persons who have entered into committed relationships of affection and fidelity. Following the approval of the Formula of Agreement in 1997, the Reformed Church in America strongly requested that the United Church of Christ enter into a dialogue of discovery about the radically different positions of the churches; it was expected that this conversation could lead the RCA to officially admonish the UCC for its position. It may come as no surprise that the motives and results of that conversation are not very different from the one that preceded it by 150 years. The United

[21] *New Brunswick Review*, May 1854–February 1855, 325.

Church of Christ, while publicly cordial, could not help but wonder why the Reformed Church in America was intruding in what the UCC believed to be a private, internal matter. The RCA, on the other hand, remained convinced that the UCC had compromised the purity of the gospel. While correspondence between the two was not suspended, it was limited by the RCA General Synod of 2000.

Although the conflict of the 1840s and the intense debate of the 1990s remain separated by more than one hundred fifty years, there remain some common elements that can assist the church as it faces the future. Church union and cooperation must be based on mutual respect and support, not feelings of superiority or inferiority; denominational dialogue needs to find common ground as well as to accept divergent views; Christian dialogue requires years, often decades, to discern the mysterious and inspiring Spirit of God; and finally, no one person or church, no matter how learned, can possess the truth, for the truth of God possesses us. What remains crucial in this and all ecumenical relationships is discerning what is essential to the gospel and what remains within the prerogative of a church, as it attempts to respond faithfully and relevantly to a world in need of the presence and peace of Christ.

CHAPTER 9

A Century of Change and Adaptation in the First English-Speaking Congregation of the Christian Reformed Church in Holland, Michigan[1]

Jacob E. Nyenhuis

Fourteenth Street Christian Reformed Church (CRC) was established on 25 June 1902 as the first English-speaking CRC congregation in Holland, Michigan. The history of Fourteenth Street Church is an account of the people who have gathered at the corner of Fourteenth Street and Central Avenue for over one hundred years to worship and then to go forth to serve Christ and community. It also reveals how change and adaptation came to a congregation originally made up exclusively of Dutch-Americans in a community founded by Dutch immigrants fifty-five years earlier.

The key theme of Fourteenth Street Church's history is the story of God working in and through individual believers to create community and to accomplish God's purposes. It is a story of grace and glory, of struggle and victory, of joy and sadness. It is a personal story of

[1] An earlier version of this paper was presented at a conference of the International Society for the Study of Reformed Communities, held in Edinburgh, Scotland, 27 June to 3 July 2003. It in turn drew heavily upon my *Centennial History of the Fourteenth Street Christian Reformed Church, Holland, Michigan, 1902-2002* (Holland, Mich.: Fourteenth Street Christian Reformed Church, 2002), which was produced in a limited edition for the church's centennial. This paper has benefited from helpful critiques offered at the ISSRC conference, as well as from those of both my beloved wife and my esteemed colleagues at the Van Raalte Institute.

a group of believers, but it also is a universal story of faith and hope.

The congregation experienced dynamic growth during the early years. The middle years were marked by conflict over how to deal with its burgeoning membership. This conflict eventually resulted in a painful separation. Those who remained behind to erect a new building also had to rebuild the reputation of the congregation within the classis and denomination. The years following the dedication of the new building in 1958 were characterized by a gradual process of healing and renewal. The last quarter century has seen a clarification of vision and adaptation to a changing environment. As the church moves forward in its second century, there is a new energy and a renewed dedication to its mission.

Beginning, Growth, Division, Renewal

The impetus for this new congregation arose in the Ninth Street (now Pillar) Christian Reformed Church already in 1899, but the majority was not yet ready to establish a daughter church, so they temporized for a time. Ninth Street CRC occupied the stately pillared building that had been erected by First Reformed Church under the leadership of the city's founding father, the Reverend Dr. Albertus C. Van Raalte.

The roots of Fourteenth Street Church actually go all the way back to the *Afscheiding* (Secession) of 1834 in the Netherlands. They extend upward through Dr. Van Raalte's emigration to America in 1846 and to Western Michigan in 1847. These roots grew larger through the Settlers' Church (later First Reformed Church) which Dr. Van Raalte established in the colony at Holland and later through the fledgling denomination that came to be known as the Christian Reformed Church.[2]

This new denomination had been founded 8 April 1857 by people who had originally resisted the more ecumenical Van Raalte in his efforts

2 The seceding churches met six times over a period of two years before they agreed upon a name for themselves. At the meeting of Classis held in Grand Rapids on 2 February 1859, they unanimously chose the name "Holland Reformed" (Art. 4, quoted in Henry Beets, *De Chr. Geref. Kerk in N[oord] A[merika]* [Grand Rapids: Grand Rapids Printing, 1918], 122). At the Classis meeting of 6 February 1861, they chose the name "True Dutch Reformed" (ibid., Art. 9*)*, but in October 1864 they decided henceforth to use the equivalent Dutch title, "*Ware Hollandsche Gereformeerde Kerk*" (ibid.). A proposal from Classis Illinois in 1872 was adopted at the Synodale Vergadering (Synodical Assembly) of 1880, and the name was changed once more, to "*Holland Christian Reformed Church*" (Beets, 123).

to affiliate with the American church. They had been uncomfortable in the Reformed Protestant Dutch Church, or Dutch Reformed Church, which in 1867 was renamed the Reformed Church in America. Among the founders of the new denomination were those who had felt that the union with the American church had occurred too quickly. They also were disturbed by reports of developments in the Reformed churches in the East, such as lodge membership, replacement of catechetical instruction with Sunday School, and the substitution of hymns for psalms in the worship services. These evidences of Americanization caused four of the congregations to withdraw from the union of 1850 to return to "their former stand point." [3]

In 1882, just fifteen years after the CRC was founded, the majority of the congregation of Van Raalte's original church also withdrew from the Reformed Church, by a vote of eighty-six to eighteen. In the ensuing court battle, the seceders won the right to the stately church building. Two years later, the congregation affiliated with the new denomination and became Ninth Street Christian Reformed Church. At the root of this separation was the struggle over how best to adapt to the culture in which they now lived. It was a struggle waged over and over again by this and other immigrant groups. At the end of the nineteenth century, that struggle found its expression in conflict over the language of worship. The immigrant families had worshiped all their lives using the Dutch language. They were accustomed to hearing the Word of God read and explicated in Dutch, and they praised God by singing the Psalms in Dutch. The children of immigrants, however, and their descendants were being educated in public schools where they were learning the English language so they could survive and prosper in their homeland. For them, it was difficult to understand the Dutch Scriptures and sermons.

In 1899, therefore, the consistory of this congregation that had resisted Americanization began to discuss the need for a congregation that conducted all its services in the English language.[4] When they

[3] For a more extensive treatment of factors that led to the secession of these congregations from Classis Holland of the Dutch Reformed Church (RCA) to form what was to become the CRC, see Earl Wm. Kennedy's essay, "Richard Baxter: An English Fox in a Dutch Chicken Coop?" elsewhere in this festschrift.

[4] Minutes of the Consistory of Ninth Street Christian Reformed Church, 1 November 1899, cited in G. J. Steggerda, "History of the Fourteenth Street Christian Reformed Church," *Twenty-Fifth Anniversary of the Fourteenth Street Chr. Ref. Church, Holland, Michigan* (Holland, Mich.: Fourteenth Street Christian Reformed Church, 1927), 3.

brought the idea to a congregational meeting on 27 November 1899, the consistory found that the congregation was not yet ready for such a drastic step. Instead, they decided to hold evening worship services in English.[5] This decision was first implemented at the evening service on 28 January 1900.[6] This solution seemed satisfactory at first, but it merely laid the groundwork for the eventual establishment of a new congregation that would use the English language in all its worship and educational programs. By 9 May 1901, the Ninth Street consistory called a special meeting to consider the matter further: a committee was appointed to canvas both the Ninth Street and Central Avenue CRC congregations, but they reported to the consistory that there were not enough people yet ready to organize a new congregation.[7]

It is worth noting that the Americanization of the RCA in Holland had not progressed very rapidly either, although Hope Reformed Church had been established in 1862 as the first English-speaking Reformed Church. Hope Church was founded by members of the faculty of Hope College who had come from English-speaking Reformed Church congregations in the East. Third Reformed Church, however, did not switch to the use of English in worship services "until 1896, exactly forty-nine years after the colony of Holland was founded."[8] Despite this fact, Third Church was considered to be "the most progressive Dutch-immigrant church in the community in this matter."[9] During the first twenty-five years of the community's existence, moreover, there were three Dutch-language newspapers, but not a single one in English. The move toward English services at Third Church had been led by its pastor, Rev. Henry Utterwick (1872-80), who had begun teaching catechism in English, but abandoned even that practice in 1879 because of the congregation's strong opposition to English services. He resigned his pastorate a year later.[10]

5 Minutes of the Congregational Meeting of Ninth Street Christian Reformed Church, 27 November 1899, show that the vote passed fifty-five to nine, with some abstentions (Steggerda, 3).

6 The issue of organizing an English-speaking congregation was again introduced at a congregational meeting less than a year after the first services in English, but no action was taken and the members were asked to think about it (Minutes of the Congregational Meeting of Ninth Street Christian Reformed Church, 17 December 1900; Steggerda, 3).

7 Minutes of the Consistory of Ninth Street Christian Reformed Church, 2 September 1901 (Steggerda, 3).

8 Elton J. Bruins, *The Americanization of a Congregation,* 2nd ed. (Grand Rapids: Eerdmans, 1995), 35-36.

9 Bruins, 36.

10 Bruins, 38.

First Reformed Church did not begin services in English until 1906, when it initiated morning services in English, but they "continued an afternoon Dutch service until 1923."[11] Other Reformed churches postponed the move to English services "until the decade after World War I" and as late as 1924 a new "Dutch only" church was established as Seventh Reformed, although its appeal diminished over time and the congregation disbanded after World War II.[12] Considering these developments within the congregations of the Reformed Church in Holland, Michigan, it is somewhat surprising that the impetus for an English-speaking Christian Reformed Church began as early as it did in Ninth Street CRC, the former First Reformed Church.

Less than two years after the first evening worship service was conducted in English at Ninth Street Church, a meeting of interested parties from Ninth Street and Central Avenue Churches was held. This meeting, on 21 January 1902, led to the appointment of a committee to undertake efforts to organize an English-speaking CRC in Holland. Within six months of that meeting, the decision to organize was made, a site was acquired, G. J. Daverman of Grand Rapids was chosen as architect, bids were let, and a date for organization was set. Thus, on 25 June 1902, Fourteenth Street English Christian Reformed Church was organized.[13] A month later, a pastor was called, and on 5 September 1902, Rev. Douwe R. Drukker was installed as pastor.[14]

The records of Fourteenth Street Church show that once the flood gates were opened to worshiping in English, there was no stopping the torrent that followed. From the initial thirty-nine families, the congregation grew rapidly. By the end of the pastorate of Rev. Drukker in 1911, the number of souls had more than quadrupled, from 231 to 930,[15] and the number of families from 39 to 184.[16] This dramatic

11 Bruins, 41.

12 Ibid.

13 Minutes of the Congregational Meeting, 25 June 1902.

14 Minutes of the Congregational Meeting, 23 July 1902, reveal that Rev. Douwe R. Drukker, of Drenthe, Michigan, CRC, was called at a salary of $800 (or $700, if the Domestic Mission Board should fail to grant the new congregation's request for aid), plus $150 for renting a house (379 Central Avenue was later chosen as the first parsonage).

15 Nyenhuis, *Centennial History*, 12; the figure of 930 for 1911 comes from the *Twenty-Fifth Anniversary* booklet (6) and does not correspond to the official figures in the *Yearbook of the Christian Reformed Church*, which reports only 865 members (Nyenhuis, 161-62).

16 Henry Beets, "Life Sketch," in *The Beauty of the Lord and Other Sermons: A Selection of Sermons Preached by the Reverend D. R. Drukker*, ed. Raymond B. Drukker (Eerdmans, 1927), 16.

growth was also attributable to the excellent preaching of Rev. Drukker, whose classmate, Rev. Dr. Henry Beets, reported that "from his days . . . as a student . . . to the very end of his ministry, he was constantly in demand . . . and may well be called the most popular preacher in the denomination in his days."[17]

Rev. Drukker was succeeded by Rev. Peter A. Hoekstra, the grandfather of Robert P. Swierenga, the Albertus C. Van Raalte Research Professor at the Van Raalte Institute and dean of Dutch-American scholarship. Rev. Hoekstra had been ordained less than two years earlier as pastor of the Moline, Michigan, CRC, a Dutch-speaking congregation. That new congregation had grown dramatically during his brief tenure as their "beloved first pastor," and there was similar growth at Fourteenth Street Church during his ministry there. The clerk of the church reported on Hoekstra's installation and subsequent inaugural sermon, declaring that "Hoekstra gave the congregation a 'forward look, and colored the future with bright hopes, if we maintain our Reformed principles.'"[18] The mortgage on the church was burned exactly ten years after the church had been established.[19] A biography of Rev. Hoekstra asserts: "Under Hoekstra's congenial leadership, the congregation grew by leaps and bounds until the sanctuary was so full that chairs were set in the aisles, but the fire chief put an end to this on the grounds of safety."[20] Therefore, just two years after Rev. Hoekstra arrived as pastor, Maple Avenue Church was established as a daughter church, the second English-speaking CRC congregation in Holland. The number of families from Fourteenth Street Church who became charter members of Maple Avenue Church was identical to the number of charter families of Fourteenth Street Church eleven years earlier. Nonetheless, the church's "records show that fully 150 families still belonged to our congregation after the departure of our families to Maple Ave. Church."[21]

17 Ibid., 15. Beets also reports that Rev. Drukker, on the occasion of the twenty-fifth anniversary of his ordination, had written "that during these twenty-five years of ministry, he had preached and lectured 3,284 times, united 255 couples in the bonds of matrimony and had officiated at 233 funerals. We may add that up to that time he had received 51 calls–among them four from congregations he had served before" (18).

18 *Banner,* 25 July 1912, as quoted in Robert P. Swierenga, "The Anne (Andrew) Hoekstra Family," (working paper, Van Raalte Institute, January 2003), 9.

19 *Twenty-Fifth Anniversary*, 6.

20 Swierenga, 10.

21 *Twenty-Fifth Anniversary*, 7.

Rev. Hoekstra held together a diverse congregation by means of his irenic spirit and his diligent efforts, but the divisions within the congregation became more visible with the pastorate of his successor, Rev. Herman Hoeksema (1915-20). Hoeksema had grown up in Groningen, the Netherlands, the son of "a pious mother beset with an alcoholic, philandering husband," who deserted the family. After his father left, "young Herman took to the streets, stealing bread, running with a gang, defying all order and propriety. His mother's faith eventually turned him around and his blacksmith training gave him a skill."[22] He subsequently emigrated to Chicago in 1904, worked there for four years, then went to Calvin College and Seminary, where he excelled. It is said that his "Calvinism was logical, unswerving, and remorselessly consistent."[23]

The militant Hoeksema came to Fourteenth Street Church right out of seminary, after three ordained ministers had declined the call. Rev. Hoeksema claimed that "under his predecessor some 90 percent of the families in the congregation opposed Christian education and were very lukewarm in their support of Holland Christian School,"[24] which had been established the same year as Fourteenth Street Church. Rev. Hoeksema "brought the disagreements to a head by pushing Christian education and doctrinal orthodoxy."[25] The membership of the congregation declined considerably between 1917 and 1918, because his approach alienated a number of the families, with the result that "there was a grand exodus . . . mostly to Trinity RCA, and primarily over the issue of the Christian School."[26] By the time that he left in 1920,[27] however, the membership had rebounded to slightly more than it was when he arrived.

22 James D. Bratt and Christopher H. Meehan, *Gathered at the River: Grand Rapids, Michigan, and Its People of Faith* (Grand Rapids: Eerdmans, 1993), 119.

23 Bratt and Meehan, 120.

24 Swierenga, 10.

25 Ibid.

26 Interview by the author with two nonagenarian members of Fourteenth Street Church, Kathryn Fredricks and Elizabeth Sterenberg, 2002.

27 He left to assume a pastorate at Eastern Avenue CRC in Grand Rapids, where he again became embroiled in debate over orthodoxy, this time over the issue of common grace, i.e., whether there is a certain favor or grace of God which He shows to all His creatures. Rev. Hoeksema believed very passionately that the "Three Points of Common Grace" adopted by the Synod of the Christian Reformed Church in 1924 were theologically

While still at Fourteenth Street Church, Rev. Hoeksema had sparked controversy in the local press by his successful efforts to have the American flag removed from the sanctuary during worship services. Since the nation was involved in World War I at that time, it is not surprising that this action sparked strong feelings. As a result, Rev. Hoeksema carried a pistol for self-protection and "even threatened to use [it] one night on some vigilantes near his home."[28] The *Holland Sentinel* of 15 July 1918 records an amusing story about the American flag at Fourteenth Street Church. The previous Sunday, the congregation was surprised to see "Old Glory" reappear in the sanctuary, suspended across the wall behind the pulpit. The pastor stated before the worship service began that "the decorations were placed there unbeknown to him or the members of the church consistory." The only other reference to the flag came during the pastor's prayer, "when he stated that such an act of entering the church was an act of rowdyism." A note left on the pulpit Bible, not mentioned in the newspaper, was dated 13 July 1918, and signed by the "American Protective League." The note, which is preserved in the church's archives, states: "This flag must and shall remain in this place." The flag was removed, however, as surreptitiously as it arrived, sometime between 1:00 and 7:00 p.m.[29]

In the 1920s there was another tremendous growth spurt, from 842 in 1920 to 1,211 in 1927. That year the enrollment in Sunday School reached 542, making it the second largest Sunday School in the denomination. The Sunday School's highest attendance record (506) was reached in 1933. Minutes of congregational meetings record frequent discussions of proposals to expand the building to accommodate the burgeoning congregation. Land was repeatedly acquired adjacent to the existing property, either to add on to the building or to expand

---

in error, and he pursued his views relentlessly. His congregation became hopelessly divided and, in the end, he was deposed from the ministry in the CRC. He therefore led the organization of a break-away denomination, the Protestant Reformed Church (*One Hundred Years in the Covenant: Eastern Avenue CRC, Grand Rapids, Michigan, 1879-1979* [Grand Rapids, Mich.: Eastern Avenue Christian Reformed Church, 1979], 30-40).

28 Bratt and Meehan, 119.

29 After the publication of my *Centennial History*, a retired colleague solved the mystery by confirming that, in his youth, his father, James Dyke van Putten, who had served for many years as a U.S. diplomat and later became the first professor of political science at Hope College, had been the ringleader for this prank.

the parking lot.[30] Shortly after the fiftieth anniversary, additional property was acquired, but this time at some distance, to escape the potential expansion of the business district of the city.[31] In 1954, the congregation voted 103-57 to purchase a large piece of property on Twenty-sixth Street from Huldah Nies Bequette at a price of $20,000.[32] The intent was to erect an entirely new building on the Nies property to meet the needs of this rapidly expanding congregation. In the end, however, this purchase did not prove to be as beneficial as anticipated, for it led to a serious split in the congregation.

The minutes of both the consistory and the congregational meetings are replete with information about proposals, counter-proposals, decisions, reversals of decisions, and the resulting hurt feelings and alienation. Life-long members of Fourteenth Street Church who lived through that era report that many enduring friendships were damaged or destroyed by the conflict, and many families were divided about whether to stay or leave.

Not quite a year after the decision to buy the property on Twenty-sixth Street, on 21 March 1955, a majority of the congregation (102-85) rejected the consistory's recommendation to build a new church on that property. Then, at a special congregational meeting on 19 September 1955, the decision was reversed and the majority again voted in favor of building on the Twenty-sixth Street property, but at a meeting on 14 November, the majority again reversed the decision, creating the final impetus for splitting the congregation. A week later, a delegation informed the consistory that they would petition Classis Holland in January 1956 for permission to organize a new congregation.[33]

At a meeting on 16 January 1956, chaired by Rev. Henry Baker, a member of the Classical Visitors Committee, the congregation voted to give the property on Twenty-sixth Street to the new congregation and

[30] One example was the purchase of the "Molengraff property directly west of the church" and the creation of a committee of seven contractors from the congregation to determine the feasibility of expansion (*Holland City News*, 27 April 1916). Three years later the congregation approved the expansion of the church building at a cost of $12,000 (Minutes of the Congregational Meeting, 26 February 1919, and *Holland City News*, 27 February 1919).

[31] Ironically, the continuing expansion of Holland Hospital and medical office buildings has encroached more on Faith Church than the business district has on Fourteenth Street Church.

[32] Minutes of the Congregational Meeting, 26 April 1954.

[33] Minutes of the Consistory, 21 November 1955.

to "assure a fair distribution of funds."[34] On 9 February, the prospective members of the daughter church met, made plans for beginning their own services on 12 February, and chose the name Faith CRC for their new congregation. All but one of the members of the consistory at this time left to become part of Faith CRC.

The repercussions from the separation continued for a long time afterward. Not only did about a third of the congregation leave to establish Faith Church, but there followed a steady stream of requests for membership transfers, some to Faith Church, but many to other churches, both Reformed and Christian Reformed. Finding a new pastor proved difficult: from April 1956 until 28 April 1958, sixteen calls were extended to pastors before Rev. Dr. Simon John De Vries accepted the call.

In the meantime, the remaining members undertook the building of a new church building. In August 1956 the architectural firm of Stapert-Pratt-Bulthuis and Sprau, Inc. of Kalamazoo was hired to design a new building.[35] The architectural plans were unanimously approved by the congregation on 10 December 1956. On 10 June 1957, the congregation approved a project budget of $225,000, and voted (115-10) to award the general building contract to Russell Lamar.[36] Six days later, the congregation held their final worship service in the old building, after which the organ was dismantled for later reassembling. The old building was then razed.

For the next thirteen months, services were held in the Christian High School Gymnasium. On 20 July 1958, services were held for the first time in the new building and the new church was dedicated on 21-22 September 1958. It is important to note that this church building was the first in Holland to be fully accessible to members and visitors with physical disabilities, long before the Americans with Disabilities Act (ADA) was approved by Congress.

Nearly twenty years later, a Long-Range Planning Committee was appointed to "analyze present building needs and project future building needs of the congregation," but their proposals were soundly defeated in March 1980.[37] A month later, an apartment building at the

34 Minutes of the Congregational Meeting, 16 January 1956.

35 Church bulletin, 12 August 1956, reported that the consistory, on 30 July 1956, had authorized the New Church Building Committee to engage the services of this firm.

36 Minutes of the Congregational Meeting, 10 June 1956.

37 Minutes of the Consistory, 5 December 1977; Minutes of the Congregational Meeting, 3 March 1980, show that it was defeated 52 to 130.

corner of Fifteenth Street and Central Avenue, immediately adjacent to church property, became available. Many people saw this as an answer to prayer, and the congregation approved its purchase at a cost of $93,500—and by a much more convincing margin than that by which they had rejected the earlier proposal.[38] That acquisition failed, however, to meet the congregation's expectations, so it was eventually sold.[39] This sale ended a vision for the building's use for community outreach and other programs.

The following year a new Building Expansion Committee was appointed and, in June 1988, their recommendation for an expansion that would add classrooms and offices was approved by the congregation.[40] This addition greatly enhanced the educational program and the refurbished Fellowship Room has served as a focal point for socializing after the worship services, for monthly church potlucks, and for many other activities that promote spiritual growth and a sense of community.

After this expansion, Fourteenth Street Church became active in the Inter Parish Council (IPC) and increased their involvement with the community. The IPC included ten local congregations—Roman Catholic, Episcopal, United Methodist, Reformed Church in America, and Christian Reformed—all located in or very near the center of town. The IPC sought to establish common ground for outreach efforts and sponsored joint worship services, such as a Lenten Luncheon Series and a community-wide Service of Christian Unity. Churches of the IPC also joined together to sponsor the building of a Habitat for Humanity House a few years before it disbanded in 2005.

At the beginning of the third millennium, in early 2000, Rev. Marvin Hofman became the congregation's fifteenth pastor. During his tenure, both spiritual and numerical growth has been evident. Whereas membership had risen dramatically during the church's first twenty-five years, had declined gradually during the next twenty-five, then dropped precipitously with the split in 1956, it continued to decline over the years until it had fallen to only 303 members in 1998. The trend was reversed during the interval between pastors (1999-2000),

[38] Minutes of the Congregational Meeting, 28 April 1980, show that the vote was 121 to 17.

[39] The sale of the apartment building to Heritage Homes for $50,000 was unanimously approved (Minutes of the Congregational Meeting, 18 August 1986).

[40] Minutes of the Congregational Meeting, 7 June 1988.

and membership had risen to 339 by the beginning of the church's centennial year in 2002.

On 7 May 2006, after three years of study by three different committees, the congregation again voted on a plan to expand the church building. Eighty percent of the votes cast at that meeting favored the expansion and remodeling of the current facility at a cost not to exceed one million dollars. The theme of "Gathering and Growing God's Family" was adopted for a three-year period to give focus to the vision for the congregation. A Vision Coordinator from the Council was appointed to help implement the theme and the pastor has been using it in planning worship services.[41] Conversations continue about the goal and nature of the expansion program.

Adaptation to a Changing Environment

Fourteenth Street Church came into existence to enable people to worship in a language that was familiar to them. The neighborhood where the church was first built consisted at the time almost exclusively of descendants of either the original immigrants or later waves of immigrants, so there was little ethnic diversity. Over the years, however, the composition of the neighborhood has become increasingly diverse. Fourteenth Street Church's response to those changes shows varying degrees of both isolation and adaptation.

From the very beginning, Fourteenth Street Church showed a commitment to outreach, but to regions far from home. This is evident, for example, in its support for the denominational missions program from the outset. In 1925 Fourteenth Street Church joined with Central Avenue CRC in the calling and support of a missionary: Rev. Albert H. Selles served intermittently in China until 1942. In 1948 Rev. Edward A. Van Baak was called for service in China, and subsequently to Japan. The Church later supported missionaries to many different places in this hemisphere, as well as to Ceylon, Japan, Liberia, Nigeria, and Cambodia.

At the local level, the congregation has supported the classical home missions program for well over fifty years. Already in 1952, it was reported that "seven of our members have given of their time and

[41] "A Path to Build," a booklet distributed on 23 April 2006 (cover mistakenly carries the date of 23 April 2003, reflecting the year that the first committee was appointed). See also Minutes of the Congregational Meeting, 7 May 2006.

talents as volunteer workers for a number of years. We also maintained a salaried part-time worker . . . 1946-49."[42] These efforts were nurtured through the years by many different groups within the congregation. In March 1959, the consistory approved a statement of purpose for a new Committee on Evangelism and Outreach that had been approved at their previous meeting. Its purposes were:

> 1) To work with the Sunday School and Societies to promote interest in and support for evangelistic activity, both locally and in distant places; 2) To advise the Consistory on matters of missions, evangelism, and community relations coming before us; and 3) To devise and supervise for our congregation a program for increasing our Christian witness in the community through such means as civic betterment, social work among distressed peoples, and neighborhood evangelism.[43]

When Rev. R. O. Broekhuizen came to Fourteenth Street Church in 1973, he brought a vision and a passion for evangelism. During his tenure, various programs and activities were undertaken to encourage local evangelistic efforts. By 1975, the church newsletter reported that "the 14th Street Witnessing Teams have been instructed every other week by Rev. Milton Doornbos."[44] It was also reported that a weekly Bible study had begun with a person contacted by one of these teams.

At the same time, attention was turning toward a ministry to refugees from Southeast Asia. Sponsorship of a Vietnamese refugee family was approved and a family was taken under the care of the congregation in 1976. Some members of the congregation became actively involved in the Community Education program in English as a Second Language, forming enduring relationships with individuals and families from Southeast Asia. In December 1979, a Cambodian family arrived under the church's sponsorship. Members of the Refugee Resettlement Committee worked diligently to assist the family in getting settled, finding work, enrolling the children in school, and so forth.

These efforts at outreach, particularly the stress on personal evangelism, did not win the support of all members of the congregation.

42 *Fiftieth Anniversary Historical Booklet of the Fourteenth Street Christian Reformed Church* (Holland, Mich.: Fourteenth Street Christian Reformed Church, 1952), 30.

43 Minutes of the Consistory, 2 March 1959.

44 *Focus,* April 1975.

Rev. Broekhuizen was not to be deterred, however, from a commitment to missions that he had made already in college. He came to Fourteenth Street Church from a "mission church" in Washington, Pennsylvania. He later declared that he had come to see that there should be no "distinction between 'Mission Churches' and 'Established Churches,'" so he accepted the call to the latter "in a very 'religious' community."[45] In his first week in town, he "found two truths: I met unsaved people in the community and I met people in the congregation who had a deep desire to see lost people saved. My vision was to lead the individual members of the congregation into individual soul winning of lost persons as a consistent part of daily life. . . . But I did not succeed in leading 14th Street to become a vibrant conversion center."[46]

Although Broekhuizen did not realize his vision as fully as he had hoped, he did nurture a spirit of evangelism and outreach in many members of the congregation. One consequence was the establishment of an outreach ministry, Cornerstone Ministries, just three blocks from the church, at Central Avenue and Seventeenth Street. This program, which was founded by two members of Fourteenth Street Church, serves teenagers and young adults. It has been supported by Fourteenth Street Church since 1980.

During the pastorate of Rev. Clifford E. Bajema (1983-88), the Council and the congregation sought a closer relationship with Iglesia Hispana, which is now known as Vida Nueva Christian Reformed Church. The first formal engagement with Iglesia Hispana had begun in August 1980, when the consistory approved the extension of an invitation to them to participate in a joint worship service on 5 October 1980.[47] Six years later to the day, the two congregations held joint services in both the morning and the evening.[48] There were duplicate communion services at Iglesia Hispana in the morning and a single combined service at Fourteenth Street Church in the evening. Joint worship services also took place in 1988 on Maundy Thursday (20 March 1988) and on Pentecost Sunday (22 May 1988). In January 1989, the Council approved a recommendation from the elders that the church create "the office of special elder and deacon . . . with the specific

45 R. O. Broekhuizen to Jacob E. Nyenhuis, January 2002, quoted in Nyenhuis, *Centennial History*, 36-37.

46 Ibid.

47 Minutes of the Consistory, 4 August 1980.

48 Minutes of the Consistory, 9 September 1986.

task of offering help and assistance to the Iglesia Hispana CRC."[49] In June 1989, the Council approved a joint Cadet Program (similar to the Boy Scouts) with Iglesia Hispana and terminated a similar program with Pillar Church.[50] During the latter half of the 1980s, the two congregations not only held joint bilingual services, but also joint potlucks on various occasions. For a time, members of Fourteenth Street also were assigned on a rotating basis to attend worship services at Iglesia Hispana.

All these efforts were intended to strengthen ecclesiastical and personal ties and to develop a deeper mutual understanding and respect. The pastors of the two congregations began to speak openly of a merger of the two congregations. Regrettably, however, the fear of assimilation into the much larger Fourteenth Street congregation caused Iglesia Hispana to resist moves toward integrating the two congregations. In fact, they withdrew completely from the inter-congregational services and activities. On 10 September 1991, the Council of Fourteenth Street Church received an invitation from Iglesia Hispana to send representatives to their worship service on 22 September 1991 to celebrate their organization as an independent congregation.

It is unfortunate that the pastor and Council of Fourteenth Street Church failed to seek to restore the once-congenial relationship between the two congregations. The foundation for friendships and mutual encouragement had been well laid, but there appeared to be a loss of vision for this cross-cultural engagement with fellow believers. The opportunity for forging a partnership of equals under God was lost, and the two congregations once again consisted essentially of people of a single ethnic group, although Fourteenth Street Church does have a Cambodian family as members and a number of African-Americans attend from time to time.

In 2000 Fourteenth Street Church joined in a different kind of partnership, which again provided opportunity for some cross-cultural experience and dialogue. After Rev. Marvin Hofman indicated a desire to purchase his own home rather than live in the parsonage near the church, the congregation was faced with the question of whether to sell the parsonage or to seek to use it for another purpose. After deliberation, the congregation in December 2000 approved a partnership with the Good Samaritan Center's Community Housing

[49] Council Minutes, 10 January 1989.
[50] Council Minutes, 13 June 1989.

Program (CHP), donating the use of the parsonage until 2006.[51] As a result, a family was selected by the Good Samaritan Center to live there, learning how to become successful home renters or owners. The CHP provided various people to work with this family to help them develop the necessary skills and experience.

Fourteenth Street Church has also joined the Core City Christian Community Development Program (CCCCD), which is headed by Rev. Wayne Coleman, formerly the pastor of the Church of the Burning Bush (COBB). After Rev. Hofman came to Fourteenth Street Church, he initiated contact with Rev. Coleman at the nearby Church of the Burning Bush, located on Sixteenth Street. Rev. Coleman was invited to participate in leading some worship services at Fourteenth Street, and a number of members of Fourteenth Street attended worship services and met with parishioners at this storefront ministry. COBB was also the center for an active after-school tutoring program for African-American students, headed by Mrs. Ruth Coleman. At first the program was located at the COBB facility, where members of Fourteenth Street Church and others volunteered their time and skills. The LEAP tutoring program moved to Fourteenth Street Church several years ago, after COBB was disbanded, and a number of members continue to volunteer for this twice-a-week program. After COBB was disbanded, the CCCCD Program was initiated by the Colemans. The CCCCD includes such programs as emergency food and counseling on how to escape dependency on drugs and alcohol. At the meeting of Classis Holland on 17 January 2002, delegates from Fourteenth Street Church and Faith CRC presented a vision for ministry to African-Americans.[52] Interestingly, this newest effort linked Fourteenth Street Church directly with Faith Church for the first time since their painful separation forty-six years earlier.

Fourteenth Street Church's ministry to children of the neighborhood took a major step forward in 1996, when the congregation agreed to participate in the KidsHope USA program. This program links the pastor and other church members in one-on-one relationships with at-risk students in the Holland Public Elementary Schools. Approval was given to join the program, to authorize

[51] Approval was granted for an initial two-year partnership, which began in the summer of 2001, but was renewed until 2006, when a decision was made to sell the parsonage to help with funding the expansion of the church building.

[52] *Classis Holland Ministry News* 1, no. 6 (January-March 2002).

appointment of a director, to appoint a Steering Committee, and to establish an annual operating budget for the program.[53] Fourteenth Street Church's first partner was Lincoln School, with twenty-four tutors actively engaged with students needing special assistance and attention. The decision of the Board of the Holland Public Schools to close Lincoln School in 2001 due to shrinking enrollments and severe budgetary pressures caused the end of that very special relationship. Many students had come into Fourteenth Street Church's Boys' Club and Joy Club (which include grades three through eight) as a result of the KidsHope USA partnership with Lincoln School. These children from the neighborhood represented a much more diverse ethnic group than that of the children from the congregation, so this program contributed significantly to improving cross-cultural understanding. After the closing of Lincoln School, the church found a new partnership with Jefferson School, but that school is not in the neighborhood, so the church's outreach to neighborhood was sadly diminished. The subsequent decision of the Holland Public Schools to restructure the elementary schools into unified bi-level schools (K-1, 2-3, 4-5), called Focus Schools, not only destroyed the neighborhood school concept, but also limited the involvement of Fourteenth Street Church and other churches with children over an extended period of time. In 2006, another restructuring occurred: East Middle School was converted to a K-8 school enrolling students in kindergarten through eighth grade. Fourteenth Street Church was assigned to this school, so the prospect of building long-term relationships with the students has been restored.

Other forms of outreach to the community include or have included: an AIDS Food Pantry, Angel Tree, and a neighborhood block party. Angel Tree is a ministry coordinated by teen volunteers to provide Christmas presents to children of people in prison. A block party for the neighborhood has been organized annually by the Evangelism Committee for a number of years. It was an important part of the Centennial Celebration in 2002, with a block party held the weekend after the initial celebration on 15-16 June. The church's parking lot served as a fine spot for drawing in neighbors to help to celebrate this milestone in the life of the congregation.

[53] Minutes of Council, 6 April, 14 May, and 13 August 1996, and Minutes of the Congregational Meeting of 28 April 1996.

Although there has been adaptation to the changing environment around the church, there also have been changes and adaptations within the sanctuary itself. These adaptations are particularly evident in changes in worship. The language of worship has often been a cause for conflict. First, it was Dutch versus English. Then it was the language of patriotism during WWI. For the past two decades or so, it has been the language of music and worship style. The issue of music, however, has never been far from the center of things. The singing of Psalms rather than hymns was strongly reaffirmed with the founding of the CRC. As early as February 1904, there were reports of difficulties between the choir and the organist (Consistory Minutes, 2 February 1904), which led to the resignation of the organist.

The organ has played a central role in the church's worship for over a century, although it is often supplemented and sometimes supplanted in the worship services. Over the past quarter century, the church has adapted to changing tastes in music, not by abandoning past traditions, but by modifying those traditions. Hence, the congregation has developed a fairly eclectic music style. The organ and the piano are the dominant instruments, but musicians also use electric guitars, chamber ensembles, brass ensembles, and individual instruments, such as flute and violin. Children's choirs and the adult choir provide musical leadership fairly regularly, but puppet shows, skits, and sacred dance are also employed to enhance worship. By showing hospitality to a diversity of worship styles, Fourteenth Street Church has minimized the "worship wars" that have fractured many congregations.

A Story of Faith and Hope

The story of this congregation is distinctive in many respects. Not only was Fourteenth Street Church the first English-speaking CRC in Holland, but the church has been located on the same site for over a century, adapting to a changing environment, yet maintaining its central character and purpose. Whereas a number of other downtown churches have either closed or moved from the core city, Fourteenth Street Church remains committed to ministry at its original location. After a period of some decline in membership, the congregation is again thriving. This revitalization of the congregation is cause for praise and gratitude.

The single word "Ebenezer" was placed above the rostrum when the first church building was erected and was restored each time that the original building was remodeled. By calling to mind the stone erected by Samuel (which he called "Ebenezer," or "Stone of Help") after the Lord had routed the Philistines (I Sam. 7:12), this motto served as a constant reminder that God is the rock upon which this church was built. When the new church building was erected in 1958, however, a simple cross was installed at the center of the front wall, behind the choir loft. The empty cross continues to remind worshipers that Christ's death was superseded by his resurrection, that in Christ's victory over sin and death we have a sure hope of eternal life.

In the report on the twenty-fifth anniversary of the church in the *Banner* of 8 July 1927, the writer declared: "Truly, as a congregation we can say, 'Hitherto hath the Lord helped us,' and He is still 'Our hope for years to come.'" That confident assertion was reaffirmed as still relevant at the time of the centennial. Fourteenth Street Church has adapted to its changing environment, but it has not lost sight of its mission, nor has it ceased to anchor its hope in the Lord who is their rock and their salvation (Ps. 62:2). The congregation's struggles with growth, with dissension, with schism, have been overcome by a persistent faith in God's love and mercy and a firm belief that they have been called to serve God in their community from the same corner where they first put down their roots. Their struggles and their victories, like those of individual members, are at once intensely personal, yet also universal. Faith and hope are joined at the comer of Fourteenth Street and Central Avenue in Holland, Michigan. The faithfulness of God sustains this faith and this hope.

CHAPTER 10

What Happened to the Reformation?: The Contentious Relationship between History and Religion

J. Jeffery Tyler

The interplay of religion and history has often been provocative and fractious in everyday life and scholarship. Convictions of faith divide families, friends, and nations. Four centuries ago the religious wars of Europe helped to shape the Enlightenment, a complex movement that sought to overcome the violent excesses of spiritual fervor and limit religion as a detriment to political unity. Today ethnic cleansing, sectarian violence, and worldwide terrorism remind us of the sort of anxiety that must have troubled Enlightenment philosophers as they surveyed the devastation unleashed in the name of true faith. In the early twenty-first century we are all the more aware of the volatility of religiously-sponsored conflict, especially when rooted in ancient rivalries and long-remembered histories of bloodshed and unrequited revenge. It may not be surprising that our explanations for the past, present, and future are less daunting and less controversial if matters of religion are carefully put aside. Does not the field of history serve best when highlighting the development of democracy, human rights, and free market capitalism? Likewise are not faith and devotion kept pristine and inviolate when sequestered in church history and theology, in personal piety and soulful living?

Yet the recent and phenomenal success of Dan Brown's *The Da Vinci Code* shows the degree to which the complex relationship between history and religion can still ignite popular curiosity and generate extraordinary wealth. This blockbuster novel has awakened widespread interest in the true shape of ancient Christianity and its impact on Western history.[1] It is precisely his passion for religion *and* history that is so entirely natural and essential to the very substance of Christianity. Since the Evangelist Luke and early church historian Eusebius of Caesarea (d. 339) Christians have claimed that a crucial connection exists between faith and history, for God created history, works in history, and entered history decisively in Jesus the Christ. Though complicated and controversial, the interplay of history and religion is vital for scholarship on Christianity and for the expression of faith in everyday life.

For more than a half century, Elton J. Bruins has embodied this crucial and creative exchange between religion and history in ministry and academia, teaching and research, writing and administration. In his service to the Reformed Church in America, Hope College, and most recently as founding director of the A. C. Van Raalte Institute, Elton Bruins has brought history and religion, academy and church together in fruitful and enduring ways, demonstrating that scholarship and intellectual rigor can be combined with vibrant faith and vigorous church service. In this way, Bruins represents a crucial period in this unfolding of history and religion, a period when much of secular scholarship has turned away from theology and religion as substantial and viable explanations for historical influence and change.[2] Indeed, the faculty of church-related colleges and seminaries are among those who have kept alive the vital tie between history and religion, even as religion and theology drifted to the edges of what many considered serious scholarship.

1 Dan Brown, *The Da Vinci Code* (New York: Doubleday, 2003). Regarding the claims of the novel, its impact, and suggested background reading, see J. Jeffery Tyler, "*The Da Vinci Code*, Jesus, and History: Imagining Christianity Past and Present," *Reformed Review* 59 (2006): 261-82, <www.westernsem.edu/Brix?pageID=18737>.

2 Early on, Bruins demonstrated his ability to move between the fields of religious studies and history in his *The Americanization of a Congregation*, 2nd ed. (1970; Grand Rapids: Eerdmans, 1995). This volume is much more than a whitewashed chronicle of a pivotal congregation in the Reformed Church in America. On the basis of archival sources and American history, Bruins reveals how a church of Dutch descent came to grips with the profound influence of American culture.

Few academic fields illustrate the tension between history and religion more profoundly and the issues at stake more clearly than the era in Western history long described as the Reformation.[3] During the last half-century, scholarship has sharply downplayed religion and theology as significant sources of historical change. An account of this vital and volatile dialogue among scholars in recent decades is a fitting and worthy way to honor the tireless and winsome research and teaching of Elton J. Bruins, who long taught a beloved course on Calvin and Calvinism and in research and writing continues to unfold the legacy of the Reformation.[4]

The "Traditional" Reformation Story and Its Demise

In 1956, Roland H. Bainton, already in his thirty-seventh year on the faculty of Yale University, published a concise volume titled *The Age of the Reformation*. Appearing six years after his highly praised Luther biography, *Here I Stand*, Bainton's reformation reader was the thirteenth volume in the Anvil Original series, a sequence of books related almost exclusively to modern history.[5] Most telling in Bainton's title are the two

[3] An example of this sort of scholarship and perspective, now thoroughly out of fashion among professional historians, is Will Durant's long popular and ambitious eleven-volume series the Story of Civilization, which categorized Western history in terms of great intellectual epochs, such as volume four, *The Age of Faith* (New York: Simon and Schuster, 1950); volume five, *The Renaissance* (New York: Simon and Schuster, 1953); and volume six, *The Reformation* (New York: Simon and Schuster, 1957). The legacy of Will and Ariel Durant continues to be celebrated by the Will Durant Foundation: <www.willdurant.com>.

[4] The course was titled "Studies in Calvinism" and described as "a survey of the teachings of John Calvin and the development of the Reformed tradition in Europe and North America" (*Hope College Catalog*, 1979-80, 260).

[5] Roland H. Bainton, *The Age of the Reformation* (Princeton: D. Van Nostrand, 1956); this volume is still in print in 2006 in an edition published by Krieger Publishing. *Here I Stand: A Life of Martin Luther* was first published in 1950 (New York: Abingdon-Cokesbury) and remains in print to this day. It has appeared in multiple editions, with a variety of publishers and in numerous languages, including Chinese, Finish, German, Greek, Italian, Japanese, Korean, Spanish, and Swedish. As of 1982 one million copies had been sold (Cynthia Wales Lund, *A Bainton Bibliography*, Sixteenth-Century Essays and Studies, vol. 47 [Kirksville, Mo.: Truman State University Press, 2000], 10-12). In addition to Lund's comprehensive and richly annotated bibliography, Bainton's work has been explored by Steven H. Simpler in *Roland H. Bainton: An Examination of His Reformation Historiography*, Texts and Volumes in Religion, no. 24 (Lewiston, N.Y.: Edwin Mellen, 1985).

direct articles; it was *the* age in which *the* one and singular Reformation proved to be historically decisive. In his lengthy introduction, Bainton wrote of the sixteenth century not only as "the Age of the Reformation," but also as "an age of faith"; he sketched the decisive impact of the Reformation on society, democracy, economics, marriage, and culture.[6] His narrative introduction and companion sources presented a classic narrative, stretching from Luther to the Reformed Churches and onward to the Anglicans, the Catholic Reformation, Confessions and Edicts, and sixteenth-century politics.

With some significant alterations, Bainton's presentation of the Reformation as a historical turning point on the road to the modern world and as a religious event that shaped Western history continues to have many admirers and a few successors.[7] In a notable example, Lewis W. Spitz, in his 1985 survey *The Protestant Reformation 1517-1559*, echoed Bainton's view:

> Few periods in the long history of Europe have had such a momentous impact upon the western world as the four decades

[6] Bainton, *The Age of the Reformation*, 11-12, 83-92. Bainton's designation of the Reformation as "an age of faith" might be read as "a Protestant age of faith," although Roman Catholics are covered in a brief chapter. This Protestant age of faith seems to answer similar claims about the medieval period as the true age of faith; see *The Age of Belief: The Medieval Philosophers*, ed. A. Fremantle (New York: Houghton Mifflin, 1954). Bainton published *The Age of the Reformation* just four years after his narrative history, *The Reformation of the Sixteenth Century* (Boston: Beacon, 1952). In the latter volume Bainton presents the Reformation as the transition from the Middle Ages to the Modern World, and although focusing on religious influence, he also summarizes the political, economic, and domestic impact of the Reformation. This work as well remains in print as of 2006.

[7] Across the Atlantic, English historian G. R. Elton produced a survey that paralleled that of Bainton and a more wide-ranging reader: see *Reformation Europe 1517-1559* (London: Fontana, 1963) and *Renaissance and Reformation 1300-1648* (New York: Macmillan, 1963). Two collections of sources, produced by Hans J. Hillerbrand during the 1960s, typify the continuing vitality of the dominant Reformation account, although greater attention was given to the Anabaptist or so-called "Radical Reformation"; see *The Reformation: A Narrative History Related by Contemporary Observers and Participants* (New York: Harper and Row, 1964) and *The Protestant Reformation*, ed. H. J. Hillerbrand (New York: Harper and Row, 1968). Showing the staying power of these books, Elton's reader was still in print in the 1980s while his *Reformation Europe* appeared in a fresh edition in 2000. Hillerbrand's *The Protestant Reformation* is in print as of 2006, whereas his earlier reader was republished in 1978.

> lying between the years 1517 and 1559. It began when a very personal matter, Luther's struggle for a right relationship to God, became a popular cause. Its end was marked by an auspicious public event, for Europe entered one of its rare interludes of peace. . . . The Protestant Reformation was a conjuncture of critical importance for the whole course of modern history.[8]

With great enthusiasm and perhaps an unfortunate lack of restraint, Spitz further targeted those historians who did not share his passionate estimation of the Reformation. He castigated scholars who analyzed economic and social forces, but were unable to understand the dynamic and volatile changes brought on by politics, religion, and ideas. He singled out those "social historians who are disdainful of all but statistical evidence and the condition of the masses." In contrast, Spitz pointed out that "many of the eventmakers in history have been uncommon men, the world's most persistent minority group. History is the story of *homo sapiens* gifted with a capacity for thought and spiritual aspirations."[9] Spitz's nearly hyperbolic assessment of the Reformation is telling, for by the mid-1980s the classic Reformation narrative he shared with Bainton no longer reigned. Spitz would likely face silence or scorn from most early modern historians.

In fact, Spitz's book had barely appeared on bookstore shelves, when social historian Thomas A. Brady Jr. gave sharp reply. Much of Brady's 1985 review was fiercely critical of Spitz's lack of historical framework, narrow focus on Lutheranism, and numerous errors in historical detail.[10] But Brady also lambasted Spitz's "halting command

8 Lewis W. Spitz, *The Protestant Reformation, 1517-1559*, Rise of Modern Europe (New York: Harper and Row, 1985), 1, 5.

9 Spitz, 2. One hears the echo of Spitz's main contribution to historical scholarship, his classic *The Religious Renaissance of the German Humanists* (Cambridge: Harvard University Press, 1963).

10 Thomas A. Brady Jr., review of *The Protestant Reformation, 1517-1559*, by Lewis W. Spitz, *Sixteenth Century Journal* 16 (1985): 410-12. In 1978 Brady had already taken on an even more formidable adversary in his *Ruling Class, Regime, and Reformation at Strasbourg, 1520-1555*, Studies in the Medieval and Reformation Thought, vol. 22 (Leiden: Brill, 1978). In 1962 Bernd Moeller published *Reichsstadt und Reformation* (Gütersloh: G. Mohn, 1962; English edition, *Imperial Cities and the Reformation: Three Essays* [Philadelphia: Fortress, 1972]), which argued for the urban environment in Germany as crucial to the growth and spread of the Reformation. According to Moeller, medieval civic corporatism—the city as a sacred society—embraced and shaped the Reformation as it took root in the cities. As with Spitz,

of [the] sources, literature, and issues [of social history]" and criticized "his distaste for the history of everyday life and the common people." According to Brady, "Spitz treats all social and economic topics like a child gagging on his spinach" and fails to pursue what all responsible historians do: namely, attend "to the complementarity of events and structures, ideas and social forces, and theology and popular religion" (411).

The confrontation between Brady and Spitz exposes the ever-expanding shift in the history of the sixteenth century within and outside the United States. Although Spitz held a revered position among many who admired the classical rendition of the Reformation, Brady and his peers were continuing to reshape the landscape of scholarship.[11] In fact, theologians and historians had already been divided for some time about the significance of the Reformation in Europe.[12] By the 1970s an ever-increasing majority of scholars had rejected the account of European and Western history originally promoted by Bainton and others, an account that gives preference to theologians and reformers. Emphasis on social causes and structures, long-term political and

---

Brady is repulsed by claims based on religious abstraction and thus here Moeller's "sacred society" draws Brady's fire. He argues that Moeller lays "little weight on . . . [urban] internal structures" and overestimates the "late medieval town . . . as a distinct society, politically, socially, and culturally . . . separate from the greater, essentially aristocratic, land-based society around it" (5, 16). Brady does identify one central redeeming quality in Moeller's work: "The strength of Moeller's view of the urban reform—a strength which none of his non-socialist critics has engaged—is his return to an historical interpretation of the theology of the Reformation era according to social principles of determination" (10). In the end, Brady argues that the importance of Moeller's view of civic corporatism "can be gauged only by an understanding of what the objective, unidealized city was, a question not of social theology, but of historical sociology" (19).

11 This shift is most evident in professional societies. The field of Reformation Studies was long dominated by the *Verein für Reformationsgeschichte*, which was founded in 1902 in Germany and continues to sponsor a journal, *Archive of Reformation History*. The *Verein* expanded to the United States in 1947 as the Society for Reformation Research (with records, accounts, and journals currently maintained at Hope College). By the end of the twentieth century, however, the influence of the Society for Reformation Research had been eclipsed by the Sixteenth-Century Studies Conference and its now dominant publication, *Sixteenth Century Journal*, in which theological papers and articles are a distinct minority.

12 See A. G. Dickens and John M. Tonkin, *The Reformation in Historical Thought* (Cambridge: Harvard University Press, 1985), especially 234-321.

economic trends, would become dominant thereafter. The history of elites (theologians, philosophers, etc.) would be downplayed and diminished, especially as significant agents of change, and a preference for larger demographic groupings would come to the fore as a more accurate gauge of historical development.[13] Although a systematic study still must be undertaken, it may well be that university history departments have tended to embrace scholars who have been trained primarily in sociological and anthropological methods. In contrast, intellectual historians—philosophers, theologians, and church historians—have been increasingly cloistered in seminaries and small colleges, in religion and theology departments.[14] Commenting in 1978 on the increased use of sociology, social historian Robert Scribner wrote: "This trend has gathered such momentum that some church historians have begun to call for a reversal of its course, to argue that the Reformation as a religious phenomenon should be rescued from the incursions of the social historian."[15] In short, theologians and church historians have become outsiders in a field of historical study they once dominated and, one might even say, created.[16]

13 A crucial example of this development is the work of Robert W. Scribner. See his collection of articles *Popular Culture and Popular Movements in Reformation Germany* (London: Hambledon Press, 1987) and especially the article therein, "The Reformation as a Social Movement" (145-74). See the overview chapter in Scribner and C. Scott Dixon's *The German Reformation* (1986; reprint, New York: Palgrave, 2003), 65-88, which includes a section on Reformation myths (67-70).

14 This situation has been further complicated by the appearance of several generations of historians who often have minimal formal training in theology; sixteenth-century sermons, biblical exegesis, and doctrinal treatises are therefore difficult to decipher, interpret, and evaluate. This trend has reinforced the conception of theology and religion as irrelevant to significant historical change in the sixteenth century.

15 Scribner, "The Reformation as a Social Movement," 145.

16 Andrew Pettegree describes similar developments in the historiography of the Reformation, focusing mainly on the British Isles. He points out Geoffrey Elton's *Reformation Europe* (as in n. 7 above) as a watershed in scholarship and then unfolds how Reformation history has subsequently changed and evolved. Elton's book also marked the liberation of Reformation studies from the confines of church history and confessional research (pitting Protestants against Roman Catholics), and the full appearance of the Reformation on the stage of mainstream history (Andrew Pettegree, "Introduction: The Changing Face of Reformation History," in *The Reformation World*, ed. A. Pettegree [London and New York: Routledge, 2000], 1-6).

Where does Bainton's "Reformation" stand today? The current situation among most historians can be summarized in a series of concise *theses* (a good Reformation word!).

1) There was no world-changing "age of reformation," especially a distinctively religious era that ushered in the modern world. Although Reformers, their theology and debates, had some impact, in the end neither religious impulses nor theology were the decisive factors in historical continuity and change. Scholars today seldom designate this period as an era of Renaissance or Reformation; "Early Modern" is the phrase most often used to describe the time between the Middle Ages and the Modern world.[17]

[17] There are many subtle ways to measure this shift. For example, the University of Chicago series of primary source volumes, Readings in Western Civilization, which stretches in content and chronology from ancient Greece to twentieth-century Europe, has no single volume devoted to the Reformation. The final chapter of volume 5, *The Renaissance* (Chicago: University of Chicago Press, 1986), offers readings from Luther, Erasmus, Calvin, the Council of Trent, and an anonymous diary (325-426).

In his 1991 survey, *The European Reformation* (Oxford: Clarendon Press, 1991), Euan Cameron wrote of the Reformation as "the religious transformation which overtook European society in the sixteenth century" (1). He also maintained that "the coalition of churchmen's protests and lay peoples' political involvement lasted just long enough to make sweeping and irreversible changes in all sorts of aspects of sixteenth-century life" (2). Thus, here we find in a book devoted with great affection to the complexities of the Reformation a tacit admission that the "transformation" was largely limited to the "religious dimension" and that its effect endured "just long enough" to elicit some change. No longer present is the sweeping claim about the Reformation as a great hinge or turning point from the medieval to the modern world. This diminution of the Reformation is further in evidence in a later volume also edited by Cameron, *Early Modern Europe: An Oxford History* (New York: Oxford University Press, 1999); herein the Reformation is described along with the Renaissance and in a mere forty-eight pages of the 402-page volume.

Moreover, in their survey on Germany, Robert Scribner and C. Scott Dixon open with a chapter titled: "The Impact of Reform" (note: not the impact of Reformation). Scribner and Dixon identify the following areas decisively influenced by religion: church life, clergy, poor relief, marriage, education, women, popular culture, and confessionalization (*The German Reformation*, 55-63).

One sees this academic divide in the two leading reference works. The first example illustrates a more traditional conception of the period: *The Oxford Encyclopedia of the Reformation*, ed. Hans. J. Hillerbrand, 4 vols. (New York: Oxford University Press, 1996). The second is the title born of compromise

2) *The* Reformation never existed; rather, numerous reformation movements emerged during the sixteenth century, each with its own distinctive theology, reform program, elite-generated literature, learned and popular cultures; today one must speak in the plural of "reformations."[18]

3) Such reformations were not limited to the sixteenth century; their roots reached back into the Middle Ages. Theological debates among Protestants and Roman Catholics were more medieval in tone and content than modern. The long-term resolution of religious issues and substantial change in religious culture can be measured only by including the seventeenth and even the eighteenth century; the sixteenth century does not stand alone historically.[19]

4) Reform movements and theological literature did at times act as accelerants, igniting the economic, political, and social grievances of sixteenth-century Europeans; there is much to be learned from religious and theological phenomena, provided one does not give these phenomena primary causation in historical change.

5) Measurable historical change did occur within the period traditionally attributed to the Reformation; significant development is evident in state-building and social discipline of European populations. Monarchs, princes, and city councils employed state churches and

between historians of various outlooks: *Handbook of European History 1400-1600: Late Middle Ages, Renaissance, and Reformation*, ed. Thomas A. Brady Jr., Heiko A. Oberman, and James D. Tracy, 2 vols. (Leiden: Brill, 1994, 1995).

18 See for example Carter Lindberg, *The European Reformations* (Oxford: Blackwell, 1996) and the companion volume *The European Reformations Sourcebook*, ed. C. Lindberg (Oxford: Blackwell, 2000) and James D. Tracy, *Europe's Reformations 1450-1650* (Lanham: Rowan and Littlefield, 1999). Tracy contends that "religious belief is a motive force in history, but only one among many, so that the outcome of a religious movement can never be explained solely on the basis of religion" (3).

19 Here the traditional narrative from Luther to Calvin, the Anabaptists to the Counter-Reformation, no longer holds together as a definitive epoch. Steven Ozment places the Reformation in a context that reaches back to the mid-thirteenth century: *The Age of Reform 1250-1550: An Intellectual, and Religious History of Late Medieval and Reformation Europe* (New Haven: Yale University Press, 1980). James Tracy contends that the Protestant Reformation is best grasped "as the high point in a series of 'reformations' that convulsed the Latin or western half of Christendom from the eleventh to the eighteenth centuries" (Tracy, 3). For the most recent survey, summarizing this perspective, see Peter G. Wallace, *The Long Reformation: Religion, Political Conflict, and the Search for Conformity, 1350-1750* (New York: Palgrave, 2004).

religious confessions as a means of social control and political indoctrination. Historians now use the term *confessionalization* to describe government exploitation of church institutions and religious confessions to enforce acceptable norms and civil behavior. The shape of confessionalization was remarkably similar whether in Roman Catholic, Lutheran, or Calvinist lands and cities.[20]

6) A Reformation or reformations may have occurred among elites—the literate and well educated, theologians, philosophers, humanists, and civic officers—who were almost exclusively male. But there was little long-term effect on a vast majority of the population—peasants and artisans, merchants and day laborers, domestic servants and beggars. Some scholars have argued that the "reforms" of the sixteenth century did not substantially alter religion in general in the long run. Sixteenth-century documents show that, in the end, *the* Reformation failed.[21]

7) There was a very limited reformation for women. The diverse female roles of the later Middle Ages were reduced among Protestants to the vocations of marriage and motherhood, thus strengthening patriarchy and setting the stage for the fierce persecution of marginal women, which we now call "the witchcraze."[22]

[20] The primary theorist of confessionalization and perhaps the most influential historian of the sixteenth century in Germany as of 2006 is Heinz Schilling. See for example his "Confessionalization in the Empire: Religious and Societal Change in Germany between 1555 and 1620," in Schilling's *Religion, Political Culture and the Emergence of the Early Modern State: Essays in German and Dutch History*, Studies in Medieval and Reformation Thought, no. 50 (Leiden: Brill, 1992), 205-45. For an excellent survey of the social discipline thesis, see R. Po-Chia Hsia, *Social Discipline in the Reformation: Central Europe 1550-1750* (New York: Routledge, 1989).

[21] The creator of the failure thesis, Gerald Strauss, sums up: "A century of Protestantism had brought about little or no change in the common religious conscience and in the ways in which ordinary men and women conducted their lives. Given people's nebulous grasp of the substance of the faith, no meaningful distinction could have existed between Protestants and Catholics—a distinction arising from articulated belief, conscious attachment, and self-perception" (*Luther's House of Learning: Indoctrination of the Young in the German Reformation* [Baltimore: Johns Hopkins University Press, 1978], 299).

[22] See Merry E. Wiesner, *Women and Gender in Early Modern Europe*, New Approaches to European History (Cambridge: Cambridge University Press, 1993), especially 21-25, 218-35; see also Lyndal Roper, *The Holy Household: Women and Morals in Reformation Augsburg*, Oxford Studies in Social History (Oxford: Clarendon Press, 1989) and *Oedipus and the Devil: Witchcraft, Sexuality and Religion in Early Modern Europe* (New York: Routledge, 1994).

The Reformation Revived?

Despite the apparent triumph of social history in the study of the sixteenth century, variations of the classic Reformation narrative have endured and lingered. In fact, it has been difficult for scholars to promote the rather bland Early Modern title and come up with sociological categories and descriptions that match the staying power, descriptive color, and marketing magnetism of Reformation as either a noun (the Reformation/reformations) or as an adjective (e.g., Reformation Germany). Moreover, economic, political, and social historians have been willing to concede that religious ideas, reform movements, and sectarian conflicts were something of a common denominator throughout Europe from 1400-1700. *Reformation* is a useful term to delineate this religious commonality, even if for some historians religion and religious ideas in particular correspond more to what we might call similarities in local color; for example, religion is to the sixteenth century what Tulip Time is to twentieth-century Holland, Michigan. In this view, religion gives the age a certain hue and contributes to its texture and flavor. Such texture and flavor deserve to be researched, but do they matter significantly as explanations of historical change? For example, did variation in interpretations of the Lord's Supper truly divide communities, shape royal policy, and lead to revolt? Peasant and pauper, pastor and prince, may have had varied and fiercely held convictions about the Eucharist. But did such convictions make a difference in daily life? Did not religious language serve at least as a guise for deeper and more profound political and economic grievances?[23]

In response to decisive shifts in research and historiography certain scholars have not only continued to emphasize theology, religious history, and literature in their programs of research and writing, but have also sought new ways to connect with social history. Their efforts have preserved and revised more traditional approaches, while reasserting the primacy of what was once called "the Reformation" in the field of history.

In many ways Steven Ozment appears to be the heir apparent to Roland Bainton. Ozment began his career in the 1960s as an intellectual historian of the Middle Ages and Reformation.[24] Since 1975 Ozment

[23] This question brings to mind a favorite and cryptic proverb of Elton Bruins: "Politics is everything, but everything isn't politics."

[24] See Ozment's *Homo Spiritualis: A Comparative Study of the Anthropology of Johannes Tauler, Jean Gerson and Martin Luther (1509-16) in the Context of Their*

has attempted to bring together his earlier focus on a Reformation rooted in medieval theology, philosophy, and spirituality with a later interest in the City Reformation and social history.[25] He has devoted his career to measuring the impact of the Reformation not only on church and theology, but also on family history and private life in the sixteenth century.[26] In his 1992 book, *Protestants: The Birth of a Revolution*, Ozment made the following assertion:

> The birth of Protestantism is . . . a story about modern historians and their audience. No other great event in Western history is more ignored by historians and the general public today than the Protestant Reformation. If given the option, most historians would prefer to write, and most people to read, a book on the American, the French, or the Russian revolution than one on the birth of Protestantism. Why are we more comfortable with the other revolutions that have shaped our world than we are with the great religious one? Unlike them, the Reformation is not so straightforward a contest for economic justice and political freedom. It forces us to think about history and human life in more varied and complex ways. We find in it not only a spiritual movement driving society and politics, but one that makes injustice and bondage within the inner life as portentous as those which afflict people's physical lives. For people living then, the struggle against sin, death, and the devil became as basic as that for bread, land, and self-determination.[27]

Theological Thought, Studies of Medieval and Reformation Thought, no. 6 (Leiden: Brill, 1969) and *Mysticism and Dissent: Religious Ideology and Social Protest in the Sixteenth Century* (New Haven: Yale University Press, 1973).

[25] Ozment describes this shift in *The Reformation in the Cities: The Appeal of Protestantism to Sixteenth-Century Germany and Switzerland* (New Haven: Yale University Press, 1975), 1-2.

[26] See the following works in Ozment's corpus on family and private life: *When Fathers Ruled: Family Life in Reformation Europe* (Cambridge: Harvard University Press, 1983), *Flesh and Spirit: Private Life in Early Modern Germany* (New York: Viking, 1999), and *Ancestors: The Loving Family in Old Europe* (Cambridge: Harvard University Press, 2001). His microhistories and source volumes in a similar vein are: *Magdalena and Balthasar: An Intimate Portrait of Life in 16th-Century Europe* (New York: Simon and Schuster, 1986), *Three Behaim Boys: Growing Up in Early Modern Germany* (New Haven: Yale University Press, 1990), and *The Bürgermeister's Daughter: Scandal in a Sixteenth-Century Town* (New York: St. Martin's, 1996).

[27] Ozment, *Protestants: The Birth of a Revolution* (New York: Doubleday, 1992), 2-3.

In this irenic and engaging paragraph, Ozment reasserts the primacy of the Reformation as a crucial and definable era in history, in fact, as a revolution. He alludes to questions of spirituality and theology that do not fit current historical constructs and are thus overlooked or dismissed. And he contends that the issues of the Reformation were indeed decisive matters for all people, not merely for a literate, educated, and socially isolated elite. In his passion for the Reformation, command of languages, and productivity, Ozment continues the legacy of Roland Bainton and Lewis Spitz. Moreover, he has held prestigious chairs in history and has published frequently with recognized academic presses; his books sell. But many social historians of early modern Europe have not been convinced by the Reformation Ozment portrays.[28]

[28] For example, Thomas A. Brady Jr. was among the first to question Ozment's grasp of urban and social history, describing Ozment as a "self-confessed 'recent convert'": Brady opines, "Despite his *apparent* interest in social history (Ozment spares only one line for socialist historiography, the longest continuous tradition of social study of the Reformation), he wants to turn the study of the urban reform back to the old paths and lead it back under the sovereignty of Luther" (Brady, *Ruling Class, Regime and Reformation at Strasbourg 1520-1555*, Studies in Medieval and Reformation Thought, no. 22 [Leiden: Brill, 1978], 9).

Despite their differences, in 1982 Ozment and Brady could still collaborate on a volume edited by Ozment, *Reformation Europe: A Guide to Research* (St. Louis: Center for Reformation Research, 1982). In his article therein, Brady begins his final comments with a flourish that seems aimed at Ozment: "When the strident voices of the polemicists are still, when the grand systems of long-dead theologians fall away. . . ." Brady then concludes: "Neither confessional nor racial-cultural explanations of the place of the Reformation in European history have survived the fire of historical criticism. Perhaps the social-historical explanation will" [and not Ozment's version!] (Brady, "Social History," in *Reformation Europe,* 176).

The breach between Ozment and Brady appears to have become all the more permanent after Brady went after Ozment's *When Fathers Ruled* in a review of an entirely different book: "Reformation studies are plagued by books and articles which advance this or that sampling of sources, often pamphlets or treatises, as representative, typical or particularly revealing of the motives and mentalities and anxieties of an earlier age. One then infers revolutions which never happened, relying on the romantic-idealist notion that the meaning of a process may be grasped truly only at its origin. Such procedures have allowed historians to discover revolutionary change in the Reformation era at almost every hand, while sober analysis of archival sources usually dispels the myth" (review of *Let No Man Put Asunder*, by T. M. Safley, *Sixteenth Century Journal* 15 [1984]: 226; cited in Heiko A. Oberman, *The Impact of the Reformation* [Grand Rapids: Eerdmans, 1994], 22).

In contrast to Ozment, who seeks to revive the grand and venerable Reformation narrative, Scott Hendrix has modest and yet considerable goals.[29] Over against those who see only multiplicity and variety—a gaggle of reformations, Lutheran or Calvinist, Roman Catholic or Radical, City or Communal, German, French or English—Hendrix proposes a singular reform program characteristic of all the so-called "reformations." "The most important unifying element [of the Reformation] was the vision of replanting Christianity that was judged by Protestant reformers to be riddled with idolatry and by Catholic reformers to be in need of more explicit Christian faith and devotion."[30] Such an effort assumed a scathing critique of a debased, corrupted form of medieval Christianity and sparked a missionary zeal to plant and spread a true and pure faith. Despite variation in theology and religious practice, Lutherans, Zwinglians, Calvinists, Radicals, and Roman Catholics shared a common desire to Christianize Europe; disagreements among the various reform movements can be attributed to "differences in strategy."[31] According to Hendrix, the Reformation in Europe completed the medieval project of Christendom—the Christianizing of Europe on the local as well as the pan-European level.[32] Moreover, the Reformation had a profound impact on social institutions such as marriage and the clerical estate while fueling a missionary movement that envisioned the conversion of the non-

[29] Hendrix has devoted much of his career to the works of Martin Luther and Lutheranism more generally. See his *Ecclesia in Via: Ecclesiological Developments in the Medieval Psalms Exegesis and the "Dictata super Psalterium" (1513-1515) of Martin Luther*, Studies in Medieval and Reformation Thought, no. 8 (Leiden: Brill, 1974); *Luther and the Papacy: Stages in a Reformation Conflict* (Philadelphia: Fortress, 1981); and, with Gunther Grassmann, *Fortress Introduction to the Lutheran Confessions* (Philadelphia: Fortress, 1999). Seminal articles by Hendrix, which reflect his broader research on the sixteenth century, appear in *Tradition and Authority in the Reformation* (Brookfield: Variorum, 1996).

[30] Scott H. Hendrix, *Recultivating the Vineyard: The Reformation Agendas of Christianization* (Louisville: Westminster John Knox, 2004), xviii.

[31] Scott H. Hendrix, "Rerooting the Faith: The Reformation as Re-Christianization," *Church History* 69 (2000), 561, 569.

[32] Via his study of the Christianizing project in sixteenth-century Europe, Hendrix hopes to make clear how the many reformations are like the trees in a larger forest we call the Reformation; recent scholarship has been focused on the individual reformations without seeing the common goal shared by all the reformations (Hendrix, *Recultivating the Vineyard*, especially xv-xxiii).

Christian in Europe, including the Jews, and the spread of the faith in the wake of world exploration. The impact of *the* Reformation was both European and global.[33]

Whereas Scott Hendrix finds commonality among the reformers in their shared vision of Christianization, Brad Gregory turns, in his award-winning book, *Salvation at Stake*, to religious sensibilities reflected in the practice and literature of sixteenth-century martyrdoms. This comparative study of Protestant, Roman Catholic, and Anabaptist martyrs delineates the various ecclesiastical and civic justifications for capital punishment, the process of memorializing the martyred faithful, and debates about true and false martyrs. Gregory's work is not only a study of martyr literature, but also a strident effort to reassert the relevance and impact of religious belief and behavior in our understanding of the sixteenth century. He writes:

> Martyrdom is a sharp wedge with which to penetrate the beliefs and behaviors of devout early modern Christians. It leads through distinct traditions, across national and linguistic boundaries, among the privileged and the humble, the learned and the unlettered, men and women, clergy and laity . . . [the views of such people] were beliefs about the way the world is. People could heed them as facts in the hope of their salvation, or ignore them to their certain damnation. Properly understood, they were literally more than a matter of life and death.[34]

Moreover, Gregory bristles at those who read current worldviews and scholarly assumptions back into the sixteenth century, who deny the sources and voices of the past because their religious convictions or outlook no longer speak to or even offend readers today:

> Desiring a different past cannot unmake its realities. This misdirected impulse exposes the real danger involved in contemporary attempts to "construct a usable past." "Usable" by whom? and for what? . . . It is scholars who deploy reductionist theories who go further–in the wrong direction. When they consider martyrdom at all, they seem uninterested in exploring what it meant to the martyrs and their contemporaries. Instead,

[33] Hendrix, "Rerooting the Faith," 575-77; *Recultivating the Vineyard*, 79-81, 148-74.

[34] Brad S. Gregory, *Salvation at Stake: Christian Martyrdom in Early Modern Europe* (Cambridge: Harvard University Press, 1999), 342-43.

> modern or postmodern beliefs underpin explanatory theories that assume a post-Enlightenment, materialist, and atheistic metaphysic, one now in its afterlife, characterized mostly by an indifference toward religious claims. . . . [But] the act of martyrdom makes no sense whatsoever unless we take religion seriously, on the terms of people who were willing to die for their convictions. When we do, the intelligibility of martyrdom hits us like a hammer.[35]

Gregory concludes his book by pointing out that it is precisely the very doggedness of sixteenth-century believers with their conflicting versions of Christianity and their willingness to kill and die for them that served to shape a secular society. Absolute and contradictory claims about Christianity in the end undercut the authority of religion and made religion increasingly irrelevant to the development of the modern state. Yet this later development does not detract from the reality that the Reformation was a matter of life and death—in this life and the next—for sixteenth-century people at every level of society.[36]

Beyond the efforts of American scholars Ozment, Hendrix, and Gregory, it is worthwhile to turn to the work of Berndt Hamm, Professor of Modern Church History at the University of Erlangen-Nürnberg. Since the 1970s Hamm has been one of the most influential and provocative German scholars of the Middle Ages and Reformation. Although he is known for his expertise as a historical theologian, Hamm's broader interest in social and art history have made him a player throughout early modern studies within and beyond church history and theology.[37] Hamm's chief contribution to church history has been his

35 Gregory, 350.

36 Gregory, 351-52.

37 Berndt Hamm's many contributions have just recently become available to the English-speaking world in a collection of his seminal articles: *The Reformation of Faith in the Context of Late Medieval Theology and Piety*, ed. R. J. Bast, Studies in the History of Christian Traditions, no. 110 (Leiden: Brill, 2004). His works on historical theology include *Promisso, Pactum, Ordinatio. Freiheit und Selbstbindung Gottes in der scholastischen Gnadenlehre* (Tübingen: Mohr, 1977); "Johann von Staupitz (c. 1468-1524) - spätmittelalterlicher Reformer und 'Vater' der Reformation," *Archiv für Reformationsgeschichte* 92 (2001): 6-42; *Zwinglis Reformation der Freiheit* (Neukirchen-Vluyn: Neukirchener Verlag, 1988).

Hamm's broader historical interests are reflected in his monograph *Bürgertum und Glaube: Konturen der städtischen Reformation* (Göttingen: Vandenhoeck and Ruprecht, 1996) and in his role as chief editor of

identification of a form of religiosity he has termed "theology of piety" (*Frömmigkeitstheologie*). This theology, which we might call practical, is typical of the later Middle Ages; it is rooted in pastoral experience, the consoling and guiding of souls, and is dedicated to the shaping of a Christian life which will lead to salvation. Medieval authors of this theology of piety did not limit their target audience to the erudite and educated. They targeted the laity as well as theologically untrained clergy and devotees of the monastic life.[38] This pastoral dimension of theology was in turn clearly taken up by the theologians and leaders of the Protestant Reformation in the sixteenth century. Yet this theology of piety does not stand alone in some sort of religious or intellectual vacuum. In fact, throughout the later Middle Ages a growing passion for a theology of piety paralleled, reflected, and shaped a new outlook in Europe, a change of view rooted in an age of turbulence, discord, and uncertainty. In their theology of piety, theologians illustrate Hamm's broader contribution to European history more generally, a development he has titled "normative centering" (*normative Zentrierung*). Normative centering was a comprehensive movement in thought and practice toward simplification, assurance, and certainty. Hamm describes this trend as "the alignment of both religion and society toward a standardizing, authoritative, regulating and legitimizing focal point."[39]

---

two ongoing critical edition projects—on the one hand Hamm's more predictable work as editor of the multi-volume set of Martin Bucer's correspondence (*Martin Bucer Correspondence/Briefwechsel*, published by Brill) and on the other hand more surprising, Hamm's oversight and editing of the writings of Lazarus Spengler, secretary of the city of Nuremberg during the sixteenth century (in two volumes published thus far, *Lazarus Spengler Schriften* [Göttingen: Gütersloh, 1995, 1999]).

38 See "Frömmigkeit als Gegenstand theologiegeschichtlicher Forschung. Methodisch-historische Überlegungen am Beispiel von Spätmittelalter und Reformation," *Zeitschrift für Theologie und Kirche* 74 (1977): 464-97; and *Frömmigkeitstheologie am Anfang des 16. Jahrhunderts: Studien zu Johannes Paltz und seinem Umkreis* (Tübingen: Mohr, 1982).

The successful dispersion of Hamm's *concept of Frömmigkeitstheologie* is reflected in the conference volume *Spätmittelalterliche Frömmigkeit zwischen Ideal und Praxis*, ed. B. Hamm and T. Lentes (Tübingen: Mohr Siebeck, 2001) and in *Frömmigkeit - Theologie - Frömmigkeitstheologie. Contributions to European Church History: Festschrift für Berndt Hamm Zum 60. Geburtstag*, eds. G. Litz and H. Munzert, Studies in the History of Christian Thought, no. 124 (Leiden: Brill, 2005).

39 Berndt Hamm, "Normative Centering in the 15th and 16th Centuries: Observations on Religiosity, Theology, and Iconology," in *The Reformation of Faith*, 3.

Examples of normative centering include not only the late medieval emphasis on a theology of piety, but also the great *sola*-principles of the Reformation: scripture alone, faith alone, grace alone, and Christ alone. Hamm perceives similar movements toward normative centering in politics, law, humanism, and the fine arts. In his view, the theology of the later Middle Ages and Reformation participated in and reinforced the greater normative centering occurring in Europe.[40] Doctrinal issues and religious concerns lay at the very heart of a larger shift in European culture. The Reformation itself is a later variant of this theology of piety and a significant influence on the history of the sixteenth century.

Any exploration of the Reformation and its impact on Western history must consider the decisive work of Heiko A. Oberman, a historian who bridged the Middle Ages and Reformation as well as European and American academia.[41] Oberman's original approach

[40] "The 15th-century sources constantly confront us with the fact that the 'normative centering' of the Reformation hardly materialized out of thin air: *de facto* it assumed and drew upon a late-medieval dynamic of simplification and intensification and continued in some ways, a regulating, normativizing sequence of standardization. An entire range of witnesses that includes theologians, church reformers and preachers, jurists, politicians, city chroniclers and scribes (*Stadtschreiber*) along with humanists and artists testifies to the concept of a simplified, reduced set of core principles identified as *the* roadmap for the pilgrimage in this world and as the guaranteed route to salvation in the next" (Hamm, "Normative Centering," 9).

[41] Oberman's career was shaped by professorial positions at Harvard University, the University of Tübingen in Germany, and the University of Arizona. His opus includes three seminal works on late medieval theology, the intellectual climate in late medieval and Reformation Europe, and his classic, a biography of Martin Luther: *The Harvest of Medieval Theology: Gabriel Biel and Late Medieval Nominalism* (1963; Grand Rapids: Baker Academic, 2001); *Masters of the Reformation: The Emergence of a New Intellectual Climate in Europe*, trans. D. Martin (Cambridge: Cambridge University Press, 1981; German edition, 1977); and *Luther: Man Between God and the Devil*, trans. E. Walliser-Schwarzbart (New Haven: Yale University Press, 1989; German edition, 1982). Not to be overlooked are collections of Oberman's key articles: *The Dawn of the Reformation: Essays in Late Medieval and Reformation Thought* (Edinburgh: T. & T. Clark, 1986), *The Impact of the Reformation* (Grand Rapids: Eerdmans, 1994), and *The Reformation: Roots and Ramifications* (Grand Rapids: Eerdmans, 1994). For a succinct and richly informative overview of Oberman's contributions, see Scott H. Hendrix, "The Work of Heiko A. Oberman (1930-2001)," *Religious Studies Review* 28 (2002): 123-30.

was rooted in the history of ideas, historical theology, and medieval philosophy in particular. Early on in his career Oberman became sensitized to larger historical issues, such as the way in which historical periods are defined and described. Oberman's research led to the discovery of the Later Middle Ages as a period of great ferment and harvest, as opposed to the dominant scholarly paradigms, which described the end of the Middle Ages as a time of waning and decline.[42] During the 1960s and 1970s Oberman broadened his scholarship to include the Reformation and the sixteenth century. In his own mind, he became ever less the scholar of ideas and theology alone and ever more the European historian. Oberman increasingly sought confrontation and fervent debate with social historians while defending the validity of the Reformation as a historical reality and the impact of ideas. His ultimate goal was a scholarly breakthrough which combined the resources of social and intellectual history.

As a result, Oberman developed his "social history of ideas," an approach which sought to identify and measure the origin of ideas and their effect on social change as well as to find the intersection of social forces with intellectual trends. Oberman envisioned

> the redirection of intellectual history toward a social history of ideas that reflects two insights: the uniqueness and singularity of the matrix from which new ideas first emerge; and the fermentation phase when audiences become active recipients and develop their own networks of discourse.[43]

This approach takes into consideration the conditions of life in which ideas came to life and the means by which intellectual leaders and their followers in turn made such ideas active in history. The "fermentation phase," noted above, cannot simply be reduced to social forces or structures. In the end, social historians must take seriously the impact of ideas as history unfolds and especially in decisive periods such as the Reformation.

[42] See Oberman, *The Harvest of Late Medieval Theology*, 5-7. Oberman was in debate primarily with Johan Huizinga's portrait of the later Middle Ages; see Huizinga, *The Autumn of the Middle Ages*, trans. R. J. Payton and U. Mammitzsch (Chicago: University of Chicago Press, 1996) and the review essay by James Kennedy, "The Autumns of Johan Huizinga," *Studies in Medievalism* 9 (1997): 209-17.

[43] Heiko A. Oberman, *The Impact of the Reformation*, ix.

To grasp Oberman's social history of ideas one must understand his equally important concept of "mentality"—the intellectual perceptions and worldviews that shaped how people understood and responded to the environment in which they lived. In fact, Oberman came to believe that a distinctive European mentality had emerged in Europe, stretching from the Black Death in the mid-fourteenth century to the Peace of Westphalia (1648), a mentality embracing the periods sometimes described as the later Middle Ages, the Renaissance, the Reformation, and the Early Modern.[44] In his exploration of mentality Oberman found unlikely and perhaps unwilling support from scholars engaged in historical anthropology, historians of ritual, group behavior, and social movements in the sixteenth century. Oberman contended that the research of social historians paralleled his own understanding of the impact of religious ideas and mentality.[45]

What most stoked Oberman's ire was not thorough-going social history, however divorced from religious concerns it might be, but rather the tendency of some historians to assume and claim a kind of lock-step social process as the inevitable engine of historical change, a process which the past and its records simply did not prove. Historians absorbed with seeking the roots of modernity are particularly culpable. From this perspective the sixteenth century, for example, might only

[44] Heiko A. Oberman, "The Devil and the Devious Historian: Reaching for the Roots of Modernity," in *Heiniken Lectures 1996* (Amsterdam: Royal Netherlands Academy of Arts and Sciences, 1997), 34.

[45] "By moving from established political history to cultural and mentality studies, historians reestablished the crucial importance of religion, although they frequently marginalized it under the misleading category of popular religion" (Heiko A. Oberman, *The Two Reformations: The Journey from the Last Days to the New World*, ed. Donald Weinstein [New Haven: Yale University Press, 2003], 2.

Ulinka Rublack has provided the most recent survey of the Reformation, which focuses on social history and echoes Oberman's own sense of mentality. Rublack's book gives a rich and thick description of Protestant mentalities, arguing that both the material culture (e.g., churches, homes, ceramics, and medals) and the biblical focus of Lutherans and Calvinists have not been explicated in their complexity. Protestants neither denied the emotions nor the senses in their focus on the scripture; rather, they "tried to define a new spiritual aesthetics which would involve sensual reading as a process of chewing on words and literally incorporating them or psalm singing as a practice of transcendence" (Rublack, *Reformation Europe*, New Approaches to European History, no. 28 [Cambridge: Cambridge University Press, 2005], 193).

be useful and "historical" to the degree that it anticipates the modern world.[46] Theology and religious expression can then be discarded as remnants of a more primitive age, dead ends and cul-de-sacs on the road to modernity.[47] Oberman asserted that social historians outstretched their evidence and data, failing to admit their supposed processes were not the immutable forces of history. Instead an honest concession is needed: such processes are fallible, partial, and human-made interpretations.[48] In reality history is much more complex, unpredictable, and contingent. Historical change is not so easily predicted and plotted, the agents of continuity and discontinuity could be surprising and sudden, social and religious.[49]

46 Sixteenth-century folk certainly believed that religion mattered, even if from our viewpoint we may think it did not or no longer does. Patrick Collinson writes aptly about the sixteenth century: "There is no doubt that we take a voyage into another country where they do things differently when we try to comprehend the mindset and worldview of the age of the Reformation. We cannot pick and choose between the beliefs of those early modern Europeans that we find acceptable" (Collinson, *The Reformation: A History* [New York: Modern Library, 2004], 215).

47 Clearly the suppositions of many social historians have been rooted in a twentieth century that appeared to be moving toward an ever more secular and non-religious future. Given the durability and resurgence of religious devotion worldwide (apart from Europe) in the early twenty-first century, perhaps religious ideas and behavior will gravitate back to a place of serious consideration as part of historical causality.

48 One might say that social historians tend to trust the utter reliability of their own ideas about history even as they regard the ideas of people in the past as historically insignificant.

49 Oberman, "The Devil and the Devious Historian," 34-37, 42. Despite their differences Oberman and social historian Thomas A. Brady Jr. were close friends. Brady published his first book, *Ruling Class, Regime, and Reformation*, in Oberman's monograph series Studies in Medieval and Reformation Thought and, much later, a collection of his articles in the same series, *Communities, Politics, and Reformation in Early Modern Europe*, SMRT, no. 68 (Leiden: Brill, 1998), dedicating it to Oberman and writing of their friendship: "For more than a quarter of a century, we have stood, as we say, 'back to back,' acknowledging and benefiting from one another's strengths without ever feeling obliged to mute, much less to deny, our differences. It is a genuine pleasure to be able to dedicate this volume to him, small recompense for his unstinting criticism and unflagging support" (xix). In his last book, Oberman described Brady as "one of [social history's] finest spokesmen" (3) and yet continued to debate with him to the end of his career and life (Oberman, *The Two Reformations*, 19-20, 99, 100).

Conclusion

The past five decades in Reformation scholarship have witnessed not only the ascendancy of social history, but also the decline, resilience, and revival of historical research that continues to take seriously ideas, religion, and theology. Although research universities have dominated the field of history, certain doctoral programs, seminaries, and church-related colleges have continued to nurture and sustain the "Reformation." No doubt, fierce exchanges with social historians have compelled scholars of religion and Christianity to sharpen their methods and refine their research in order to participate in larger debates and academic gatherings. Perhaps with the gradual passing of a generation forged in the trenches of a scholarly conflict pitting history against religion, a fresh wave of historians will emerge, following in the footsteps of Hendrix, Gregory, Hamm, and Oberman.[50] They may yet reach a point at which a new historical vision and consensus emerges, which harvests and synthesizes the best of Reformation and Early Modern scholarship.[51] Even now learned appraisals of "early modern Europe" continue to reflect the enduring vitality of Reformation as an

[50] It is important to note that all of the scholars reviewed above, who attempt to reassert the place of religion, religious ideas, and Reformation, are directly related to Oberman. Ozment completed his doctorate under Oberman at Harvard, Hendrix with Oberman at the University of Tübingen; Hamm wrote his dissertation and habilitation under Oberman at Tübingen; Gregory wrote a master's thesis with Oberman at the University of Arizona. Each scholar reflects both Oberman's scholarly focus on the impact of ideas and religion *and* his concern that his students pursue their own leads and ideas. For a model that brings social, legal, and religious history together, see the work of another Oberman doctoral student, J. Jeffery Tyler, "Refugees and Reform: Banishment and Exile in Early Modern Augsburg" in *Continuity and Change: The Harvest of Late Medieval and Reformation History. Essays Presented to Heiko A. Oberman on His 70th Birthday*, ed. A. C. Gow and R. J. Bast (Leiden: Brill, 2000), 77-97.

[51] See, for example, the new reference volume, *A Companion to the Reformation World*, ed. R. Po-Chia Hsia (Oxford: Blackwell, 2004). This book represents marvelous collaboration among a variety of historians and captures an emerging vision of the Reformation in a global context, beginning with late-medieval antecedents, covering the German Reformation heartland, moving out to various European manifestations of Reformation, stretching into the seventeenth century, and then out into the larger world, tracing the impact of the Reformation on India, China, and Japan. Likewise, another volume similarly titled and edited by Andrew Pettegree, *The Reformation World* (2000), reflects a similar geographical spread and includes chapters

apt adjective and noun.[52] As social historians deepen our understanding of gender, culture, and social structure, they show increasing openness to religious influence and impulse. Moreover, the giants of the traditional Reformation narrative—Martin Luther (d. 1546), Huldrych Zwingli (d. 1531), John Calvin (d. 1564), Ignatius of Loyola (d. 1556), and Menno Simons (d. 1561)—now appear in ever more complex cultural, political, and religious contexts, their uniqueness recognized due to personal charisma and unique local landscapes.[53] This new era of increasing cooperation and collaboration echoes the enduring legacy of Elton J. Bruins, who throughout his career has established bridges between religion and history, faith and scholarship, college and community, church and academy. Indeed, the sturdy pillars of those bridges rest upon Bruins's archival digging, meticulous filing, persistent writing, and great personal warmth. The dexterity of his mind is perhaps best reflected by Bruins's willingness, as founder and first Director of the A. C. Van Raalte Institute, to challenge some of Van Raalte's mythological standing at Hope College and to restore credit to the college's first

---

on the Reformation and art, music, architecture, education, popular culture, science, and medicine.

Yet other efforts to explore and restore theology and religion as decisive players in early modern scholarship are still underway; note, for example, the Society for Reformation Research Roundtable, "Is Theology Still Relevant to Reformation Research?," Sixteenth-Century Studies Conference, Salt Lake City, 28 October 2006.

52 In his recent survey (2004), Patrick Collinson describes the Reformation as a "meteor strike," a "turning point," and as "the blast furnace in which the modern state was forged"; he points out that the Reformation is distinctive to Western Christianity; nothing quite like it appears in Eastern Orthodoxy (*The Reformation*, 3-4, 8, 206). Diarmaid MacCulloch has written a narrative of the Reformation remarkable in its scope, detail, and insight. A final section of his book describes the impact of the Reformation on "Patterns of Life," including time measurement, life and death, sex and love (MacCulloch, *The Reformation: A History* [New York and London: Penguin, 2003]). Although viewing history through the lens of social history, Ulinka Rublack still titled her book *Reformation Europe*.

53 Ulinka Rublack, for example, describes with eloquence the ways in which both Luther's and Calvin's ideas and reform programs were a product of their theological genius *and* the remarkable particularities of Wittenberg and Geneva (Rublack, *Reformation Europe*, 195-98).

president, Philip Phelps.[54] The quality of Bruins's spirit shines in his ongoing efforts to strengthen the bridge between church and academy, a bridge envisioned and realized by sixteenth-century reformers. Elton J. Bruins is a worthy heir of the Reformation, and of Reformation scholarship past and present.

[54] See Bruins, "Early Hope College History as Reflected in the Correspondence of Rev. Albertus C. Van Raalte to Rev. Philip Phelps Jr., 1857-1875," in *The Dutch Adapting to North America, Papers Presented at the Conference of the Association for the Advancement of Dutch American Studies, June 23 and 24, 2001*, ed. R. H. Harms, 1-8; and Bruins, "Who Founded Hope College?" (paper presented to Hope College faculty members, 2001).

CHAPTER 11

Civil War Correspondence of Benjamin Van Raalte during the Atlanta Campaign, 1864

"My opinion is that much will have to happen before this campaign is concluded. Whoever lives through it will have much to tell."[1]

Jeanne M. Jacobson

Benjamin Van Raalte, second son of the founder of Holland, Michigan, served throughout the Civil War with the Twenty-fifth Michigan Volunteers. He was an acute observer and careful chronicler of events, and his letters indeed have much to tell. Reading them, we are indebted to the soldier who wrote them, to the family who received them (most were written to his father, Albertus Christiaan Van Raalte himself), and to historian and scholar Elton J. Bruins, through whose decades-long efforts letters have been located, copied, and translated, with the copies carefully archived and made available through the A. C. Van Raalte Institute.[2]

Letters from Benjamin Van Raalte to his parents were signed, "Your loving B. Van Raalte." Here he will be referred to, in economical

1 Ben Van Raalte to Albertus C. Van Raalte, Paldon County, Georgia, 31 May 1864, Holland Museum Archives, Holland, Mich.

2 Twenty-one of Benjamin Van Raalte's letters are transcribed here, in whole or in part. The original letters can be found in the Holland Museum Archives, along with a translation from Dutch into English by Clarence Jalving. Ben headed his letters with place and date; here that ordering is reversed (date, then place) to emphasize the sequence of events in the Atlanta campaign as Ben experienced it during the spring and summer of 1864. Letters are reproduced with the permission of the Holland Historical Trust, holder of the Holland Museum Archives.

and friendly fashion, as Ben. In addition to his letters, excerpts are used from another contemporary source: *National History of the War for the Union: Civil, Military and Naval* by Evert A. Duyckinck.[3] This mammoth work was compiled and composed during the war, "founded on official and other authentic documents, illustrated with battle scenes by sea and land, and full-length portraits of naval and military heroes." Duyckinck was a wealthy New Yorker, bibliophile, patron of aspiring writers, editor, publisher, prolific author, and an ardent supporter of the United States and the Union cause.[4]

Current histories of the Civil War abound, and internet sites—far more abounding—can provide detailed information at the touch of a finger, but there are significant advantages in studying documents of the time. As that period recedes in time, those who write about it must condense and select. In order to be fair, historians may strive to give an impartial picture of people and events; in order to arouse interest, writers may include startling or sensational items. Balanced treatment may lead to an emphasis on failures and frustrations; attention may be gained by focusing on quarrels or private lives. Inspiration, as well as greater detail, may be found in study of writings produced in the time period.

Ben Van Raalte was not troubled by the need to be impartial, and he never doubted that his letters, if they reached home, would be eagerly read. He enlisted in the United States army in 1862 and rose to the rank of sergeant. He not only loved his family, he respected them, and this is evident in what he wrote. Dominie Albertus Van Raalte was a devoted father, deeply religious, and a staunch patriot in his adopted country. He was also inclined to be impatient with his sons. (Married daughter Mina, and younger daughters Christina, Maria, and Anna, who lived at home during the Civil War years, did not experience his impatience, at least not in written form.) On 24 August 1862, he wrote to his friend and colleague Philip Phelps: "The Town Holland has been aroused to encourage volunteering to avoid the draft. . . . Sixty-one from this town are sworn in: a clean sweep of our boys; now the married men are allowed to stay at home. . . . Dirk has no desire or courage: Benjamin

3 Evert A. Duyckinck, *National History of the War for the Union: Civil, Military and Naval* (New York: Johnson, Fry and Company, [1861?]. See especially vol. 3, chap. 100, "General Sherman's Georgia Campaign—Chattanooga to Atlanta, May-September, 1864."

4 Edmund G. Burrows and Mike Wallace, *Gotham: A History of New York City to 1898* (New York: Oxford University Press, 1999), 686-87, 701-6.

has enlisted: It did cost Mrs. Van Raalte a severe struggle, but now she has rest. The Boys have organized a company.[5] Dr. Dowd is Captain; a wounded volunteer, Martin De Boe, just coming back[6] was elected 1st Lieutenant, and Jacob Doesburg for 2nd lieutenant."[7] Had that letter been written a few days later, Dirk would not have been censured: he is listed, age eighteen, in the original company, and his father was one of the notables who gathered to see them depart from Kalamazoo.

The men of the Van Raaltes' company were from Ottawa County, ranging in age from seventeen to forty-three. Original officers were young: Dr. William E. Dowd was 28, Martin De Boe, 25, and Jacob Otto Doesburg, son of the editor of a local newspaper, 24. Two did not remain long with the company. When Doesburg returned home, Dirk wrote sarcastically, "Last week our very beloved, high esteemed friend, Mr. Otto Doesburg left us. He himself says it's due to ill health but I say it's because of being homesick and fear of the bullets."[8]

On both sides, throughout the war, healthy men left the army, through legitimate means or desertion, and other men, once healthy, sickened and died. Histories report that the Civil War death toll from both armies exceeds the nation's loss in all its other wars from the Revolution through Vietnam. Over 110,000 Union men died in battle, and more than 250,000 died from disease. On the Confederate side, casualties were numerically lower, but proportionately greater.[9] Ben

5 The website <www.michiganinthewar.org/infantry/25thinf.htm>, accessed 26 July 2006, lists officers and enlisted men of the original company (some names misspelled), with ages and places of residence. See <http: //www.army.mil/ cmh-pg/books/AMH/AMH-12.htm>, accessed 26 July 2006, for "The Civil War, 1864-1865." A map of the terrain described in the letters transcribed in this article is on p. 217.

6 I.e., returning after serving a term in the war. Fort Sumter was attacked at on 12 April 186l. In the North, volunteers signed up for three-month terms of service. The first battle of the war was fought in Virginia, at Bull Run, on 21 July 1861.

7 The practice of volunteers electing their regimental officers worked reasonably well for the Twenty-fifth Michigan, but problems occurred elsewhere. See Dennis K. Boman, "Conduct and Revolt in the Twenty-fifth Ohio Battery: An Insider's Account," *Ohio History* 104, summer/autumn 1995: 163-83. Online at <ohiohistory.org>, accessed 10 Sept. 2006.

8 Dirk Van Raalte to his parents, 16 February 1863, Calvin College Archives.

9 See "The Price in Blood! Casualties in the Civil War" at <http:// civilwarhome.com/casualties.htm>, accessed 21 Aug. 2006. "The Price in Blood" is one item in a remarkably thorough and balanced website titled *Shotgun's Home of the American Civil War*, whose webmaster states his view

wrote, "Our boys like our captain. There is none better in the whole regiment. The doctoring which he does is worth a lot to our boys."[10] Doctoring put William Dowd in close contact with sick men, and he died of dysentery on 17 February 1863, not yet thirty years old. Martin De Boe succeeded him as captain, and John Kramer replaced J. O. Doesburg as lieutenant.[11]

From September to early December 1862, the regiment was stationed at Louisville, Kentucky; thereafter it fought at Munfordville and served on provost and picket duty and guarded trains at Bowling Green. The war changed the Van Raalte sons, as it did all soldiers. At twenty-two, Ben was a strong, hard-working, cheerful young man, managing to be independent within the strong constraints of a close family and devout parents. Letters he wrote in 1862 and 1863 were from a younger, less experienced soldier than those included here, and attempts at reassuring and placating his parents were a recurring theme. Pens and inkbottles were sent to the front, where they were lost or abandoned. Clothing and blankets were sent, and Ben balanced gratitude with reminders that he had to carry all his possessions as he marched. His father investigated purchase of a bulletproof vest. Ben wrote loyally, "regarding your bullet-proof vest, I hardly know what to say. When I left home I thought I couldn't get along without some armor and a revolver but I have forgotten about that long ago. The longer one is a soldier, the less danger one feels and for that reason I am indifferent. However, if you have bought one, I will wear it, but if we go into action I would be the butt of some jokes about 'the iron-clad soldier.'"[12] The idea was abandoned.

---

thus: "I am a Southerner by birth and a Rebel by choice. As I read and study, I pull for Lee, Jackson, and Longstreet. As I live, I thank Grant, Lincoln, and Democracy."

[10] Ben Van Raalte to Christina de Moen Van Raalte, 15 November 1862, Holland Museum Archives.

[11] A photograph of Jacob O. Doesburg can be located in the "Archives of Michigan Civil War Soldiers" found on the website <www.haldigitalcollection.cdmhost.com>, accessed 26 July 2006. Items are in alphabetical order, and many of the men listed in the Glossary of Names are pictured there, including some not from Michigan. Ben Van Raalte to Albertus C. Van Raalte, 14 July 1864, wrote: "We were overjoyed to have Lieut. Kramer drop in and feeling fine," Holland Museum Archives.

[12] Ben Van Raalte to Albertus C. Van Raalte, Bowling Green, Ky., 23 March 1863, Holland Museum Archives, Holland, Mich.

Most of Ben's letters were written to his father; for others, salutations are given. He wrote in Dutch to his parents, and in English to siblings. Farewell phrases—"Best regards to all"—are omitted in transcriptions given here. Comments about topics follow some letters, including information about officers Ben mentions frequently. Information about all officers mentioned in letters and text is given in the Glossary of Names. Ben wrote names of people and places as he heard them. These alternate spellings of names and place names are footnoted at their first use (see note 20) and written correctly thereafter.

When Ben heard reports of events he had not seen, he used phrases such as "so I hear." When he made predictions, he used phrases such as "in my opinion." It is a tribute to his knowledge and good sense that his opinions were sound, and, moreover, in accord with what is known about the views of his commanding officers. Sherman and his friend and superior officer, U. S. Grant, knew the importance of taking Atlanta, and the northern newspapers that were not biased toward the rebel cause made this clear to readers:

> In the first place, it is Atlanta itself—a modern, well-built city, now approaching its twenty-first year, but still sooner to reach its freedom birthday. . . . From its protected situation, deep in the interior of the Confederacy, it was chosen at the outset as a great military depot of supplies and of material of war, and, furthermore, as a great military workshop. . . . Here are arsenals, foundries, furnaces, rolling-mills, machine-shops, laboratories, factories, which have been busily supplying the Confederacy with munitions of war for the past three years. . . . We, with our surplus Springfields and Lowells,[13] do not appreciate how illy the enemy can spare this single city. . . . Next, Atlanta is one of the chief railroad centres in the Confederacy. . . . It is the key of all that lies behind its back, or, rather, it is the gate which closes up all that region from assault. . . . [F]or penetrating Central Georgia, Atlanta is the true starting point. . . . Once carried, Atlanta is the new advanced position and [the army's labor to reach it] is done once for all.[14]

13 The cities of Springfield and Lowell in Massachusetts were two of many Northern cities whose factories supplied munitions for the Union army.

14 An article in the *New York Times,* 26 July 1864, quoted from Duyckinck, *History of the War*, vol. 3, 374-75, which includes the entire text of the article.

The second volume of General Sherman's memoirs[15] opens with five chapters devoted to the Atlanta campaign. Duyckinck summarizes the relative strengths of the two armies as the struggle began. "[Sherman] had opposed to him the second army in the Confederacy . . . commanded by Joseph E. Johnston, one of the most experienced of the rebel officers. . . . Numerically, the force of General Sherman was superior. . . . But to compensate for any inequality, the enemy had the advantage of position, their thorough knowledge of an intricate field of operations, an interior line of communication for supplies and reinforcements, while Sherman, at every move departing farther from his base as Johnston approached his, risked everything on the issue of the campaign."[16]

Differing dates are given for the start of the campaign that contributed so greatly to ending the war. The "official date" is 1 May 1864,[17] when the first skirmish occurred at Old Stone Church near Ringgold, Georgia. *The Atlas of the Civil War* dates the first phase of the Atlanta Campaign from 7 May to 20 May.

Battles of the Atlanta Campaign, 1864[18]

Rocky Face Ridge: 8-13 May
Resaca: 14 May
Cassville: 18-19 May
Dallas and New Hope Church: 26-28 May
Kennesaw Mountain: skirmishing 10-19 June; battle 27 July
Peachtree Creek: 20 July
Attacks around Atlanta: 21-28 July
Ezra Church: 29 July
Utoy Creek: 6 August
Jonesborough: 31 August - 1-2 September CSA forces evacuate Atlanta; Union forces occupy the city

Source: James M. McPherson, *The Atlas of the Civil War,* New York: Macmillan, 1994, 174-79.

15 William T. Sherman, *Memoirs of General William T. Sherman*, Civil War Centennial Series (1875; reprint, 2 vols. in 1, Bloomington, Ind.: Indiana University Press, 1957).

16 Duyckinck, *History of the War,* vol. 3, 375.

17 See "Chronology of the Atlanta Campaign" at <www.ngeorgia.com/history/atlcamp>, accessed 3 Aug. 2006.

18 The website <www.pathsofthecivilwar.com>, accessed 18 Sept. 2006, provides an amazingly detailed interactive battlefield map. Users select a

7 May 1864. Camp by the wayside Georgia some what Near Tunnelhill[19]

Reveille sounded at 2:00 AM this morning and at daybreak we left Red Clay. Marching went very slowly today—very gradually we are getting nearer to the enemy. They say that the Rebs have left Tunnelhill and this morning our troops went forward on all roads. . . . It is very warm here. The soil is sandy and the water is not very good. I can't give you much news because camp talk is not very reliable so I will not say anything which I haven't seen. The Rebel pickets were driven back but I do not know how far. I saw only one prisoner today and it is my opinion that the Rebs will leave Dalton. If not, there likely will be some fighting. When we stop to rest our lines are in good position with the artillery there to back us up. I do not think they will catch Schofield napping. Our Brigade is now commanded by Brig. Gen McNeil. We like him real well. We expect to see Col. Moore[20] *soon. Our Lt. Col is a fine man and we are very fond of him—whatever the boys do is O.K. with him. I had to laugh on our march from Mossy Creek. The soldiers were very tired on the evening of the third day of marching and while they were resting the order of "Fall in" was heard. No one got up to obey the order—just looked at each other and remained where they were. Then he rode through the ranks, smiled and said, "Boys, fall in—I presume you all know what that means." It didn't take long for them to get up then.*

I must close now. It's nice being a soldier if only one didn't get so tired. It appears that we will stay here tonight but one never can tell. Up to the present we are all well—my health has never been better than now. . . . We are now through marching or at least are used to it. I haven't been real tired since the night we arrived at London. When we arrived we had only thirteen guns in our company when we had to stack arms. That held true of the whole division. Some came straggling in in the morning. It was hot

---

year between 1861 and 1865 to get a map of the selected year's battles, and then, by positioning the mouse over a marked site on the map, can read the name of the battle and, by clicking on the site, read factual information about the battle.

[19] This small town, located in northwest Georgia, was called "Tunnel Hill" until 1848 when it was incorporated into "Tunnelsville" (<www.northga.net/whitfield/tunnel.html>, accessed 24 Sept. 2006).

[20] Ben Van Raalte's spelling: *More*.

that day and the march was forced, scandalously so. Do not repeat this as I do not like to say anything against the company. At such time some of the soldiers get quite indifferent and say—I am not going any farther, let happen what may, I don't want to die. Some just can't stand the pace and so it happens many are taken prisoners on a retreat.

Ben wrote letters to family frequently, and by 1864 the names of many officers would have been familiar to them. Here he favorably mentions Schofield, McNeil, and Moore, and also writes, "Our Lt. Col is a fine man and we are very fond of him." The unnamed officer was Benjamin Orcutt,[21] a native of Kalamazoo, who served as Lieutenant Colonel under Colonel Moore, and led troops when Colonel Moore was commanding elsewhere. Orcutt had fought in the Mexican War; afterwards he served two terms as Sheriff of Kalamazoo County, married, and had three sons. Returning to Kalamazoo in 1865 after the Civil War, he was again elected sheriff. Less than two years later, he was shot and killed by an escaping prisoner.[22]

General John M. Schofield[23] was a career army officer, beginning the war as major of a regiment of Missouri volunteers. Early in the war he was awarded the Medal of Honor for gallantry. A strong and upright leader, he graduated from West Point in 1853, ranking seventh in a class of fifty-two. In 1863, after guerilla raiders crossed from Missouri into Kansas and ravaged the town of Lawrence, burning, plundering, and killing civilians, Schofield was denounced for "inefficiency" in pursuing the raiders, and the protesters went to Washington and were able to meet with the president. Lincoln listened with his usual patience and replied thoughtfully and in depth, concluding, "Without disparaging any, I affirm with confidence that no commander of that department has, in proportion to his means, done better than General Schofield."[24]

21 "Archives of Michigan Civil War Soldiers" on the website <www.haldigitalcollection.cdmhost.com>, accessed 20 July 2006, includes two photographs of Benjamin Orcutt.

22 "Officer Down Memorial Page Remembers" on <www.odmp.org>, accessed 10 Sept. 2006.

23 The website <www.sunsite.utk.edu/civil-war/wpungen.html>, accessed 3 Aug. 2006, lists "Union Generals from West Point," and the website <www.sunsite.utk.edu/civil-war/wpcongen.html>, accessed 3 Aug. 2006, lists "Confederate Generals from West Point." The generals in both lists are given with their dates of graduation and rank in class. Men who became Civil War generals but "departed before graduation" are listed separately.

24 Duyckinck, *History of the War*, vol. 3, 276.

After the war Schofield served briefly as Secretary of War, succeeding Edwin Stanton. In 1873 Secretary of War William Belknap directed him to investigate the strategic potential of a United States presence in the Hawaiian Islands. Schofield recommended that a naval port be established at Pearl Harbor, and Schofield Barracks in Hawaii is named for him. All cadets at the United States Military Academy at West Point and the United States Air Force Academy are required to memorize this statement, written by Schofield:

> The discipline which makes the soldiers of a free country reliable in battle is not to be gained by harsh or tyrannical treatment. On the contrary, such treatment is far more likely to destroy than to make an army. It is possible to impart instruction and give commands in such a manner and such a tone of voice as to inspire in the soldier no feeling, but an intense desire to obey, while the opposite manner and tone of voice cannot fail to excite strong resentment and a desire to disobey. The one mode or the other of dealing with subordinates springs from a corresponding spirit in the breast of the commander. He who feels the respect which is due to others cannot fail to inspire in them respect for himself. While he who feels, and hence manifests, disrespect towards others, especially his subordinates, cannot fail to inspire hatred against himself.[25]

During the Atlanta campaign, General Sherman divided his troops into three columns or wings, which he called his three armies. Schofield commanded the Army of the Ohio until the close of the war. On 7 May 1864, Ben wrote, "It is my opinion that the Rebs will leave Dalton. If not, there likely will be some fighting. . . . I do not think they will catch Schofield napping." His next letter, written 21 May 1864, corroborates this opinion. Though the Confederate troops didn't move immediately, they left Dalton, as they had retreated from other points on the way to Atlanta, but only after there was a fight. Though General Schofield was not napping, there were guns he could not see, masked by brush and debris.

Brigadier General John McNeil was born in Canada and lived before the war in St. Louis, Missouri, where he became a prosperous businessman and served in the state legislature. When the rebellion broke out, his associates expected him to join the Confederate army,

[25] <www.en.wikipedia.org/wiki/John_M._Schofield>, accessed 12 Aug. 2006.

but he declared for the Union, losing much of his wealth thereby when southern debts to northerners were repudiated. In the spring of 1862 he was a colonel, assigned to command the District of Northeast Missouri, charged to clear the area of guerillas. Palmyra had been occupied by Confederate forces, and McNeil's troops retook the town.

When McNeil was appointed to lead the Twenty-fifth Michigan troops, Ben wrote, "We like him real well."[26] Thus it is startling to discover that the internet contains sites denouncing him for "the Palmyra Massacre"—which consisted of the execution, by firing squad, of ten Confederate soldiers who had been paroled after swearing not to take up arms against the Union again, but who had violated that parole, a capital crime. An elderly citizen of Palmyra, a Union supporter, had been kidnapped (he was later found murdered) and the Provost Marshal sent a message to Col. Joseph C. Porter, a Confederate officer, announcing that the imprisoned soldiers would be executed if he was not returned unharmed. Jefferson Davis threatened to execute ten Union prisoners unless McNeil were handed over to him. *Harper's Weekly* and the local loyalist paper defended Colonel McNeil, and the area was pacified.[27] McNeil had been sent to the area with explicit directions from General Schofield:

> SAINT LOUIS, *MO., June* 12, 1862.
> Colonel McNEIL, *Palmyra, Mo.:*
> I want you to take the field in person, with as much of your force as can be spared, and exterminate the rebel bands in your division. . . .
> Don't rest until you have exterminated the rascals.
> J. M. Schofield, *Brigadier-General*[28]

Ben's letters refer often to his company's colonel, Orlando Hurley Moore. O. H. Moore (1827-90), a career soldier from Schoolcraft, Michigan, led the Twenty-fifth Michigan troops throughout the Civil

26 Ben Van Raalte to Albertus C. Van Raalte, 7 May 1864, Holland Museum Archives.

27 <www.en.wikipedia.org/wiki/John_McNeil>, accessed 12 Aug. 2006. On the website <www.civilwarstlouis.com>, accessed 12 Aug. 2006, in a section titled "The Palmyra Massacre," a picture of General Schofield, with the dispatch he sent to McNeil, is featured.

28 Thus Schofield angered some Missouri residents because he did not pursue raiders past Missouri borders, but his name remains untarnished. McNeil also took legitimate action, but "the act earned him the unshakeable title of 'Butcher of Palmyra'" (<www.en.wikipedia.org/wiki/John_McNeil>, accessed 12 Aug. 2006).

War.[29] After the war, General Sherman wrote his memoirs, concluding with a chapter on "Military Lessons of the War," in which he explained the proper organization of an army, with its composition from the army itself through corps, division, brigade, regiment, and company. "The regiment is the family," he wrote. "The colonel, as the father, should have a personal acquaintance with every officer and man, and should instill a feeling of pride and affection for himself, so that his officers and men would naturally look to him for personal advice and instruction."[30] Colonel Moore was such a man. Ben's earliest letters describe a system of daily routines that taught the new soldiers while keeping them active, usefully busy, and informed. In May 1865, the war was over but Moore continued his sensible care. On 2 May 1865, Ben wrote from Raleigh, North Carolina, "Col. Moore is again with the Regiment. We have two hours of daily drill."

The most famous event for Moore and his soldiers occurred in July 1863.[31] In the Confederate ranks there was a troop of raiders, valued because they created havoc through surprise attacks. Their leader, John Hunt Morgan, officially served under General Braxton Bragg, but acted on his own. Like other soldiers, Moore's men knew about Morgan; unlike many, they were well prepared. Months before Morgan attacked them, Ben wrote, "We are daily awaiting an attack by Uncle Morgan. His purpose is to cut off communications between Nashville and Louisville. We sleep at night with our guns at our sides so we can be ready at a moment's notice. Every morning at four or four-thirty we form a line of battle which is done to teach us to fall in quickly and not be half asleep in case the old boy should come as he has the habit of doing at daylight."[32]

29 <www.michiganinthewar.org/infantry/25thinf.htm>, accessed 12 Aug. 2006. A website with information about Colonel Moore and pictures of civil war artifacts is <www.kvm.kvcc.edu/content/collections/civil_war_artifacts.htm>, accessed 12 Aug. 2006. Included in the displays are Moore's photograph, officer's dress coat, portable field desk, and tea service presented to him by the city of Louisville in 1868, in recognition of his leadership at Tebbs Bend.

30 Sherman, *Memoirs,* vol. 2, 385.

31 <http://www.state.ky.us/agencies//khc/tebbs.htm>, accessed 3 Aug. 2006. Jeanne M. Jacobson, Elton J. Bruins, and Larry J. Wagenaar, *Albertus C. Van Raalte: Dutch Leader and American Patriot.* Hope College (Holland, Mich.: Hope College, 1996), 124.

32 Ben Van Raalte to Albertus C. Van Raalte, Munfordville, Ky., 22 December 1862, Holland Museum Archives.

In early July 1863, Colonel Moore learned that Morgan was near, at the head of over two thousand troops. He rode out immediately to select the best site for defense, moved his troops quietly, and set them to preparing the terrain. Morgan attacked on 4 July, and after exchange of fire and attack by Confederate artillery, sent a demand for surrender. Moore replied, "Present my compliments to General Morgan and say, this being the Fourth of July, I cannot entertain the proposition to surrender."[33] A Confederate officer urged, "You see the breach we have made upon your works with our battery; you cannot expect to repulse General Morgan's whole division with your little command; you have resisted us gallantly and deserve credit for it, and now I hope you will save useless bloodshed by reconsidering the message to General Morgan." To this the Colonel replied: "Sir, when you assume to know my strength you assume too much. I have a duty to perform to my country, and therefore cannot reconsider my reply to General Morgan." Not only did he not surrender, he outwitted the rebels, and under his leadership his troops defeated the vastly larger Confederate force. "Confederate General John Hunt Morgan, at the beginning of his 'Great Raid' into Ohio and Indiana, encountered 200 men of the 25th Michigan Infantry under Colonel Orlando Moore. Morgan, known as the 'Thunderbolt of the Confederacy' for his lightning quick guerilla raids, had superior numbers in terms of troops and weapons, but Moore had the better location protected by an earthen fortification. Moore employed one of the cleverest ruses in Civil War military history. Knowing that his closest aid was 30 miles away, he tricked the Confederates into thinking that reinforcements were continuously coming in by ordering his men to ride their horses back and forth."[34] Another strategy was ordering Company I of the Twenty-fifth Michigan (Ben's company) to remain hidden and hold their fire; thus when he ordered Captain De Boe to attack, the Confederates believed reinforcements had arrived. With this indication of a strengthened force, Morgan requested permission for a truce to bury the dead, but fled before that was completed. He

[33] <http://www.homepages.rootsweb.com/~janwhite/25thInf.html> and <http://www.michiganinthewar.org/infantry/25thinf.htm>, both accessed 21 Aug. 2006. Visitors to Campbellsville, Ky., may tour the Morgan-Moore Trail commemorating the battle. See <http://www.campbellsville.com/virtual/tebbsbendmap.htm>, accessed 21 Aug. 2006.

[34] <http://www.civilwar.cloudworth.com/battles-and-battlefields-rest-of.php>, "Tebbs Bend—Small But Significant Kentucky Civil War Site," accessed 16 Aug. 2006. This website labels itself as "an apolitical news service for historians and history buffs."

sent a jocular message to Moore: "I promote you to brigadier general." (Moore commented that all he wished was to continue as colonel of his men.) A Confederate soldier in Morgan's troop wrote in his diary, "We learned from some of our wounded boys that came to us some time after, that Colonel Moore was very kind to our wounded left on the battle field."[35]

When news of the battle reached him, Dominie Van Raalte wrote an ebullient letter to his friend Philip Phelps: "Our boys 200 in number had a tremendous fight with Morgan's division on the fourth of July: the fire and 8 charges they had to endure of 2000 men during 3½ hours: Morgan did ask permission to bury his dead, but did not finish his work (our boys had to bury yet 25 of his men) but left them in haste. . . . Col. Moore had chosen an excellent position on a hill with trees and logs: sometimes they were overwhelmed and they had to back out to be able to use their guns. . . . They did call our boys ground hounds because they fired out of the ground: they said their number wounded and killed were 250. . . . 5 of ours were killed and 20 wounded . . . and yet they were constant under a rain of bullets: the leaves brush and bark of the trees was so abundant, it did hinder constant in their eyes: the Colonel's horse and pantaloon was hit. The Colonel loves very much the Holland Company. . . . We feel that God's hand did cover them; Morgan's division could have eaten them up. Morgan seems to have been discouraged on account of that unusual number of wounded and dead; our boys did hit them all in the head or breast. I tell you we have had a very pleasant thanksgiving day."[36]

21 May 1864. Camp Near Cassville, Georgia[37]

Since I am still well I wish to take this opportunity to write a letter. It seems we are going to remain here today, why I do not know. The rumor

[35] Quotation from "The Wartime Diary of John Weatherred" found at <www.jackmasters.net/we1863.html>, accessed 18 Aug. 2006.

[36] Albertus C. Van Raalte to Philip Phelps Jr., 7 August 1863. Van Raalte was a highly literate man, and a prolific correspondent. His native language was Dutch, which became evident when he wrote rapidly in English, as he does here, when he slips in a Dutch word here and there (all of them translated in this edited version).

[37] At this time General Joseph E. Johnston was commander of the Confederate forces. Expecting an attack by Sherman at Cassville, he had prepared a strong but hidden defense; Sherman did not take the bait. The translator wrote "Carsville," but Ben had "Cassville," the correct spelling of a place in

is that we must get ready for a twenty day march but there are so many rumors making the rounds lately. It seems to me we should now stay right on the Rebs heels. They left Cassville at midnight in great haste and all the civilians of the town left with them. We didn't have time to make a stand as they were very strongly fortified, having blockaded the streets of the town so we couldn't do any damage with a cavalry charge. They retreated quite slowly as they had a river to cross and didn't go any faster than they had to.

But now I will go back a few days to the 7th, the day we left Red Clay. There was some skirmishing that day driving back the Reb pickets. The 8th the fighting was heavier on the ridge and our division reached the ridge in the afternoon but couldn't engage the enemy as darkness fell. That night we slept on Rocky Face and stayed there until 11:00 the next morning when another Corps joined us. Then we turned back and formed our line of battle in the valley, then forward skirmishing. The Rebs withdrew gradually until they reached their breastworks. Then the skirmishers retreated and the brigade received orders to storm the works. This we did and held good lines but soon we were within range and they opened up with deadly firing. Then we received orders to lie down which we did very gladly and quickly. They had masked batteries or rather hidden cannon which our general didn't know about. The shells dropped behind us, between us and in front of us but none of our company was killed or wounded. Those on the right retreated, crawling on the ground. Then our artillery got into position and stilled the Rebs laughter in a hurry. Two of our regiment were killed and four or five wounded. The 4th Corps seemed to be engaged in fighting on the ridge at the same time. That night we stayed in battle line and in the morning got orders to retreat about a mile and a half. The following day we were relieved by the 4th Corps and went to the extreme right above Dalton where we had a battle on the 14th. About noon we were ordered to make a charge and it was terrible. Their breastworks were too strong to capture by storm and our regiment lost about forty dead and wounded. I never expected to see any of our company again. We lost C[ornelis] Van Dam and J[ohn] Pilon is missing. We couldn't find him on the battlefield. . . . Now I must finish because I am too sleepy to write any more. The last two

Northern Georgia that was used by both Hood and Polk during the Atlanta campaign (<www.ngeorgia.com/history/atlcamp.html>, accessed 21 Aug. 2006).

weeks we have had hardly any rest—on the go practically day and night. The next time I will make a better report.

31 May 1864. Camp Near Pumpkinvine Creek,[38] Paldon Co., Ga.

I am happy to report that I am in good health and hope you are also well. Sunday evening we left the front and were sent to the rear to get some rest. It was impossible to get any at the front either day or night. We were relieved by the first division which has not been at the front as yet. They are all new recruits. Now we are about four miles to the rear and guarding the trains. Last week we fought nearly all week but our company was lucky and didn't lose a man to the bullets. One evening we were shelled very heavily and a piece of shell hit Wilterdink in his side but fortunately he had a Testament in his pocket which saved his life. It hurt him a lot but he stayed with the company. Another was hit but his knapsack saved him. Several others were hit—too many to tell about. One day our company was ordered to clear a ridge and after a couple of hours of sharp fighting we did so. That day I had plenty of chances to shoot at Rebs but they also had shots at me. I got a bullet through my blouse at the belt line. It was quite a fight but we made a charge and they retreated and are in their breastworks again. It appears they wish us to besiege them because they make no general attacks. Our rifle pits are opposite their works but so far they have always been repulsed with heavy losses. I think they will get tired of that after a while. My opinion is that much will have to happen before this campaign is concluded. Whoever lives through it will have much to tell.

Morning of 1 June.

It is very warm today. Cannonading is going on continuously and reinforcements are rolling in daily. We haven't been sent back to the front yet but expect to be sent back any moment. The Rebs are finding themselves in a tight spot. Last night I got your letter in which you said that you know the news almost as well as we, if not better. Yes, at the front where you would expect to know it, one hears nothing but the music of bullets.

Ben's next letter again includes his characteristic phrase "in my opinion": "I think that we in the western army have suffered very small

[38] Ben Van Raalte's spelling: *Punkinvine.*

losses considering the success we have had. Gen. Sherman seems quick and decisive and still a very cautious person, in my opinion. Just the man we need."[39] In 1861, as the country was becoming divided into South and North, it was neither popular nor safe to combine caution and decisiveness, nor was it a time, on either side, where foresight was welcomed. Those who warned Southerners against secession and war were not heeded, and sometimes suffered for their prescience.

> *Let me tell you what is coming.* . . . Your fathers and husbands, your sons and brothers, will be herded at the point of the bayonet. . . . You may, after the sacrifice of countless millions of treasure and hundreds of thousands of lives, as a bare possibility, win Southern independence . . . but I doubt it. I tell you that, while I believe with you in the doctrine of states rights, the North is determined to preserve this Union. They are not a fiery, impulsive people as you are, for they live in colder climates. But when they begin to move in a given direction . . . they move with the steady momentum and perseverance of a mighty avalanche.[40]
>
> *You people of the South don't know what you are doing.* This country will be drenched in blood, and God only knows how it will end. It is all folly, madness, a crime against civilization! You people speak so lightly of war; you don't know what you're talking about. War is a terrible thing!
>
> You mistake, too, the people of the North. They are a peaceable people but an earnest people, and they will fight, too. They are not going to let this country be destroyed without a mighty effort to save it. . . . Besides, where are your men and appliances of war to contend against them? The North can make a steam engine, locomotive, or railway car; hardly a yard of cloth or pair of shoes can you make. You are rushing into war with one of the most powerful, ingeniously mechanical, and determined people on Earth—right at your doors.
>
> You are bound to fail. Only in your spirit and determination are you prepared for war. In all else you are totally unprepared, with a bad cause to start with. At first you will make headway, but as

39 Ben Van Raalte to Albertus C. Van Raalte, 9 June 1864, Holland Museum Archives.

40 Geoffrey C. Ward, *The Civil War: An Illustrated History* (New York: Alfred A. Knopf, 1992), 27 (emphasis mine); see also <www.graceproducts.com/houston/life.html>, accessed 21 Aug. 2006.

> your limited resources begin to fail, shut out from the markets of Europe as you will be, your cause will begin to wane. If your people will but stop and think, they must see in the end that you will surely fail.[41]

The writer of "Let me tell you what is coming" was the venerable hero Sam Houston, victor over Santa Anna in the Texas War of Independence, first President of the Republic of Texas, Senator from the State of Texas, and three times Governor of the State of Texas. He was governor when the Texas legislature voted to secede. When he refused to swear allegiance to the Confederacy, he was deposed, no longer admired, but vilified. "You people of the South don't know what you are doing" are the words of William Tecumseh Sherman, first head of the Louisiana State Military College (now Louisiana State University), a position he resigned when Louisiana seceded, going immediately north to volunteer for the Union army.

As Ben perceived, Sherman was quick, decisive, and cautious—though not cautious in protecting himself. Duyckinck describes "General Thomas' memorable report of his tour of inspection in the West with Secretary Cameron. On the 16th of October [1861] . . . the party arrived in Louisville and had an interview with General Sherman, who gave a gloomy picture of affairs in Kentucky. . . . On being asked the question what force he deemed necessary, he promptly replied, 'two hundred thousand men.'"[42] Other officers derided him, and newspapers spread the falsehood that he was crazy. Sherman was withdrawn from his command. But Lincoln had faith in Grant, and Grant had faith in Sherman, and by the time Ben Van Raalte encountered Sherman, he was second in rank only to General Grant.

9 June 1864. Camp East of Dallas Georgia

Up to the present we are well which is worth a lot to a soldier. Many are sick here but still not as many as one would expect. . . . At the present time there are many generals who seem to have no regard for human lives and think of nothing but gaining honors and promotions, like our friend Judah. Contrary to orders he kept on trying to take Reb. positions by storm. When he marched us through Knoxville he made the remark that the second

[41] Among many internet sources where the quotation can be found, it is given on the website: <www.reference. com/browse/wiki/ William_Tecumseh_Sherman>, accessed 21 Aug. 2006 (emphasis mine).

[42] Duyckinck, *History of the War,* vol. 2, 90.

Division would get him a star but it didn't work out that way. They would rather see him in a bottomless pit. Our division is now under the command of Gen. Hascall[43] *who formerly was in command of the second Brigade. He is a quiet man but sees all that goes on. The Brigade is now commanded by Colonel Bond of the 111th Ohio. There has been a big change in our brigade. Our General McLean*[44] *was transferred to the third Division, first Brigade, of our Corps because it was the largest brigade commanded by a Colonel. Now we are the only regiment still in the brigade of all the old regiments when it was organized. . . . Now the brigade is under the command of Colonel Cooper of the sixth Tennessee. The brigade now has five regiments—the 6th and 3rd Tennessee, the 91st Indiana, the 45th Ohio and the 25th Mich. We are sorry to see our general go. He was a lovable man and everyone held him in high regard and our regiment stands to lose much. Our Lt. Colonel is an exceptionally fine man but a poor commander and we need them in a fight. Colonel Moore was unsurpassable in that respect. I believe that if Colonel Moore had been with us at Resaca,*[45] *the results might have been different. There was one regiment in the second Brig. viz. the 111th Ohio. Colonel Bond didn't follow up with his regiment and told Judah if he wanted to storm the positions then he himself would have to lead the charge. . . . When we saw that the charge was unsuccessful he* [i.e., Judah] *said that the division had to take the position and keep reforming until they took them. But no one listened to him and he stayed in the rear. The fighting became heavier and heavier as we made the attack and in the evening our brigade kept coming back, each man for himself. They gathered together and that evening Judah was as flannel-mouthed*[46] *as could be. He said "25th, you have lost all but your honor." We didn't appreciate his speech much, especially when we learned that the charge had been made contrary to orders.*

11 June

Yesterday morning we left camp and went back four miles to the front. Now we lie under the breastworks of the Rebs again but we have

43 Ben Van Raalte's spelling: *Haskels.*

44 Ben Van Raalte's spelling: *McClane.*

45 Ben Van Raalte's spelling: *Resacca.*

46 "Flannel-mouthed" is American slang for smooth-talking in an insincere or deceptive way. The British convey a similar idea with the verb "to flannel." Both uses are derived from the smoothness of flannel fabric.

thrown up works opposite theirs. After a little skirmishing they fell back to their works and they are quite strong there. Yesterday one of our batteries shelled them but there was no answer until evening when they opened up. No damage was done. During the night they dropped a couple of shells on our works—apparently they were afraid we might sleep too soundly. It is now 7 o'clock and very quiet—only an occasional shot is heard. I do not know when this letter will be mailed but hope you get it. Our company used up 500 rounds in one day of skirmishing.

12 June 1864. In the field, Allatoona Mountain

Up until now we are still well. Yesterday our batteries shelled the Rebs heavily and this morning they are very quiet. They shell us now and then but so far have not done much damage. We have lots of rain and the roads are practically unpassable. Hooker is again making flanking movements and the Rebs had to retire from our right yesterday. Our men made two or three charges and the Rebs had to get out of their works. The third division was to make a charge also but the rain prevented them and this morning they said the ground was too muddy and soft.

. . . Yesterday we built some strong breastworks so if the Rebs start shelling again we will have some cover. The Rebs must think that the Yanks have a lot of nerve to build so near them. In the lines of our division we have 25 cannon which can open up on them any minute. I sometimes wish that some of those Copperheads in the colony could be here to take part in the fighting and see whether or not they would think so much of the Rebs. I would think they would then say that the bombs they are throwing are not very healthful nor are exactly kindly to the Union. Now I must close. Just as I am finishing our cannon are beginning to say "Boom, boom, Southern Rights!" Others call "Guardhouse."[47]

20 June 1864. Camp 25th Mich. In the field

In haste but with much pleasure I can announce that we are still well. The Rebs have been flanked again and are slowly retiring. The fighting began at noon on the 15th. We were opposite Lost Mountain, a

[47] When the cannon spoke, they were, Ben imagined, attacking the rebel cause, and reminding rebel soldiers of the Guardhouse, a holding pen for prisoners.

little to the left. Schofield went forward in the shape of a horseshoe leaving the mountain to his left. We pressed the Rebs so hard they no longer felt safe on the mountain and on the night of the 17th they had to fall back. Since that time we drove at them from all points. It is hard going because of the rains. It rained night and day. Old Hooker was active too and cannonading was very heavy. The people at home think we are making slow progress as we are still far from Atlanta but they wouldn't say so if they were here and taking part in the fighting. You must realize that all the roads are strongly fortified and if we didn't proceed slowly and cautiously there would not be much left by way of an Army to take Atlanta. We must first feel out the enemy positions—should you run into a group of masked batteries it is far from pleasant. We have had very small losses so far, especially on the right. The fighting was very heavy on the 15th and we came close to a Reb battery but they didn't do much harm. It was getting late and they couldn't see us too well. The entire woods was filled with smoke. The soldiers were dissatisfied that they were not permitted to go on but they were ordered back. We were so close that they could not do much damage to us. The Rebs are getting discouraged and they reserve their best troops for the skirmish line to prevent desertions. The first Georgia Regiment is opposite our brigade in the skirmish line and they are about played out. One day sixty deserters came over and now there are more every day so that nearly a whole company has been taken as prisoners. A hundred or more were buried in the field. This is one of their best units so you can imagine what will happen when we meet the others. Now they have to retreat in the mud which isn't so pleasant. The Yanks are full of pep and say, "The Rebellion must and shall be put down, mud or no mud!" Yesterday we waded through such deep creeks that we had to hold our ammunition above our heads. I am writing under difficulties so please forgive the writing in this letter. I hardly get any letters and do not know when this letter will go but at least it is ready.

23 June 1864. Camp 25th Mich. Near Marietta, Georgia

Just a few lines to let you know we are well. Yesterday we again made excellent progress. Last night we arrived just in time or the Rebs might have turned Hooker's lines. They had massed their troops and came forward in three strong battle lines, trying to penetrate our lines but the Yanks were not asleep. The batteries had already been placed in position and the soldiers had made good progress in throwing up breastworks. You can imagine that at such times the soldiers work as fast as possible—I wish you could see it. When the Rebs were within 50 yards we gave them a dose of grape and canister and musketry and the old boys were soon retreating. When they were close we could hear the Rebel officers yelling "Forward, take that battery" but the Johnnies didn't dare—they were under cross fire. Hooker ran around like a fighting cock[48] *and kept yelling "We can hold them" with Schofield saying "Just in time." I have heard that the Rebs are now retreating but I don't think very far. Things are going against them. From here we can see sixty Rebs lying in a heap. I must close now as the bugles are sounding again. I will write as often as possible just to let you know how things are.*

Joseph Hooker is mentioned in more of Ben Van Raalte's letters than any other officer, yet Ben was never under his command. Hooker esteemed himself highly, and had a correspondingly low opinion of those placed above him. In 1862, when General Ambrose Burnside requested that his troublesome subordinate be transferred, Hooker had also been writing to Lincoln, who was having difficulties finding effective generals. He replaced Burnside with Hooker, but with a cautionary letter:

> Executive Mansion
> Washington, D.C.
> January 26, 1863.
>
> Major General Hooker:
> General. I have placed you at the head of the Army of the Potomac. Of course I have done this upon what appear to me to be sufficient reasons. And yet I think it best for you to know that there are some things in regard to which I am not quite satisfied with you. I believe you to be a brave and a skilful soldier, which, of course, I like. I also believe you do not mix politics with your profession, in which you are right. You have confidence in yourself, which is a valuable, if not an indispensable quality. You are ambitious, which, within reasonable bounds, does good rather than harm. But I think that during Gen. Burnside's

[48] Ben would have had opportunities to observe fighting cocks. Many soldiers acquired roosters as they marched through farming country, and cockfighting was a popular spectator sport in many camps.

> command of the Army, you have taken counsel of your ambition, and thwarted him as much as you could, in which you did a great wrong to the country, and to a most meritorious and honorable brother officer. I have heard, in such way as to believe it, of your recently saying that both the Army and the Government needed a Dictator. Of course it was not for this, but in spite of it, that I have given you the command. Only those generals who gain successes, can set up dictators. What I now ask of you is military success, and I will risk the dictatorship. The government will support you to the utmost of its ability, which is neither more nor less than it has done and will do for all commanders. I much fear that the spirit which you have aided to infuse into the Army, of criticising their Commander, and withholding confidence from him, will now turn upon you. I shall assist you as far as I can, to put it down. Neither you, nor Napoleon, if he were alive again, could get any good out of an army, while such a spirit prevails in it. And now, beware of rashness. Beware of rashness, but with energy, and sleepless vigilance, go forward, and give us victories.
>
> Yours very truly
> A. Lincoln.[49]

The first major test of Hooker's leadership came at Chancellorsville.[50] Union forces were large and well sited, but Lee's relatively small Confederate army defeated them. General Darius N. Couch, Hooker's second in command, had to take the leadership when Hooker became, or chose to become, incapacitated. Couch refused thereafter to serve under him. Lincoln offered Hooker's position (commander of the armies) to Couch, who declined and suggested General George Meade. Hooker's nickname, "Fighting Joe" (which he disliked), resulted from a newspaper dispatch where punctuation was omitted between the word fighting and his name.[51] After Chancellorsville, General Lee referred to him as "Mr. F. J. Hooker." In his *Memoirs*, General Sherman cites an instance of Hooker's apparently incorrigible untruthfulness:

49 <www.swcivilwar.com/hookerletter.html>, accessed 10 Sept. 2006.

50 Darius N. Couch, "Outgeneraled by Lee," in *Battles and Leaders of the Civil War*, ed. Ned Bradford (1887-88 in 4 vols.; New York: Appleton-Century-Crofts, 1956), 323-36.

51 A biography of Joseph Hooker can be found at <www.civilwarhome.com/hookbio.htm>, accessed 10 Sept. 2006.

I rode the whole line, and ordered General Thomas in person to advance his extreme right corps (Hooker's); and instructed General Schofield, by letter, to keep his entire army, viz., the Twenty-Third Corps, as a strong right flank in close support of Hooker's deployed line. . . . I had got back to my bivouac about dark, when a signal message was received: "Kulp House,[52] 5:30 p.m. General Sherman: 'We have repulsed two heavy attacks, and feel confident, our only apprehension being from our extreme right flank. Three entire corps are in front of us. Major-General Hooker.'" Hooker's corps belonged to Thomas's army; Thomas's headquarters were two miles nearer to Hooker than mine; and Hooker, being an old army officer, knew that he should have reported to Thomas and not to me; I was disturbed by the assertion that he was uneasy about his right flank, when Schofield had been ordered to protect that. The rebel army was only composed of three corps; I had that very day ridden six miles of their lines, and Hooker could not have encountered "three entire corps." . . . Early the next day I rode down to the Kulp House; on the way I passed through [a] division of Hooker's corps, which I learned had not been engaged at all in the battle the day before; then I rode along [two other] divisions and the men were engaged in burying the dead. . . . I met Generals Schofield and Hooker together and I showed General Schofield Hooker's signal-message of the day before. He was very angry, and pretty sharp words passed between them, Schofield saying that his head of column (Hascall's division) had been, at the time of the battle, actually in advance of Hooker's line; that the enemy struck his troops before Hooker's; and he offered to go out and show me that the dead men of his advance division (Hascall's) were lying farther out than any of Hooker's. . . . As we rode away General Hooker was by my side; and I told him that such a thing must not occur again, and from that time he began to sulk. General Hooker had come from the East with great fame as a "fighter." He seems jealous of all the army commanders, because in years, former rank, and experience, he thought he was our superior.[53]

[52] Jay Wertz and Edwin C. Bearss, *Smithsonian's Great Battles and Battlefields of the Civil War: The Definitive Field Guide Based on the Award-Winning Series by Mastervision* (New York: William Morrow, 1997),171. Sherman's use of "Kulp House" has not been changed here; however, it was Kolb House, a farm and home owned by the widow of Valentine Kolb.

[53] Thus, Hooker believed himself superior to every general in the Western theater, including Sherman. See Ulysses S. Grant, *Personal Memoirs of U. S. Grant*, ed. E. B. Long (1885-86 in 2 vols.; Cleveland: World, 1952), 581-82.

General George H. Thomas was the antithesis of Hooker—honest, loyal, courageous, and modest. During the bloody three-day battle at Chickamauga in 1863, General Rosecrans ordered retreat and fled with other officers, leaving Thomas the only officer with rank above division commander. He gathered his remaining troops, and chose the site to position them, placing himself where he could see and command—and fight. An aide sent to give information about his position asked where he would find him when he returned, and General Thomas shouted "Here!" He and his troops remained to protect retreating soldiers and the wounded, staving off repeated Confederate attacks and preventing a Union rout. Thereafter he was known as "The Rock of Chickamauga." Thomas was recommended to replace Rosecrans; the appointment was offered to him personally by an aide to President Lincoln. Thomas, though greatly moved, declined, saying, "I should have long since liked to have an independent command, but I would not like to be exposed to the imputation of having intrigued to supplant my previous commander."[54] He was made General of the Army of the Cumberland, which he led throughout the Atlanta campaign, after which he was chosen by Sherman to follow John Bell Hood, with General Schofield, into Tennessee, where Hood's army suffered a massive defeat.

28 June 1864. Camp Near Marietta, Georgia

Last night I received your letter of the 19th. Through the Lord's mercy we are still well and there are no dead or wounded in our group. We have not been in a general engagement as yet but thousands of bullets whistle about our heads. Yesterday there again was heavy skirmishing and farther toward the left heavy fighting. It was Hooker and the fourth Corps so I hear, with the Rebs advancing three and four lines deep. Our skirmishers withdrew and allowed them to come real close before they let loose with the cannon. Then they fired them all at once and shattered their lines. The fourth Corps then attacked five lines deep, supported by two other Corps and drove them back a mile. Yesterday saw action along the whole line. Sherman seems to wish to proceed slowly and carefully in order to save his troops which is a good thing. The Rebs cannot break our lines anywhere—they try it here and there but it is as if they are bumping against a stone wall. This is a hard campaign—hard work and little sleep. We have fortified the

[54] Otto Eisenschiml and Ralph Newman, *The Civil War: An American Iliad* (New York: Mallard, 1991), 531.

entire area and at night we advance the line of battle to the skirmish line.[55] *Naturally we go very quietly and then construct our rifle pits so that in the morning we are strong enough to withstand the Johnnies attack. Then the cannon get busy and soon there is plenty of trouble for the Rebs. How they can hold out is beyond my comprehension nor do I know how things are going inside their ranks. They do not seem to dare to fire their cannon while ours don't seem to care how much ammunition they use. That is to say that if the Rebs fire one cannon, ours will answer with twenty-five shells and then they are silenced. And if one of their skirmishers fires a shot they are answered with twenty of ours. If the citizens of Holland were to visit us now they would feel rather strange I am sure, as the bullets make such sweet music. I suppose it isn't right to make fun of it but sometimes I must laugh. I believe you would too. The captain's and the colonel's cooks are always in the rear and when they come with food you should see the boys scramble. One thing is sure, if you have been under fire in a real battle, you would rather not go back in again right away. Some of our boys had become a little timid after Resaca but that is now past. The soldiers who are now at the front have the right stuff—the cowards use all kinds of excuses to avoid battle and for that reason the good soldier has little chance. Our armies are full of pretenders and they are the heroes and blowhards. Well, enough of that. Yesterday about six of our regiment were wounded. The fact is the Rebs are strong here—the saying goes that this is one of their strongest units. We are going to besiege them. It is very hot and we have had lots of rain this month. They say it is caused by all the shooting.*

3 July 1864. Camp Near Kenesaw[56] Mountain Georgia

P.S. I write as often as I can but am very busy. Have Mother send me some carrystraps, good strong ones, and a pair of socks. I appreciate the book. I haven't received paper and envelopes as yet. Next pay day I will settle with you. Although I may annoy you, I think a little money is always good

55 Sentence retranslated by the editor.

56 *Kennesaw* is the modern spelling, but *Kenesaw* was the contemporary form and both Ben and Sherman used this spelling. Baseball's first commissioner was Judge Kenesaw Mountain Landis, named for the battle in which his father fought for the Union. A painting done in 1891, titled "Battle of Kenesaw Mountain," is shown in Harold Holzer and Mark E. Neely Jr., *Mine Eyes Have Seen the Glory: The Civil War in Art* (N.Y.: Orion, 1993), 131.

for a soldier to have with him. One never knows when it will be needed. Cannonading is keeping up steadily. The rumor is that the Rebs have left Kenesaw mountain. Our last breastworks we built are extra strong. Latest news—The Stars and Stripes are waving over Kenesaw Mountain.

The Battle of Kennesaw Mountain was fought on 27 June; it was a Confederate victory and Union losses were high. But it is indicative of the pattern of the Atlanta campaign that Ben's 3 July postscript is also correct. On 3 July, the United States flag flew over the battle site.

12 July 1864. Camp in the field Near the Chattahoochee river

Since we are not fighting I want to take this opportunity to write a letter. We are lying on a ridge about two miles from the river and have fortified our position strongly. We have chopped down the woods in front of us so that we have a good view. There are no Rebs here to bother us and it is quite a change to be able to stick our heads above our breastworks rather than keeping them down or, if we build a fire, to have our coffee pots shot off them. We can go about our tasks as if there wasn't a Rebel near. It always gives me great pleasure when I notice how afraid the Rebs are of us and our bullets. We notice this particularly when we examine their breastworks. The officers dug holes behind the breastworks and there the old boys sought shelter. We can also see the places where our shells landed and plowed up the ground. Our men know how to place their batteries so the enemy positions come under cross fire of which they are very afraid. Sometimes we see tunnels which they have dug out like a bunch of rabbits. We usually wait to begin our shelling until we have built our breastworks but sometimes the Rebs open up with a couple of shells. Then our boys raise the bet immediately and let go with about twenty-five shells which soon ends matters for the Rebs. Our boys enjoy this—quite a different life than at home on the 4th of July. Yesterday, the Fourth Corps was crossing. It is under the command of Gen. Howard who has only one arm. In front of us is another high ridge but not as high as the one we are on so our cannon have command of it. . . . I have sometimes thought it strange that we don't establish a position on this ridge with fortifications but Gen. Sherman undoubtedly has good reasons for not doing so. He is in favor of sparing his troops and does much of his fighting by flanking movements and then fortifying positions. While it is true that we are going slowly, still we have made more than a mile a day in this campaign, with breastwork after breastwork to be taken from the Rebs. If they had not had the entire route fortified we would long ago have destroyed Johnston's[57] *army. But we cannot go too fast—our rear must be kept open also. They use Negroes to fortify their rear—last week we captured at least 800 of them. We now and then hear a little cannonading to the right of us.*

14 July 1864. Camp 25th Mich. Near the Chattahoochee River, Ga.

Last evening I received your letter of the 2nd with joy. Just at that time we were also overjoyed to have Lieut. Kramer drop in and feeling fine. It was just nine months ago that he left. The boys were all eager for news. He told me that you were looking very well again which made me happy. The boys then wanted to know how things were in the colony and he said that it had grown tremendously—we would hardly know the place any more. But in the same breath he said that the place teemed with copperheads. I am sorry to hear it. Kramer was surprised to see the high morale existing in the army. He said the Copperhead newspapers told such lies and printed such favorable Rebel news to bring fear into the hearts of the people, but I think the shoe is beginning to pinch because they are afraid of their businesses and of the Army. Well, one thing is certain—there is no copperheadism in the army—it is true blue. Gen. Sherman's army is the cream of the country and is bound to crush the rebellion. It doesn't make any difference under what circumstances all that bad news is published in the Northern papers. It is nothing but favoring the Rebs and a pack of lies. The Rebels have not once had the advantage in this campaign but rather the contrary. Sometimes we have had heavy losses but that has been exaggerated in the Northern papers. Our soldiers are not discouraged because of it or sad about it. On the contrary, they feel they will make it up next time. Such is the Army—the good soldiers who are truly fighting for the cause are found in the front lines and the slackers and good-for-nothings are found in the rear. Then there are those cowards who get their discharge and have so many complaints to make that everyone gets scared. With few exceptions they favor the copperheads. For that reason I am sorry that the North believes them because it isn't very pleasant for us, besides encouraging the Rebs. Much of the Rebellion has been licked and one thing is certain—they do not fight with the courage of our soldiers. They fight in despair and they can see with

[57] Ben Van Raalte's spelling: *Jhonson*.

their own eyes that many soldiers are deserting and that from their best troops. Besides nearly all of their men are under arms, at least all that can carry a gun. Their strength is diminishing and ours is getting stronger daily. All the losses which they suffer cannot be replaced. I have seen bodies through this campaign who choked to death on the matter of the Southern Confederacy. While they may be people, they are rebels and remain rebels and they must be exterminated even if it is to the last man. One can notice they are a little touched because they fear the old Starry Flag.

We went forward about two miles today. Our Corps is on the extreme left joining the fourth Corps under command of Gen. Howard, the one-armed general. We are all well and have again erected strong fortifications. We have fortified all of Georgia, thus a pleasant prospect for the Rebs. It is terribly hot here and Kramer said that Michigan didn't know what heat was. He feels like a new recruit but will soon get used to it.

P.S. We get few letters from home but I think I have most of yours at the present time. There are 23 men in our company, some on other duties. D. Van Raalte, hospital attendant; two Bloms are cooks, one for a captain and one Reg. Hdqrs. cook; P. De Vries and K. Dykhuis, stretcher bearers to carry the wounded;[58] *Wilterdink, regimental butcher; H. TerSligter, Brig Provo. Guard; two musicians. Total present: 33 men and two commissioned officers.*

If I need anything I will write for it. Mother must not send me anything unless I ask for it. Remember we carry our clothes closet on our backs. Mother may send me a pair of carrying straps.

Ben was often critical of newspapers ("the Copperhead newspapers told such lies and printed such favorable Rebel news to bring fear into the hearts of the people")—another matter on which he and General Sherman agreed. Newspapers eagerly sought war news, and were not above slanting or falsifying the facts. Moreover, accurate information could alert the opposing side to what was being planned. This is the last topic General Sherman addressed in his memoirs:

> Newspaper correspondents with an army, as a rule, are mischievous. They are the world's gossips, pick up and retail the camp scandal, and gradually drift to the headquarters of some general, who finds is easier to make reputation at home than with

[58] Clause retranslated by the editor.

his own corps or division. They are also tempted to prophesy events and state facts which, to an enemy, reveal a purpose in time to guard against it. Moreover, they are always bound to see facts colored by the partisan or political characters of their own patrons, and thus bring army officers into the political controversies. . . . Yet, so greedy are the people at large for war news, that it is doubtful whether any army commander can exclude all reporters. . . . Time and moderation must bring a just solution to this modern difficulty.[59]

In his next letter, dated 21 July 1864, Ben writes, "They say Johnston is being relieved and Hood is replacing him." The rumor was accurate; the change in command had already happened. Confederate President Jefferson Davis, who disliked General Johnston, removed him from command on 17 July, stating in a brief dispatch that Johnston had failed to arrest the advance of the enemy and that he had no confidence that Johnston could defeat or repel Sherman. Johnston replied: "I assert that Sherman's army is much stronger, compared with that of Tennessee, than Grant's compared with that of northern Virginia. Yet the enemy has been compelled to advance much more slowly to the vicinity of Atlanta than to that of Richmond and Petersburg, and penetrated much deeper into Virginia than into Georgia."[60]

21 July 1864. Camp 25th Mich. Near Atlanta, Ga.

We have had skirmishes with the Johnnies the last few days and have driven them back. The 19th we took Decatur—there was no defense but cavalry and they left in a hurry leaving everything behind. Yesterday we chased the Rebs all day and took many prisoners. We are now about two miles from Atlanta—we can see the city well by climbing trees but that is dangerous with so many bullets flying through the air. Some time during the night we dug rifle pits. The Rebs have their rifle pits four or five hundred paces away. Yesterday Shields shelled them severely but they made no reply. Yesterday I enjoyed the fighting—the Rebs running from the Yanks—sometimes they start running when we start yelling. Yesterday we acted as support for the battery. The ground is sandy here but heavily wooded. It looks like the road to Grand Haven. At noon of the 18th we were at

59 Sherman, *Memoirs*, vol. 2, 408-9.
60 Eisenschiml and Newman, *Civil War*, 618-20.

Crosskeys—from there we came here by way of Peachroad. Gen. Sherman held his own yesterday—he came frequently to have a look. McPherson started moving this morning also. Atlanta will soon be ours. The Rebs say they are fighting for the whiskey their officers get. They laugh about it and say they are whipped but some are still fighting because of vindictiveness. I do not have much time to write at present. We are doing good business nowadays. The Union is getting stronger—poor Rebs—they get no rest. They say Johnston is being relieved and Hood is replacing him. Forgive my poor writing—I have no desire for it.

The day after Ben wrote this letter, General James McPherson was killed, and Sherman was desolated. On 22 July, the two were conferring at Sherman's headquarters, when gunfire erupted. McPherson mounted and sped towards his troops. He found the Sixteenth Corps struggling against a fierce assault; after giving orders to its commander, he rode further along the line. Confederate skirmishers, hidden in a stand of woods, called on him to halt, but he wheeled his horse and made a quick dash to his right. Shots were fired; McPherson staggered in the saddle for a short distance and then fell. In his official report of the death of McPherson, Sherman wrote, "The country generally will realize that we have lost not only an able military leader, but a man who had he survived, was qualified to heal the national strife which has been raised by designing and ambitious men."[61]

26 July 1864. Camp 25th Mich. Near Atlanta, Ga.

We are directly in front of the city and the Rebs have very strong fortifications. Yesterday we went ahead about a mile but the fighting was very heavy—the Rebs made terrific charges and the amount of firing was deafening. They made three charges and in one of them Gen. McPherson was killed which is a heavy loss. The Rebs drove us back and took some of our cannon and many prisoners. Soon after that we were reinforced by another group of our Corps and others and we made a charge, recapturing all the cannon and the prisoners which they had taken from us besides taking two thousand of them prisoner. The dead and wounded all fell into our hands. I do not think Gen. Hood gained anything yesterday with his charges. They also made a charge against Gen. Hooker and suffered very

[61] Sherman, *Memoirs*, vol. 2, 75-78; Eisenschiml and Newman, *Civil War*, 620-22.

heavy losses. There was activity all along the line yesterday and I guess they wanted to try us out. We could see them forming but I guess they didn't dare to risk it. This morning a deserter came to us and told us that they had received orders three times to charge but the officers could not agree. When they did come to an agreement the privates didn't dare to or didn't want to charge. Cannonading was heavy yesterday—we shelled the city and the fortifications but they shelled us heavily also. We had to build our breastworks under heavy fire, shell fragments flying about our ears. We have to play woodchuck nowadays. I will become an expert shovel handler here. Yesterday morning Rinke De Vries was wounded lightly by a shell fragment. It didn't draw blood but became very swollen but in a day or two he should be back on duty again. We have made our fortifications extra strong as the Rebs have very heavy artillery. I am expecting very heavy shelling as we lie directly in front of a Reb fort but we can also dump so many shells on them that it will be a joy to behold. Maybe they will get tired of it but they may also throw over some "camp-kettles." That's what the boys call those big shells. The story is that we took five thousand prisoners to Marietta this morning. Also that Gen Hardee[62] was wounded and taken to the sixteenth Corps hospital. That is good news but maybe it isn't true. There is so much talk floating around. Now I must finish, hoping that we may be spared and that Atlanta may soon be in our possession.

P.S. We get very few letters—why, I don't know. Lieut. Kramer sends his regards. Yesterday we captured seven stands of collers.[63] The Johnnies must be vanquished. Our boys are in good spirits. My headquarters is at present in the rifle pits, in case the Rebs start shelling.

62 Ben Van Raalte's spelling: *Hardie*. Sherman also used that spelling in his memoirs.

63 Ben's spelling for *colors*. According to John Schmale, "The US Army Regulations called for each regiment to have 'two silken colors. The first, or the national color, of stars and stripe; the name and number of the regiment to be embroidered with silver on the centre strip. The second, or regimental color, to be blue, with the arms of the United States embroidered in silk on the centre. The name of the regiment in a scroll, underneath the eagle. The size of each color to be six feet six inches fly, and six feet deep on the pike. The length of the pike, including the spear and ferrule, to be nine feet ten inches. The fringe yellow; cords and tassels, blue and white silk intermixed.' It was a great honor to be the color bearer but in battle the mortality rate for color bearers was quite high since the goal of the opposing force was to shoot the color bearer and seize the enemies' colors" (quoted in <http://www.illinoiscivilwar.org/cwflags.html>, accessed 14 February 2007).

28 July 1864. Camp 25th Mich., Near Atlanta, Georgia

Dear Mother,

Through the Lord's mercy we are still in good health. During the past days we have been busy all of the time building fortifications. Day before yesterday our lines were changed completely. Three Corps which had been on the left flank were transferred to the right flank, presumably to cut off the railroad. The cavalry is also out on another expedition but on the whole we are not informed of the various movements. The Rebels are very quiet this morning, so much so that some thought they had left the front but that wasn't the case. I sometimes think they remain quiet to tempt us and then, if we attacked, to make another Resaca of it. But we are too smart to fall into such a trap. We advanced our skirmish line and then it proved they were still there and they began answering our artillery fire. Yesterday we saw them forming a column when our right flank was marching. We could see them plainly with the naked eye. We threw some bombs in their ranks. The Rebs have very strong fortifications here with rows of sharpened sticks in front of them. Occasionally we shoot some holes in them with our cannon but then they are right out with their shovels to fix them up. We couldn't accomplish anything by charging their fortifications and I think Gen. Sherman will work out their capture by various flanking movements.... Our works are now so strong that the Rebels are welcome to come and try to take them. They were laid out by the engineers and are so constructed that we can open with cross fire. We also have sharpened spikes and layers of brush in front of them so that it is impossible for a man to penetrate. We haven't used our heavy cannon yet. The Rebels don't do much firing with their heavy artillery, why I do not know. I guess they are gaining respect for the Yankees—respect for our cannon they already have. They are not stingy with their light artillery and, because of the large numbers of our men, some are bound to become wounded even if they are shooting wild. However, we do the same thing as busily as we can.

P.S. Rinke De Vries is recovering nicely. I was just getting ready to seal my letter but the Rebels wouldn't let me. They suddenly opened up with the cannon in the fort so that all was bedlam for a little while. But our artillery soon silenced them. While it lasted the shell fragments were singing around our ears. The Rebs did very little damage—the tents were knocked down and one man lost a leg.

30 July 1864. In the field in front of Atlanta, Georgia

Dear Sister:[64]

A few days ago I received your kind letter and was glad to hear that you was in good health and to hear what good times you have had at the wedding. That must have been quite a good time indeed. Well, we have such good success in this Army that we often feal as much rejoiced as we should be at a wedding. The Rebels have had such heavy losses in front of Atlanta that it is awful. They fight most desperate, make charge after charge and repulsed time after time and still they keep on. Gen Hood seems to be great for charging—it is great foolishness to try to take strong works by storm for any general. We had satisfaction of that at Resaca—the party behind the works has all the advantage and if they stand firm the works cannot be taken. The Rebs have had a loss of least twenty thousand since the twenty-second. . . . We have taken a large number of prisoners and every charge they make the dead and wounded has fallen into our hands. Our losses have been but small as our fighting has been mostly behind the works. I hope that Gen. Hood will stay in command, then the Southern Confederacy will soon play out. I often wonder how it is that the Rebs don't charge our Corps—it must be that our works are too strong. We have never had the luck to fight behind the works but have had to take it in the open field. Our Corps is now the extreme left. Gen. Howard has taken the old command of Gen. McPherson and has had great success. He is our one-armed general, a splendid looking man—I think the best looking on the job. Gen. Sherman looks like an old broken-down farmer but a sharper. I have had the pleasure to see most all our generals in this Army. In this campaign there has been heavy fighting on our right. This afternoon we have not yet heard the results but the report is that we took a large number of prisoners. We are getting so closely on them that they are very uneasy. Our boys do not give them rest night nor day. Our boys throw shells night and day and once and a while they reply with a hundred pounder or such a matter. A day or two ago they opened all their guns on us. I tell you that they made us lay low and struck a few tents for the boys. It was fun to hear our guns

[64] Ben's letter was written in English to his younger sister Christine. The author is using the transcription made by Clarence Jalving, translator of the other letters. *Ed.*

open. They gained the day and the Johnnies had to knock under. . . . The boys are in good health and good spirits. The brass bands play every night to spite the Rebs.

1 Aug. 1864. Camp 25th Mich., In front of Atlanta, Ga.

At the moment everything is quiet except for skirmishing—that always goes on. Early this morning there was heavy musketry at the right. Bombarding continues steadily first here and then somewhere else but the heavy fighting has, up to the present, been on the right wing except for the 22nd*. Gen. McPherson's* [former] *command is on the left—that was on the Decatur Railroad. But now our wing has been shifted and our Corps is now on the extreme left but nevertheless our pickets hold the railroad. At present there is no more than one strong skirmish line in the old breastworks of McPherson. But our plan is not to fight them there in case they attack but to fall back to the fortifications where we will have a cross fire. They won't be able to drive us out of there. The Rebs sometimes resort to false alarms, making a pretense of coming at us with a lot of yelling but then do not come. The Reb. casualties have been heavy in front of Atlanta. A few days ago a lieutenant surrendered and he told us that he couldn't stand the slaughter any more and that Gen. Hood could stand only two more killings. Gen. Howard experienced one of the killings so that leaves only one. Our boys had to laugh to hear the lieutenant talk.*[65] *Up to this time our losses have not been heavy.*

Yesterday evening I received your letter of the 20th*. The calling up of 500,000 suits me fine. I have no sympathy for those at home who are being drafted. In Holland they appear to be very scared. Doesburg is putting the fear of death into the hearts of the ignorant masses. They should burn his printing office—he speaks as if everyone who signs up is going to die. It is enough to put the death fear into anyone who has never seen a war. I am not surprised that the young people are running away. He is no better than a Rebel—his writings are shameful for our Holland people. I saw an article in the paper that he was making an estimate of the number of soldiers Lincoln had had in the service and how many survivors there were. It was such a large figure I hardly dare mention it. The way he figured*

[65] Jacobson et al., *Albertus C. Van Raalte*, 130. The "killings" were losses of limbs through amputations or immobilizing wounds. Officers who rode horses in battle could continue to fight strapped into the saddle with one arm and one leg on opposite sides of the body.

Lincoln had, through his stupidity, doomed all these men to eternity. But he overlooked the thousands of deserters and those who died of illness. Also those who bought their way out. I can name a couple for him—his own sons, the one a deserter and the other purchasing a substitute. Just a coward.

Colonel Cooper of the sixth Tennessee is now Brigadier General. The first Brigade had earned a rest. We were continually at the front so we got little rest. But now I think things will get better since he has received his star—he has earned it. He was the first captain of Co. A of the sixth Tennessee to elude capture by the Rebs. There are no better troops. He looks like a Drenthe farmer.

P.S. The sharpshooters still manage to put some bullets through our tents. The packages you sent arrived in good shape.

Promotion was due to Cooper's excellence, but General Sherman's hot temper speeded the process. The account is given in his *Memoirs*. On 24 July, he was informed by dispatch that two men formerly under his command had been promoted. "Both of them had gone to the rear— [one] by reason of sickness and [the other] dissatisfied with General Schofield and myself. I answered on the 25th, closing with this language: 'If the rear be the post of honor, then we had better all change front on Washington.'" He received an immediate reply from President Lincoln himself—the promotions had been made based on commendations, including his own, sent many months earlier. On 28 July, a dispatch directed him to nominate eight colonels for promotion as brigadier generals. "I at once sent a circular note to the army-commanders to nominate officers and on the 29th I telegraphed the names. . . . These were promptly appointed brigadier generals, [and] were already in command of brigades or divisions; and I doubt if eight promotions were ever made fairer, or were more honestly earned, during the whole war."[66]

7 Aug. 1864. In the field in front of Atlanta, Ga.

Yesterday I wrote you that we were being relieved by the 14th A.C. [Army Corps] *and we were moved to the extreme right. There was heavy fighting there. I had remained behind to assist in making up the payroll but joined the group in time to take part in the fighting. In the forenoon the third division had engaged in heavy fighting. We marched slowly to the*

66 Sherman, *Memoirs*, vol. 2, 94-95.

right and about half past three we received orders to put our knapsacks in a pile, each company a pile. At that time a battery was shelling us but did no damage as the distance was too great. We soon got the news—our brigade had to make a charge and attempt to capture the battery. Well, when we had formed our lines the order rang out "Go for them, boys." For about half an hour the fighting was heavy and bloody and we did not succeed in capturing the battery although we did drive the Rebs back about a mile and a half. I do not know what the losses were in the regiment but our company lost three: Alexander Jonkheer, fatally wounded; Cornelius Den Herder, lightly wounded and Darwin C. Huff received a flesh wound. Through God's mercy, the rest of us came through and were spared but we feel deep sympathy for our boys. The Rebs had a great advantage over us yesterday but their breastworks were not too strong and that helped a lot. We had no support on our right and so had to fall back a little way. If we had had one more brigade we would have been able to capture Armstrong's cavalry. I just heard that the losses in our regiment were twelve wounded and two dead. I must close now because we just received orders to pack up. The Rebs have fallen back somewhat. We are otherwise in good health.

13 Aug. 1864. Near Atlanta Ga.

I am happy to be able to write and to announce that I am still in good health. It is now the third day that we have lain in our breastworks and we have had a very good rest. Yesterday our third Division was out on our flank in order to give the cavalry a good position. Compared to some we have had, this is a quiet place with not much doing on the front. Last night the Rebs tried to annoy us by shelling the camp but didn't do any damage. The shells whistled through the camp and it isn't very pleasant to be teased this way at night. But we usually pay them back with some of our best shells. Our Corps has suffered much in this sector and another change has been made in our brigade or division. The brigade was becoming so small that they took the fourth brigade and divided it among the other three. There was some talk that Colonel Moore would be restored to his old command of our group—that would suit us fine. Gen. Cooper is slated to go back to Knoxville to become provost marshal and Colonel Swayne[67] is to command our brigade.

[67] Ben Van Raalte's spelling: *Swane.*

I think the people in Holland are getting sharp and doing everything they can to stay out of the draft. That was a smart move to draw lots ahead of time so if they were drawn they could still go as volunteers. I wish they were in the field now although new recruits are of very little value. There are usually four recruits on the sick list against one old soldier. Still everything helps and another 500,000 men could make a big difference.

I am sorry that Grant's campaign has not been as successful as we had hoped. Sherman seems to be taking his time. I hear that heavy cannon are arriving daily by train. There is heavy cannonading on the left as far as we can hear. We built a flank to our breastworks as the Rebs seemed to have us in a cross fire this morning. I don't know how it happened but it sometimes occurs on the flanks. Sometimes the breastworks run very crooked because of the lay of the land. They must always be built on the highest elevations. Georgia is becoming a country of breastworks as each army fortifies itself. The farmers will have quite a job to level them all. It seems as if the Rebs have received reinforcements because their lines are nearly as long as ours. Only on the flank not much is to be seen besides cavalry.

Now I must close. It is still very hot and we are having lots of rain. Everything in our path is being destroyed. The boys tear down the houses to construct breastworks. So it goes with everything. It is so dark I can hardly see any more. Our company is quite well at present.

14 Aug. 1864. In front of Atlanta, Ga.

Since we were paid today I will write a letter and enclose some money. Most of the boys send theirs by Adams Express but, since they do not guarantee it anyway, I would just as soon take the risk of sending it in a regular letter. To put the amount down on the company list doesn't suit me either because if you do that the whole colony will know what you sent and it is none of their business. They are in a hurry with paying off because they worked all night at it. It is very hot today and now it has started to rain. I heard that a whole brigade of Rebs had surrendered voluntarily. That would be wonderful if they continue to surrender voluntarily. I do not have much news to tell you. We receive very few newspapers and hear very little news. We can't see very far here—it is mostly woods.

I cannot understand why letters are so slow reaching us. It seems our letters go out all right but those coming in not so good. There is still cannonading at the front on the left and now and then a single shot in our sector. If our citizens could pay a visit to the front it would look quite different from what they had imagined. It seems as if they are chopping along the entire line night and day. We don't hear it but anyone not used to it would be very surprised to hear bullets whistling past his head. It has now been since the 7th of May that we have heard shooting every day with bullets whistling past our ears. When one thinks about it then it is surprising that anyone should still be alive with so much lead flying about.

The company is in reasonably good condition. No serious illnesses—some a little ill but going out again. R. De Vries is beginning to assume duty again and the company is pretty well sifted. The few who had buck fever keep hanging around the hospitals and doing some work there to stay away from the bullets. By reason of the changes made in the brigade the Provost Guards were sent to their regiments and so Ter Sligte again joined our company. He has had it pretty soft until now and hasn't heard any lead fly. He has always been at headquarters in the rear. Capt. De Boe doesn't seem to improve very rapidly.

[Encl.] $40.00

Two items in this letter deserve explanation, though "buck fever" may be familiar to those who hunt and recall some trepidation before their first shot. In the second chapter of his autobiography, Theodore Roosevelt gives a definition: "Buck fever means a state of intense nervous excitement which may be entirely divorced from timidity. It may affect a man the first time he has to speak to a large audience just as it affects him the first time he sees a buck [deer] or goes into battle. What such a man needs is not courage but nerve control, cool-headedness. This he can get only by actual practice."[68]

The Adams Express Company, established in 1841, split into two companies–Adams Express and Southern Express–during the Civil War, with Adams Express separated into three divisions in order to provide mail service for the army. Probably the most important service the company provided was the delivery and receipt of mail to and from the soldiers in the field. In addition, the company carried money and sent packages; packages sent to soldiers were carried at half price. On

[68] Theodore Roosevelt, *Theodore Roosevelt: An Autobiography* (New York: Macmillan, 1913), see especially chapter 2, "The Vigor of Life." The book can be viewed in its entirety on <www.bartleby.com>, accessed 18 Sept. 2006.

paydays many men would send part, or all, of their pay home to support their families.[69]

16 Aug. 1864. Near Atlanta, Ga.

Loving Mother:

I am happy to enjoy good health and able to write you a letter. We have orders to be ready to move, possibly a change of position again. It is very warm. Yesterday I had the pleasure of receiving two letters from home, one from Christine and one from Father. As a rule we receive few letters lately. One would think that the Rebs were in our rear. . . . Now I must close as I have to pack. We have orders to be ready. I am sending $12.00 in this letter for the clothing which you sent.

24 Aug. 1864. In front of Atlanta, Ga.

Last night I received your letter of the 13th and was happy to learn that you were all well with the exception of Mina's child. I am sorry about Mina's child. Through God's blessing we are all well. It is very hot but we can stand it just as well as we could in Michigan. The Rebels seem to be fidgety today and are doing a lot of shelling without doing any damage. Our men just ignore it and let them go ahead. We'll catch up later. Otherwise it has been very quiet the last few days. We hear that A. J. Smith has arrived here with 30,000 reinforcements and that can change the program a lot. There is also a rumor that our Corps is to go out on a raid tomorrow. It wouldn't surprise me that, if these reinforcements have arrived, a flanking movement will be attempted. We have always been Sherman's flanking machine. It is also said that Sherman is in Washington. It looks to me that there is something in the wind because of the preparations which are being made. I do not believe that Atlanta can be taken by storm. Cutting off communications could make them very uneasy. They have a large army here and although the railroads have been torn up they can repair them. A couple of good lines of breastworks over the roads would change matters. If the reinforcements have come this is likely to happen soon because such a large army needs a tremendous amount of supplies. We know that from our own experience. If you could see the rations used by our army in ten

[69] Marshall J. Pixley, "The Adams Express Company" on <www.floridareenactorsonline.com/history2.htm>, accessed 18 Sept. 2006.

days it would look like such a mountain you would think it never could all be used. I imagine you did not get much of our mail while the railroad was broken up and our communications were cut off. Possibly what I sent has fallen into the wrong hands but that can't be helped. There is so much that falls into wrong hands that this little bit won't make much difference. You should see what goes on in the Army. The officers know how to use the expense account to their advantage.

. . . It does my heart good that Co. I is so down on the copperheads in the colony. They say that if they could re-enlist it would never be for Holland—they would represent Kentucky. Now those at home are doing all in their power to stay there and have been around to collect money from parents who have all their children in the war. They are too old to be in the service themselves but collect money in order to buy substitutes for those who would have to go. . . . Nice people. They can buy substitutes and let others pay the bill, or have it put on the taxes. If I may give advice, never give anyone any money in order to stay home. It would be better to perish. I must close now. Capt. De Boe sends his greetings. He feels fine and the talk of his resigning was never true.

"I am sorry about Mina's child," Ben wrote. His older sister, Johanna Maria Wilhelmina (Mina), married the Rev. Pieter Oggel in 1860, and their daughter Christina Johanna Oggel was two years old in the summer of 1864. On 19 August, five days before Ben received his father's letter, she died.[70]

There would be other bad news for the Van Raalte family. 26 August 1864 was, or seemed to be, a quiet day. Dirk Van Raalte and Cornelis Bouman, who worked at the regimental hospital, were able to ride out for pleasure. Surprised by Confederate soldiers, Bouman was captured and sent to the dreaded Andersonville prison.[71] Dirk spurred

70 Elton J. Bruins, Karen G. Schakel, Sara Frederickson Simmons, and Marie N. Zingle, *Albertus and Christina: The Van Raalte Family, Home and Roots* (Grand Rapids: Eerdmans, 2004), 100-2, 105.

71 John L. Ransom, *John Ransom's Andersonville Diary* (New York: Berkley, 1994); MacKinlay Kantor, *Andersonville* (New York: World, 1955). See also Mark Mayo Boatner III, *The Civil War Dictionary* (New York: David McKay, 1959), for a description of the prison (quoted in Jacobson et al., *Albertus C. Van Raalte*, 133). Cornelis Bouman was released, along with other Union prisoners, by the Confederates when Sherman's troops were approaching Andersonville: a comrade wrote that he was in terrible shape, his clothes were in tatters, and he was filthy (Johannes Van Lente to his family, 3

his horse forward, and the Confederates shot and wounded him. With his right arm shattered he outrode pursuit and reached safety. Ben was allowed to go to him immediately, and accompanied him to the hospital. Dirk's arm was amputated at the shoulder, and Ben stayed with him and cared for him. In a joint letter from the Twenty-third A.C. Hospital in Marietta, Georgia, Dirk began by writing reassuringly to his parents: "I write with my left hand and Benjamin holds the paper smooth. You must not worry about me." In his part of the letter, Ben wrote: "They say that Atlanta has fallen and I am sorry I was not there. I have been everywhere throughout the whole campaign but Dirk's needs come first."[72]

On 1 September 1864, Confederate troops left Atlanta, leaving its citizens behind, and the next day Sherman's troops marched in. The corps led by General Henry Slocum was the first to enter. Sherman telegraphed President Lincoln, "Atlanta is ours, and fairly won." Sherman then sent a message to Hood, requesting a ten-day truce to enable him to arrange for evacuation of civilians. "Situated in the heart of the enemy's country, and valuable only as a base of further operations," Duyckinck wrote, "[Sherman] could not consent that [Atlanta] should be occupied by a doubtful or disaffected population, composed largely of families many of whose members were in the rebel service. . . . He accordingly announced to General Hood his intention of removing the remaining inhabitants, offering to them the choice of going North or South, and to give them the opportunity of doing so, proposed a cessation of hostilities for ten days. Servants or negro slaves were to be allowed, if they wish to do so, to accompany their masters or mistresses; otherwise to be sent away or employed by the quartermaster."[73]

General Hood protested "in the name of the God of humanity against the expulsion of the people of Atlanta from their firesides," and accused Sherman of "transcending the studied and ungenerous cruelty of acts ever before brought to the attention of mankind, even in the

March 1865, in Janice Van Lente Catlin, *The Civil War Letters of Johannes Van Lente* [Okemos, Mich.: Yankee Girl Publications, 1992]). Ben later wrote: "Bouman has had a hard time of it. He wouldn't have lasted another week as prisoner of the Rebels but it seems he is going to make it" (Ben Van Raalte to Albertus C. Van Raalte, 2 May 1865, Holland Museum Archives).

[72] Dirk and Ben Van Raalte to Albertus C. Van Raalte, Marietta, Ga., 30 August 1864, Holland Museum Archives.

[73] Duyckinck, *History of the* War, vol. 3, 403-4.

darkest history of war."[74] Sherman, as vigorous with words as in action, replied:

> General J. B. Hood,
> Commanding Army of the Tennessee Confederate Army
>
> General—I have the honor to acknowledge the receipt of your letter of this date at the hands of Messrs. Ball and Crew, consenting to the arrangements I had proposed to facilitate the removal South of the people of Atlanta who propose to go in that direction. I enclose you a copy of my orders, which will, I am satisfied, accomplish my purpose perfectly. You style the measures proposed "unprecedented" and appeal to the dark history of war for a parallel as an act of "studied and ungenerous cruelty." It is not unprecedented, for General Johnston himself very wisely and properly removed the families all the way from Dalton down, and I see no reason why Atlanta should be excepted. Nor is it necessary to appeal to the dark history of war when recent and modern examples are so handy. You yourself burned dwelling-houses along your parapet and I have seen today fifty houses that you have rendered uninhabitable because they stood in the way of your forts and men. You defended Atlanta on a line so close to the town that every cannon-shot and many musket shots from our line of investments, that overshot their mark, went into the habitations of women and children. General Hardee did the same at Jonesboro, and General Johnston did the same last summer at Jackson, Miss. I have not accused you of heartless cruelty, but merely instance these causes of very recent occurrence, and could go on and enumerate hundreds of others, and challenge any fair man to judge which of us has the heart of pity for the families of a "brave people." I say it is a kindness to these families of Atlanta to remove them now at once from scenes that women and children should not be exposed to, and the brave people should scorn to commit their wives and children to the rude barbarians who thus, as you say, violate the laws of war, as illustrated in the pages of its dark history.
>
> In the name of common sense, I ask you not to appeal to a just God in such a sacrilegious manner—you, who, in the midst of peace and prosperity, have plunged a nation into war, "dark

[74] Ibid., 404.

> and cruel war," who dared and badgered us to battle, insulted our flag, seized our arsenals and forts that were left in the honorable custody of a peaceful ordnance serjeant, seized and made prisoners of war the very garrisons sent to protect your people against negros and Indians, long before any overt act was committed by the (to you) hateful Lincoln Government, tried to force Kentucky and Missouri into the rebellion in spite of themselves, falsified the vote of Louisiana, turned loose your privateers to plunder unarmed ships, expelled Union families by the thousand, burned their homes, and declared, by act of your Congress the confiscation of all debts due Northern men for goods had and received. Talk thus to the marines,[75] but not to me, who have seen these things, and who will this day make as much sacrifice for the peace and honor of the South, as the best born Southerner among you. If we must be enemies, let us be men, and fight it out as we propose to-day, and not deal in such hypocritical appeals to God and humanity. God will judge us in due time, and he will pronounce whether it be more humane to fight with a town full of women and the families of a "brave people" at our back, or to remove them in time to places of safety among their own friends and people.[76]

Jefferson Davis gave a fiery speech at Macon, proclaiming, "Our cause is not lost! Sherman cannot keep up his long line of communications and retreat. Sooner or later he must fall back, and when that day comes the fate that befell the army of the French Empire on its retreat from Moscow will be re-[en]acted."[77]

By 1864, war weariness was a factor in the presidential election campaign. The capture of Atlanta brought a resurgence to Northern morale, and on 8 November 1864, President Lincoln was resoundingly

[75] Hood would certainly have understood what Sherman meant when he said, "Talk thus to the marines, but not to me." "Tell that to the Marines" is nineteenth-century slang. *Oxford English Dictionary*, s.v. "marines," defines it as "a colloquial expression of incredulity," and cites its use by Lord Byron in "that will do for the [Royal] marines, but the [British] sailors won't believe it" ("The Island," 1823) and by Anthony Trollope in "Is that a story to tell to such a man as me! You may tell it to the marines!" (*The Small House at Allington*, 1864).

[76] Duyckinck, *History of the War*, vol. 3, 404.

[77] Ibid., vol. 3, 483. When he heard this, Grant said, "Where will he get the snow?"

re-elected, receiving 212 of 233 electoral votes, 55 percent of the popular vote, and strong support from the men in the Union forces. On 20 December 1864, Sherman reached Savannah, completing his march to the sea. Abraham Lincoln was inaugurated on 4 March 1865, amid much rejoicing. On 9 April, General Lee surrendered his Confederate army to General Grant. On 11 April, the United States flag was raised again over Fort Sumter. On 14 April, an obsessed egomaniac shot the president. Abraham Lincoln died the following morning without regaining consciousness, and the hope of a generous, calm reconciliation between South and North died with him.

2 May 1865. Raleigh, N.C.

Yesterday I received your letter of the 17th and noted that you are both well and that Dirk had received his discharge. They would have preferred to have him stay with the regiment but all is well now. Bouman[78] *has had a hard time of it. He wouldn't have lasted another week as prisoner of the Rebels but it seems he is going to make it. It is peaceful and quiet here—quite a contrast from last summer and spring. Sherman's army has left for Richmond and there is talk that our division is going to Danville. But nothing is certain. Raleigh is a nice place and businesses are starting up again. . . . The death of the President is heavily mourned—that was a great loss. Col. Moore is again with the Regiment. We have two hours of daily drill. The recruits hit it just right—it's too bad they didn't come earlier—then they could have seen some fighting and now they see nothing.*

On the 19th of May, Sherman received new orders from the War Department.

> I received a copy of War department Special Order ordering a grand review, by the President[79] and cabinet, of all the armies then near Washington; General Meade's to occur on Tuesday, May 23rd, mine on Wednesday, the 24th. By invitation I was on the reviewing-stand, and witnessed the review of the Army of the Potomac commanded by General Meade in person. The day was beautiful, and the pageant was superb. Washington was full of strangers, who filled the streets in holiday-dress, and every house was decorated with flags. The army marched by divisions in close

[78] See Jacobson et al., *Albertus C. Van Raalte,* 132-33.
[79] Andrew Johnson, seventeenth president of the United States.

column around the Capital, down Pennsylvania Avenue, past the President and cabinet, who occupied a large stand prepared for the occasion, directly in front of the White House. I had telegraphed to Lancaster for Mrs. Sherman, who arrived that day, accompanied by her father, the Hon. Thomas Ewing, and my son Tom, then eight years old.

During the afternoon and night of the 23rd, the Fifteenth, Seventeenth, and Twentieth Corps crossed Long Bridge, bivouacked in the streets about the Capital, and the Fourteenth Corps closed up to the bridge. The morning of the 24th was extremely beautiful, and the ground was in splendid order for our review. The streets were filled with people to see the pageant, armed with bouquets of flowers for their favorite regiments or heroes, and every thing was propitious. Punctually at 9 a.m. the signal-gun was fired, when in person, attended by General Howard and all my staff, I rode slowly down Pennsylvania Avenue, the crowds of men, women, and children densely lining the sidewalks, and almost obstructing the way. When I reached the Treasury-building, and looked back, the sight was simply magnificent. The column was compact, and the glittering muskets looked like a solid mass of steel, moving with the regularity of a pendulum. As I neared the brick-house opposite the lower corner of Lafayette Square, someone asked me to notice Mr. Seward, who, still feeble and bandaged from his wounds,[80] had been removed there that he might behold the troops. I moved in that direction and took off my hat to Mr. Seward, who sat at an upper window. He recognized the salute, returned it, and then we rode on steadily past the President, saluting with our swords. All on his stand arose and acknowledged the salute. Then, turning into the gate of the presidential grounds, we left our horses with orderlies, and went upon the stand where I shook hands with the President, General Grant, and [members of the cabinet]. I then took my post on the left of the President, and for six hours and a half stood while the army passed in the order of the Fifteenth, Seventeenth, Twentieth, and Fourteenth Corps. It was, in my judgment, the most magnificent army in existence—sixty-five thousand men,

[80] The assassination of Abraham Lincoln was only part of a plot which was almost as stupid as its results were terrible. Cabinet members were to have been killed as well, and one of the conspirators did break into the home of Secretary of State William Seward and stabbed him as he slept.

> in splendid physique, who had just completed a march of nearly two thousand miles in a hostile country, in good drill, and who realized that they were being closely scrutinized by thousands of their fellow-countrymen and by foreigners. Division after division passed, each commander of an army corps or division coming on the stand during the passage of his command, to be presented to the President, cabinet, and spectators. The steadiness and firmness of the tread, the careful dress on the guides, the uniform intervals between the companies, all eyes directly to the front, and the tattered and bullet-riven flags, festooned with flowers, all attracted universal notice. Many good people, up to that time, had looked upon our Western army as a sort of mob; but the world then saw, and recognized the fact, that it was an army in the proper sense, well organized, well commanded and disciplined, and there was no wonder that it had swept through the South like a tornado.
>
> Some little scenes enlivened the day and called for the laughter and cheers of the crowd. Each division was followed by six ambulances, as a representative of its baggage train. Some of the division commanders had added, by way of variety, goats, milch-cows, and pack-mules, whose loads consisted of game-cocks, poultry, hams, etc., and some of them had the families of freed slaves along, with the women leading their children. Each division was preceded by its corps of black pioneers, armed with picks and spades. These marched abreast in double ranks, keeping perfect dress and step, and added much to the interest of the occasion. On the whole, the grand review was a splendid success, and was a fitting conclusion to the campaign and the war.[81]

After the surrender of the Confederate army, Ben's regiment was mustered out on the 24th of June, and sent north by rail to Jackson, Michigan, where, on 2 July 1865, the regiment disbanded. Of its original 968 soldiers, 22 were killed in action, and 13 died of wounds, 129 died of disease. Benjamin Van Raalte returned to Holland and became a successful farmer and businessman. He married Julia Gilmore, whose brother had earlier married Ben's sister Christine; they had children and grandchildren, and his line continues. He was second commander of the A. C. Van Raalte Post of the Grand Army of the

[81] Sherman, *Memoirs*, vol. 2, 376-78; Grant, *Personal Memoirs*, 579-80.

Republic, succeeding John Wilterdink, and remained active in the GAR throughout his life. Ben died peacefully in his sleep on 14 August 1917, exactly fifty-five years after the date he enlisted to fight for the Union.[82] The Old Starry Flag had regained the lost stars, and more were added as the nation grew westward.

[82] Bruins et al., *Albertus and Christina*, 115; Jacobson et al., *Albertus C. Van Raalte*, 201.

GLOSSARY OF NAMES

Ben's boast to his sister Christine, "I have had the pleasure to see most all our generals in this army," was, uncharacteristically, wildly inaccurate.

John R. Bond enlisted as first lieutenant in the Twentieth Regiment, Ohio Volunteer Infantry, in September 1861, and rose to the rank of colonel, leading the 111th Ohio Volunteer Infantry when it was mustered in September 1862 with 1050 men. References to Bond can be found in the letter of 9 June 1864.

Braxton Bragg, C.S.A[83] (1817-76) graduated from West Point in 1837, fifth in rank in a class of fifty. He joined the Confederacy as a brigadier general and was soon appointed a full general by his friend Jefferson Davis. Bad-tempered and quarrelsome, he was disliked by troops and other officers.

Ambrose Burnside (1824-81) graduated from West Point in 1847, ranking eighteenth in a class of thirty-eight. Militarily, his failures outweighed his successes. As head of the Department of the Ohio, he presided over military trials, including that of John Hunt Morgan.

Joseph Alexander Cooper (1823-1910) was, before the war, a strongly anti-secessionist farmer living in Tennessee. When Tennessee seceded, he secretly gathered other Union supporters who crossed with him into Kentucky, where they were sworn in as the First Tennessee Infantry with Cooper as a captain. Later he was promoted to colonel, and, on 30 July 1864, to brigadier general. See the following letters for references to Cooper: 11 June; 1 and 13 August 1864.

Darius Nash Couch (1822-97) graduated from West Point in 1846, ranking thirteenth in a class of fifty-nine. During the Mexican War he contracted illnesses that pained him all his life, but he nevertheless led his troops in battle when more senior generals retreated and withdrew. He wrote copiously about his experiences, capturing scenes in a few words: "I have seen the dead who die in peace but how different is the stamp of death upon those who die in battle."

[83] Confederate States of America. Persons not designated C.S.A. are from the Union.

Ulysses Simpson Grant (1822-85) graduated from West Point in 1843, ranking twenty-first in a class of thirty-nine. His biography, featured on the website <www.americanhistory.si.edu/ westpoint>, accessed 24 Dec. 2006, does justice to his heroism and goodness. "As a cadet Grant excelled only in horsemanship, but he proved a brave and resourceful junior officer in the Mexican War. In 1848 he and Julia Dent married. They became inseparable and had four children. The oldest, Frederick, was also a West Point graduate (1871). Grant disliked peacetime army service and resigned in 1854, despite few prospects in civilian life. With the Civil War, Grant emerged as one of history's greatest generals. He won the surrender of three enemy armies—at Fort Donelson (1862), Vicksburg (1863), and Appomattox (1865)—a feat accomplished by no other general. No one else so effectively united strategic vision, operational finesse, tactical focus, exemplary leadership, moral courage, and unassuming modesty. Twice elected president, Grant completed his masterly memoirs four days before his death from throat cancer."

Henry Wager Halleck (1815-72) graduated from West Point in 1839, ranking third in a class of thirty-one. From biographies of graduates, we can infer that scholarship was not directly correlated either to fighting ability or uprightness; Halleck ("Old Brains") is the prime example. Given command of all Union forces in the West after victories by his subordinate, U. S. Grant, he led troops only once—to take Corinth, Mississippi—advancing about one mile a day. Corinth was abandoned before he arrived. Halleck's actions toward Grant and Sherman were duplicitous and unconscionable.

William Joseph Hardee, C.S.A. (1815-73) graduated from West Point in 1838, ranking twenty-sixth in a class of forty-five. A career officer, he authored *Rifle and Light Infantry Tactics*, which was used as a text for many years. In 1861, he resigned to join the Confederate Army, where he became known as "Old Reliable." After a fashion, Ben shows respect for him by treating the rumor that he'd been wounded as good news. He served under Bragg, whom he disliked, and then under Joe Johnston, whom he admired. He requested a transfer when Jefferson Davis replaced Johnston with Hood.

Milo Smith Hascall (1829-1904) graduated from West Point in 1852, ranking fourteenth in a class of forty-three. When the Civil War began, Hascall enlisted as a private in a three-month regiment; by the end of the year he was a brigade commander. In the Atlanta Campaign,

General Hascall led the second division of the Twenty-Third Corps. He resigned from the army in October 1864. Letter of 9 June 1864 has a reference to Hascall.

John Bell Hood, C.S.A. (1831-79) graduated from West Point in 1853, ranking forty-fourth in a class of fifty-two, a poor student with disciplinary problems. He resigned from the army to join the Confederacy. By 1864 his right leg had been amputated and his left arm was useless. Jefferson Davis promoted him to full general—the youngest man on either side of the war to be given command of an army. General Lee had advised against this, describing Hood as "all lion and no fox." Mentioned in letters of 26, 30 July and 1 August 1864.

Joseph Hooker (1814-79) graduated from West Point in 1837, ranking twenty-ninth in a class of fifty. Cited in letters of 12, 20, 23, 28 June and 26 July 1864. Biographical information is given after Ben's letter of 23 June.

Oliver Otis Howard (1830-1909) graduated from West Point in 1854, ranking fourth in a class of forty-six. Ben—consistently a good judge of character—admired him. References to Howard can be found in letters of 12, 14, 30 July and 1 August 1864. Like Grant and Sherman, Howard was a good and remarkable man who was, and is even today, savaged as well as celebrated in print. His biography, like theirs, is featured on the website <www.americanhistory.si.edu/westpoint>. "Howard completed four years at Bowdoin College before attending West Point. Unlike many Northern graduates, he stayed in the army. Two years later he married Elizabeth Ann Waite. They had two children. Howard soon returned to West Point to teach mathematics, a tour of duty cut short by war. He rose rapidly to corps command, despite losing his right arm in an 1862 battle. Strong religious, civil rights, and temperance views led to his choice as head of the new Freedmen's Bureau in 1865. His record as commissioner was, like his army record, mixed. But a real concern for African American education made him active in founding Howard University. Spending the 1870s in several western Indian campaigns, Howard became West Point superintendent in 1881."

Albert Sidney Johnston, C. S.A. (1803-62) graduated from West Point in 1826, ranking eighth in a class of forty-one. He resigned from the army to join the Confederacy, and was highly esteemed as an officer. He died on 6 April 1862, at the bloody battle of Shiloh. While leading a charge, he was wounded, taking a bullet behind his right knee. The ground was covered with injured and dying men, and General Johnston, believing he was only slightly hurt, sent his personal physician to attend to the Union wounded. The bullet had nicked an artery; he bled to death in minutes. Like Union General James McPherson, he was a man who, had he lived, could have helped the nation heal.

Joseph Eggleston Johnston, C.S.A. (1807-91) graduated from West Point in 1825, ranking thirteenth in a class of forty-six. He was quartermaster general and brigadier general in the U.S. army when he resigned to join the Confederacy. During the Atlanta campaign he conducted a canny defense, but was removed from command. He and General Sherman were opponents in war, and friends in peace. Johnston was an honorary pallbearer at Sherman's funeral, standing, hatless, outside the church on a bitterly cold day. Urged to have a care for his health, he said, "If I were in Cump's place and he were standing here in mine, he would not put on his hat." He died of pneumonia, ten days later. See letter of 21 July 1864 for a reference to Johnston.

Henry M. Judah (1821-66), son of an Episcopalian minister, graduated from West Point in 1843, ranking thirty-fifth in a class of thirty-nine. His army career was troubled and troublesome; on occasion he was too drunk to stay on his horse. General Schofield disciplined Judah for poor performance and alcoholism, but—unwisely—gave him a chance to redeem himself at Resaca. He was the only Union general Ben despised. Judah is mentioned in the letter of 9 June 1864.

Robert Edward Lee, C.S.A. (1807-70), son of Revolutionary War cavalry hero "Lighthorse Harry" Lee, graduated from West Point in 1829, ranking second in a class of forty-six. When the South seceded, elderly hero General Winfield Scott offered Colonel Lee command of the United States Army, but Lee resigned to join the Confederacy. After many initial successes, General Lee failed at Gettysburg in an attempt to invade Northern territory. He was able to slow—but not stop—Grant's progress, and in 1865, he surrendered his army to General Grant at the small town of Appomattox Court House, Virginia.

Nathaniel Collins McLean (1815-1905), son of Supreme Court Justice John McLean, graduated from college at the age of sixteen and became a lawyer. When rebellion came, he joined the Union army and was commissioned a colonel, later being promoted to brigadier general.

He served under many generals, including Joseph Hooker, whose leadership—or lack thereof—angered McLean and others. He was in active service throughout the war, except for two brief leaves of absence. McLean is cited in the letter of 9 June 1864.

John McNeil (1813-91) served directly under General John Schofield. He is described in the text after the 7 May 1864 letter and elsewhere.

James Birdseye McPherson (1828-64) graduated from West Point in 1853, ranking first in a class of fifty-two. When the Civil War began, he was commissioned captain in the Corps of Engineers, serving as General Grant's chief engineer—valuable experience when he later commanded the Army of the Tennessee in Georgia's mountainous terrain. The highest-ranking Union officer killed in the Civil War, he is buried in Clyde, Ohio, where the McPherson Cemetery is named in his honor. McPherson is mentioned in letters of 21, 26, 30 July and 1 August 1864.

George Gordon Meade (1815-72) graduated from West Point in 1835, ranking nineteenth in a class of fifty-six. Chosen to replace Hooker in army command only three days before Gettysburg, his planning and leadership there were skilled. At the Grand Review of the Armies in May 1865, General Meade rode at the head of the Army of the Potomac. Referred to in Sherman's *Memoirs*, 376-78, cited above.

Orlando Hurley Moore (1827-90) was the colonel commanding the Twenty-fifth Michigan Infantry troops and others throughout the war. Mentioned in letters of 7 May, 9 June, 13 August 1864, 2 May 1865, and described in the text after the 7 May 1864 letter.

John Hunt Morgan, C.S.A. (1825-64) enlisted in the Confederate Army at the start of the rebellion and rose to the rank of brigadier general. He was a raider, a leader of "guerilla" soldiers. His Civil War career was brief. In July 1863, he surrendered himself and his troops, and was sent to the Ohio Penitentiary. He escaped in November, returned to raiding, and was killed the following September. Raiding, always brutal, became an opportunity for outlawry, robbery, and violence, and continued after the war ended.

Benjamin Franklin Orcutt (1814-67) is referred to, but not mentioned by name, in Ben's letters of 7 May and 9 June and is described in the text after the 7 May 1864 letter.

William Starke Rosecrans (1819-98) graduated from West Point in 1842, ranking fifth in a class of fifty-six, and served in the Corps of Engineers. He served briefly and unsuccessfully as commander of the Army of the Cumberland.

John McAllister Schofield (1831-1906) graduated from West Point in 1853, ranking seventh in a class of fifty-two. After the Atlanta campaign, he and General George Thomas pursued Hood into Tennessee. Described in text after the 7 May 1864 letter and mentioned in the letters of 7 May and 20 and 23 June 1864.

Philip Henry Sheridan (1831-88) graduated from West Point in 1853, ranked thirty-fourth in a class of fifty-two. He lied about his age to gain early admission, but while there was suspended for a year for misbehavior. When the Civil War began, he was made an infantry captain and later a quartermaster. He preferred fighting to staff duty, and showed it; in 1862 he was appointed colonel of a cavalry division. Sheridan was short, but he was tall in the saddle. Grant gave him command of all cavalry in the Army of the Potomac. "Sheridan's Ride," a ballad by Thomas Buchanan Read, celebrates his twenty-mile gallop from Winchester, Virginia, in time to rally troops and defeat a surprise Confederate attack at Cedar Creek. After the war, he succeeded General Sherman as commander-in-chief of the armies.

William Tecumseh Sherman (1820-91) graduated from West Point in 1840, ranking sixth in a class of forty-two. (Academically, he ranked third, but was placed lower because of accumulated demerits.) Like his close friend U. S. Grant, Sherman is featured on the website <www.american history.si.edu/westpoint>. "After West Point, the Ohio-born Sherman served at Southern posts as an artillery officer before the Mexican War brought him to California. Returning east in 1850, he married Ellen Ewing, daughter of the man who had raised him after his father's early death. They had eight children. Sherman resigned from the army in 1853, but struggled in civilian life until 1859, when he happily became head of the Louisiana Military Seminary. Secession drove Sherman North and the outbreak of war brought him back to the army. He rose to prominence with Ulysses S. Grant in the Vicksburg and Chattanooga campaigns. When Grant moved east to take command of all Union armies, Sherman launched the drive through Georgia and the Carolinas that devastated the Confederacy and made him famous. After the war, he succeeded Grant as the army's commanding general."

Joseph C. Shields commanded the Nineteenth Ohio Independent Light Artillery, known as "Shields' Battery," joining the Atlanta campaign in 1864. He and his troops were heavily engaged in fighting throughout the campaign. After Atlanta was abandoned by Confederate forces, Captain Shields resigned from the army. See the letter of 21 July 1864 for a reference to Shields.

Henry Warner Slocum (1827-94) graduated from West Point in 1829, ranking twelfth in a class of forty-six. He served throughout the Civil War, though he threatened to resign rather than serve under Joseph Hooker. In 1864, Sherman selected Slocum to replace Hooker, and when Atlanta was abandoned, Slocum's corps was first to enter the city. He and General Howard commanded two armies in Sherman's March to the Sea and Carolinas Campaigns. After the war he was elected three times to Congress.

Andrew Jackson Smith (1815-97) graduated from West Point in 1838, ranking thirty-sixth in a class of forty-five. Son of a veteran of the Revolutionary War and the War of 1812, he was named for his father's commander at the Battle of New Orleans. Vigorous, versatile, and popular with troops, he was repeatedly ordered to crisis points. When Confederate cavalry attacked in Tennessee, Grant telegraphed: "If A. J. Smith has reached Decatur, he had better be ordered by rail to Nashville to get on the track of Wheeler and drive him south." Later Sherman telegraphed Smith from Atlanta: "I have been trying for three months to get you to me, but am headed off at every turn. Halleck asks for you to clear out Price. Can't you make a quick job of it and then get to me?" See letter of 24 August 1864.

Wager Swayne (1834-1902) was a member of a Virginia family which moved to Ohio because they were opposed to slavery. He entered the Union army in 1861 as a major, rising in rank to colonel and then general. He served under General Sherman during the Atlanta campaign and thereafter. He was wounded in 1865, and his right leg was amputated. After the war he served in the Freedman's Bureau, under General Howard. Cited in the letter of 13 August 1864.

George Henry Thomas (1816-70) graduated from West Point in 1840, ranking twelfth in a class of forty-two. When Southern states seceded, fellow officers Robert E. Lee, Albert Sidney Johnston, and William J. Hardee resigned to join the Confederacy; Thomas, though a Virginian, remained loyal to the United States. From that time his family treated him, not as dead, but as if he had never existed—turned his picture against the wall, destroyed his letters, and never spoke to him again. Moreover, at first, some Union officers distrusted him because he was a Southerner. Only his wife was loyal and loving. Throughout the Civil War he never took a day's leave; she visited him at the front. General Thomas walked slowly because of an injured back, and was deliberate in taking action, but he was powerful and courageous—and successful—in battle.

CHAPTER 12

Albertus C. Van Raalte as a Businessman

Robert P. Swierenga

If Albertus Van Raalte had not followed his father into the Dutch Reformed Church pastorate, he surely would have been a businessman. He had the instincts of an entrepreneur and was a risk taker. It was a life-long pattern. Van Raalte had a dynamic view of money and always tried to put ready cash to work, expecting to earn market rate of interest on his investments. From his late twenties and continuing until his last years, Van Raalte was involved in various business ventures in manufacturing, milling, retailing, newspaper publishing, and especially real estate and mortgage lending.[1]

[1] I am indebted to Richard Harms, Earl Wm. Kennedy, and Jack Nyenhuis for their suggestions and comments on this chapter and to Nella Kennedy for checking all the translations. Previous accounts of Van Raalte's business dealings are: Elton J. Bruins, "Albertus Christiaan Van Raalte: Funding His Vision of a Christian Colony," in *The Dutch and Their Faith: Immigrant Religious Experience in the Nineteenth and Twentieth Centuries, Proceedings of the Eighth Biennial Conference of the Association for the Advancement of Dutch American Studies* (Holland, Mich.: Hope College, 1991); and W. de Graaf, "Een afgescheiden dominie als zakenman: Dr. A. C. van Raalte," *De Hoeksteen: Tijdschrift voor Nederlands Kerkgescheidenis* 12 (February 1983): 3-12, translation by Ralph W. Vunderink in Van Raalte Papers, A. C. Van Raalte Institute (VRI), Hope College, Holland, Mich.

Elton Bruins, who has devoted his scholarly career to Van Raalte's life and work, notes that many pious colonists in Holland considered it "unseemly" for their pastor to be so involved in "worldly pursuits." But Bruins insists that the dominie's business activities were "absolutely crucial to the success of his pioneering endeavors." He realized very quickly, says Bruins, that "there simply could not be a Christian Colony if this community were not able to develop economically by providing land for the farm families and business opportunities for the villagers." So Van Raalte's proclivities for business nicely dovetailed with his vision for the colony.[2]

Ommen Factories

In the decade before Van Raalte emigrated, 1836-46, while planting Seceder congregations throughout his home province of Overijssel in the Netherlands, he took an active interest in businesses that hired unemployed *Afgescheidenen* (Separatists, members of the Christian Seceded Church), many of whom were blacklisted or boycotted for their faith. In 1839, the year the young dominie and his family took up residence in the parsonage at Ommen, he bought a fishing vessel at Scheveningen to help several men to support their families. In April 1840 he invested funds his wife Christina had inherited from her well-to-do family, the Benjamin de Moens of Leiden, in several clay works in Ommen and the nearby village of Lemele. The aim was to employ Seceders in the manufacture of bricks, roof tiles, fine porcelain, and earthen cookware. The properties included two brick kilns, three houses for workers, an office, and a barn for horses and wagons. The buildings and lands were valued at *fl* 50,000 ($20,000), a princely price.[3]

Van Raalte bought the factories, which employed thirty men, women, and children, in partnership with his wife Christina's brother, Dr. Carel G. de Moen, a surgeon and gynecologist (and later a Seceder pastor), and C. Dros, a Leiden soap manufacturer. The contract was to run for fifteen years and the principals adopted the name "De Moen & Co." De Moen moved his medical practice to Ommen to assume management of the factories, since Van Raalte was frequently away for days at a time "riding the circuit" as the "Apostle of Overijssel," ministering to newly-founded congregations throughout the province.

[2] Bruins, "Van Raalte," 53.

[3] De Graaf, "Een afgescheiden dominie als zakenman," 8-9.

The firm began operations in March 1841, after the mayor and councilmen of Ommen gave final approval.[4]

Meanwhile, Van Raalte cast about for additional capital to expand the operation. He first solicited another Seceder dominie, his fellow Leiden theology classmate, Rev. Hendrik P. Scholte, who had inherited a successful business in Amsterdam from his father. Van Raalte requested a loan "for de Moen and me" of *fl* 5,000-*fl* 10,000 [$2,000-$4,000] at 5 to 6 percent interest. He noted that *fl* 15,000 [$6,000] "of our own money is out of our reach, and we cannot invest in the business." Where this money was tied up is unknown. Van Raalte also noted that he had donated *fl* 2,200 [$880] for a church building in Ommen, because the parishioners were too poor to fund it. Finally, should Scholte be disinclined to invest in the firm, would he intercede with Judith van IJsseldijk-Zeelt, a wealthy widow friend and Seceder benefactor living on a country estate near Amsterdam? In the end, neither one took part in Van Raalte's venture. Scholte was likely miffed that Van Raalte only a few months earlier had joined in a vote by the Seceded Church Synod of 1840 to oust him over church order and theological issues.[5]

Van Raalte's problems were compounded when de Moen in 1841 indicated his desire to sell his interest in the firm and enter the gospel ministry. Van Raalte could hardly have been surprised, since he had encouraged de Moen to take this step. He turned to another brother-in-law, his sister Johanna's husband Dirk Blikman Kikkert, a prosperous Amsterdam shipbroker, who agreed to buy out de Moen, move to Ommen, and take charge of the firm. De Moen had apparently bought out Dros, the third partner, some time before. In the contract of December 1841, Blikman Kikkert provided one-half of the capital, secured by a mortgage on the property, and was entitled to one-

4 "Contract between Albertus C. van Raalte and C. G. de Moen in regards to pottery factory, Ommen," 13 April 1840, copy provided by Melis te Velde and translated by Simone Kennedy, VRI. The brick and tile factory was in Lemele and the fine porcelain and pottery factory was in Ommen.

5 Van Raalte, Ommen, to Scholte, 26 October 1840, Central College Archives; published in Cornelis Smits, *Documenten uit het archief ds. H. P. Scholte bewaard te Pella, Iowa, U.S.A.*, vol. 3 of *De Afscheiding van 1834* (Dordrecht: J. P. van den Tol, 1977), 179-81; letter translated by Elizabeth Dekker. For information on Mrs. Zeelt, see *Iowa Letters: Dutch Immigrants on the American Frontier*, ed. Robert P. Swierenga, trans. Walter Lagerwey (Grand Rapids: Eerdmans, 2004), 11, 223-24. On Scholte's ouster, see Lubbertus Oostendorp, *H. P. Scholte: Leader of the Secession of 1834 and Founder of Pella* (Ph.D. diss., Free University of Amsterdam, 1964), 123-26.

half the profits, plus an extra 5 percent "for the care, execution, and administration of the affairs of the partnership," renamed Blikman Kikkert & Co.[6]

Unfortunately, the business did not go well, at least in the early years, possibly because of poor management and the decision of the philanthropic owners to pay wages above prevailing rates. It was said that the workmen's pay was "exceptionally high." Van Raalte's brother-in-law, Anthony Brummelkamp, a key Seceder leader who remained in the Netherlands, reported that the profit from the "association with Blikman" was less than the eventual interest of the capital invested in the company. He advised him to sell the business before he lost more money. The Bentheim Seceder preacher, Jan Barend Sundag, who was a critic of Van Raalte in general, noted: "By establishing a pottery factory, he [Van Raalte] lost most of his money." Van Raalte himself admitted more than a decade later that the project had been "unhappy for me."[7]

There are no known documents indicating that Van Raalte sold his interest in the firm, either before or after he immigrated to Michigan in 1846, which is in sharp contrast to the five extant documents that carefully detail the founding of the firm and ownership change in late 1841. The likelihood is, therefore, that Van Raalte did not sell his interest, but rather left the struggling firm in the hands of Blikman Kikkert and took very little or no money from the venture.[8]

6 Blikman Kikkert bought out De Moen's interest in the land and buildings at Ommen and Lemele on 7 December 1841, according to the contract signed with Van Raalte on 1 February 1842 and published in De Graaf, "Een afgescheiden dominie als zakenman," 12-13.

7 Quotes from H. Reenders, "Albertus C. van Raalte als leider van Overijsselse Afgescheidenen," in *'Van scheurmakers, onruststokers en geheime opruijers . . .': De Afscheiding in Overijssel*, ed. Freek Pereboom, H. Hille, and H. Reenders (Kampen: IJsselakademie, 1984), 193-94, translated by Elizabeth Dekker; Van Raalte to Brummelkamp, 11 September 1852, Elton J. Bruins's personal files, copy of letter provided by George Harinck who found it in George Puchinger's personal papers, translated by Nella Kennedy and Henry ten Hoor. The *fl* 25,000 mortgage amount is in Albert Hyma, *Albertus C. Van Raalte and His Dutch Settlements in the United States* (Grand Rapids: Eerdmans, 1947), 123. Blikman Kikkert's role in the business is described in Hyma and in Jan Wesseling, *De Afscheiding van 1834 in Overijssel* (Barneveld: De Vuurbaak, 1985), 202-3, relevant passages translated by Elizabeth Dekker.

8 This contradicts De Graaf, "Een afgescheiden dominie als zakenman," who wrote: "There are sound reasons to accept that the financial basis for the American undertaking was laid to a great extent during Van Raalte's stay in Ommen, where he was a pastor and 'businessman' who knew how to

The Holland Colony

In the Holland Colony Van Raalte was first and foremost a dominie, the pastor of the First Reformed Church of Holland and first president of the Classis of Holland, the regional ecclesiastical body of the immigrant churches that was formed in 1848. Besides extensive church administrative work, his main task was to conduct worship services and baptize, marry, bury, and nurture his congregants. But the survival of the settlement depended on economic development and Van Raalte as the leader was increasingly drawn into "worldly pursuits." He had his hand in everything, from opening roads and building bridges, starting a sawmill and tannery, developing Holland harbor, editing the local newspaper the *Hollander*, and attending to legal and medical concerns, to directing the local grammar schools and the Holland Academy (later Hope College) for higher education.

Securing land for the Colony demanded his primary attention, because speculators, if given an opening, would buy up all the available land in the Black River watershed and force the Dutch to pay a premium. Since the nearest towns—Grand Haven, Allegan, and Grand Rapids—were fifteen to thirty miles distant, and the settlers lived amid dense forests, they needed sawmills to rip lumber for homes and barns, and gristmills to grind grain for their daily bread. Van Raalte, perforce, had to partner with associates to erect mills. Holland harbor also had to be developed. Exploiting the woodlands was the primary source of cash for the poverty-stricken immigrants, but forest products could not be sold unless ships could get them to outside markets, notably Chicago. Van Raalte drew up petitions to both the state and federal governments to request public funds to construct piers and dredge the mouth of Black Lake (renamed Lake Macatawa in 1935).[9]

Tax Deeds

The success of the entire venture to plant a Christian colony in Michigan hinged on controlling the surrounding lands, so that the Dutch settlers would have room to establish farms for themselves and for their children. This required tremendous sums of hard cash, of which the new immigrants had precious little. "What I could not

---

gain interest from money he already possessed. He would not be entirely impecunious" (8).

9 Hyma, *Van Raalte*, 187-91.

do if the association had $3,000," Van Raalte said in January 1847. Speculators were already buying up the strategic land at the neck of Black Lake, Van Raalte reported, but there were still thousands of acres of federal and state government lands upriver available cheaply. Obtaining clear titles unencumbered with tax liens, squatters' claims, and faulty land surveys was also a challenge, especially to a foreigner who did not know the intricacies of the American land system.

Besides his leadership duties in church and colony, Van Raalte devoted most of his time and energy in the first years to buying, financing, surveying, and titling land. The first major purchase is the most intriguing: it involved buying delinquent tax certificates at the Ottawa County courthouse during his initial scouting trip in January 1847. County treasurers were authorized by an 1845 law, under the direction of the state Auditor General, when owners failed to pay their realty taxes in a timely way, to sell to willing third parties tax liens against the property, which included back taxes to 1840, interest penalties, and administrative costs. The Auditor General, upon the purchaser presenting the treasurer's certificate, was bound to execute a quitclaim deed that killed the original title and gave the tax buyer full ownership.[10]

With the help of treasurer Henry Pennoyer, Van Raalte in January 1847 bought tax liens on forty-three parcels, totaling 2,750 acres, plus three "water lots" in the village of Superior on the north shore of Black Lake, for a total of only $200! These lien certificates, almost all on lands in Park Township owned by non-residents, ripened into quitclaim deeds. Subsequently, owners of thirteen parcels bought their property back from the dominie to his great benefit. In a typical case, an owner paid Van Raalte $79 on a tract he had bought at tax sale for only $19 three years earlier, thus quadrupling his money. Van Raalte hired the Detroit firm of J. L. Whiting & Adams to do the necessary legal work on his tax titles.[11]

10 *Laws of Michigan, 1845*, no. 64 (20 March 1845), 79-83. Auditor's quitclaim deeds were deemed "*prima facie* evidence of the correctness of all proceedings prior to the execution of the deed" (81). Such quitclaim deeds did not convey as secure a title as warrantee deeds, however, because original owners might still claim a "color of title" based on supposed procedural flaws, and thus cloud the tax title. For a study of tax sales, see Robert P. Swierenga, *Acres for Cents: Delinquent Tax Auctions in Frontier Iowa* (Westport Conn.: Greenwood Press, 1976).

11 Computed from State Auditor Tax Land Deeds, 23 October 1847, and Van Raalte's notations thereon; State Auditor of Michigan to Van Raalte,

This plunge at the county tax auctions by a novice investor during his very first month on Michigan soil gave the dominie a leg up on the road to financial success. In September 1847 Van Raalte returned to the tax auction and bought another twenty-three parcels, containing 1,044 acres, for $28.59.[12] He continued to buy tax liens over the next four years. Acquiring "acres for cents" required careful bookkeeping and attention to taxes and titles, but it paid handsomely. In a very revealing letter to Brummelkamp in 1852, Van Raalte noted: "I have more than 1,500 acres of tax titles from six to eleven years [of delinquent taxes], among which are the most expensive possessions along the Lake, and among others the lots near the mouth of our Lake where it flows into Lake Michigan. The rest all lie in or near the colony."[13]

Investing in tax liens was controversial, especially for a minister of the gospel. Any process that wiped out property rights by legal fiat, often for pennies on the dollar, had negative overtones, even though tax lien investors were performing a valuable service to the county government by ensuring the timely payment of realty taxes, and the losers were often non-residents for whom locals had little sympathy. Yet buyers at frontier tax auctions had somewhat the reputation of vultures.[14]

One owner who lost his title to Van Raalte went after him with a vengeance and created a "dangerous crisis," but the dominie stood his ground. He told Brummelkamp about the incident in an 1852 letter:

---

tax deed, 22 January 1848, $19.45, sold by Van Raalte to A. B. Hubbard of Norwich, Conn., 12 July 1851, for $78.84; Van Raalte to Pennoyer, Grand Haven, 30 September 1847, reprinted in *Holland City News*, 10 January 1891; J. L. Whiting & Adams, Detroit, to Van Raalte, 1 January 1850; Van Raalte to Gilman Chase, Michigan Auditor General, 5 August 1854, all in Van Raalte Collection, Calvin College Archives (hereafter CCA). Van Raalte did not buy liens on lands of poor Dutch settlers in default, for whom the dominie supposedly would "hold them in trust," as Hyma hypothesized (*Van Raalte*, 214). Rather, the former owners of his certificates were non-residents, such as A. H. Hubbard, James Anderson, and James Brayton of Ionia; Simon Newman of Kalamazoo; George W. Jewitt of Ann Arbor; John H. Ostram and Thomas A. Hubbard of Utica, N.Y.; William R. Palmer and Thomas A. Walker of New York; and others whose residences are not yet determined.

12 Computed from Michigan State Auditor Tax Land Deeds, 6 January 1849.

13 Van Raalte to Brummelkamp, 11 September 1852.

14 See Swierenga, *Acres for Cents*, 4-6, for a discussion of the "folklore view" of delinquent tax sales.

> A gentleman from a rich firm, had years before bought a piece of land across our Lake for 19 dollars per acre, yet had given it up, or let it go for the taxes because he thought that it never would be inhabited here, or for other reasons. He learned that I was the owner by tax title, came here in hopes of having those lands back, and offered me twenty percent above the money I spent. However, I told him that . . . I considered titles of a series of years as safe enough and looked upon them as my possession.
>
> Whereupon the man tried to scare me, threatening me a lawsuit for every tree that was chopped down, for which I certainly would have to pay a fine of $5,000. Outraged, I told him with blazing words that he had miscalculated the person and the means by which to achieve his objective, and that I did not want to exchange any words with him. . . . But that gentleman, stirred by a pushy determination that showed he was never accustomed to be stopped in his course, found matters different here from what he had expected. Maybe his tough reception was a blessing for the people (although I got a troubled conscience for my temper), for such Nimrods don't usually bring well-being.[15]

Land Purchases

Van Raalte's most important land acquisitions came directly from the federal public domain and from Internal Improvement lands that Congress granted to the State of Michigan to fund river navigation, canals, and harbor projects. In April 1847 he entered at the U.S. Land Office in Ionia (the regional office for western Michigan) a 240-acre tract in the south half of Section 29, Township 5, Range 15 west, which he designated the site of Holland. He paid $1.25 per acre for the land, the minimum "Congress price." This was the first of many so-called "private entries" at Ionia. From April 1847 to August 1849, the dominie purchased thirty parcels (2,108 acres) of "Congress land" around Holland at the same minimum price, for a total of $2,600. In a few cases he paid less, by using Mexican War military bounty land warrants that Congress issued to reward veterans and made assignable to third parties. Federal land offices accepted this so-called land paper in lieu of cash on certain restricted categories of lands and in keeping with specific regulations. Depending on market forces, land warrants

[15] Van Raalte to Brummelkamp, 11 September 1852.

traded publicly at discounts up to 50 percent. Van Raalte bought warrants from land agent John Ball of Grand Rapids and thereby acquired government land for as little as 75 cents per acre.[16]

Buying key tracts of land before speculators did was a major challenge, as Van Raalte found out in the fall of 1847, when the state put on the market lands that Congress had donated to fund internal improvements. The dominie set off on foot to Allegan, from where he planned to catch the stage for Kalamazoo and then the train to the State Land Office at Marshall. He pushed himself to the limit, but missed the stage at Allegan, so he borrowed a horse that proved so weak he had to walk beside it all the way to the train depot at Kalamazoo. When he finally reached Marshall after three harrowing days, he found prices had "terribly risen." "Worse," he told his wife in a letter, "speculators already took all the lands I had in mind." With the help of a sympathetic Marshall lawyer named Clark, Van Raalte learned that a key buyer was a Grand Rapids contractor on the Michigan Canal who had claimed the public lands as compensation for his work under the Internal Improvements land grant to the State of Michigan.[17]

Van Raalte persuaded Clark to accompany him to Grand Rapids, a two-day ride by rented carriage, to dicker with the man. Here they found that the contractor was willing to sell, but he could not give a good title because the law required that the project be finished before titles could pass, which was at least four years away. With the intervention of "some very important people in Grand Rapids," however, Van Raalte and Clark persuaded the contractor to allow the lands to revert to the state, "which meant that I could then buy them. . . . I have suffered through days full of worry," Van Raalte wrote his wife, "but I am thankful that God has saved our people from such destruction." The two men then

16 All tracts were in Holland and Zeeland townships, except five tracts in Blendon and Fillmore townships (Ionia Public Land Office, Ottawa County Books of Original Entry); Van Raalte to Ball, Grand Rapids, 4 October 1847, John Ball Papers, no. 44, folder 435, Grand Rapids Public Library; Hyma, *Van Raalte*, 163-64. For the operations of the land warrant market and their use by investors, see James W. Oberly, *Sixty Million Acres: American Veterans and the Public Lands before the Civil War* (Kent, Ohio: Kent State University Press, 1990); and Robert P. Swierenga, *Pioneers and Profits: Land Speculation on the Iowa Frontier* (Ames, Iowa: Iowa State University Press, 1968).

17 Van Raalte, Yellow Springs, to Mrs. C. J. Van Raalte, 2 November 1847, Joint Archives of Holland (JAH), Hope College, Holland, Mich., translated by Elizabeth Dekker and Simone Kennedy.

returned to Marshall by way of Yellow Springs. Before heading back to Holland, Van Raalte went on to the State Capitol at Detroit "to do business." The entire trip took more than two weeks. But it resulted in his obtaining ten tracts, totaling 744 valuable acres, in Holland Township for $930 ($1.25 an acre). In May 1848 he purchased another two hundred acres from the State lying in Zeeland Township, and in April of 1849 he bought eight more tracts totaling 325 acres in Holland and Laketown townships. Altogether, he bought more than thirteen hundred acres at the Marshall Land Office for over $1600.[18]

While Van Raalte was accumulating federal and state lands, he tried to gain title to lands around Holland that eastern investors had purchased before the Dutch came. Nathaniel Silsbee of Salem, Massachusetts, owned a key 261-acre tract at the mouth of Black Lake, and the dominie sought to contact him within two weeks of his arrival with the first contingent of colonists in February 1847. Van Raalte had his friend, Rev. Isaac Wyckoff of the Second Dutch Reformed Church of Albany, New York, write an acquaintance in Boston to visit Silsbee and tell him that "Mr. Van Raalte is anxious to secure these lots" and wants the first option to buy. Silsbee agreed and sold the land in September 1847 for $923, or $3.54 per acre, nearly three times the purchase price, but Van Raalte believed the key tract well worth it and he could buy on time—$100 down and six years for the remainder. The Village Association paid the down payment and the annual principal and interest payments of $80 in 1848 and 1849.[19]

That same month Van Raalte bought 320 acres from Peter Schermerhorn of New York City for $810, or $2.53 per acre, again with $200 down and six years to pay the remainder.[20] In November 1847

[18] Ibid. From 1 February 1848 to 1 January 1867, the Michigan State Land Office in Marshall issued Van Raalte twenty-three deeds totaling 1,309 acres, all in Ottawa County.

[19] George Minot, Boston, to Hon. N. Silsbee, Salem, Massachusetts, Holland Museum Archives (HMA), Holland, Mich.; Charles Noble, Monroe, Michigan, to Silsbee, 10 April 1847, HMA; Van Raalte's account book with Nathaniel Silsbee for the tract, 1 September 1847, Van Raalte Collection, CCA; *Dorpslands Dagboek* [Village Daybook], April 1847-December 1849, Van Raalte Collection, CCA; Hyma, *Van Raalte*, 164-65. Silsbee paid cash at the Ionia Public Land Office on 3 October 1836 for this 102-acre tract (Ottawa County Book of Original Entry, Ionia Public Land Office).

[20] Schermerhorn purchased 320 acres on 23 July 1836 (Ionia Public Land Office, Ottawa County Book of Original Entry); Receipt, William Schermerhorn for Peter Schermerhorn from A. C. Van Raalte per George Young, 16 September 1847 (Young was an elder in the First Reformed

he purchased from insurance agent Courtland Palmer, another New York City land investor, a huge 1,656 acre-tract for $3,840, or $2.32 per acre, paying down $400 from Village Trustees funds, with the rest on mortgage at 7 percent interest.[21] In 1853 Palmer sold the mortgage to merchant James Suydam and druggist Samuel B. Schieffelin of New York City, both wealthy laymen in the Marble Collegiate Reformed Church who contributed much to denominational causes. For several payments Van Raalte sent personal drafts (akin to modern checks) to De Witt, who cashed them at various merchants, deposited the funds in a bank, and saw to it that the two men received their money.[22]

Van Raalte also kept an eye on the lands of the Ottawa Indians of the Old Wing Mission in nearby Allegan County and at the Indian "Landing" on Black Lake, on the assumption that they would sell their lands and move north to get away from the swarming Dutch colonists. In September 1847, he asked Pennoyer, "How is it with the lands of the Indians? I wisch [*sic*] that they came for sale. When you can do something to get this ready, I would be very much obliged." Within six months, Van Raalte's wish was granted. The Indian chief,

---

Church of Grand Rapids); P. Schermerhorn, New York City, to H. D. Post, Postmaster, Holland, Michigan, 2 October 1848, HMA.

21 Palmer's father, William R. Palmer, together with his associates John H. Ostram and Thomas A. Walker of Utica, New York, entered the tract at the U.S. Land Office at Bronson, Michigan, on 11 February 1836 and quitclaimed it to Courtland Palmer on 18 November 1847 (Abstract of Title, Ottawa County Abstract & Title Co.; Ottawa County Deed Registers, Book B, 437-40; Book G, 425). It appears that Courtland Palmer and his associate Thomas H. Hubbard of Utica had lost the land to Van Raalte at the 1847 tax sale, and Van Raalte bought their quitclaim deed to give him a warrantable title (Thomas De Witt, New York City, to Van Raalte, 23, 30 April 1849). Hyma, not having the 11 November 1847 deed in hand, mistakenly states that Van Raalte obtained "some 3,000 acres of land for about $7,000" and he signed a guarantee bond for $4,000, on which he would default if he did not pay $2,740 in five equal annual installments of $568 (*Van Raalte*, 163). The deeds (Book B, 441, recorded 18 November 1847, and Book G, 425, filed 8 December 1853) list sixteen tracts, totaling 1,656 acres (not 3,000) for a price of $3,840.47. That the down payment was only $400 is stated in a Village Daybook entry for 7 November 1847: "Borrowed from J. Slag $505.00 against the Village for paying Van Raalte's advance for Silsbee's land, $105.00, and of the partial buying price of the Blocks of Village land from Palmer on the south side of Black Lake at interest of seven percent."

22 Mortgage Assignment, Courtland Palmer to James Suydam and Samuel B. Schieffelin, New York, 10 March 1857, Van Raalte Collection, CCA.

Peter Wakazoo, decided to relocate to the region of Little Traverse Bay, and the Indians set about selling their lands. In May 1848 Van Raalte purchased forty acres at Old Wing Mission from six Ottawas, including Chief Peter Wakazoo, for $226. He paid the Indians $5.65 per acre for this improved farmland. The same month Van Raalte paid Wakazoo $26 for the Indian church at the Landing.[23]

Altogether, from 1847 through 1849 Van Raalte purchased, either for himself or on behalf of the Village Trustees, 11,800 acres for $14,000 (Table 2, Table 3).[24] Most amazing is the range and sophistication of the land dealings. He clearly received excellent coaching and personal assistance from key government officials, such as Ottawa County treasurer Henry Pennoyer and John Ball, the Grand Rapids land surveyor, dealer, and speculator.[25] When the federal census marshal in 1850 recorded the value of realty in Holland Township, Van Raalte's lands at $2600 were worth 30 percent more than those of the next wealthiest resident. For his part, Van Raalte introduced his clerical colleagues, the Reverends Cornelius Vander Meulen in Zeeland and Seine Bolks in Overisel, to the intricacies of real estate investing as a way to augment their meager salaries. The Ottawa County deed registers record more than one hundred Vander Meulen transactions between 1848 and 1876.[26]

Sources of Capital

Where did Van Raalte find the $14,000 for his land purchases? Public land offices and county treasurers demanded payment in specie

23 Van Raalte to H. Pennoyer, Grand Haven, 22 November 1847; Van Raalte to Brummelkamp, 30 January 1847, translated by Gerrit Vander Ziel, typescript, p. 15, Van Raalte Collection, CCA.

24 This acreage total is inflated because several tax-deeded tracts covered the same parcel for different years of delinquency, and seventeen tax-deed tracts were sold back to original owners within months of the purchase. Van Raalte also sold his farmlands as soon as possible to new immigrants. By 1853 his list of lands in Holland Township assessed for taxes totaled only fourteen hundred acres, plus hundreds of town lots.

25 John Ball purchased in Ottawa County alone sixteen tracts totaling twenty-eight hundred acres in the 1830s and thirty tracts totaling two thousand acres in 1843-53; all but two of the latter were entered with land warrants (compiled from Ionia Public Land Office, Ottawa County Book of Original Entry).

26 Compiled from Ionia Public Land Office, Ottawa County Books of Original Entry; Ottawa County Deed Registers.

(gold or silver coin), which carried a premium over bank notes, or buyers could pay with military bounty land warrants that were available at discount on the open market. But the private eastern sellers—Silsbee, Schermerhorn, and Palmer—took back mortgages of $4,300. The Village trustees provided $500 and he borrowed another $2,600; specifically, $200 from Zeeland farmer-capitalist Jannes Vande Luyster, $700 from Holland ship carpenters Jan Slag and his son Harm, $400 from farmer Hendrik Hiddink, $300 from Judge John B. Kellogg of Allegan, and $1,000 from the Rev. Isaac Wyckoff and the Second Albany (N.Y.) Reformed Church. The Wyckoff loan was earmarked entirely for building a pier at Holland harbor, which indicates the complexities of sorting out community development expenses for land purchases.[27]

The Arnhem Emigration Association raised $2,000 (*fl* 5,000) before members embarked for America, and Brummelkamp personally gave $800 (*fl* 2,000). Except for $700 used to buy communal lands, these monies were expended in the first two years for the needs of the village—constructing crude cabins for fresh arrivals, opening streets and roads, erecting bridges, surveying lots and lands, clearing building lots, building and furnishing the log church, real estate taxes, and the like.[28]

Mortgages and loans (excluding the Wyckoff loan) totaled $6,400, leaving Van Raalte to pay the remaining $8,100 for land purchases. His sales of city lots and outlying lands from 1847 through 1849 totaled $5,100 (Table 2), which covered all but $3,000 of his land purchases in those years. He needed about $500 to cover the family's travel costs and to build a home of sawed lumber (not a crude log cabin like all the rest). Living expenses in Michigan he presumably paid from his $600 salary as pastor, although the congregation frequently was in arrears because of budget shortfalls.[29] I conclude, therefore, that upon arrival

27 All the loans were at 7 percent interest, except the Wyckoff loan at 6 percent (Village Daybook, April 1847-December 1849, entry of 16 December 1849; Hyma, *Van Raalte*, 149, 151; Ottawa and Allegan County deed record books. The Wyckoff loan was paid off on 24 September 1853. Hyma, *Van Raalte*, 162-65, gives a figure of $8,000 as the amount Van Raalte paid for his land purchases, but this is surely too low. Jannes Vande Luyster Account Book, 1847, shows Van Raalte borrowed $100 in June at 5 percent interest and another $100 in December at 7 percent (HMA).

28 The expenses are detailed in the Village Daybook, 1847-49 (CCA).

29 Of Van Raalte's $600 annual salary, he received only $251 in 1852 and $240 in 1853 (First Reformed Church Consistory Minutes, 22 November 1853, Art. 3).

in Michigan Van Raalte required no more than $3,500 for passage fare, his home, and the costs of real estate purchases, such as surveying, legal fees, taxes, and other management expenses in the first twelve to eighteen months, after which sales more than covered his expenses.

The Village Board of Trustees, of which Van Raalte was the president, was also involved in buying and selling city lots to the colonists, nearly half with one-quarter down and three years to pay the remainder at 7 percent interest. From 1847 to 1849, the Village Daybook cash account lists income of $1,935 on the sale of 160 lots, less $201 for land purchases, leaving a net of $1,735. [Actual sales of lands and lots totaled a net of $4,366, but almost all were sold on land contracts with small down payments (Table 3 and Table 4).] Village expenses of $3,330 for surveying, clearing lots and streets of trees, and building the Log Church, among other needs, required all of the income and more, leaving a deficit on the books of $2,000 in 1849. The $2,600 due on land contracts would more than cover this deficit, except that most colonists could not meet their payment schedules. In short, the village treasury could not fund the major land purchases of the colony.[30]

How much money did Van Raalte carry with him from the Netherlands? Historian Albert Hyma of the University of Michigan, the first biographer to have access to the Van Raalte Collection at Calvin College, asserted boldly that the dominie carried $10,000 to America as his share in the Ommen pottery business. Says Hyma in *Albertus C. Van Raalte and His Dutch Settlements in America* (1947): "We may *presume* [italics added] that upon his departure for America he sold his interest in the firm and used the capital ($10,000) for his great adventure."[31] The tip-off that this information is suspect is Hyma's use of the telltale phrase, "We may presume." Hyma also notes that in April 1847, barely three months after arriving in Michigan, Van Raalte only had $400 left, after paying traveling expenses and buying land.[32]

I conclude that Hyma and other scholars who have accepted his $10,000 figure have greatly overestimated the size of Van Raalte's

30 Village expenses, other than lots and lands, totaled $4,650 ($2,116 in 1847, $955 in 1848, $211 in 1849, $971 in 1850, and $397 in 1851). Compiled from Village Daybook, vol. 1, 1847-49; and vol. 2, 1849-51 (CCA).

31 Hyma, *Van Raalte*, 124.

32 Ibid. Elton Bruins ("Van Raalte," 54) adds the $2,000 from the Emigration Association and Brummelkamp, to bring Van Raalte's initial capital to $12,000, but only $700 of the $2,000 was used to buy land.

moneybag.[33] He likely carried little more than $3,000, with which he gained title to thousands of key acres in Holland Township, including the town of Holland, and thereby ensured the future of the entire colony. With a relatively small purse, he gained a treasure in lands that increased in value to $200,000 ($4 million in today's dollars). He became a rich man indeed! But his investments were highly leveraged in the early years and the strain showed at times.

City Lots

When Van Raalte in 1847 purchased land for the colony and had the city of Holland platted into sixty-nine blocks and 687 lots of various sizes, he titled the land personally and jointly with his wife, because the People's Assembly, a town meeting form of government, was not incorporated and could not act in legal matters. This ensured that colonists would receive clear titles, with no clouds on them. Hence, the chain of title in virtually every deed in Holland City and many surrounding farms carries Van Raalte's name at or near the top. Many deeds carried a stipulation barring on "said premises" the manufacture or sale of liquor and any "gaming, dancing, or theatrical performance."[34]

In late 1849, after the People's Assembly had fallen several thousand dollars in debt, the trustees asked Van Raalte to assume all debts and the costs of any future title issues, and in return the Assembly allowed him to take personal ownership of 546 city lots then remaining unsold. By this time only 141 lots (20 percent) had been sold. Van Raalte accepted this huge liability with some reluctance, so he said,

33 De Graaf in "Een afgescheiden dominie as zakenman," states: "There is reason to assume that at his departure from the Netherlands he had at his disposal $10,000" (8) and, "We may agree with Dr. Hyma that he sold his shares in the brick-factory before his departure to America and targeted their amount for his 'great adventure,' which yielded such precious fruit in America" (11).

34 An example of this restriction is in Warrantee Deed, A. C. Van Raalte to John Van Vleck, 7 May 1857, Ottawa County Deed Register, Book M, 308-9; Van Raalte to Brummelkamp, 30 January 1847, Vander Ziel typescript, pp. 15-16, 22; Van Raalte to John Ball, Grand Rapids, 9 October 1850, Grand Rapids Public Library, no. 44, folder 435; Bruins, "Van Raalte," 54-56. Subsequent to the initial survey, as Holland City developed, Van Raalte platted new additions that added more than four hundred lots. He sold 842 during his lifetime (Table 2) and bequeathed another 268 to his heirs in 1875-76, bringing the total number of lots to 1,110.

but he realized full well the potential windfall of owning lots that would rise sharply in value as the town developed. "I figure that I could live on the income of the Village properties alone," Van Raalte told Brummelkamp in 1852.[35] Indeed, over the next twenty-five years, his sales totaled $100,000, and he had a portfolio worth another $100,000 to bequeath to his children in the months before his death in November 1876. Taking the risk of ownership of the city lots provided Van Raalte with the foundation for his family wealth, and the landed security with which to lure investors for his business ventures.[36]

In Van Raalte's detailed record of land sales in the years 1847-51, farmland near the city sold for $3 per acre in 1847 and three-acre city lots for $40. Some lot buyers paid cash, but most put $10 down and signed a mortgage for the rest at 7 percent interest. As the city grew and land values increased from normal development, he pushed lot prices up to $45 in 1849, $48 in 1850, $70 in 1855, $120 in 1865, and $400 by 1874. Raw farmland nearly tripled from $3 to $8 per acre by the eve of the Civil War and surpassed $10 an acre after the War. His annual tax bill climbed steadily as well; it was $146 in 1850, $200 in 1852, $228 in 1856, and $660 in 1868.[37]

The value of the properties climbed apace. Barely six years after immigrating to the Michigan frontier, Van Raalte had accumulated a landed estate that was the envy of many. It included more than five hundred village lots and a thousand rural acres. In 1853 the assessed valuation of Van Raalte's real estate, tract by tract, as determined by the county assessor for tax purposes, totaled $5,500 for Holland Township lands and $11,600 for Holland city lots, for a grand total of $17,100.[38] The market value was considerably larger. Building lots

[35] Van Raalte to Brummelkamp, 11 September 1852.

[36] Van Raalte's property bequests to his children, compiled from the Ottawa County Deed Registers, total 268 city lots, with an estimated value of $400 each, or $107,200, and 1,246 acres, with an estimated value of $12 each, or $14,950–grand total $122,150 (Philip Phelps Scrapbook, 23 November 1872; Van Raalte to P. Phelps, [?] February 1873; Phelps to Van Raalte, 29 August 1873; lot sales account book, 1873-76, Van Raalte Papers, VRI; Gerrit Van Schelven, "Historical Sketch of Holland City and Colony," *Holland City News*, 26 August 1876; Bruins, "Van Raalte," 55).

[37] Village Daybook, 1847-49 and Village Daybook, *Tweede Stuk* [Second Part], December 1849 - 9 September 1851, Van Raalte Collection, CCA.

[38] Tax receipts, Holland Township Treasurer's Office, 20 January 1850, 15 December 1852, 23 January 1856, 8 January 1869; Assessment of the Property of A. C. Van Raalte for 1853 in Town Holland, Ottawa County, Van Raalte Collection, CCA.

in Holland that he sold for $40 in 1848 were worth on average $60-$70 in 1852, Van Raalte told Brummelkamp, and they will "without doubt double their value in four years." And a "small strip on the water's edge" is worth $250. I am amazed, he admitted, in "the peculiar position in which I see myself as the owner of such really unimaginable wealth."[39] Land sales provided Van Raalte's primary source of income and nicely supplemented his church salary, which often went unpaid or underpaid, on the unspoken assumption that his parishioners were in far worse financial straits than he was.

Raising Capital

Van Raalte was constantly seeking capital for the Colony. In 1849 he sent a positive report about the successes and challenges to Rev. Carel de Moen, his wife's brother in the Netherlands. It included an appeal for investment capital:

> Although taken as a whole, we are a poor company of people, and the funds of even the well-to-do among them have dwindled away in supplying the thousands of needs of a new settlement as in bottomless pits. Financial needs are pressing; thousands of dollars could be invested with rich returns, even appearing to be indispensable. Yet we are taught, on the other hand, that it is not money or capital that helps us grow, but the caring, omniscient, Almighty hand does more than we can understand.[40]

Two years later, in 1851, Van Raalte expanded on his economic philosophy in a letter about conditions in the Holland Colony penned to Rev. Helenius de Cock, another Seceder cleric in the Netherlands:

> Dealings, vocations, or trade opportunities, retail and wholesale, are not lacking here. At a glance, i.e., an experienced glance, one can find business everywhere—not just where one can make a living, but where, as Americans say, one can make money. Twenty-five years ago nothing could be found around Lake

[39] Van Raalte to P. Den Bleyker, Kalamazoo, 9 January 1851, Den Bleyker Papers, Michigan Historical Collections, Bentley Historical Library, University of Michigan (hereafter BHL), translated by Nella Kennedy; Van Raalte to Brummelkamp, 11 September 1852.

[40] Van Raalte to De Moen, 11 February 1849, published in "De Toestand der Hollandsche Kolonisatie in den Staat Michigan . . ." (1849), translated by Johannes W. Visscher and Nella Kennedy.

> Michigan, except for a log cabin in a couple of places for the purpose of trading with the Indians. Now there is profit with the large cities and villages. The people who came here were generally people who began with nothing, or on credit, or with a couple of thousand dollars at most. They are capitalists now. It is a common occurrence that people become propertied in the course of eight to ten years. It is not considered important if one fails, for one begins with "A" again [i.e., one starts over again], and is granted credit soon.
>
> Among the capitalists there are some who have gone bankrupt two or three times in fifteen years (even if they began with little or nothing, with everything on credit), and are wealthy again in fifteen years. It is a strange country, incomprehensible to Europeans who know nothing of growing along with the development of cities. And yet, that is the key to why the new settlers in the West could come to prosperity so fast, even though they hardly possessed anything to start with. The flood of the influx of peoples brings value to the land in a short amount of time, and the land brings forth much in a short time, bringing about the necessity for all branches of trade, manufacturing, and others.[41]

Van Raalte by this time was involved in a number of business ventures, for which there is little or no documentation in the extant documents. In the summer of 1847 he became the initiator and principal owner of a sawmill, along with Messrs. Benham, Brist, and Gibbs, known as the Colony Mill, which was built along a stream running through the present-day Van Raalte Farm. The stream was dammed up to provide enough waterpower to mill four thousand board feet a year for several seasons. Van Raalte also owned half interests in a tree nursery "with the English," a potash (potassium carbonate) and saleratus (baking soda) factory with another Englishman (Henry D. Post), including a store to sell soap and candles, and a tannery with Peter Pfanstiehl, named P. F. Pfanstiehl & Co., and then with John Keeler (Kerler), a Bavarian, renamed Keeler & Co. Van Raalte sold his half interest in 1854 for $200 to John Scheur (Schurr) of Holland, and the factory became Scheur & Co.[42]

41 Van Raalte to De Cock, 's-Hertogenbosch, 26 September 1851, Van Raalte Collection, CCA, translated by Nella Kennedy.

42 Ottawa County Deed Register, Book E, 471; Gerrit Van Schelven Historical Collection, "Pioneer Industries," Letter of Hoyt J. Post, 27 November 1899,

Francis Denison of Kalamazoo, one of the supporters of the Dutch colony, urged Van Raalte to set up an ash factory as early as May 1847. "Procure as many Iron Kettles as you have men to use them," Dennison advised. "I know of no other way in which you can clear up the farms and get a living from the labor of your men at the same time." Van Raalte took heed and Post & Co. (Van Raalte was the "Co.") became the first manufacturing plant in the Colony. Settlers from up to ten miles around carried on their backs bundles of ashes to the factory at the head of Black Lake, to exchange for money for groceries and supplies. Each wooded acre produced $6 worth of ash. With a crew of five or six employees, the factory manufactured a good quality hard soap and later potash, which was shipped to New York, and black salt for the Chicago market. The firm made a profit of $10,000 a year, and the colonists earned their first cash income. The partners sold the ash factory in 1854 to George Colt of Williamsburg, New York, and later Kalamazoo.[43]

These ventures, all backed by mortgage security on his lands, and the cash required for paying land mortgages and annual county taxes, caused the dominie to feel the pressure. "Most perilous for me," he wrote his brother-in-law de Moen in May of 1851, "is that all public land purchases and enterprises with the financial costs are mine to pay, [as well as] the debts incurred through that. I am burdened by that. Although it is opined that my duties are enviable, they are too much mixed with care and danger." Yet, Van Raalte concluded, "I have been blessed in earthly means and God has steadily given me abundance."[44] The Silsbee mortgage was clearly one of those concerns, because in August Van Raalte wrote Silsbee's son and executor of his estate pleading for more time to make the final payment of $409 until he could sell some other lands. Several church families lived on the land and Van Raalte did not want to see them evicted. "This is a singular country," the dominie explained to the New Yorker. "We have enough to eat and still to get money back is next to impossible."[45]

HMA; Denison, Kalamazoo, to Van Raalte, 15 May 1847, photocopy in Hyma, *Van Raalte*, 179; *De Hollander*, 16 November 1852, 16 November 1854, 29 May 1857. The Scheur (Schurr, Schuur) purchase of 31 October 1854 is recorded in Book 1, 20. Keeler was a twenty-eight-year old from Milwaukee.

43 Denison to Van Raalte, 15 May 1847.

44 Van Raalte to De Moen, Den Ham (Ov.), 23 May 1851, Melis te Velde Collection, JAH, translated by Nella Kennedy.

45 Van Raalte to Silsbee Executor, 19 August 1851, quoted in Hyma, *Van Raalte*, 164-65.

Den Bleyker Fiasco

Paulus Den Bleyker, a Dutch immigrant who settled in Kalamazoo in November 1850, was the epitome of the kind of capitalist and entrepreneur Van Raalte envisioned for developing Holland, and early in 1851 the dominie set to work mightily to recruit him. Historian Henry Lucas called Den Bleyker the "first capitalist" in the West Michigan Dutch settlement; Hyma dubbed him the "richest Hollander in Michigan." He came to America with $30,000.[46]

Van Raalte had capitalist instincts, but Den Bleyker had actual capital and much of it. He made his money draining the Eendracht Polder on the Island of Texel and then selling the lands reclaimed from the Zuider Zee. Den Bleyker sympathized with the Seceder ideals that had compelled Van Raalte and his followers to emigrate and decided to join them in the exodus. When he reached Kalamazoo—a city not much bigger than Holland but with a Dutch contingent of only four hundred—he saw unlimited opportunities to make money as a land developer. He purchased for $12,000 a 330-acre farm twelve miles from the city with wheat fields ready for harvest, and another 180-acre farm on the edge of town for an additional $12,000, this from Epaphroditus Ransom, ex-governor of Michigan and a Kalamazoo capitalist. The wealthy Dutchman platted part of the Ransom farm as "Den Bleyker's Addition" and expected the sale of lots to more than recoup his initial investment.[47]

When Ransom learned that Den Bleyker had another $20,000 ready for investment, he asked him to be a partner in a banking and land mortgage company, and he wrote Van Raalte to help entice the newcomer. At this point Den Bleyker also wrote Van Raalte for a character reference on Ransom. So the dominie, who knew the governor and had found him trustworthy, was put in the position of a go-between. He gave Den Bleyker a positive reference, but could not let

[46] Henry S. Lucas, *Netherlanders in America: Dutch Immigration to the United States and Canada, 1789-1950* (Ann Arbor, Mich.: University of Michigan Press, 1955; reprint, Grand Rapids: Eerdmans, 1989), 280; Hyma, *Van Raalte*, 181; Louis G. Vander Velde, "Glimpses of the Early Dutch Settlements in Michigan," *Michigan Historical Collections, University of Michigan*, no. 1 (November 1947): 1.

[47] Lucas, *Netherlanders in America*, 280-84; Hyma, *Van Raalte*, 181-85, citing letters in Den Bleyker Papers, BHL. Kalamazoo had 2,500 inhabitants in 1850, 6,100 in 1860, and 9,000 in 1870.

the opportunity pass to try to win him and his money for the Holland Colony.[48]

Van Raalte also visited dominies Cornelius Vander Meulen of Zeeland, where Den Bleyker's brother worshipped, and Hendrik Klyn of Graafschap, a friend from the Old Country, and both clerics wrote personal letters to Den Bleyker. Vander Meulen urged him to come settle among his own people and benefit from the lower cost of living. Klyn warned him to be careful in dealing with strangers and quoted the scriptural injunction, "Be wise as serpents and innocent as doves" (Matt. 10:16 RSV). Better to invest in wholly safe and profitable ventures in Holland.

Van Raalte likewise wrote and warned Den Bleyker against getting too involved financially with Americans, who "scorn us as an uncivilized, dull, slow people," and might well take advantage of him as a greenhorn. "Think: Opportunity makes the thief!!!" Moreover, besides the great risk, Ransom's banking venture offered him 10 percent, while Ransom made 15 percent, "keeping 5% of it as his salary." In Holland, Van Raalte insisted, "I want to give you that same 10% and will guarantee your interest and capital in real estate that is double its worth." Further, Den Bleyker "must begin business among the Dutch folk" he could trust, and in a location with a great future, since Holland harbor is destined to become the distribution center of the Upper Great Lakes to eastern markets.[49]

Specifically, Van Raalte suggested a double steam-driven sawmill and gristmill, which would together cost $10,000 and return 20 to 100 percent on the money. The run-down sawmill of Oswald Vander Sluis was woefully inadequate. And the colonists, now numbering five thousand, had to drive oxen for two days to get grain ground. They "will shout for joy" to have a local mill. "I would want to start these with you," Van Raalte declared, either as an active or silent partner. "I can show you how this could be carried out."

Van Raalte then played the high notes on his keyboard:

> Perhaps you wonder at this language, not knowing my position. Yes, even I myself am frequently astonished at the position in

[48] Van Raalte to "Friend Bleker" [Paulus Den Bleyker], Kalamazoo, 23 December 1850, BHL, translated by Elizabeth Dekker and Simone Kennedy.

[49] Van Raalte to Den Bleyker, Kalamazoo, 9 January 1851, BHL, translated by Nella Kennedy (letter was marked "Strictly Confidential!!!!!"); see also Van Raalte to De Moen, Leiden, 23 May 1851.

which I find myself. Although I did come here with some capital, it never occurred to me that I would become involved in so many business matters. But I find that the Lord has wanted to bless me and [he] placed me uniquely as the possessor of large properties. Otherwise I would not have been able to stand where I have stood in order to work on laying the foundations for these people. Especially because of these exceptional blessings and many business interests, I can invest capital at a high rate of interest, and give security by way of real estate. . . .

I shall now reveal, confidentially, something about this. At first I traded in land for and in the name of the colony. But after all was said and done, no one wished to be involved anymore for fear of possible loss and other rationales. But this unreasonable foolishness actually became a blessing to me. . . . This people deserted me and broke contracts with me. At first this was difficult, but now it is to my advantage. That is how it went with the village of Holland also.

And besides, I was very fortunate in the purchase of valuable lands. So that now, without having desired this, I own wonderful land along the water; besides thousands of acres of farmland, including strips of cultivated land and a good amount of natural meadowland and hayfields, as well as lime beds, all the land of the village of Holland, and three water power sources. Along with the English I began a tree nursery. Three years ago I began, with another Englishman, a saleratus and potash factory in which soap and candles are also made. Another Hollander and I are in partnership in a tannery business, which is an excellent business; all that is made of leather will be made here. From this and that you can see what my circumstances are and the basis on which I can talk to you about this.

I am convinced that you can enter into business here with pleasure and without danger, business that you could oversee, in which under God's blessing, you can turn over capital and profit. . . . And if you choose to live here among Hollanders, you can live under the privileges and institutions of God's church. This is important above all, not only for the benefit of one's own temporal and spiritual prosperity, but also for that of his children. . . .

P.S. One more thing, I began with little capital, which always hinders enterprise. Moreover, in the beginning there are always

> problems to be worked through. And yet, the profits were never less than 30% and 40%. With greater capital, interest is increased much more, and especially if you can double the capital. This can happen when the business affairs have developed more and the money market becomes better. The tannery brings large profits, up to 80%. These percentages would be much higher if various businesses work in combination. This is our plan and where it also naturally leads. This actually is the hidden art of American business, by which capital can be increased in a few years.[50]

This frank letter, which appealed both to Den Bleyker's pocketbook and his Christian conscience, won over Den Bleyker, but he came to regret the decision. Van Raalte had downplayed the risks of investing on the American frontier, even in the tight Dutch colony among fellow believers. In March 1851, Den Bleyker made the decision to move to Holland and invest in the project, taking a mortgage on Van Raalte's lands as security. The dominie provided the mill site along Black Lake, and his associate, Henry D. Post, Holland merchant and postmaster, agreed for $200 plus traveling expenses to contract for machinery and build the mill. Post bought a powerful steam engine built by Gates & Co. of Chicago and soon joined the firm as a partner. Despite some stumbling blocks in funding the company, named Post & Co., the gristmill successfully went into operation in August and the sawmill a few months later.[51]

But Den Bleyker never moved with his family to Holland, although he purchased a fine house in town. Heavy rains in May washed out the corn sprouts and sharply reduced the crop, so the Den Bleyker Mill, as it was called, lost money instead of making generous profits. Then to his chagrin, Van Raalte wrote that he was unable to repay Den Bleyker's loan and help cover the losses.

Post & Co., meanwhile, had to deal with the financial fallout. In November 1851, the partners Van Raalte and Post sold the bankrupt

[50] Van Raalte to Den Bleyker, 9 January 1851. I quote this letter at length because of its revealing insights about Van Raalte's business acumen and persuasive powers.

[51] For this and the next paragraph, see Van Raalte to Den Bleyker, 28 February, 11, 18 March, 21 April, 3 June, 8, 22 August 1851, BHL; Van Raalte to De Moen, 23 May 1851, JAH; Henry D. Post and Paulus Den Bleyker, agreement, 19 June 1851, HMA; *Grand Haven (Mich.) Grand River Times*, 21 July 1852; *De Nederlander* (Kalamazoo), 20 August 1852.

company with its "considerable" indebtedness of $5,800 (owed to sixteen creditors) for a token sum of $1 to two of the largest creditors, [Jonas C.] Heartt & Co. of Troy and George Colt of Williamsburg, both in New York. The agreement required the partners to turn over the lands and property put up as collateral, which must have pained Van Raalte greatly. It included five lots and forty acres, together with their ashery and saleratus factory and all fixtures, a house and steam mill, 600 bushels of ashes, 15,000 pounds of black salts, 120 saleratus boxes, a team of oxen and lumber wagon, and 200 cords of wood. A few weeks later, Van Raalte indemnified Post by giving him nine mortgages on ten Holland village lots, valued at $420. Van Raalte pegged his total losses in the venture at $2,000 to $3,000. This was Den Bleyker's first and last business venture in Holland, much to Van Raalte's keen disappointment.[52]

Going bankrupt in the Den Bleyker venture was a sobering experience for Van Raalte and he learned how easy it was to lose property put up as collateral. The early 1850s were also personally dark ones for Van Raalte and his family. His wife Christina was sickly and two babies died in infancy, the local newspaper editor charged him with highhandedness in colonial affairs, and conflict began in the Classis of Holland that culminated in 1857 in a church split.[53]

Mortgage Troubles

The disastrous milling venture weighed heavily on Van Raalte and threatened the financial future of his family for several years.

[52] "Schedule A" of Post & Co indebtedness, dated 3 November 1851, lists the sixteen creditors (photocopy in Hyma, *Van Raalte*, 150); Indenture between Post & Company and Heartt & Company and George Colt, executed 3 November 1851, Ottawa County Deed Register, Book A, Miscellaneous Records, 22-25; Henry D. Post to A. C. Van Raalte, Bond, 13 December 1851, Van Raalte Collection, CCA; Van Raalte to Brummelkamp, 11 September 1852; Henry D. Post and George Post of New York City (Post & Co.) to George Colt, assignee of Henry D. Post and A. C. Van Raalte, "formerly doing business under the name of Post & Co.," Deed, $559, 16 February 1854, Ottawa County Deed Register, Book G, 654-55, and Book H, 227-28. In 1853 Theodore White of Grand Haven bought the Den Bleyker sawmill for $4,200 and operated it successfully with a partner, Nicholas Vyn, of Holland, under the name White, Vyn & Co. (later Plugger, Vyn & Co). See Lucas, *Netherlanders in America*, 284.

[53] Bruins, "Van Raalte," 63-64; Robert P. Swierenga and Elton J. Bruins, *Family Quarrels in the Dutch Reformed Churches in the Nineteenth Century* (Grand Rapids: Eerdmans, 1997), 61-89.

"One dark storm or other darker clouds are packing together above me, threatening me with destruction," he wrote his colleague, Rev. John Garretson, Secretary of the Board of Domestic Missions of the Reformed Church in New York City. His indebtedness in late 1852 was $4,000 and losses on the Den Bleyker Mill likely pushed the total to $5,000.[54] Most critical were the annual mortgage payments due on the valuable tracts of lands he had purchased in 1847 from Silsbee and Schermerhorn. Final payments on these mortgages were due in 1853 and he lacked the monies. He might even have to sell his home and farm to cover these large financial obligations. This predicament forced him to write pathetic letters pleading for more time to avoid foreclosure. He owed the Silsbee estate $900 and Schieffelin (who had purchased Schermerhorn's mortgage) $1,600. Van Raalte assured Silsbee's son and executor: "I will surely pay you just as fast as possible. I hate debts."[55]

To gain concessions from Schieffelin, who still owed money on the land contract with Courtland Palmer, Van Raalte had his ministerial colleagues, Garretson and Rev. Thomas De Witt, pastor of the Marble Collegiate Church, act as intermediaries. He asked both to use their "influence" on Schieffelin to find a way to avoid foreclosure. "I am willing to make every sacrifice to avoid this forced sale," Van Raalte implored Garretson. "It would hurt my position, it would be ruinous to my family . . . I beseech you to work and pray for me." In a follow-up letter a month later, Van Raalte detailed the wider implications of his predicament. If Schieffelin foreclosed, it would wipe out the titles of several immigrant families who had bought parts of the tract from Van Raalte and begun farms. He was willing to give up his home and farm for "these ruined families," despite the distress it would cause "my dear wife," but "it can not make up their loss, it can not heal the breach, it can not cure the evil." Worse yet was the spiritual cost. "It will crush the hearts of the pious and strengthen the hands of the ungodly; the evil heart and Satan will make use of the ignorance of the many to undermine my influence as a minister of the Gospel." If Schieffelin could not make any concessions, Van Raalte as a last resort offered to come to New York, deeds in hand to Holland village lots, to give

54 Van Raalte to Brummelkamp, 11 September 1852.

55 Hyma, *Van Raalte*, 164-65 (quote 165); Van Raalte to Garretson, New York, 18 April 1854, Correspondence, Board of Domestic Missions, Reformed Church in America, box 11, Denominational Archives, New Brunswick, N.J. (hereafter BDM), copy in VRI.

to Schieffelin, who could then "hunt up" some sixteen friends to buy them cheap at $100 apiece, and thereby cover the debt.[56]

In both cases the dominie found the lenders sympathetic to his cash squeeze and willing to give more time. Suydam and Schieffelin paid off the Palmer mortgage, which ended the immediate threat of foreclosure, and they agreed to take interest only on Van Raalte's note. "They have done a most noble act towards me," the dominie wrote to Garretson. "Last summer I was in great danger of a most ruinous destruction on account of a mortgage over a great deal of lands which I could not pay in time. They have taken the mortgage and did pay them to Mr. Palmer. May God reward them abundantly with temporal and spiritual blessings." A year later Garretson offered Van Raalte financial help from Mission Board funds, but he declined "because my creditors, the brothers Suydam and Schieffelin, are very patient with me and are so patient to receive only the interest for the present."[57]

Van Raalte paid off the Silsbee mortgage in 1855. In 1857 he gave Suydam and Schieffelin a new mortgage note on his own eighty-acre farm as security for $874 still owed on the original loan, with interest of 7 percent per annum. In 1864 Van Raalte still owed the note plus interest, amounting to about $1,000. At this point Schieffelin took back two new $500 mortgages bearing 7 percent interest, one each signed by Albertus and Christina, and he then assigned them to John Brower, treasurer of the General Synod of the Reformed Church. The $1,000 debt was now placed on the church books and Van Raalte thereafter paid annual interest on the notes to the denominational treasurer. In 1872 the denominational treasurer paid off Schieffelin and the mortgage was cancelled, but Van Raalte continued to make periodic payments to the denomination on his and Christina's bonds until his death in 1876, and his son Dirk continued to pay interest and principal until the notes were finally paid off in 1885! So the Courtland Palmer mortgage of 1847 essentially evolved into a forty-year loan on the dominie's home and farm![58]

56 Van Raalte to Garretson, New York City, 22 June, 15 July 1853, BDM.

57 The legal description was the NE1/4 SW1/4 and NW1/4 SE1/4 Sec. 28 T5N R15W, 80 contiguous acres. Van Raalte to Garretson, 18 April, 10 May 1854, BDM.

58 James Suydam et al. to Albertus C. Van Raalte, 10 March 1857, Release of Mortgage, Ottawa County Deed Records, Book D, p. 17; Trustees of Nathaniel Silsbee, Salem, Essex County, Massachusetts, to Van Raalte, Indenture Deed, 5 June 1855, Ottawa County Deed Records; Samuel B.

Subsequently, both Suydam and Schieffelin contributed to Van Raalte's signal project, endowing Hope College and placing the fledgling school on a firm fiscal foundation. After Van Raalte's colony at Amelia Courthouse, Virginia, failed in 1871, Schieffelin came to his rescue a second time and purchased 162 acres from him for $5,160. The tract, known as the "court house property," was a choice piece of land well worth $31.85 an acre. Van Raalte had purchased the land in November 1869.[59]

The financial setbacks that Van Raalte experienced in the early 1850s impacted his preaching negatively and this became a subject of concern in his congregation. In 1853 his elders felt it necessary to tell him that "the power of his preaching seems to have disappeared," and they advised him to "lay aside some other activities . . . in order to be more active within the congregation."[60]

This admonition and the financial problems dissuaded him from new business ventures for six years. Then he was drawn in again by Albertus, his firstborn son, who inherited his father's entrepreneurial instincts but not his capabilities. In 1859 the dominie bought for Albertus, then twenty-two years of age, the Holland Nursery tree farm of Homer Hudson in Georgetown Township for $1,060, including "all the fruit trees standing thereon." Father Van Raalte made the final mortgage payment on the property in 1865.[61] In 1863 Albertus began

---

Schieffelin to Van Raalte, 4 April 1857; Van Raalte to Schieffelin, Mortgage Indentures, 10 March 1857, 20 May 1864; Schieffelin to John B. Brower, Treasurer of the Reformed Protestant Dutch Church, Assignment of Mortgage, 20 May 1864; Schieffelin to Van Raalte, Satisfaction of [1857] Mortgage, 23 August 1864; Albertus Van Raalte to Schieffelin, by General Synod of Reformed Church in America, Satisfaction of [1864] Mortgage, 5 September 1872. Copies of all legal documents and Schieffelin correspondence cited are in CCA. The Van Raalte bonds are noted in Treasurer Brower's report for 1871-72 in *Acts and Proceedings of the General Synod of the Reformed Church in America*, June 1872, 418.

59 Van Raalte to Schieffelin, Indenture Deed, 3 April 1871, Van Raalte Collection, CCA.

60 First Reformed Church Consistory Minutes, 28 March 1853, Art. 3-4.

61 Indenture Deed for two tracts, totaling seventeen acres, in Sec. 28 T5N R15W, from Homer E. and Clarinda Burt Hudson to Albertus C. Van Raalte, 19 April 1859, Ottawa County Deed Register, Book 0, 617, and Book P, 109; A. C. Van Raalte to Homer E. Hudson, Notes, 19 April 1859, 18 November 1865, and Deed Book P, 489. Van Raalte had purchased a half interest in Hudson's tree nursery on 31 December 1851 in the names of his five oldest children. In 1859 he bought Hudson's half, giving Albertus Van Raalte sole control (Deed Book E, 361).

a second venture by entering into partnership with Warren Wilder, a Grand Haven millwright, in a lumber and shingle mill in Olive Township, under the company name Wilder & Van Raalte. A year later, in March 1864, the dominie joined the firm, and each partner invested $1500. Van Raalte's share came by buying land in Olive Township from Wilder. The junior Van Raalte raised some of his capital by selling two thousand acres of land to Wilder for $400, and the pair pledged to "devote their whole time to the business." The dominie was only responsible "to put in his place a person (a Competent Bookkeeper) at his expense to be his representative in the business," renamed Wilder & Company.[62]

Less than four months later, the dominie bought out Wilder's interest for $1700 ($500 down and three years for the remainder at 10 percent interest), and Albertus was on his own. But his business acumen was questionable. The younger son Ben, then serving in the Civil War, called the decision to go into the mill business during wartime "a silly thing." Albertus might succeed if "he is lucky," but "I am sometimes afraid that he feels like a man standing on ice—a little unsteady. I personally do not like the mill business but, if it is handled right, a good living can be made at it." Whether Albertus made a go of the mill is doubtful; five years later he abandoned his wife and five children and was never heard from again.[63]

Serving Two Masters?

Financial pressures from his generally poor business affairs continued to consume Van Raalte. His land holdings made him a wealthy man on paper, yet he complained of being "land poor," because his money was tied up in unproductive land and he had to raise cash for the annual tax bill. In 1860 he was by far the wealthiest man in

[62] Albertus and Helena Van Raalte to Warren Wilder, Indenture Deed, 15 March 1864, Deed Book Y, 127; Warren Wilder, Albertus C. Van Raalte, and Albertus Van Raalte, Contract, 16 March 1864; A. C. Van Raalte to Warren and Olivia Wilder, 27 July 1864, Deed Book U, 307-8 and Book Y, 141; *De Hollander*, 29 February 1860.

[63] Warren Wilder, Albertus C. Van Raalte, and Albertus Van Raalte, Agreement, 27 July 1864, Van Raalte Collection, CCA; Ben Van Raalte, Johnsonville, Tennessee, to A. C. Van Raalte, 17 November 1864, HMA; Elton J. Bruins et al., *Albertus and Christina: The Van Raalte Family, Home and Roots* (Grand Rapids: Eerdmans, 2004), 67-69.

Holland Township, which made him one of the few men subject to the temporary Civil War income tax law in 1862.[64]

He admitted the pressure in a confidential letter to Rev. Giles Van de Wall, his former associate and teacher at the Holland Academy, who was serving as a missionary in South Africa.

> I am burdened with temporal difficulties that are great and that demand all of the time of a strong person. . . . On the one hand, I have to see to it that idle property yields a return or I will have to sell it to pay the taxes. On the other hand I say, "Is it proper for me to busy myself with worldly matters, since I should devote myself to preaching the Gospel?" And still I am responsible for the needs of my family. I am in a quandary. . . . [This] often leads me to say, "Is it not my duty to look for another field of labor, where I am not hampered by earthly difficulties?"[65]

A decade earlier, Van Raalte expressed even more angst about wealth in a letter to Brummelkamp:

> I came here naked, but I have been able to live with a large family and was able to spend as one who had capital. But despite my continual resistance, yes, bitterness toward God and man, I find myself placed with possessions, which if it pleased God could make me a capitalist. And yet, they were thrown around my neck for my lack of trust and to kill me. They are possessions that the worldling by turns praises and envies, and still those same possessions seem to become my grace or my destruction because of the debts connected to this and from my position, at least to be for me a source of distressing cares. Often I ask Why? Why? Yet I have the root of all devilish evil in me and also the root of the desire to become rich. . . . Sometimes I say in impatience, let everything break up and go to pieces as it will. However, in a calmer moment, I see it is not without God's providence that I was placed in this important position.[66]

64 Van Raalte had to pay $400 in 1862 under the new federal income tax law (Bruins, "Van Raalte," 58).

65 Van Raalte to Van de Wall, 29 June 1862, Van Raalte Collection, CCA, translated by Nella Kennedy.

66 Van Raalte to Brummelkamp, 11 September 1852.

These telling letters shows that Van Raalte wrestled with his calling as a minister of the gospel and his desire to enjoy a standard of living above that of most of his parishioners. He was torn between serving "two masters." Yet, he was the only university-educated man among thousands of immigrants, and this alone justified an upper-middle-class lifestyle, according to his Old World standards.

More Land

Although land dealings brought complications in his life, Van Raalte could not resist buying more, despite the debt to the denomination still owed on his home. Between 1859 and 1874, he invested $10,000 in more land (Table 1). In February 1865, he purchased all the swamplands held by the Harbor Board for $3,500, with $200 down and the remainder in three years at 7 percent interest.[67] Improving the harbor had been a priority from the outset. The second purchase of swamplands was "for my boys," the dominie noted. The same year he paid Holland merchant Peter Pfanstiehl $2,160 for six parcels totaling 1,440 acres. To seal the deal, Pfanstiehl demanded two choice town lots in return, for which he paid $290. Van Raalte sold several other town lots to raise more cash, but not enough to pay off the Pfanstiehl contract. Within days the he was writing Philip Phelps, president of his favorite endeavor, the Holland Academy, and complaining that the "pledge of the Pfanstiehl lots drives me to a corner." He hoped Phelps could induce the trustees to buy eight half lots located adjacent to the campus for "Professorial residences" at a price of $140 each. "This chance never comes back," Van Raalte reminded Phelps, "once the lots are sold and occupied by a miserable mixture of houses of every description. . . . Is it possible in some way to secure them for the object?" The school trustees did not bail him out.[68]

Van Raalte was so entrepreneurial-minded that he viewed colleges such as Hope in broad economic terms. Colleges, he said,

[67] A. C. Van Raalte with Holland Harbor Board, Contract, 4 February 1865, Van Raalte Collection, CCA. The first part of the purchase was made on 25 November 1862 from John Roost, for $1,492, Ottawa County Deed Register, Book W, 496. In 1867, Van Raalte still owed the Harbor Fund $2,000 for the lands. See "Statement of Debts and Credits of the Township of Holland . . . on the first day of April A.D. 1867," HMA.

[68] Peter F. Pfanstiehl and his wife Helena Mastenbroek to Albertus C. Van Raalte, Indenture Deed, 18 October 1865, Ottawa County Deed Register, Book Z, 166; Van Raalte to Phelps, 7 November 1865, Van Raalte Papers, JAH.

> produce the greatest indirect profits and benefits. . . . [They] make property values rise. They promote the growth of a community. They create markets and life. They attract capital and the best kind of inhabitants to such a place. Imagine for a moment of how much capital would this place have been deprived annually if the educational work of late years had not been promoted? What would our characters be worth? What would real estate prices be?[69]

How prescient this view was. Hope College has done that and much more for Holland.

Van Raalte helped the college wring profits from its landed endowment. In 1869 James Suydam donated $5,000 for the college to buy a choice tract, the Point Superior Farm on Black Lake (now Marigold Lodge). When Van Raalte learned of the gift and the possibility of $2,000 more to clear all debts on the property, he suggested renaming it the Suydam Farm. He also asked his son Ben to go into partnership with him to raise peach trees on a high-lying portion of the property. He offered Ben $30 a year to manage the project, plus all expenses for seed pits, fertilizer, and fencing. If done properly, in three years the Van Raaltes would have peaches aplenty for their table and even more to sell for the benefit of the College.[70]

After Van Raalte retired in 1867 as pastor of First Reformed Church, until his death in 1876, he was free as a private citizen to devote more time and energy to financial matters. This was especially the case after his return to Holland in 1869, following an unsuccessful attempt to plant a new Dutch colony at Amelia Courthouse, Virginia, which caused him to lose several thousand dollars. He had financed that venture in large part by selling for $5,000 in 1867-68 three building lots and a steam-powered sawmill to Thomas Padgett of Rochele, Illinois, director of the Port Sheldon Lumber Company.[71]

The largest transaction in his entire life took place in 1871 when the Michigan Lake Shore Railroad paid $11,000 for forty-five choice lots for a new depot and right-of-way alongside the college campus.

69 A. C. Van Raalte, New York City, to Benjamin Van Raalte, 13 November 1869, Van Raalte Collection, CCA.

70 Van Raalte to Phelps, 5, 22, 23 November 1869, Van Raalte Papers, Hope College Collection, JAH; A. C. Van Raalte to Benjamin Van Raalte, 13 November 1869.

71 Van Raalte to Padgett, 1 June 1867, $1,000, Ottawa County Deed Register, Book 5, 171; Van Raalte to Padgett, 27 October 1868, $4,000, Book 3, 398. The property was Lots 3, 4, and 6 of Sec. 16, T6N R16W.

Van Raalte was inclined not to sell when the railroad first came calling, but Holland residents were caught up in a fevered campaign to bring rail service to town and had even voted to bond themselves to entice the company not to bypass the town. In the years from 1870 to 1876, Van Raalte sold seventy-nine town lots and one thousand acres of farmland for $50,000 (Table 2). The largest sale, for $10,000, three months before his death, was to son Dirk B. K. Van Raalte for the purchase of the dominie's homestead and farm, with the proviso that the two youngest daughters, Maria and Anna, could continue to live in the house until their marriages.[72]

A Proposed Bank

In his business activities, the biggest problem Van Raalte and his partners faced was the lack of capital for development, which was a ubiquitous problem on the American frontier. For manufacturing and trade to flourish, Holland needed a bank to issue reputable (rather than wildcat) bank notes, and for some time he considered chartering a bank under the aegis of the state banking act of 1857. Nathan Kenyon had opened the first private bank in Holland in 1856 and Kommer Schaddelee followed suit in 1871 with an exchange bank. Both accepted savings deposits, paid in currency on merchant's drafts and private bank notes submitted for exchange, and issued notes (paper money). But private bank notes lacked credibility and were worth no more than the reputation of the issuer. Van Raalte hoped to form a local bank that could tie in to the national banking system created by Congress during the Civil War, which was empowered to issue to bank notes, dubbed Greenbacks.[73]

The disastrous Holland Fire of 8 October 1871 forced Van Raalte to seek to implement his banking plan. The flames spared his home, church, and college, but the entire business district and the residential heart of town was lost. Holland could not be rebuilt without capital.

[72] Compiled from Ottawa County Deed Registers, 15 July 1871, Book 14, 250-51; Book 15, 140-41; Book 29, 410 (Van Raalte deed to son Dirk). Chester Warner of Chicago, a principal in the railway, is listed as the purchaser on $4,000 worth of the deeds.

[73] "Our Banking System," *Holland City News*, 26 October 1872; Darlene Winter, "100 Years Ago Today," *Holland Sentinel*, 20 December 1986; *Sheboygan (Wis.) Nieuwsbode*, 24 May 1871; Randall Vande Water, "First Bank Was a Home," *Holland: Happenings, Heroes and Hot Shots*, 4 vols. (Holland, Mich., 1995-97), 3:26-29.

"I must go ahead or give up," he told Phelps, then in New York City to raise money for Hope College. Van Raalte envisioned a National Bank capitalized at $50,000 to $100,000, but the way to reach that goal was unclear. If he sought help to obtain a charter from Americans in Grand Haven, such as U.S. Senator Thomas F. Ferry, the news would get out and "sharpers" and "society-enervating leeches or blood suckers" would try to take over.[74]

Van Raalte's "ripe plan," as he called it, was brilliant. He would partner with Arent Geerlings, a "practical miller" with a solid reputation, whose City Mills and feed store (Werkman, Geerlings & Company) were both destroyed by the fire. With $16,000 to $20,000 in start-up capital, half coming from mortgages on Van Raalte's farmlands, he and Geerlings could begin a small bank that might be able to attract capital from "eastern friends," i.e., Dutch Reformed capitalists in New York. They would "take stock in it" by depositing government bonds, from which they would continue to clip 6 percent coupons. With the bonds as collateral, the bank would issue bank notes as loans to farmers and manufacturers. This would increase the local money supply and "bring business life back" after the fire. Hope College could also invest its endowment monies in the bank and borrow from it to erect buildings.

The bank could operate out of a rebuilt feed store in Holland, with branches in outlying villages. Supplying feed and other necessities to farmers is "a safe and good business," Van Raalte reasoned, and the bank could piggyback on that cachet and expand into banking and investment services. "We could expect the first years more than barely to keep alive," but the business would expand "as fast as small deposits grow on the hands," Van Raalte told Phelps. "All my property is given to it, even self preservation compels me. . . . Most sickening will be our situation without capital." Van Raalte then came to the bottom line. "If you could effect a loan for me of 20 m [thousand] on ample security on real estate, this would perhaps provide matters. They tell me Life insurance companies are doing this sometimes." Despite the dominie's desperate tone and the bleak situation facing the city, his appeal to "eastern friends" went unheeded. No money for a charter bank in

[74] Van Raalte to Phelps, 23 October, 8 November 1871, Van Raalte Papers, Hope College Collection, JAH; Adrian Van Koevering, *Legends of the Dutch* (Zeeland, Mich.: Zeeland Historical Record, 1960), 475.

Holland was forthcoming until 1889, although relief funds for the townspeople did arrive.[75]

Conclusion

In his economic endeavors, Van Raalte can better be described as a promoter and fundraiser than a businessman. He raised tens of thousands of dollars in the East for colonial lands, Holland harbor, the Colonial Church, Hope College, and various business ventures.[76] His prime goal at the outset was to ensure the success of the Colony, not to play the role of capitalist and accrue wealth. Yet his entrepreneurial mindset, capitalistic attitude toward money, and eagerness to take risks in various enterprises inevitably drew him into business life. Only his duties as pastor constrained him from taking a more hands-on role; he could be a partner and co-investor but not the person in charge.

Lots and lands, however, did lend themselves to his direct management, since he could squeeze sales, legal work, and tax payments in between his pastoral duties. His dabbling in factories and mills did not prove profitable, whereas real estate dealings made him a fabulously wealthy man. Land in and around Holland gained value while he slept, due to the rapid and steady development of the community. He got in "on the ground floor" and parlayed a modest investment in land into a portfolio worth $5 million in today's dollars. It was Van Raalte, not Den Bleyker, who deserves the title of "wealthiest Hollander in Michigan."

[75] Henry S. Lucas, *Dutch Immigrant Memoirs and Related Writings*, rev. ed., 2 vols. (Assen, the Netherlands: Van Gorcum, 1955; reprint, Grand Rapids: Eerdmans, 1997), 2:495; Van Raalte to Phelps, 23 October, 8 November 1871; Vande Water, "Holland Had State Bank in 1889," *Holland: Happenings, Heroes, and Hot Shots*, 2:62-64. The *Holland City News* gave some credence to Van Raalte's efforts. Its 10 August 1872 issue reported: "We learn that movements are being made toward establishing a National Bank in this city, and that it promises a success."

[76] Bruins, "Van Raalte," 55-57, lists the dominie's fundraising efforts.

Table 1: A. C. Van Raalte Land Purchases, 1847-76

Year	$ Total*	No. Buys	Acreage	Lots
1847	7346	80	7288	0
1848	2536	41	3010	0
1849	3981	18	1349	1
1850	103	5	720	0
1851	393	14	840	0
1852	35	13	1024	0
1853	0	0	0	0
1854	50	1	83	0
1855	0	0	0	0
1857	0	0	0	0
1858	11	1	320	0
1859	1180	2	17	2
1860	950	3	240	2
1861	660	3	120	1
1862	9	3	0	3
1863	910	3	1582	0
1864	1480	13	1040	0
1865	2160	12	1440	0
1866	400	1	0	0
1867	540	2	0	2
1868	0	0	0	0
1869	0	0	0	0
1870	300	1	0	1
1871	1100	2	80	1
1872	0	0	0	0
1873	0	0	0	0
1874	400	1	40	1
1875	0	0	0	0
1876	0	0	0	0
Total	24,504	219	19,193	14

*Van Raalte bought some lands, especially in 1847, with small cash down payments, and sellers took back mortgages for the remainder. The mortgage payments of principal and interest are not included.

Table 2: A. C. Van Raalte Land Sales, 1848-76

Year	$Total*	No. Sales	Acreage	City Lots
1848	1984	27	1211	2
1849	2158	20	563	14
1850	923	19	70	22
1851	2558	26	454	36
1852	3844	44	146	98
1853	1511	18	730	18
1854	995	8	199	10
1855	2540	18	234	17
1856	1130	11	40	13
1857	2619	19	212	36
1858	710	7	0	15
1859	750	6	110	5
1860	4070	28	59	67
1861	2559	18	80	20
1862	1993	20	112	53
1863	2440	25	70	32
1864	4016	29	120	46
1865	4866	25	40	30
1866	2250	3	1571	2
1867	10701	32	16	66
1868	5390	13	120	21
1869	4485	12	105	15
1870	3620	8	0	43
1871	16567	17	192	92
1872	4035	12	0	12
1873	3630	9	350	12
1874	3010	8	220	4
1875	5075	13	80	16
1876	14981	12	160	24
1878	240	1	0	1
Totals	116,650	509	7264	842

* These sums are the gross amount of land sales. On an unknown number of sales, Van Raalte accepted down payments and extended credit at interest for several years. This interest income is not included here.

Table 3: Village Board of Trustees Land Purchases, 1847-51

Year	$ Total	No. Buys*	Acreage	Lots
1848	201	3	140	1

Table 4: Village Board of Trustees Land Sales, 1847-51

Year	$ Total	No. Sales*	Acreage	Lots
1847	1810	35	0	38
1848	2230	49	0	59
1849	548	12	0	68
1850	618	8	0	8
1851	563	3	80	1

*These sums are the gross amount of land sales. In twenty-one sales, the Trustees accepted down payments and extended credit at 7 percent interest for several years. The subsequent payments of principal and interest are not included.

CHAPTER 13

Will the Circle Be Unbroken?: An Essay on Hope College's Four Presidential Eras[1]

James C. Kennedy

A president constitutes the very face of an institution. Presidents are the ones who get credit for successful building projects or get blamed for failing endowments. And they are the ones considered responsible for the school's academic reputation, and its commitment to the stated vision of the college. In matters over which they exercise much control, and in matters where they do not, presidents set the standard by which colleges and universities are measured.

But writing the institutional history of a college or university is more than writing the history of presidents, as historians have realized in recent decades. Presidents do not, after all, shape these institutions alone, reliant as they are on a wide range of external and internal circumstances and actors. Presidents may have their plans, but these plans are often thwarted by reality, or lead to results they have neither expected nor desired. Presidents sometimes fail to overcome the enormous challenges, often of a structural kind, that were arrayed against them. And even if we should take presidents as important agents in institutional history, we must realize that much of what they achieved, or failed to achieve, was not a matter of formal policy, stored in archives, but by less formal processes, perceived in less formal

1 I want to thank Earl Wm. Kennedy and Carol Simon for their reading of earlier versions of this contribution.

accounts, including interviews with those who witnessed what was never written down. Furthermore, our more democratized sentiments have—rightly—developed a new concern for other kinds of players, including the roles played by women or students, often left out of most traditional histories. In sum, there are many important reasons to write about an institution's history—including Hope College's history—along lines that do not overestimate the role of presidents and their formal policies.

Perhaps these concerns, however, permit us to think about Hope College's presidents in a different and broader way: not only as agents of history (though that they certainly must remain) but as representatives of the world in which they respectively lived. They may be regarded as representatives of the college constituencies they served, and, more generally, as representative of developments and shifts in American Christian higher education. Seen this way, Calvin Vander Werf—one of the college's most controversial presidents—was not merely an *Einzelgänger* who substantially shifted the religious direction of the college, but was at the same time representative of a much longer trend in Protestant higher education. In fact, much of his outlook was shared by his immediate predecessors, Wynand Wichers and Irwin Lubbers, presidents who, like Vander Werf, believed in "the forward look" that sought to take Hope College out of its isolation and give it a respected place in the American educational firmament.

From this perspective, Hope's presidents acted as representatives of a "generation," in which they exhibited important lines of continuities with some of their predecessors and successors. "Generation" in this context does not necessarily mean that they were all born at the same time, but the term is meant to signify that for roughly a generation (thirty to forty years) at a time, Hope's presidents shared a similar outlook on the mission of the college, which itself reflected the priorities of the college's key constituencies. Seen this way, the college's past can be divided into four periods of three presidents each. Each of these periods reflect, despite important continuities, a tangibly different religious program and set of religious sensibilities, with each set of presidents adumbrating the religious climate of their times. This does not mean, of course, that they were indistinguishable from each other, or that they were mere marionettes of their age; each president set his own indelible stamp on the college. But each president shared essential commonalities with his rough contemporaries in each of these four periods. Perhaps it would not go too far to say that each cohort, in a loose sense, has constituted four generations of "representative men," each lasting three to four decades, and each with its own distinct set of religious concerns.

This essay is an effort to read the history of Hope College in this way. It has the advantage of seeing the history of the college in a perspective that is different from standard institutional histories, with its accent on discrete presidencies, or other kinds of institutional histories, like those of George Marsden or James Burtchaell, with its emphasis on a single development (e.g., the gradual disappearance of Christianity at the institutions they study).[2] This approach allows for a long view of Hope's history while at the same time paying attention to important breaks and junctures in that history. This does not mean, of course, that this is the only way to periodize the history of the college; indeed, the book *Can Hope Endure?*, which I wrote with my former colleague Carol Simon, does not use this periodization.[3] Nor should one claim that the four periods of three presidents each is sacrosanct. Indeed, the inclusion of G. Henry Mandeville in the first set, who served as acting president for only two years, is already indicative of a certain literary license, suggesting a symmetry that is all too tidy for earthly reality.

Nevertheless, this approach is a useful means for one to reflect upon Hope's nearly 150-year history, and perhaps to ruminate about its future. This essay shows that all presidents attempted to negotiate a center between competing ideals and constituencies, confirming the story in *Can Hope Endure?* that Hope College throughout much of its history attempted to steer a "middle way" between more progressive and traditional currents. At the same time, the content and direction of this "middle way" shifted every generation or so, as evidenced in the four presidential eras outlined below.

The Clerical Patrons: Phelps, Mandeville, Scott (1862-92)

As Elton Bruins—who himself played an instrumental role in the college's religious history—has argued, it is really Philip Phelps (1862-78), not Albertus Van Raalte, who deserves recognition for founding

2 George M. Marsden, *The Soul of the American University: From Protestant Establishment to Established Nonbelief* (New York: Oxford, 1994); James T. Burtchaell, *The Dying of the Light* (Grand Rapids: Eerdmans, 1998).

3 James C. Kennedy and Caroline Simon, *Can Hope Endure?: A Historical Case Study in Christian Higher Education* (Grand Rapids: Eerdmans, 2005).

Hope College.[4] It was Phelps, after all, who repeatedly urged the creation of such an institution, and who served from 1859 as the fourth principal of the Holland Academy, which in 1862 accepted its first entering class for what would formally be recognized as Hope College four years later. Thus it was Phelps who both managed and structured the curriculum of the liberal arts college from 1862 until his effective removal as president in the late 1870s.

But Phelps constituted part of a larger pattern that was decisive for the future of the college: the dominating presence of teachers and clergymen from the Eastern wing of the Reformed Church in America. The Christian Reformed Church, in contrast, could draw on few such resources, and though they could depend on pastors from the Netherlands, the establishment of Calvin College as the liberal arts institution it is today was retarded by the absence of these Eastern figures so central to Hope's history. For most of Hope's nineteenth-century history, the college was not only dependent on Eastern money, but on Eastern leadership, which included but also went beyond the ability to raise funds. The college depended to a very important extent on Eastern teachers, frequently from Rutgers College and New Brunswick Seminary, who possessed the necessary expertise in both secular and religious fields. Teachers like the future president Charles Scott (acting president 1880-85; formally 1885-92) were expected to be conversant in both. It is easy to see how Hope acquired its American character from its inception, even as Phelps tried to accommodate the Western immigrants' emphasis on theological education; for these thirty years, from the Civil War until the early 1890s, it was headed by Eastern clergymen who offered leadership to a Western constituency.

More than their successors, the first three presidents of Hope College constituted a generation in the most literal sense of the term. All three of them were born in New York State in the 1820s; they all became clergymen through completing a course of study at New Brunswick

[4] For a documentary underpinning of this thesis, see Elton J. Bruins, "Early Hope College History as Reflected in the Correspondence of Rev. Albertus C. Van Raalte to Rev. Philip Phelps Jr. 1857-1875" in *The Dutch Adapting in North America: Papers Presented at the Thirteenth Biennial Conference for the Association for the Advancement of Dutch-American Studies*, ed. Richard H. Harms (Grand Rapids: AADAS, 2001). Paper may be found as well in the Hope College Collection, H88-0019, Joint Archives of Holland (hereafter, JAH).

Seminary around 1850 and thereafter served Eastern RCA churches; and they all died within a decade of each other, in the years straddling the turn of the twentieth century. They were not, of course, Dutch in any way resembling Van Raalte or the Western Church; instead, their appreciation for the ethnicity of the church came primarily in their articulated esteem for the history of the Reformed Protestant Dutch Church (renamed the Reformed Church in America in 1867). This might have come naturally to some more than others; Mandeville came from a family of Reformed Church pastors in New Jersey and New York; Phelps's mother had ties to the Reformed Church, and Scott, raised a Presbyterian and of Scottish descent, came into the Dutch church as an adult, after having studied at Rutgers and, later, undergoing a conversion experience that prompted him to enter New Brunswick Seminary. But for all three, a primary point of their dealings with the Western settlers lay in the denomination's longer history stretching back to the Classis of Amsterdam in the Dutch Republic. It was this still tangibly ethnic history, more than theology alone, which served for them as the important source of solidarity with the Westerners. "Palsied be the hand that sunders these golden chains, and takes that immigration away from the historical faith of their Fatherland," Scott pronounced in 1884, unhappy with the increasing number of new settlers joining the CRC.[5]

All three presidents, too, were intellectually formed in the years before the Civil War, in the years before Darwin, higher criticism, and academic specialization, when knowledge seemed of a whole piece and when the evidences of God in creation were not widely doubted. All professed academic interest for the whole field of knowledge, though perhaps Scott, who was appointed in 1866 Professor of Chemistry and Natural History and Lector of Sacred and Church History at Hope College and its Theological Department, is the best example of this wide range of interests. In an obituary the eulogist praised him as a scholar and noted:

> His mind was bright and active, and his faculty for acquisition was well balanced along all lines of study. He was a linguist, a mathematician and a scientist. As a student and teacher he was noted for his love of accuracy. Of course, his great life work lay in

5 Charles Scott, "Address," in *Centennial of the Theological Seminary of the Reformed Church in America, 1784-1884* (New York, 1885), 252.

> his ministry and teaching. But he also had side lines of pursuit. Especially he was a laborious antiquarian and local, secular and church historian.[6]

Seen this way, Hope College's initial contours as an academic institution were very much shaped by the mid-nineteenth century mold that in turn had shaped its first presidents. In a context in which the Western churches were heavily reliant on Eastern support, its leading institution necessarily looked a lot like the Protestant colleges with which its leaders were familiar. And any significant variation—such as Phelps's unfilled aspirations for a Hope Haven University—was likely to run into trouble.

Religiously, the three presidents can safely be classified as orthodox, with a strong interest in missions that was perhaps most deeply felt by Phelps, though Scott, too, was strongly supportive of missionary endeavor. The great age of Hope's foreign missions efforts still lay in the future, although the first Hope graduate to do foreign mission work, Rev. Enne Heeren (a brother-in-law of future president Ame Vennema), left for India in 1872, and the great RCA missionary, Samuel Zwemer, graduated during the Scott presidency. Until the 1890s, though, the emphasis in practice lay with solidifying Hope as a center for home missions and for serving the Reformed Church, particularly the "West" (it was Scott who wrote the history of the RCA's home missions in the 1870s).[7] Scott himself stressed the importance of Hope for the whole denomination, noting that theology "has lost its power" in colleges like Princeton, Yale, and Rutgers (for which Scott had raised $10,000 in the early 1860s), whereas at Hope it remained "the crown of scholarship," and he predicted, accurately, that its graduates in the future "will fill the [ministerial] vacancies of the East."[8]

Although they were all denominational loyalists, the three clergymen eschewed sectarianism and were not particularly doctrinaire. Perhaps Mandeville is illustrative of their theological outlook. Often overlooked as president because he merely served as Acting President for two years (1878-80) while continuing as a minister at Harlem Reformed Church in New York City, Mandeville nevertheless played a decisive role in restoring the college's finances, through his long stints on the

6 Edward Tanjore Corwin, *Manual of the Reformed Church in America*, 4th ed. (New York, 1902), 711.

7 Scott, "Address."

8 Ibid., 253.

Council of Hope College and, soon after laying down his presidential tasks, becoming Secretary of the RCA's Board of Education (1883-1900). In his Baccalaureate Sermon, "The Bible and Civilization," given on the Hope campus in 1879, Mandeville expressed his confidence that Christianity was the great underwriter of advancing civilization, despite the presence of scientific skeptics and those who wished to remove the Scriptures from public schools. And in a statement that probably confirmed the worst suspicions of the Eastern Church of some more Calvinistic Westerners, Mandeville proclaimed:

> Never *was Christianity more clearly recognized* as *broader, larger, grander than any Church or than all Churches* and the Word of God as more comprehensive and glorious than any system of theology, Arminian or Calvanistic [*sic*], Wesleyan or Augustinian [italics original].[9]

Mandeville, who exercised most of his presidency from his New York base, was more "Eastern" and possibly more theologically latitudinarian—he was rumored to be a Freemason—than either Phelps or Scott, who spent many years working among and with the Westerners. Still, the emphasis on personal piety and collective Christian action, rather than a theologically or doctrinally critical stance, helped determine the spiritual trajectory of the college long after Scott resigned as president in 1892. The Western Church would not countenance the emerging theological liberalism that manifested itself at New Brunswick and the Eastern classes by the 1920s, but it retained much of the cheerful, practical orthodoxy embodied by its first presidents.

In their leadership, Hope's first three presidents were primarily patrons or trustees, overseeing the development of a nascent regional institution largely intended for immigrants and their children. And as guardians of the nascent Western church's interests, they constituted an important mediating role between the Eastern and Western sections of the church. Only after their successes, including the financial stability brought by Mandeville and Scott, and only after a generation of Hope graduates, was the Western Church able to take charge of its own institution.

9 G. Henry Mandeville, "The Bible and Modern Civilization. Baccalaureate Sermon at Hope College, June 22nd, 1879," (G. Henry Mandeville Papers, H88-101, JAH), 3.

The Immigrant Sons: Kollen, Vennema, Dimnent (1893-1931)

On the surface Gerrit Kollen, Ame Vennema, and Edward Dimnent are, on the basis of generational considerations as well as their professional and social status, harder to place within a single category than their predecessors. The eldest, Kollen (1893-1911), was born in the Netherlands in the 1840s; the youngest, Dimnent, in 1870s Chicago. Moreover, Dimnent (1918-31) died at a ripe age in 1959, in a world vastly different from the one Kollen had departed in 1915. Moreover, only Vennema, whose long and varied service to the Eastern churches most resembles Mandeville's career, was an ordained minister during his presidential tenure (1911-18). In contrast, Kollen was the quintessentially self-made man, somewhat reminiscent of his contemporary and fellow Dutch immigrant Edward Bok, who possessed the social skills and developed the social graces to make him a welcome guest at Andrew Carnegie's Scottish estate and at the mansions of New York's upper crust. The classicist Dimnent fit neither profile. A somewhat eccentric bachelor, he was both a financial wizard and an aspiring writer-poet, who seems to have spent a good deal of time in the 1920s (as his archive suggests) writing grandiloquent letters to parents whose children had misbehaved while at Hope.

Nevertheless, key similarities unite these men. They were all born of Dutch parents who were either about to emigrate or had recently immigrated, and they remained conversant in Dutch (Vennema occasionally intersperses his English-language letters to Dimnent, written after the First World War, with fluent Dutch sentences). At the same time, they opted consciously for Americanization; all three were members, like most of their predecessors and many of their successors, of Hope Church, the Anglophone bastion (by Holland, Michigan, standards) of progressive thought. They all rose from modest circumstances, received their bachelor's education at Hope, but, with the exception of Vennema's New Brunswick degree, had little graduate education, let alone an earned doctorate. Their place of leadership within the Midwestern RCA stemmed from the fact that they were preachers (Vennema) or teachers (Kollen taught high school before becoming a professor at Hope, and Dimnent taught at Hope after graduation), but in any case from the fact that they were pious Christians. Kollen as a young man was an occasional lay preacher, and Dimnent, who as president showed a considerable familiarity with theology, was ordained—after having served as president—in 1935.

In short, they were, in contrast to their predecessors, deeply rooted in the Dutch Midwestern Reformed Church, while at the same time, in different ways, transcending it by their education and travel. But perhaps transcendence is not quite the right word, for Kollen, Vennema, and Dimnent also represented the changes that the Midwestern RCA was slowly undergoing in the dynamic period between 1890 and 1930, as its members became better educated, wealthier, more well-traveled, more ecumenical in sentiments, and perhaps a bit worldlier, as evidenced by Kollen's own social attainments or, on a different level, Vennema's electrifying experience with jazz dancing at his New Jersey church—still an abomination in most Midwestern circles—shortly after he left Hope.[10] Hope College continued to function as part of a Dutch Calvinist enclave throughout this period, but there can be no doubt that the habitus of the school changed considerably during these decades of substantial growth and ever-widening contacts with the larger world.

In any event, the priorities and sentiments of these three presidents both shaped and reflect two momentous developments that determined the character of the college during their tenures. The first was the dramatic expansion of Van Raalte's (and Phelps's) dream for their "School of the Prophets." The training of clergy and missionaries had from the very start been central to Hope's purpose and identity, but this intensified as the college grew in size, capacity, and ambition, all stimulated by the wider interest in missions by American Protestants in the decades prior to, and in the immediate aftermath of, the First World War. Hope was proud of the fact that it delivered an uncommon number of ministers and missionaries, a pride that found public expression through the 1920s. Not everyone was happy with the great emphasis placed on church service; one student recollected that Vennema thought that all male students should become ministers of the gospel, and Irwin Lubbers, as instructor at the college worried in the 1920s that Hope's profile was too one-sidedly focused on the School of the Prophets.[11] However one might view it, Hope's emphasis on Christian missionary endeavor certainly showed in the high-blown rhetoric of the times, as exemplified by Gerrit J. Diekema, Hope's most influential alumnus and Holland's most prominent politician, who

10 Kennedy and Simon, *Can Hope Endure*, 46.

11 M. Jay Flipse to Gordon Van Wylen, 20 November 1982, Ame Vennema Biographical Papers, JAH; M. Eugene Osterhaven, interview by author, 13 January 2003, in which Osterhaven recalled what Irwin Lubbers had said to him.

served in the key position as Secretary of the Council of Hope College, as the Board of Trustees was then known. In 1913, Diekema gave a speech at Vennema's inauguration, in which he set forth the responsibilities of the new president:

> Remembering our heroic ancestry and their struggles for light and liberty; remembering that what Leyden was to the Hollander beyond the sea, Hope College is to the Hollander in America; remembering our far-flung battle lines in Africa, China, Arabia, India and Japan; remembering that in the pending struggle between Christ and Islam, the cross and the crescent, it is a son of Hope [Samuel Zwemer] who as commander in chief leads the world's forces of light; remembering the blood of our heroes and martyrs shed in distant climes and under strange skies, and that within the walls of Hope there are now young men and women upon whose physical strength, moral fibre and mental equipment the destiny of nations and races of men may depend, we see for our new president golden gates of opportunity wide open and burdens of responsibility which only the strongest shoulders can bear.[12]

Nor was this sentiment mere public utterance. Dimnent, imbibing a postmillennial expectation of the imminent Kingdom of God, wrote to an Iowa pastor in 1918:

> [W]ill you not join with a few of us and bring Christ to all the world and make Hope College the radiating influence from which there shall go a tremendous enthusiasm for the Christ, a world-devastating flood of evangelism which shall bring the "new age" of which the Revelation dreams and of which Christ told . . . ?[13]

All of this went accompanied with a revivalist religious atmosphere at the college, in which the college organized specific events to encourage students to make a personal decision for Christ. This was of vital importance for Kollen, who said that a college education should hold up Christ "as a pattern for all; and his vicarious sacrifice

[12] Gerrit J. Diekema in "Service of Inauguration of the Rev. Ame Vennema, D.D., as President of Hope College," Ame Vennema Papers, JAH.

[13] Edward Dimnent to Harry Hoffs, 20 November 1918, Correspondence from Dimnent, 1918-19, file, Dimnent Papers, JAH.

as the only sufficient redeeming grace."[14] Until the First World War, the college publicly tallied the professions of faith made by its students, but thereafter, too, the college sponsored a Week of Prayer, in which, at least on one occasion, the happy result was that nearly 100 percent had made a "decision" for Christ.[15] The religious climate of the college during this period, then, can be said to be only moderately Calvinist—Dimnent thought of himself as a "mossback" more Calvinistic than most of his colleagues[16]—and more defined by a more general Protestant orthodoxy that stressed personal commitment to Christ and collective responsibility for the world, expressed by a range of worldly and religious endeavor, with missions at its apex.

But if this period was the high point for Hope as "School of the Prophets," the presidencies of Kollen, Vennema, and Dimnent also witnessed another important trend that by 1930 would ultimately eclipse the call to Christian ministry. Both Kollen and Dimnent had opted after graduating from Hope not for the ministry but for teaching, and they in doing so forecasted a future development; after 1914, the larger share of Hope's graduates chose a field other than pastor or missionary. Nor was this in the first instance a sign of incipient secularization. Hope College, after all, had been founded to give new opportunities for the surrounding Dutch Reformed community. Vennema addressed the community of Holland in his inaugural address by reminding them that:

> For half a century [Hope] has helped to build up your material prosperity . . . it does for your sons and daughters what your manufacturing plants are doing with the crude material brought to them, makes them over into something more finished and valuable. It will continue to knock at the door of the humble

[14] Gerrit Kollen, "Inaugural Address," 27 June 1894, Kollen Papers, H88-0088, JAH.

[15] Dimnent to Mrs. John S. Allen, 22 November 1920, Correspondence from Dimnent, 1919-20, file, Dimnent Papers, H88-040, JAH.

[16] Dimnent to Hoffs, 20 November 1918. In his 1913 inaugural address, Vennema proclaimed that "we are in hearty accord with the doctrines of the Reformed Church, with that form of religious philosophy commonly known as Calvinistic." But Calvinist or Reformed theology was not, as such, at the heart of his speech, which stressed Christian action in the world. Moreover, to relegate Calvinism to a "religious philosophy" suggests that Vennema had already learned to relativize the importance of the Reformed confessions ("Inaugural Address," Vennema Papers, JAH).

> toiler in city and country. . . . It will open the way for the poor young man and woman to join the ranks of the privileged ones who by all round development are preparing for larger spheres of activity.[17]

The ambitions of the Dutch community in the Midwest went hand in hand with an economy and society that required the services of Christian teachers in its public schools and other educated Christians in the business world. It is not surprising, then, that by the Vennema presidency the college was confronted with large numbers of students–including a very large percentage of women–who, though serious Christians, had no plans to work on the mission field or live in a parsonage as either a minister or his spouse. This trend was checked for a time during Dimnent's early years as president, when the Student Volunteer Band, following national trends, included some forty students in a given year. By the mid-1920s, however, active interest for missions (again following a national trend) had waned among students, effectively ending the great missionary impulse that had dominated the college since its inception, and which reached its culmination under these presidents.

It is hard, for this reason, to escape the conclusion that Hope's religious climate changed in the last half of the 1920s. Students opted for more secular vocations. Moreover, through the automobile and radio they were participating more fully in the wider world than they had before. Their new interest in dancing and movies were signs of trouble that prompted Dimnent to make his sometimes somber prognostications of their spiritual estate. As part of the larger spiritual world, Hope was not unaffected by the Fundamentalist-Modernist controversy in the 1920s, which helped put an end to a shared Protestant vision for society that emphasized both personal conversion and social uplift. It now became harder to join both of these elements together, though it would be the task of the next generation of Hope's presidents to try.

Perhaps the most emblematic symbol of these changes is the Memorial Chapel, which was completed by Dimnent in 1929 and, on which, thirty years later, was bestowed his name. Dimnent had become convinced of the need for an eclectic-medieval chapel as a way to convince all that Hope College possessed "the genuine 24-carat type

17 Vennema, "Inaugural Address."

of religion" and "to generate a depth of religious purpose which would bring our people to the right mind and will in religion."[18] Dimnent apparently sensed that religious inspiration could no longer be generated in rough-hewn edifices and revivalist religion, but required a richer aesthetic that might appeal to people with a more sophisticated—and more moderate—form of Christian faith. In sensing this trend, he well anticipated the future of the college.

The Progressive Protestants: Wichers, Lubbers, Vander Werf (1931-70)

That Hope "liberalized" in the mid-twentieth century is taken for granted by those at all familiar with the college's history. Most typically, that process of liberalization, even secularization, is intimately tied to the relatively short presidency of Vander Werf (1963-70), though a case can also be made for extending it to include the presidency of the religious moderate Irwin Lubbers (1945-63), when the college grew dramatically. But it was with Wynand Wichers at the helm (1931-45) that the college received a new kind of president who, more than his predecessors, believed that the college must break with an unfruitful conservatism and "progress" toward full participation in American civic and academic life. In this respect, Lubbers and Vander Werf were inheritors of a social and academic aspiration already set by Wichers in the 1930s.

It is clear that in all three cases we are dealing with a new kind of president, that all three of them were far more imbued with academic life than their predecessors. They came from RCA homes in the Midwest, and all three graduated from Hope (1909, 1917, and 1937, respectively), but each sought graduate education well beyond the confines of the RCA. It is well-known that Vander Werf was deeply shaped by the research university, to which he gave decades of his life (both before and after his tenure at Hope), but the same can be said, to a more modest degree, of his immediate predecessors. The historian Wichers taught both at the University of Michigan (as a graduate student) and at what was to become Western Michigan University, as well as at his alma mater. As a teacher at Hope, Wichers developed a reputation for scholarship, as evidenced by a letter sent to him by Old Testament scholar and moderately liberal Protestant James Muilenburg, urging

[18] Dimnent to Charles A. Runk, 24 May 1928, Correspondence from Dimnent, 1924-29, file, Dimnent Papers, JAH.

him, on the eve of his presidency, to make Hope College "respectable scholastically":

> I frequently felt [as a Hope student] that in strategic quarters there was almost a disdain for true scholarship. You were the only person in my four years at Hope who gave me a sense of scholarliness and kindled me with the lure of scholarship.[19]

More than in Wichers's case, Lubbers's formative experience offered him opportunities to reinterpret his cultural and religious inheritance. As a missionary-teacher in India, he wrote to his brother of his birthplace: "Cedar Grove [Wisconsin] is a great place and I often get lonesome for it but when you get away from it you will find that your opinion will change on many things and it should."[20] Though shocked at some "heathen" practices of non-Christian Indians, Lubbers developed a good relationship with a Brahmin, who gave him the equivalent of $125 as he left India. Lubbers confided in a letter: "The Brahmins are the most antagonistic of all to Christianity, as a class. This man and a few others, however, I really consider Christian at heart but they cannot break from the caste system." Lubbers's appreciation of this gesture, interpreted by his own Christian faith, may seem patronizing to some, but the tone is decidedly different from Dimnent's, who in 1918 decried the fact that "the boys come back with the crazy notions that Brahma is as good as Christ just because some heathen Hindoo fought in the trenches of France against the Hun and that Confucius is as divine as Jesus just because some Chink cooked officers' mess along side of one of our Yanks."[21]

But perhaps it was Lubbers's own further education that more decisively shaped his educational and religious vision, taking classes as he did at "modernist" Union Seminary in New York and such courses as "Christianity in the Light of Modern Knowledge" at Northwestern University. By 1930 Lubbers was advocating a consciously centrist line between those, as he put it, who had lost their faith by abandoning their

[19] James Muilenburg to Wichers, 4 March 1931, Correspondence-Election as President of the College, 1930-31, file, Wynand Wichers Papers, H88-200, JAH.

[20] Irwin Lubbers, Kodai Kanal, India, to his brother in Cedar Grove, Wisconsin, 23 May 1920, Early Years-India-Mission Service in India-Correspondence, 1919-22, file, Irwin Lubbers Papers, JAH.

[21] Dimnent to Hoffs, 20 December 1918.

creeds (modernists) and those who had lost their faith by defending them (fundamentalists).[22]

But in exemplifying these characteristics, these presidents also reflected spiritual change within the denomination, and in particular the Midwestern RCA. The Western church had "arrived" at the mainstream of American life: its Dutch roots were now largely confined to historical memory, and it could no longer fully be considered an immigrant community. The Midwestern churches, though still deeply suspicious of theological liberalism, had no strong critique, or sense of distance from, American society, and it own members were rapidly taking college degrees and finding well-paying positions.

Wichers, Lubbers, and perhaps to a lesser extent, Vander Werf interpreted their presidential task as a delicate balancing act. On the one hand, both Wichers and Lubbers, as their written material shows, were deeply aware of the fact that Christian colleges could easily lose their spiritual birthright, and they were stout defenders of the idea of "the Christian college." They were genuinely appalled at the secularizing trends in American higher education, and wished to preserve Hope College from such a fate, believing that Christian colleges offered the moral and spiritual fiber missing from secular institutions. Moreover, as sons of the Midwestern RCA, they showed the necessary respect for the religious and moral sensibilities of its Midwestern constituency, prohibiting dancing or, in Lubbers's case, intervening in college theatre productions. They were denominational loyalists dedicated to the RCA and to its institutions, and it was under their collective tenures that Hope became—in a way it has not been before or since—a school for the entire denomination, drawing between a fourth and a fifth of its students from the East. Perhaps above all, they were committed to keeping Hope a Protestant institution that generated sincere and active Christians for leadership in church and society.

At the same time, all three presidents firmly believed that the college must participate more fully in American academic life. Vander Werf, not surprisingly, was the most explicit about this obligation, opining in his 1963 inaugural address that church-related colleges were seriously in danger of becoming academically irrelevant if they did not quickly modernize. But Lubbers shared it, too, attempting in the late 1940s to modernize the college's mission statement and developing as his progressivist theme the metaphor of the passing lane, in which the

[22] Lubbers cited in *Can Hope Endure*, 101.

driver should pass whenever it was safe to do so. Wichers, too, fits in this category. In 1930 and 1931, he had been the candidate of self-conscious progressives—including Diekema and Muilenburg—who believed that Wichers could pull the college out of its overly conservative religious environment. "He knows our past history and traditions," Diekema wrote of Wichers, "but at the same time he has the forward look. Under him the College would not become fossilized."[23]

"The forward look," to emphasize this again, did not mean for either Diekema or Wichers becoming less of a Christian college. But it did mean becoming "respectable scholastically," and that was primarily measured by the school's participation, and stature, in American higher education. Wichers himself gave expression to this aim in his *A Century of Hope* (1968), the standard history of the school completed some two decades after he stepped down as president. Writing of his time as president, Wichers wrote, "Hope College was again in a position for all-out progress . . . [and its] traditional isolation now abandoned." What he meant was that the college participated in studies with other colleges and changed many of its anachronistic peculiarities in favor of practices widely in use elsewhere, such as an A-B-C-D grading system and a commencement address. More significant were Wichers's efforts to improve faculty and facilities, initiating a strong trend toward professionalization, evident at many colleges, which continued under his successors. In hindsight, Wichers's accomplishments seem modest, but he initiated a commitment to modernize the college, to bring "progress" to its inner workings, and to make it a college respected not only for its piety but also for its academic accomplishments.

For several decades, the balancing act consciously launched by Wichers seemed to work well. Hope remained a stoutly denominational college. It held mandatory chapel, developed special religious programs for the still overwhelmingly Reformed student body, and hired exclusively Protestant faculty—though there were those who feared that some of them were not Christian enough. And it grew in academic attainments; by about 1960, Hope was drawing national attention for the accomplishments of faculty and students alike, and not just in the long vibrant natural sciences.

[23] Gerrit Diekema to Charles M. McLean, 14 July 1930, Correspondence-Election as President of the College, 1930-31, file, Wichers Papers, JAH. Diekema forwarded a copy of this letter to Wichers.

But by the 1960s it was harder to mesh "the forward look" and what that seemed to require in the Space Age with a robust commitment to a Christian college with Christian students and Christian faculty. Certainly Vander Werf felt the tension and tried to retain the balance, but he was probably too committed to change, and too unpredictable an administrator, to have been able to succeed. Moreover, the elements necessary for maintaining the balance were breaking down: the Protestant recruiting pool was unequal to the hiring imperatives of the college, the percentage of Reformed students declined dramatically as the school grew in the 1960s, and the denomination—itself in deep crisis over its failed merger with the Southern Presbyterians—showed itself completely incapable of meeting the rising costs of its colleges. Vander Werf's efforts to restructure the Board of Trustees by ending the dominant role of the church classes confirmed, rather than triggered, the end of Hope College as a school controlled directly by the Reformed Church. If Hope could remain a Christian college and at the same time maintain the academic advances it had made, some formula other than seeking to combine the "forward look" with the necessary respect for its religious roots would have to be found.

The Defenders of the Faith: Van Wylen, Jacobson, Bultman (1972 to the Present)

The educational and social metamorphoses of the 1960s had, then, put an end to "the denominational college"—a college defined primarily by its affiliation with a Protestant church body. From that time on, many mainline Protestant colleges that until the 1960s had maintained at least important symbolic ties to the churches no longer took such ties as seriously. Moreover, "the Christian college"—a term used repeatedly by Vander Werf to describe Hope—soon was used to designate evangelical Protestant institutions, where formal ties to a denomination, more often than not, were secondary to their Christian identity. By the 1970s, the RCA had become too small a denomination, with too diffuse an educational vision and too thin a sense of common cause, to generate either the resources or the leaders to shape the colleges with which it enjoyed a "Covenant of Mutual Responsibilities" (1969). Christian support for colleges like Hope would have to be won less through institutional structures and more through informal networking.

The result was a tug-of-war for the school's spiritual direction—and for the leadership of the college. Since the Fundamentalist-

Modernist controversy of the 1920s, Hope's presidents had been under scrutiny: Wichers was supported by a friend because he had the advantage that "no one has questioned his orthodoxy,"[24] Lubbers had to fend off conservative suspicions in the late 1940s as he tried to modernize the college, and Vander Werf became an outright *bête noire* to his conservative religious foes. None of these experiences compares to the fierce struggle to appoint his successor in the long interim from 1970 to 1972, or, to a lesser extent, subsequent appointments to the presidency.

Calvin Vander Werf's successors were as different a trio as any of the presidential sets discussed in this article. But what is striking is that they were all, to varying degrees, *outsiders* to the RCA. This was true of Gordon Van Wylen, who had spent all of his life, prior to his appointment at Hope College (1972-87), in the Christian Reformed Church and whose views on faith and scholarship were largely shaped by his strong ties to InterVarsity Christian Fellowship. John Jacobson (1987-99) had known the RCA as a child, but had spent his adult life in the mainline Presbyterian Church, and in any event had no prior religious connection, as Van Wylen did, with the Dutch Reformed communities of the Midwest. And even James Bultman (1999-present), a Hope alumnus, professor, and coach with extensive networks within the RCA, had been born and raised in the Christian Reformed Church, which helped shape his theologically conservative outlook. After 1970, Hope College came to depend on much of its key leadership from those (initially) outside the denomination, including not only the presidents but figures such as long-time provost Jacob Nyenhuis (also from the CRC).

It is clear, then, that denominational affiliation alone could no longer determine the presidential pool, nor was *Lebenslauf* a good predictor of the successful presidential candidate (both Van Wylen and Jacobson had, like Vander Werf, spent most of their careers at state universities, whereas Bultman's *curriculum vitae* more closely resembled that of Wichers and Lubbers). Selection as Hope's president now also required the right kind of *personal* theological orientation. As in the rest of American society, the old confessional divides within (Protestant) Christianity had largely fallen away in Hope College's politics, and

[24] John Meengs to John A. Dykstra, 10 September 1931, Correspondence-Election as President of the College, 1930-31, file, H88-200, Wynand Wichers Papers, JAH.

what mattered now was where presidents positioned themselves along a liberal-conservative continuum. Meeting this requirement must have presented more of a challenge for Jacobson than for the others of his "cohort," since he was a liberal Democrat, mainline Protestant, and outsider to West Michigan, while at the same time cultivating deep affinities with conservative evangelical Christianity. And it mattered what the presidents' *particular* views were on church-related higher education—most crucially *the* litmus-test of this period: the hiring of faculty. Van Wylen had no interest in going back to a Protestants-only hiring policy, and Catholics became an important minority among the Hope professoriate—itself an indication of how little traditional confessional lines had come to matter. But drawing the line at the boundaries of the Christian faith became a matter of recurring and heated debate for the next three decades.

All three presidents of this period can in these respects be classified as "defenders of the faith," presidents who made concerted and conscious efforts to shore up Hope's Christian mission, and who in attempting to do so engaged opponents, often their own faculty, in what was sometimes a bitter struggle over the direction of the school. That struggle was not only between those who opposed and those who supported the school's Christian mission, but was often a struggle between protagonists who differed about the means and ends of attaining the ideals of a church-related college. But whatever one might think of their efforts, the presidents of the college in this last period saw it as their central task to restore and revitalize the Christian faith at the college, a faith that they perceived as under pressure on a number of fronts. In this respect, they reflected the growing concern within conservative American Protestantism that Christian institutions needed to be defended against secularizing tendencies in society. In this key respect, their appointments were not incidental but indicative of a new assertiveness among conservative Christians in the United States and among Hope's constituencies. It was, to be sure, a new assertiveness that, incidentally, was not always regarded with favor by these presidents—Van Wylen, for example, resisted suggestions to pull Hope in a more "fundamentalist" direction. But they saw their first priority not in checking conservative Protestantism, but in limiting the influences of what they considered to be the secularizing forces at the college.

In serving as "defenders," Van Wylen and his successors had the key support of conservative churches in the region (including many RCA churches, still a force of some significance), the mostly theologically conservative members of the Board, and many alumni and supporters of the college. Their efforts most notably included the effort to hire only Christians to the faculty, an effort that arrested Hope's trajectory toward secularization in the 1970s—a rather early and fairly unusual reversal of the way many church-related colleges have headed. It was a policy that would only be further tightened by Van Wylen's successors. But it also included modest curricular change (for example, a capstone course for seniors with a spiritual dimension), revitalization of the chapel program (most notably in Jacobson's appointment of the controversial Ben Patterson as Dean of the Chapel in 1994), attempts to regulate the moral life of the college (from frat life to an explicit rejection of homosexuality), new programs for the spiritual development of faculty and students, and the intensive cultivation of both old and new conservative Christian constituencies, an important source of students and funding for the college.

In some ways, Hope's return to a more visible and articulated Christian identity reflects a wider trend in church-related higher education, as evidenced by the recent explosion of interest in Christian higher education: by well-endowed benefactors like the Lilly Foundation, by Christian families and students, and by church-related colleges themselves, eager to develop a strategic niche in the educational market. But Hope's process of return—now nearly a generation old—has been longer and more sustained than many of the efforts undertaken at many Catholic and Protestant schools.

At the same time, the most recent presidents of Hope College have not, through both their own restraint and the limits on their own power, turned Hope College into an evangelical Protestant institution, though it is closer to that model now than it was thirty years ago. All were committed, in varying ways and to varying degrees, to what Bultman called "Reformed Centrism." Van Wylen envisioned the college lying somewhere between the evangelical and the mainline model, and in a similar sense Jacobson stressed the importance of an ecumenical Christian community: discernibly Christian, but not sectarian or expressly confessional. In this respect, Hope's "defenders of the faith" shared the role as mediators of a "middle way" with their predecessors. Hope's first presidents served as mediators by serving as Eastern patrons to the emerging Western church; Kollen and his successors did so as skilled and trusted representatives to the world of the Midwestern Dutch, while Wichers and his successors served as loyal but forward-looking churchmen-scholars.

But if this essay has demonstrated anything, it is that what Hope's "middle way" entails not only is subject to interpretation, but also has changed in the course of 140 years. That is certainly as true today as it ever was, and there are no guarantees that commitment to the shifting center will either be sustained, or that sustaining a centrist course will be felicitous in its effects. What will happen in the future is, as always, difficult to tell, but there can be little doubt that the next presidents of Hope College will have to negotiate a new balance, and a new mission, for a service in a world that is confronted with unprecedented problems, with a nation more fractious than ever, and with a church that is at once too certain and too uncertain about its mission for the twenty-first century.

CHAPTER 14

The Vexed Quesion: Hope College and Theological Education in the West

Dennis N. Voskuil

On 16 September 1909, during a gala celebration of the twenty-fifth anniversary of the restoration of theological training at Holland, Michigan, Professor Nicholas M. Steffens addressed "the vexed question of the relation of theology to Hope College." Aware that several of the venerable members of his audience had participated in the "heated discussions" which had swirled around the decisions of the General Synod of the Reformed Church in America to suspend theological instruction at Hope College in 1877 only to restore such instruction in 1884, Steffens was hesitant to revisit a painful period of "storm and stress" which had rocked the college and the church. "If we could eliminate those years of bitter words and angry deeds from the annals of our history," declared Steffens, "we all certainly could rejoice. But alas! this is impossible."[1]

Time appears to have softened the edges of this controversy. Today, a century removed from Steffens's address, "the vexed question" of the relation of Hope College to theological education in the West seems quaint. After all, Hope College and Western Theological

[1] Nicholas M. Steffens, "The Story of the First Twenty-Five Years of Restored Theological Instruction," in *Quarter-Centennial of the Western Theological Seminary, 1884-1909* (Holland, Mich., 1909), 41-43.

Seminary, which was birthed through Hope College, are remarkably strong but independent sister institutions of the Reformed Church in America. In fact, while the histories of these institutions normally touch upon "the vexed question,"[2] those who attend, serve, and support Hope College and Western Theological Seminary have, at best, but a faint understanding of their mutual relationship and of "the fierce struggle,"[3] to establish, restore, and retain theological training in Holland, Michigan.

The "Germ" of Theology in the West

Like thousands of Dutch Calvinists who migrated to Wisconsin, Illinois, and Iowa during the mid-nineteenth century, those who settled in West Michigan prized education—especially for the leaders of their churches. Their theological forebear, John Calvin, had established an academy in Geneva, from which the principles of the Reformed faith were promulgated throughout the world. Wherever the followers of Calvin went, such schools of the prophets were organized, since Reformed folk expected their pastors to be well-versed in Scripture and theology.[4]

2 The standard histories of Hope College are: Wynand Wichers, *A Century of Hope, 1866-1966* (Grand Rapids: Eerdmans, 1968), esp. 65-125; Preston J. Stegenga, *Anchor of Hope: The History of an American Denominational Institution* (Grand Rapids: Eerdmans, 1954), esp. 99-109. See also James C. Kennedy and Caroline J. Simon, *Can Hope Endure?: A Historical Case Study in Christian Higher Education* (Grand Rapids: Eerdmans, 2005), esp. 27-66. For an excellent short historical overview, see Elton J. Bruins, "Hope College: Its Origin and Development, 1851-2001," *Origins* 19, no. 1 (2001): 4-13. No major histories of Western Theological Seminary have been written. The following studies are helpful: Elton M. Eenigenburg, "The History of the Seminary," *Reformed Review* 19 (May 1966): 18-32; Donald J. Bruggink, "Beginning the Second Century," *Reformed Review* 44 (spring 1991): 185-202; Donald J. Bruggink, "Western Theological Seminary: The First Century, 1866-1966," *Origins* 19, no. 1 (2001): 14-21. See also Cornelius E. Crispell, "The Theological Seminary at Hope College," and Henry E. Dosker, "Western Seminary Since 1884," both in Edward Tanjore Corwin, ed., *A Manual of the Reformed Church in America, 1628-1902*, 4th ed. (New York, 1902), 199-207; and Cornelius E. Crispell, "Historical Sketch of Theological Instruction in the West," *Centennial of the Theological Seminary of the Reformed Church in America* (New York, 1885), 171-80.

3 Steffens, *Quarter-Centennial*, 40.

4 See John T. McNeill, *The History and Character of Calvinism* (New York: Oxford University Press, 1967), esp. 190-96. In his Inaugural Charge at President

When Pastor Albertus C. Van Raalte planted a colony of Dutch Reformed immigrants along the west coast of Michigan in 1847,[5] he began to lay the groundwork for educational institutions which would eventually prepare their religious leaders. Because of financial constraints, Van Raalte initially supported the organization of local school districts, and the children of the colony were urged to attend a public grammar school. Nurtured in the Netherlands by educational systems which were controlled by the church, Van Raalte and the colonists soon questioned whether the American model of public education could nurture the religious beliefs and values of their Reformed community. Moreover, Van Raalte realized that a church-controlled secondary school would be essential for those seeking to receive higher education for callings in teaching and ministry.[6]

It must be remembered that during its first three years of existence, the Dutch colony in West Michigan was ecclesiastically independent. The Classis of Holland, composed of a few fledging immigrant congregations, was not affiliated with an American denomination. In 1850, Van Raalte encouraged the Classis of Holland to unite with the Reformed Protestant Dutch Church, which traced its origins to New Amsterdam in 1628. He had become acquainted with this venerable American church even before he had set sail for the United States, and he had been assisted in his journey to Michigan by two of the denomination's prominent pastors, Thomas DeWitt of New York and Isaac Wyckoff of Albany. Hence, when Van Raalte proposed a church-controlled secondary school in 1851, he naturally sought the support of his adopted denomination.[7]

As part of its domestic mission program, the Reformed Church had long considered the possibility of planting schools in locations where it was planting churches. As early as 1836, for instance, the Classis of Schoharie introduced a resolution at the denomination's General Synod which called for the establishment of "a theological seminary, a college, and a preparatory school" in the Mississippi

Phelps's Inauguration, Isaac N. Wyckoff proposed that Hope College would be the "school of the Prophets" (*The Hope College Remembrancer*, [1866], 13).

5 See Albert Hyma, *Albertus C. Van Raalte and His Dutch Settlements in the United States* (Grand Rapids: Eerdmans, 1947).

6 See Wichers, *A Century of Hope*, 1-40.

7 See Elton J. Bruins, "The Church of the West: A Brief Survey of the Origin and Development of the Dutch Reformed Church in the Middle West," *Reformed Review* 20 (December 1966): 4-6.

Valley.[8] The General Synod of 1843 heard an appeal from the Classis of Illinois and the Classis of Michigan, both composed of congregations recently planted through the auspices of the predominantly Eastern denomination, to develop institutions of higher education in the West.[9] In his domestic missions report to the Synod of 1847, James Romeyn proposed the establishment of a high school at some advantageous point in the West, which could eventually prove "the germ of something important." In the same report, Romeyn took notice of a recent wave of Dutch immigrants: "A new body of Pilgrims has reached our shores from Holland, the land of our fathers." In response, the Synod appointed a special committee which proposed to the next General Synod that "an institution of high order for classical and theological instruction" be established under the patronage and control of the denomination.[10]

When the immigrant churches joined the Reformed Protestant Dutch Church in 1850, there was a convergence of interests and needs. During August of that year the Reverend John Garretson, corresponding secretary for the Board of Domestic Missions, visited Van Raalte's colony. A plan for an academy was subsequently proposed and Walter Taylor, an elder from Geneva, New York, where he was the proprietor of a private academy, was sent to Holland as the school's first principal. In 1853, the academy was taken over by the General Synod and placed under the management of the Board of Education.[11] Thus with the establishment of this "pioneer school" during the fall of 1851, the seed of theological education in the West had been planted.

The fledgling school in Holland was administered by dedicated teachers and principals, but overall it struggled because of insufficient financial support, inconsistent enrollment, and inadequate governance through the Reformed Church. Considering the religious bent of the

8 *Acts and Proceedings of the General Synod of the Reformed Protestant Dutch Church in North America*, June 1836, 493; also 503-4. See Gerald F. DeJong, *Non-Immigrant Churches in the Middle West before the Civil War*, a pamphlet published by the Particular Synod of Chicago (1978) for denominational efforts among non-immigrants.

9 *Acts and Proceedings*, June 1843, 232-33.

10 *Acts and Proceedings*, June 1847, 191-92; *Acts and Proceedings*, June 1848, 309-11.

11 *Acts and Proceedings*, June 1852, 267-68; *Acts and Proceedings*, June 1853, 361-62; Aleida J. Pieters, *A Dutch Settlement in Michigan* (Grand Rapids: Reformed Press, 1923), 133-34; Wichers, *A Century of Hope*, 34-35. Wichers inaccurately cites the Synod of 1851 as approving the plan for the academy. This occurred in 1853.

colonists, it is not surprising that the majority of those who attended the academy were motivated by a calling to become pastoral leaders. By the time that the third principal, John Van Vleck, resigned in 1859 because of poor health, discouragement, and disagreements with Van Raalte, there were just nineteen graduates but fourteen of those would enter the ministry.[12] Some of the graduates enrolled in Rutgers College before moving over to New Brunswick Theological Seminary in preparation for service in Reformed congregations.

In 1859, the Reverend Philip Phelps accepted an appointment by the Board of Education to become principal of the academy in Holland. Phelps had met Van Raalte during one of the dauntless pastor's visits East to raise funds for the school.[13] It was a propitious meeting, for Phelps possessed a vision for the institution which matched Van Raalte's. Through Phelps's charm, persistence, and firm leadership the fledgling academy would be developed into a college and nearly a university.

By the fall of 1862, Phelps developed a college curriculum and recruited a small freshman class for an institution which had taken as its name, "Hope College." In succeeding years an endowment of eighty-five thousand dollars was raised, the Articles of Association were approved, and a governing council was appointed by the General Synod. In June 1866, the Synod approved the incorporation of Hope College by the State of Michigan.[14] Philip Phelps was formally inaugurated as the first president of Hope College on 12 July 1866, just five days before the first commencement exercises were held. Bachelor of Arts degrees were conferred on the eight men who were members of the first class to graduate from Hope College.[15]

12 See Wichers, *A Century of Hope*, 41-52.

13 See Elton J. Bruins, "Early Hope College History as Reflected in the Correspondence of Rev. Albertus C. Van Raalte to Philip Phelps Jr., 1857-1875," in *The Dutch Adapting in North America: Papers Presented at the Thirteenth Biennial Conference for the Association for the Advancement of Dutch-American Studies*, ed. Richard H. Harms (Grand Rapids: AADAS, 2001), especially n. 14. For Phelps at Hope, see also Wichers, *A Century of Hope*, 52-112.

14 Wichers, *A Century of Hope*, 66-68; "Minutes of the Particular Synod of Chicago," 1863, 13-15; *Acts and Proceedings*, June 1863, 253; *Acts and Proceedings*, June 1864, 466-67. The 1864 Synod put off a proposal that a seminary be established with the college (467), *Acts and Proceedings*, June 1866, 89-90.

15 See Wichers, *A Century of Hope*, 68-72.

During its infancy, Hope College served primarily as a preparatory school for pastoral training. Seven of the eight initial graduates of the college had decided to pursue theological education at the college! With the support and encouragement of their mentor and friend, President Phelps, these seven sent a memorial petitioning the General Synod of 1866 to allow them to pursue theological education at their alma mater. Following discussion, the Synod referred the matter to the Board of Education and the Council of Hope College with instruction:

> That leave be granted to pursue their theological studies at Hope College, provided no measures shall be instituted by which additional expense shall be thrown upon Synod or Board of Education at this time; and provided further, that Synod reserves the right to withdraw this permission at any time that it may deem expedient.[16]

Although later Synods would seize upon the two important provisions, the Western church would have its own school of theology, the desire for which was arguably the motivating force behind the establishment of the academy and Hope College.

Considering future developments, it is important to note that the leaders of the Eastern church approved the decision to allow theological instruction at Hope College. After all, the voting delegates from churches in the East outnumbered those from churches in the West by more than fifteen to one in 1866.[17] A letter which ran in the *Christian Intelligencer,* a weekly newspaper published by the Reformed Church in New York City, on 11 April 1867, endorsed the decision of the Synod. Recognizing the need for more ministers to serve Western congregations, the writer argued that "the theological education of Western young men *at the West*" was the best strategy for meeting this need. Disagreeing with the notion that a theological school in the West would undermine the prosperity of the Reformed seminary at New Brunswick, this writer insisted that the decision of Synod would actually increase the number of candidates there.[18]

16 *Acts and Proceedings*, June 1866, 96-97.

17 The Western Classes (Holland [Michigan], Illinois, and Wisconsin) sent just nine out of 150 delegates to the 1866 Synod (*Acts and Proceedings*, June 1866, 3-6).

18 "A Seminary at the West," *Christian Intelligencer* 38 (11 April 1867): 2. The letter was written by "C. D. B."

In his inaugural address, President Phelps celebrated the first graduating class of Hope College as well as the recent decision of the General Synod to permit the college to inaugurate theological instruction. He even suggested a name for this new venture: "*Faith* Theological Seminary."[19]

The founder of the colony in Holland must have delighted in the turn of events. Although Van Raalte was in the Netherlands at the time of the inauguration, he had been a relentless advocate of Hope College and theological education in the West.[20] Later, immediately following the decision of the General Synod of 1877 to suspend theological instruction at Hope College, the Reverend Dirk Broek, in a letter published in the Holland, Michigan, Dutch language weekly, *De Hope*, suggested that Van Raalte, among others in the West, "intended nothing less than an institution for theological training."[21] William Moerdyk, a member of the first graduating class of Hope College who received his theological instruction at the college, insisted that while theological training was "the pet idea" of Van Raalte, it was strongly desired "by our people as a **whole**." The academy, the college, and the seminary, as they built upon each other, were the natural outcome of the purposes, prayers, and sacrifices of the early Dutch settlers. "The goal of all instruction was theological instruction."[22]

A Prepositional Question: Is Theology "in" or "at" Hope College?

Some form of theological instruction had been provided through the academy and the college years before the General Synod granted Hope College provisional permission to engage in theological training during the fall of 1866. At its October 1855 session, the General Synod permitted students in the Holland Academy "to pursue a portion of their studies in that institution, instead of entering at once into Rutgers

[19] Philip Phelps, "Inaugural Address," *Hope College Remembrance: First Inauguration and First Commencement* (1867), 17.

[20] Elton J. Bruins, "Hope College: Its Origin and Development, 1851-2001," in *Origins* 19, no. 1 (2001): 4-6. Van Raalte left for the Netherlands from Holland in April 1866 and did not leave from Rotterdam on his return trip until 14 September 1866—W. Raman, "Dr. van Raalte," *De Hope* 1, no. 30 (11 October 1866). See Bruins, "Early Hope College History," 3.

[21] Dirk Broek, "Something about the Cessation of the Theological Department at Hope College," *De Hope* 11, no. 45 (1 August 1877).

[22] William Moerdyk, "The Establishment of Theological Instruction at Holland," in *Quarter-Centennial of the Western Theological Seminary, 1884-1909*, 14-15.

College."[23] In effect, the academy offered some students a modicum of pre-ministerial course work, allowing them to delay enrolling at Rutgers. It is also evident that the academy, and perhaps the college later, offered some classes to those men who, for various reasons, were seeking to receive dispensations from a full ministerial training. The need for Dutch-speaking pastors may have necessitated some of these dispensations in the West.[24]

It was not until the Synod sanctioned theological instruction at Hope College in 1866 that it can fairly be said that the Western church was able to provide its own theological training–"Western theology for Western pastors for Western congregations."[25] Even then such training hardly constituted a theological seminary. At best it could be described as "elementary theology instruction."[26] Because the Synod stipulated that the denomination was to incur no additional expense and because the college continued to struggle financially, the Council of Hope College did not have funds to appoint additional faculty members to teach theology. So those who taught at the college were called upon to add to their teaching loads by offering classes for what was alternately described in the *Hope College Bulletin* of 1866-67 as "The Theological Course" and "the germinal Theological and Missionary Seminary."[27]

The students who sought theological instruction at Hope College were well aware that the education that they could have received at New Brunswick would have been "infinitely superior" to what they received in Holland, Michigan. William Moerdyk, one of the students who petitioned the Synod, later admitted that the theological department at Hope "labored under great disadvantages." Not only was the small faculty overloaded, but the facilities were woefully inadequate. "We had no laboratories, no library to speak of." Despite obvious disadvantages, these intrepid students did not second guess their decisions. According to Moerdyk, they did not despise Rutgers College or New Brunswick Theological Seminary, but they wanted institutions of their own, "and

23 *Acts and Proceedings*, October 1855, 17. See also *University Circular of Hope College at Holland, Michigan* (Albany, 1876), 97-100.

24 *University Circular of Hope College*, 84.

25 See Gerhard DeJonge, "In How Far Does the Western Theological Seminary Supply the Needs of the Western Field?" *Quarter-Centennial of the Western Theological Seminary, 1884-1909*, 50-69.

26 Cornelius E. Crispell, "The Theological Seminary at Hope College," in Edwin Tanjore Corwin, ed., *A Manual of the Reformed Church in America, 1628-1878*, 3rd ed. (New York, 1879), 123.

27 *Catalogue and Circular of Hope College, Holland, Michigan, 1866-67,* 6-7.

for noble, not for personal or sectarian or sectional reasons."

> They loved the Reformed Church and her Eastern institutions full well, but they loved their own people, their fathers, the people's future, and the future of the Reformed Church in the West, more.[28]

The provisional status of theological education in the West was evident at the Synod of 1867 when an ad hoc committee brought its report on Hope College. Although the committee included a favorable account of the theological instruction offered by the college professors, the core of the report addressed the question of whether "regular theological instruction [should] be continued at Hope College, with a view to the training of candidates for ministry." Although making it clear that the denomination should not at that time commit to any place as "the permanent location of its future Western Theological Seminary," the committee stated emphatically that "*it would be disastrous to our existing educational Institutions, and to our Churches in the West, and also to our Domestic Missionary operations there, to withdraw from Hope College, at the present time, the privilege of theological instruction.*"[29]

The report rehearsed the longstanding commitment of the Reformed Church in America to strengthen the Western field by inaugurating theological training there. Moreover, the committee took note of the financial support which the settlers in Michigan had provided for an institution they believed would be a training school for ministers.

> They gave out of their deep poverty, and with unparalleled liberality, in some cases denying themselves the comforts of life, not merely to found an academical and classical institution, but to provide theological instruction for their young men whom God should call to the Gospel ministry, not to multiply learned lawyers and doctors, but to supply their Churches with pastors.

The committee concluded that a reversal of the action of the Synod of 1866 would cause "the most bitter disappointment" in the West.[30]

28 Moerdyk, *Quarter-Centennial*, 17-18.

29 *Acts and Proceedings*, June 1867, 248-49. The entire sentence is italicized in the report.

30 Ibid., 249-50.

Insisting that a growing demand for ministers across the denomination would be met best through theological instruction in the West, the committee offered a rather tortured argument that such instruction would not interfere with the "prosperity" of the seminary in the East. Despite growing support in the West for its theological school, New Brunswick would "as an elder sister, fill as large a place in the heart of the Church as if she remained an only daughter."[31]

Having answered other potential objections to a continuing theological presence at Hope College, the committee indicated that the "only serious question" was financial. Could the denomination afford two theological seminaries at the present time? Without offering any meaningful solutions to the endemic financial concerns, the Synod of 1867 voted to continue theological instruction at Hope College. It even formally appointed Cornelius Crispell, still a member of the college faculty, to serve as the Professor of Didactic and Polemical Theology, but "without compensation." Two other professors at the college, Charles Scott and T. Romeyn Beck, were also invited to serve as "lectors" for the theological classes—again without compensation from the Synod.[32]

In another decision which would have important ramifications, the Synod divided the Board of Superintendents for Theological Education into two branches, Eastern and Western. The Western branch of the board, composed of representatives from Western classes, was to superintend theological education at Hope College. These arrangements, still provisional, were to last for three years and remained subject to the will of the Synod.[33]

The decisions of the Synod of 1867 allowed theological instruction to take root, at least for a few years. Under conditions set by the Synod, the first class of theological students, all seven pioneers of training at Hope College, graduated and received the professorial certificates on 21 May 1869 and were thereby permitted to receive calls to become pastors of congregations of the Reformed Church in America.[34]

Meanwhile issues related to faculty, financing, and governance were fostering confusion over the relationship of the college to its theological department. At a special November session of the General

31 Ibid., 251-52.

32 Ibid., 252, 271; for the specific appointment of Crispell, see *Acts and Proceedings*, November 1867, 344-46.

33 Crispell, "Theological Seminary at Hope College," 128.

34 Ibid.

Synod of 1867, the session at which Synod voted to change the name of the denomination from the Reformed Protestant Dutch Church to the Reformed Church in America,[35] important communications were received from Holland, Michigan, which bore on the relationship of the college to theological instruction. The Council of Hope College had sent an extensive communication which requested permission to move toward establishing the institution as a university, which would include various professional schools, including medicine, law, and theology.[36] It is not surprising that the Synod decided to defer discussion of this ambitious plan until the following General Synod. It also appointed a three-person committee to visit Hope College during the coming spring ("without expense to the General Synod") and to prepare a report.[37]

The Synod also received a letter from Cornelius Crispell, who had been appointed professor of theology by Synod at its June session. Crispell sought clarification regarding his appointment vis-à-vis the college. Was his appointment "in," "of," or "at" Hope College? Apparently all three prepositions had been employed in communications regarding the appointment. Crispell correctly believed that the "diversity of phraseology seemed to indicate indefiniteness of *status* of the Theological School," and that this indefiniteness was giving rise to conflicting opinions about the relationship between Hope College and theological instruction. Was the theological school in the West to be "merely a *department in Hope College*," with the same relationships to the council and faculty as other departments of the college? Or was it to be "*a department of Hope College as a University*, to be governed by its teachers of Theology as a Faculty, and governed by the Council of the College as a Board of Superintendents?" Both of these scenarios, according to Crispell, would produce "CONCENTRATION *of power in the Council*," and undermine the independence of the Professor of Theology. Crispell was arguing for the third prepositional option: a theological school, "under the care of General Synod, to be governed

35 For details of this denominational name change, see *Acts and Proceedings*, November 1867, 334-36.

36 See "Special Report of the Council of Hope College to the General Synod RCA, June 1868," Archives of the Reformed Church in America at New Brunswick, New Jersey; a microfilm copy of the first seventeen pages of this twenty-page document is in the WTS Collection at JAH (box 4P-1, W88-250a). Phelps's copy is in his scrapbook in the Hope College Archives at JAH. Essentially written by President Phelps, this is the most extensive plan for the university which had been developed.

37 *Acts and Proceedings*, November 1867, 347.

by it according to long-established usages, and to be located at present and, perhaps permanently, at Hope College."[38]

The General Synod supported Crispell's interpretation of his status at Hope College. Admitting that the original letter of appointment had been in error, it passed a resolution affirming that he was properly designated as a "Professor of Didactic and Polemic Theology *at* Hope College," and that his certificate of appointment should be revised accordingly.[39]

Crispell was certainly aware of the university plan which had been proposed in 1867, although it did not come before the Synod until the following June, when it came as a special report of the Council of Hope College.[40] Elaborate and extensive, the report bore the fingerprints of President Phelps. In essence the Council requested permission for the college to be developed as "Hope Haven University," which in addition to the existing baccalaureate program would incorporate the theological department as its first professional school, to be followed by those of law and medicine.[41]

Although sections of the report were devoted to the grammar school, female instruction, and Hope Farm, the lynchpin of the university proposal was the theological school. Here pains were taken to point out that, apart from Hope College, theological instruction in the West did not exist. Faculty, finances, and facilities for the theological department were provided through the auspices of the Council of the college. Considering these circumstances and the history of theological instruction, the Council argued that it would be unjust "to do anything else than establish its Western Theological School *in Hope College.*" Aware that the Synod had previously decided that Crispell was its professor of theology *at* Hope College, the Council argued that such a designation did not square with the realities of governance. Claiming that Hope, in effect, was already a university because of its theological department, the Council argued that it was vital for that department to be located "in" and not "at" Hope College.[42]

In its report, the Council anticipated two objections to the university proposal: first, that it would be improper to allow the institution to become overgrown; and second, that it would be

38 Ibid., 343-44.
39 Ibid., 346.
40 Ibid., 347; *Acts and Proceedings*, June 1868, 481-85.
41 "Special Report," 1-5.
42 Ibid., 2, 1-20.

presumptuous to call such an insignificant institution a university. Again, control of the theological department was pivotal:

> If Hope College is so feeble even with its theology, why enfeeble it still more by taking away the theology. Or if Hope College is too great by retaining theology, it is surely great enough to be recognized as a university.[43]

Apparently the faculty of the college had not been consulted by President Phelps and the Council as the elaborate proposal for Hope Haven University was being prepared. This certainly was a strategic mistake as three professors, all of whom were involved in theological instruction in addition to other teaching responsibilities, took measures to defeat the proposal. The June 1868 Synod received a lengthy letter from the professors that was sharply critical of nearly every aspect of the university plan. With respect to the status of the theological school, they understood that it was "not a department of Hope College but a school of Synod at Hope College, a school not governed or superintended in any way by the Council or Faculty of Hope College but by the General Synod only."[44]

What was the Synod's response to the university plan and to the prepositional debate which was stirring Hope College? Well, the June 1868 Synod did what most synods have done when faced with complex and disagreeable issues—they referred the issues to the next Synod.[45]

At the 1869 Synod, the committee on the Professorate read the pertinent communications and reviewed the presenting issues. Noting that the Hollanders were determined to have a theological school and that its permanent connection with Hope was vital to the very existence of the college, the committee acknowledged that the university proposal held appeal. At the same time the committee recognized

43 Ibid., 5.

44 T. Romeyn Beck, Charles Scott, and Cornelius Crispell to the General Synod of the Reformed Church in America, 25 May 1868. This handwritten letter (by the hand of Beck) is in the Archives of the Reformed Church in America at New Brunswick, New Jersey; a microfilm copy of this document is in the WTS Collection at JAH. In his notes on these letters Elton Bruins suggests that the professors were not consulted by President Phelps, which he calls "a major miscalculation" (Archival Collection of the Van Raalte Institute, Hope College).

45 *Acts and Proceedings*, June 1868, 480-84. See asterisk on 480 which noted the referral to the following synod.

that "for the dignity of theology" the seminary should *not* become a mere department in a university but remain *at* Hope College, but "in a measure *separate* from it, with its own internal discipline, and its own acknowledged professors, its own Board of Superintendents also, distinct from the Council or Trustees of the College."[46]

The committee acknowledged that the "mingling" of the faculty—sometimes as representatives of the college and sometimes as representatives of theology—had led to "inevitable clashing as to duties and powers," which had been "injurious" to the institution.

> We have a young institution, still weak, almost incipient; but with divided interests within it,—Jacob and Esau,—when it should be essentially one: a double faculty, a Council for the College and a Board of Superintendents for the Seminary; and with the jealousy, so fatal to the College, still remaining, that in time they may separate."[47]

Despite the inherent tensions in the arrangement, as it was then constituted, the committee could not recommend approval of the university plan. Unless under state control or possessing endowments, a university could be viable only after a period of maturity and growth. "A university of fifty students, no funds, and paper Professorships, can commend no respect, and does not meet the proper idea of that term."[48]

Employing the above rationale, the Synod passed a series of resolutions designed to clarify the status of the theological department of Hope College. Rescinding a previous decision, it appointed the Council of Hope College to act as the Board of the Theological Department—with duties and prerogatives similar to those of the Board of the seminary in New Brunswick. The Synod also elected two additional theological professors, one in evangelistic theology and one in exegetical theology, to augment the theological faculty. They were to be recognized as "the Faculty of the Theological school of Synod in Hope College." The Council of Hope was to offer the same course of study that was established by Synod for the theological school at New Brunswick. Finally, the Council was to complete an endowment for the theological department within two years.[49]

46 Ibid., June 1869, 646-48.
47 Ibid., 647.
48 Ibid.
49 Ibid., 647-48.

In a later attempt to clarify the relationship between the theological faculty and the college, the 1871 Synod amended the constitution of Hope College.[50] The prerogatives of General Synod to appoint professors of theology and regulate the theological school were carefully guarded. Crispell later suggested that protection of synodical prerogatives was necessary because of "persevering efforts" in the West to place the theological department in the same relationship to the college as other departments.[51] Yet, while the amended constitution guarded certain powers of Synod vis-à-vis theology, it continued to allow the Council of Hope College to serve as the Board of Superintendents for the theological department; hence, the theological faculty remained subject to the regulations of the college.

The ambiguous status of the theological faculty was evident even with regard to their compensation. Before 1875 the theological professors received salaries as college faculty and taught theology "without compensation." The Synod of 1875 voted to assume the salaries of her professors of theology: their service to other departments of the college was to be "gratuitous." To provide for the salaries, the Synod relied upon freewill offerings and these proved to be inadequate. The professors were often required to raise their own funds or go unpaid altogether.[52]

Viewed even from a distance, the decisions of Synod appear to be essentially sound. They were the careful measures of compromise, and they would leverage a few years of theological instruction "in" and/or "at" Hope College. Yet, the vexed question remained, and the inherent tensions between the president and the professors intensified.

Theological Instruction Is Suspended

In its report to the Synod in 1873, the Council of Hope College lamented the fact that the college had used some of the general endowment monies to pay for instruction in the Theological Department. After touting the success of the department to produce ministers of the Gospel for Reformed congregations across the

50 *Acts and Proceedings*, June 1871, 293-321.

51 Crispell, "Theological Seminary at Hope College," 124.

52 *Acts and Proceedings*, June 1875, 334-35; Crispell, "Theological Seminary at Hope College," 125-26. Concern regarding unpaid salaries is expressed by the professors through General Synod. See *Acts and Proceedings*, June 1876, 529-30.

denomination, the Council implored the Synod to take measures to relieve financial burdens. It added prophetically,

> Some have imagined that there would be hazard in informing the Synod that its second Theological school was costing something, for that when appraised of the fact, the Synod would probably order its suspension.[53]

Still, few saw it coming, even four years later. The benign report of the Council of Hope College in 1877 certainly did not anticipate any drastic actions. Of course the usual concerns about finances were expressed, and there were the usual pleas for funds, but the report was pretty much business as usual. The section dealing with the Theological Department revealed that just six students had attended during the previous year, but they were lauded for their piety and their participation in a religious awakening which had stirred congregations in the Holland area.[54]

Three delegates from Michigan who attended the Synod of 1877, Henry Uiterwijk, Christian Van der Veen, and Jacob Van der Meulen, later informed readers of *De Hope* that petitions from both President Phelps and Professor Crispell regarding the relationship of the college to theological instruction may have triggered the actions of the Synod.[55] At any rate, an ad hoc committee was appointed to address all of the issues associated with Hope College, including the chronic and pressing financial needs. It was this committee which proposed a series of resolutions related to governance, professors' salaries, endowments, and presidential prerogatives. But it was the resolution pertaining to the Theological Department that sent shock waves through the Western churches.

> Resolved, That in view of the present embarrassed condition of the finances of the college, the Council be directed for the present to suspend the Theological Department.[56]

The Synod did not vote on this resolution before engaging in a thorough discussion of the underlying issues. A full day and a

[53] *Acts and Proceedings*, June 1873, 731-32.

[54] *Acts and Proceedings*, June 1877, 702.

[55] Henry Uiterwijk, Christian Van der Veen, and Jacob Van der Meulen, Letter, *De Hope* 11, no. 42 (11 July 1877). The correspondence from Phelps and Crispell is noted in *Acts and Proceedings*, June 1877, 706.

[56] *Acts and Proceedings*, June 1877, 707.

half of Synod was devoted to the recommendation pertaining to the Theological Department. President Phelps and Professor Crispell, among others, were given opportunities to be heard "with patience." Uiterwijk, Van der Veen, and Van der Meulen, who voted with the majority, assured the readers of *De Hope* that there was "no driving or underhanded conspiracy" in the decision making. Everyone had the opportunity to express personal convictions.[57]

Following the defeat of a substitute motion to delay a decision until the will of the churches in the West was heard, the resolution to suspend the Theological Department passed by a vote of eighty-three to thirty-six. Because there were just seventeen delegates from Western classes at the Synod of 1877, the vast majority of "aye" and "nay" votes were cast by Eastern delegates. Four delegates from the West voted with the majority.[58]

Not surprisingly, the decision of the Synod to suspend theological instruction at Hope College triggered heated discussions across the denomination, but especially in the West. Those who opposed the decision desperately sought to identify the "real" reasons for the action of Synod. Many Western leaders simply did not accept the presented reason: the financial condition of the college. Dirk Broek, for instance, insisted that theological education at Hope College "hardly cost the church anything" and predicted that financial conditions would worsen rather than improve because of the decision.[59] Roelof Pieters agreed. Following a careful calculation of salary costs and the expected increased travel expenses for students who would now be obliged to go to New Brunswick, Pieters concluded that "financial difficulty cannot be the true reason, for the elimination costs the church about as much as the continuation."[60]

[57] The writers of the letter cited in n. 55, although pastors of Michigan churches, were graduates of Rutgers College and New Brunswick Seminary.

[58] See H. O. Yntema and Q. Huyser, "A Word of Information," *De Hope* 11, no. 46 (8 August 1877). Elder delegates from Classis Holland, Yntema and Huyser opposed suspension. The votes for this resolution were recorded and published in *Acts and Proceedings*. See *Acts and Proceedings*, June 1877, 598-601, 708-9. The four who voted to suspend were Uiterwijk, Van der Veen, Van der Meulen, and Hope Professor John W. Beardslee, who chaired the ad hoc committee on the college which brought the resolutions.

[59] Dirk Broek, "Something about the Cessation of the Theological Department at Hope College," *De Hope* 11, no. 45 (1 August 1877).

[60] Roelof Pieters, "Light on a Badly Illuminated Matter," *De Hope* 11, no. 50 (5 September 1877).

An often-repeated explanation for the suspension, especially in the West, was that some in the East were, as Broek put it, "jealous" of Hope College, preferring that ministers of the denomination be trained at New Brunswick. While the tensions between the Eastern and Western sections of the Reformed Church were evident in the 1870s, just as they are evident in the twenty-first century, it is difficult to ascertain the role that those sectarian tensions played in the Synod's decision to suspend theology in the West. As Broek himself noted, not all of the "nay" votes came from the West, and an Eastern friend of Hope College, Elder Samuel B. Schieffelin, proposed that the decision be delayed for a year.[61]

It must also be remembered that the leaders in the West did not agree about suspension. The reason that discussions were so heated was that the minority voice was strong and articulate. Many pastors of Western churches had been trained at Rutgers and the Theological Seminary in New Brunswick, and they were convinced that theological education in the West was not necessary.

The most articulate Western apologist for suspension was Christian Van der Veen, who submitted an extensive two-part article to *De Hope*, "Light on a Badly Understood Matter." In addition to funding concerns, Van der Veen pitched upon the turmoil which the Theological Department had brought to Hope College. The elimination of theology would allow the Council of Hope to put an end to "the quarrels which were a public scandal at times." Admitting that it was difficult to discuss, Van der Veen suggested that "the moral tone" of the college was negatively affected by the squabbling: "[I]t grieved and discouraged her best friends, and much sympathy for her was cut off by it."[62]

Van der Veen also claimed that theological education at Hope College had contributed to a "seeming chasm" between the East and the West. To stave off "that feeling of alienation," it was important that there be a focus on unity of understanding, purpose, and endeavors. And this would be "guaranteed by the education of all ministers in one school and under one influence."[63]

Looking back upon the decision, Nicholas Steffens admitted that it was occasioned by lack of funds, but that "the real cause of

[61] Broek, "Something about the Cessation of the Theological Department."

[62] Christian Van der Veen, "Light on a Badly Misunderstood Matter," pt. 1, *De Hope* 11, no. 49 (29 August 1877).

[63] Van der Veen, "Light on a Badly Misunderstood Matter," pt. 2, *De Hope* 11, no. 50 (5 September 1877).

the suspension lay deeper," in the disinclination toward theological education in the West. Some, from both East and West, were concerned that the unity of education of the ministry would be broken; others feared that New Brunswick would suffer financially; and still others thought that the denomination was too small to afford "the luxury of two theological schools."[64]

Increasingly, it seems, those Westerners who supported the suspension were isolated and put on the defensive. Nearly all of the congregations and most of their ministers agreed with the writer who blasted the decision to suspend in a letter to the *Christian Intelligencer*. This friend of Western education was dismayed that the Synod had "*wiped out* a Western Theological Seminary, not inadvertently, but of deliberate purpose after four hours of debate," and all of this had been done "out of imagined friendship for Hope College."[65] A month later the *Intelligencer* published another critique of the action of the Synod. "Let me assure you, brethren in the East, theology, *per se,* has never been the cause of our troubles, and its suspension will not remove any, but create a great many more, and these will damage the whole institution permanently."[66]

Henry Dosker admitted later that the ministers of the Western church had never been of one accord on the suspension, but that the churches were nearly unanimous in their deep disappointment. The suspension of theological training, wrote Dosker, "passed like an electric shock" through the Western congregations. "It increased the unrest and suspicion which existed in certain quarters, and it stands closely related to the disturbing events of the seven years which followed."[67]

Although the churches of the West had endured a series of jolts during the 1870s—the financial panic of 1873, the death of Albertus C. Van Raalte in 1876, and the great fire which destroyed much of Holland in 1871—the most serious challenge to the Reformed Church was the controversy over membership in the Masonic Lodge. Because the Reformed Church Synod refused to issue a blanket condemnation of lodge membership, many of the members and congregations left the denomination and became associated with the Christian Reformed Church. This issue was especially virulent during the early

64 Steffens, *Quarter-Centennial*, 40.

65 Letter, *Christian Intelligencer* 48, 9 July 1877: 4. The letter is titled "And yet—" and is simply signed "Reader."

66 R. Pieters, "Was it Wise?" Letter, *Christian Intelligencer* 48, 9 August 1877: 4.

67 Dosker, "Western Seminary Since 1884," 203.

1880s, a period when there was no theological school in the West. It is noteworthy that Calvin Theological Seminary had been established by the Christian Reformed Church in 1876, a year before the Synod suspended theological education at Hope. Composed of many of the same *Afscheiding* (Separatist) immigrants who had become associated with the RCA, the Christian Reformed Church greatly benefited from the Masonic controversy.[68]

Restoration of Theology in the West

Soon after the 1877 Synod decision to suspend the Theological Department, the Reformed churches in the West began to campaign for its restoration. The Synod of 1878, for instance, received memorials from the Classes of the Grand River, Wisconsin, and Holland, as well as the Council of Hope College, petitioning the Synod to "restore the Theological Department of Hope College as soon as possible on a firm basis."[69]

The Committee of the Professorate which noted that the suspension of the Theological Department was "a great disappointment," in the West, suggested that an adequate endowment, given perhaps in honor of Van Raalte, would speed the decision to restore theology. Concern for the financial health of Hope College, however, compelled the committee to recommend the suspension be extended indefinitely. So voted the Synod.[70]

At the Synod, the Education Committee listed possible reasons for the financial constraints of the college: mistakes by former Synods, poor financial management, misunderstandings between the East and the West, and "discord among the members of the Faculty." While acknowledging that such discord was exacerbated by the inability to define relations between the college and theological instruction, the committee suggested that it had created distrust in the East regarding

[68] See Robert P. Swierenga and Elton J. Bruins, *Family Quarrels in the Dutch Reformed Churches in the Nineteenth Century* (Grand Rapids: Eerdmans, 1999), 108-35. See also Elton J. Bruins, "The Masonic Controversy in Holland, Michigan, 1879-1882," in *Perspectives on the Christian Reformed Church. Studies in Its History, Theology, and Ecumenicity*, eds. Peter De Klerk and Richard R. De Ridder (Grand Rapids: Baker, 1983), 53-72.

[69] *Acts and Proceedings*, June 1878, 13-15. The specific quotation is taken from the petition from the Grand River Classis.

[70] Ibid., 118-19.

the condition of affairs in Holland, and that this distrust needed to be removed before the Eastern churches would support the college.[71]

The committee then dropped a bombshell. Arguing that "extreme measures" alone would be able to meet the emergency faced by the college, and that confidence in the college could be restored only if President Phelps and Professor Crispell leave their positions, the committee recommended that the Synod ask for their resignations. "It sometimes becomes necessary to sacrifice men to save institutions."[72] The Synod agreed and voted to request the resignations of the president and all those who taught theology. It was reported at the next Synod that all had tendered their resignations as requested.[73]

Although Phelps believed that his contributions to the college had been underappreciated and misunderstood, he did formally resign his presidency. At subsequent Synods he attempted to plead his case. Meanwhile he and his family continued to live in Van Vleck Hall until 1884 when the Synod asked them to leave the campus. Phelps subsequently moved to upstate New York where he pastored two small congregations, Blenheim and Breakabeen. Professor Crispell left the college in 1879 and became the pastor of a congregation in Spring Valley, New York. Professors Beck and Scott were retained and continued to serve the college. It was a tumultuous time for Hope College.[74]

In explaining its recommendation that the 1879 Synod once again deny the restoration of theology in the West, the Committee on Church Colleges hinted at one of the reasons for the tepid Eastern support for a theological department at Hope College:

> We are Americans and must do our work after our American fashion. It is a rule with us to keep distinct things that differ. It is not our American way to teach Theology at a college. An institution that mixed a Collegiate with a Theological training would be an anomaly, a monstrosity in our country.[75]

[71] Ibid., 123-24.

[72] Ibid., 124.

[73] Ibid., 124-25; ibid., June 1879, 333.

[74] See Bruins, "Early Hope College History," 12; Philip Phelps, *About Hope College* (April 1884), a twenty-two-page pamphlet in which Phelps argues his case; *Acts and Proceedings*, June 1884, 536; *Acts and Proceedings*, June 1879, 333.

[75] *Acts and Proceedings*, June 1879, 349.

The minutes of the 1879 Synod also included a letter from David Cole, the Synod's agent to Hope College, and a recent visitor to West Michigan, who suggested that misunderstanding between East and West was related to the incessant financial squabbles which had been generated yearly at Synod by reports from Hope College. Eastern delegates had become "tired of its very name," wrote Cole. On their part, Westerners, hurt by decisions of the church, uttered words of disappointment which gave the impression in the East that "they were becoming disloyal, and contemplating secession" from the denomination. This impression was false, wrote Cole. "The Hollanders *are* loyal. They love the Reformed Church with sterling devotion."[76]

While the Masonic controversy convulsed the Western church (at least one-tenth of the members of the Western Classes of the Reformed Church left the denomination),[77] there was little movement toward the restoration of theology until 1882. During the Synod meeting that year, a committee was appointed to report on "the advisability of establishing a department of theological instruction at the West at an early day." The report which followed reiterated the history of theological instruction in the West and the long-held desires to have it restored. It expressed concern that theological candidates from Holland were attending the seminaries of other denominations and might be lost to the Reformed Church. If the foothold of the Reformed Church in the West was to be maintained, the time had "already arrived for the resuscitation of the Department of Theology at Hope College." Aware that the Western church was "passing through a most perilous crisis," restoration of theology was a matter "of life or death."[78]

Acting upon the committee's recommendation, the Synod voted to resume theological instruction in the autumn of 1884, with the provision that the congregations belonging to the Synod of Chicago fully endow a Professorship of Didactic and Polemic Theology. The Synod also voted to appoint a special committee which would draw up

76 Ibid., 355-61. Henry Dosker claimed that a segment of the Eastern church continued to thwart the ministry of Western Seminary after 1884. He called it a "short sighted party" which was convinced that a Western seminary was unneeded. He compared it to the old "Conferentie" party of the eighteenth century. Dosker also wrote of a "reactionary party" in the West who continued to oppose Western Seminary. See Dosker, "Western Seminary Since 1884," 205-6.

77 See Bruins, "Masonic Controversy in Holland, Michigan," 69-71.

78 *Acts and Proceedings*, June 1883, 319-21.

a feasible plan for the restoration of theology to be considered at the next meeting of General Synod.[79]

The decision to begin the process of restoring theological education in the West elicited a mixed response. There was general approbation in the West, of course, but there were those who questioned the wisdom of the decision. A caustic article by Christian Van der Veen, published in the *Intelligencer*, reveals some of the deep-seated tension over the decision of Synod. "It seems we are once more to try the policy of giving the Western brethren what they want, partly as a salve for their injured feelings, and partly in the hope of preventing possible fresh disasters." Concerned that the other needs of Hope College would be overlooked, Van der Veen complained that "by the needless raising of the distracting issue of Theology" new obstacles would be laid in the way of the college. He expressed chagrin at "the exaggerated notions of the value of a theological department, especially after the experiences which have taught us what theology at Holland really signifies." Theology in any connection with the College could only be what it was in the past: "the foe of education; the parasite of that institution; the egg from which secession will ultimately be hatched."[80]

A report on theological instruction at Hope College came before the Synod of 1884, which met in Grand Rapids and traveled to nearby Holland to consider the needs of the college and the churches firsthand. Again it was stipulated that the Theological Department would be restored only after a full endowment of thirty thousand dollars had been raised for a professorship in theology. The Synod, anticipating that this stipulation would soon be met, proceeded to elect Nicholas M. Steffens, already a member of the academic faculty of the college, as Professor of Didactic and Polemic Theology. Steffens was to be inaugurated in this position only after the endowment was secured.[81]

By 3 December 1884, the theological endowment was met in full, and on the next day Professor Steffens was inaugurated as the first Professor of Didactic and Polemic Theology of the restored school of theology in the West. He was assisted by lectors Peter Moerdyke and Henry Dosker. Because Steffens had held classes in his home since the beginning of the semester, five students were already enrolled in

[79] Ibid., 321.

[80] C. Van der Veen, "On Hope College and the Restoration of Theology," *Christian Intelligencer* 55 (26 March 1884).

[81] *Acts and Proceedings*, June 1884, 326-30, 334-36. This was the first General Synod to meet in the Middle West.

courses: four first-year students and one second-year student, Dirk Scholten, who had left New Brunswick Theological Seminary to attend the restored institution in Holland.[82] Theological instruction had been reestablished in the West. The "darkest" period in "all the history of the Western church" had ended.[83]

Western Theological Seminary and Hope College: Separate But Not Separated

With the restoration in 1884, theological instruction at Hope College proceeded pretty much as it had before the suspension of 1877. Steffens constituted the Theological Professorate, assisted by lectors from the college. "The Vexed Question" of the relationship between Hope College and theological instruction in the West remained essentially unanswered.

At the June 1885 meeting of Synod, it was reported by the Committee of the Professorate: Western Department that the thirty thousand dollars for the endowment had been raised and that Professor Nicholas Steffens had been inaugurated on 4 December 1884. Details of the inauguration followed. In addition to the inaugural address by Professor Steffens, Charles Scott, president of Hope College, presided and preached the sermon; the Reverend Seine Bolks of Orange City, Iowa, gave the charge to the professor; and the Reverend Henry Dosker delivered a special address. It was noted that the service was attended "by a large assembly of interested friends who rejoiced together in the restoration of the Theological Department."[84]

In its first annual report to General Synod, the restored theological school celebrated the progress which already had been made. It included this positive assessment from Professor Steffens:

> A beginning has been made in earnest theological instruction; the desire of our people has been reopened, and God has blessed our first endeavors in teaching. We cannot make a grand display, but we are not without facts that are cheering and encouraging.[85]

82 Wichers, *A Century of Hope*, 111-12; *Acts and Proceedings*, June 1885, 741-42. See also *Catalogue of the Officers and Students of Hope College, 1885-86* (Holland, Mich.,1886), 22-23, for list of enrolled students.

83 See Gerhard De Jonge, *Quarter-Centennial*, 63, for quotation on darkest period.

84 *Acts and Proceedings*, June 1885, 741-42.

85 Ibid., 746-50.

The Committee on the Professorate noted that the Theological Department had been restored by the 1884 Synod as a department of Hope College, but "subject only to the General Synod" and that the Council of Hope College had been instructed to act "in a separate capacity" as its Board of Superintendents, in the manner of the board of the theological seminary in New Brunswick.[86]

Interpreting the decision of 1884, the committee concluded that the Theological Department of Hope College was essentially "a separate institution, having its own autonomy, taught by its own professors, and sustained by its own funds, and not in any way under the government and discipline of the corporation known as the Council of Hope College." As a "creature of the General Synod," it represented "the entire Reformed Church in America," yet, as "a sister institution," and being an outgrowth of the college, "this theological seminary" was "designed and expected to live and work in harmony with Hope College."[87]

In view of expected growth and "to avoid entangling alliances in the future," the committee proposed that the Theological Department "be placed under the government and control of a separate Board of Superintendents," with representatives to be selected from each of the Western Classes, the Particular Synod of Chicago, the General Synod, Eastern Synods, and the Church at large.[88] Finally, it was resolved: "That the corporate style and title of the Theological Department at Hope College, be and hereby is changed, so that it shall hereafter be known as the Western Theological Seminary of the Reformed Church in America."[89]

With the passing of these resolutions, it would appear that "the vexed question" was finally and fully resolved. Essentially this was so. Henry Dosker has observed that the establishment of a separate board, a distinct faculty, and an independent curriculum, "slowly wore out the old question which formerly had occasioned so many heartburnings."[90]

Only slowly. The appellation "Theological Department at Hope College" persisted for several years. The 1885-86 catalogue of Hope College boldly celebrated the reopening of the "Theological

86 Ibid., 745. See also *Acts and Proceedings*, June 1884, 529-30.
87 *Acts and Proceedings*, June 1885, 745.
88 Ibid., 745, 750.
89 Ibid., 746.
90 Dosker, "Western Seminary Since 1884," 204.

Department," and listed the eight students who were enrolled.[91] The following year the catalogue, on separate lines, highlighted: "Department of Theology" and "The Western Theological Seminary of the Reformed Church in America." The catalogue also provided a list of the seminary's Board of Superintendents, faculty members, students, course of study, and graduates (back to 1869).[92] This remained the pattern of Hope's catalogues for several years.

The 1890-91 Hope catalogue included the announcement, "Western Theological Seminary, of the Reformed Church in America, Department of Theology at Holland, Michigan." Thereafter Hope catalogues reference Western Theological Seminary but not the Department of Theology. The church had finally come to identify its theological school as Western Theological Seminary.[93]

The 1905-06 Hope catalogue initiated a longstanding practice of including a lengthy explanation of the relationship between Hope and Western in the section given to the Seminary. For several years this explanation varied little from the following:

> There is no connection charter, organic, financial, or otherwise, between Hope College and the Western Theological Seminary. Both are separate institutions under the care of the Reformed Church in America. Each takes pleasure in extending the other all possible courtesy and consideration and the advantages offered by the college are open to seminary students. No work done in either institution, however, is accepted by the other for a degree or certificate in lieu of its prescribed curriculum.[94]

Although the Hope College catalogue continued to include the Seminary's yearbook or catalogue through 1931, it was apparent by the turn of the twentieth century that the institutions were definitely distinct.

91 *Catalogue of the Officers and Students of Hope College, 1885-86*, 22-23.

92 *Catalogue of the Officers and Students of Hope College, 1886-87* (Holland, Mich., n.d.), [23]-26, [32]-36. *Acts and Proceedings*, June 1887, included a report from "The Board of Superintendents of the Western Theological Seminary at Hope College" on p. 257.

93 *Catalogue of the Officers and Students of Hope College*, 1890-91 (Grand Rapids, 1891), 41.

94 "Western Theological Seminary Yearbook," in *Hope College Catalogue, 1905-06*, n.p.

It must be pointed out that although the formal relationship between the College and the Seminary has been one of increasing separation since 1884, the institutions have never been fully separated. In various ways, some significant and some less so, these institutions have continued to be interrelated.

Take buildings, for example. Following the restoration of theological education in 1884, the Seminary was without its own building. The College permitted the Seminary to occupy the second floor of the Oggel House, and to use the gymnasium for recitations. It was not until 1895, when Peter Semelink provided funds to build an all-purpose building, known as Semelink Family Hall, that the Seminary had a home of its own. Consider the library. When Semelink Family Hall was built, the Seminary possessed a small collection of books but no building in which to house them. The students and faculty were served by the college library. Western did not have its own library until Professor John W. Beardslee provided personal funds to have one built: the Beardslee Library, also known as Divinity Hall, was not completed until 1912.[95] Today, although Hope and Western both possess impressive collections housed in large and attractive buildings, they continue to share library resources through computerized online catalogues.

With the construction of Semelink Family Hall, Divinity Hall, and a student dormitory, all of which were located on land which was designated for seminary use, the Seminary was gradually able to develop its own campus, but was always in such close proximity to the College that the distinctions between the two often blurred.

Even after the Seminary obtained its own space and buildings, however, it continued to use larger spaces at the College for commencement exercises and other major events. Today, commencement exercises for seminary graduates take place each year in spacious Dimnent Chapel on Hope's campus.

Beyond use of Hope College buildings for commencement, for many years Western graduates were included in the Hope College graduation programs. This was the case off and on through 1940.[96]

[95] Eenigenburg, "History of the Seminary," 26, 50-51. See *Western Theological Seminary, Semi-Centennial Catalog, 1869-1914*, 20; also, Wichers, *A Century of Hope*, 112. At this point the origin of the Seminary was dated from the first graduating class, 1869.

[96] See Hope College catalogues, 1869-1940.

Indeed, because Western was not originally incorporated as a degree-granting institution, Hope College actually conferred the degrees for the Seminary. Following World War I, the College granted Bachelor of Divinity, Bachelor of Theology, and Master of Theology degrees at its commencement services. With the establishment of the Association of Theological Schools, seminaries like Western began to grant their own degrees after World War II.[97]

It was perhaps in the area of governance that Western Theological Seminary and Hope College diverged most dramatically. Theological faculty members at Hope College were originally members of the Professorate of the General Synod, but governed locally by the Council of Hope College. When a separate Board of Superintendents was established for the Seminary in 1885, the institutions became distinct. For many years afterward, however, the president of the College was an ex officio member of the Seminary's board.[98] The Seminary board has remained through the years fully amenable to the General Synod. Even today, board members must be appointed by the General Synod. The Synod's ties to the College, however, have loosened considerably over time. In 1960 the General Synod ceded official control of the college to the Board of Trustees, and the structure of the board was substantially altered in 1967. Whereas the new structure required that six clergy and six laypersons be appointed by the General Synod, a maximum of nineteen at-large members who were not necessarily members of the Reformed Church in America could also be appointed.[99]

During the early days of theological education at Hope College, the faculty shared positions in the college and the theological school. This was the source of considerable tension, as we have seen. During the early twentieth century there was considerable movement from the

[97] For example, see *Western Theological Seminary Catalog, 1929-30*, 25-26, for degrees offered by Western but conferred by Hope and Central Colleges.

[98] Beginning in 1884 the president of Hope College was listed as an ex officio member of the Western Theological Seminary Board of Superintendents (Trustees). When the Western and New Brunswick boards were merged into a single Board of Theological Education in 1976, Hope's president was no longer listed as an ex officio member. See *Acts and Proceedings*, June 1967, 52-56, and *General Synod Directory, June 1967*, 10-12.

[99] See Harry Boonstra and Elton J. Bruins, "Gordon J. Van Wylen and Hope College," introduction to *Vision for a Christian College*, by Gordon J. Van Wylen (Grand Rapids: Eerdmans, 1988), xvi-xvii.

college to the seminary. Although such movement across the Pine Grove has diminished considerably since 1960, it still occurs occasionally.[100]

Perhaps the strongest continuing relationship between Hope College and Western Theological Seminary pertains to students who have enrolled at both institutions. Early in its history, the Seminary drew most of its students from Hope College, and that pattern has continued through the years, with a good percentage of Western graduates having been Hope graduates. Until the middle of the twentieth century, Hope was known as a pre-seminary institution—one which sent a large percentage of graduates into the ministry or the mission field.[101] Western Seminary continues to benefit from the religious inclinations of the Hope students. The outstanding faculty at Hope College continues to nurture those who sense a call to some form of ordained ministry and mission leadership, and if that faculty encourages some of its students to leave West Michigan for seminary training, a good percentage of them still choose to enroll at Western Theological Seminary.[102]

Conclusion

"The vexed question" of the relationship of Hope College and theological education has been significant in the history of both institutions. Considering the religious concerns of the Dutch Reformed folk who settled in the Midwest, this should not be surprising. The central motive for the founding of the Holland Academy and later Hope College was the desire for a Western school of theology. When theological instruction was suspended at the College, the Western church was deeply disappointed by what was generally considered a punitive decision of the Eastern Reformed Church. And when theological training was restored, the Western church embraced the nascent Western Theological Seminary—and it still embraces that institution today.

[100] Dennis Voskuil taught in the Religion Department at Hope College from 1977 until 1994, when he was appointed as president of Western Theological Seminary.

[101] See Wichers, *A Century of Hope*, 174-75, and Kennedy and Simon, *Can Hope Endure?*, 35-37.

[102] For example, between 1996 and 2005, 106 of the 460 students admitted to the Master of Divinity program at Western were Hope College graduates (Pat Dykhuis, registrar, Western Theological Seminary).

The tensions which once existed between the president of Hope College and the professors in the Theological Department have long been assuaged and forgotten, but the once intimate relationship between the two institutions continues to linger—even in West Michigan. When Western Theological Seminary broke ground for a new facility in 2003 and announced plans to raise funds for expansion purposes, the *Grand Rapids Press* ran the headline: "Hope Seminary Seeks Expansion Funds." Formally separated from Hope College since 1885, the Seminary is still identified as a part of Hope College today. President Philip Phelps would be pleased.[103]

[103] "Hope Seminary Seeks Expansion Funds," *Grand Rapids Press*, 9 May 2002, sec. B2.

CHAPTER 15

The Joint Archives of Holland: An Experiment in Cooperative Archival Preservation and Access

Larry J. Wagenaar

How do we guarantee that the story of our past survives and ensure that the past will really serve us as a prologue to the future? Preservation of archival resources is a key element in retaining our history. Sadly, archival collections are often the stepchild of flashier public programs and institutions that draw higher visitor numbers and pique the interest of major donors. In an effort to provide state-of-the-art care and access, the concept of cooperative archival preservation—bringing several institutions together to pool resources and talent—can be a boon to curators, researchers, and the public. Joint archival approaches can also result in difficult situations that require deft negotiations and involve interesting politics.

This essay discusses the formation, development, and growth of the Joint Archives of Holland, a pioneering cooperative archival program, which was the result of the direct efforts and support of Dr. Elton Bruins. The Joint Archives produced both great results and challenging inter-agency conflicts that partially diminished its full potential.

Bringing It Together

The Joint Archives of Holland was founded in 1988 when the archival collections of Hope College, the Holland Historical Trust (later the Holland Museum), and Western Theological Seminary were brought together on the lower level of the new Van Wylen Library on the college campus. This state-of-the-art facility, designed to hold the new archives and the college's rare book collection, immediately became a focal point of Dutch-American, collegiate, church, and community history. It would grow dramatically but also experience some significant challenges as it matured.

The effort to provide care in one facility for the archival collections of several institutions, one of the first of its kind, could not have come to fruition without the vision of Dr. Bruins. Aided by Netherlands Museum Director Willard C. Wichers, Hope College Provost Jacob Nyenhuis, and many others, his dream took hold through tireless advocacy efforts with key decision makers on the college campus and in the greater Holland community.

The idea of a cooperative archival program took root in a conversation between Bruins and Robert Warner, Director of the Bentley Historical Library at the University of Michigan prior to his appointment as Archivist of the United States.[1] Although Bruins had been working for some time at preserving the archives of the Netherlands Museum, Hope College, and Western Theological Seminary,[2] it took Warner's outside evaluation of the related nature of the three collections to spur the initial idea of combining them in one location.

Translating the concept of a "joint archives" into reality failed twice before it was achieved in the new college library. In 1976 efforts were underway to include a cooperative archival program in an expansion of the Herrick Public Library located on River Avenue, just south of Holland's principal shopping district. After this initiative failed, serious discussions were held about incorporating such a program in the new multi-story Cook Library being built for Western Seminary in 1980. For both of these efforts, finances became the sticking point.[3] Finally, thanks to the efforts of Bruins, Wichers, and

[1] Elton Bruins has shared this story with me on numerous occasions and at public gatherings when recounting how the initial idea of a joint archival program between the institutions germinated.

[2] *Holland Sentinel*, 14 May 1975. Bruins started working in the seminary's archives in 1967 and took over as the college's volunteer archivist after the first Hope archivist, Janet Mulder, retired in 1968. He also spent time on the museum's archives. An April 1976 article in the *Hope College Alumni Magazine* describes his work for the college.

[3] *Holland Sentinel*, 23 January 1987.

Nyenhuis, President Gordon Van Wylen approved the inclusion of an expanded archival space as part of the archives/rare book room being incorporated into the new library, which would later bear his and his wife Margaret's name. A creative solution for funding the joint archives was devised by Provost Nyenhuis to make this third effort succeed: each of the three institutions would contribute a base fee of $5,000 as equal partners; the rest of the budget was to be covered by assessments based on the percentage of the space taken up by the collection of each institution.[4] Thus the Holland Historical Trust (Netherlands Museum) and the Seminary would bear a proportionally lower cost than the college. Hope College would serve as the fiduciary agent for the program and the archivist hired would be an employee of the college.

The archives of the three institutions were in widely varying condition. The Netherlands Museum's archives were literally stuffed into the old treasurer's vault in the mayor's office of City Hall. Grace Antoon, assistant to museum director Wichers and his successor Reid Van Sluis, did her best to provide access to the collection, which had been organized to some degree by Barbara Lampen and the volunteer efforts of Bruins. Both had built on the foundational work of early Holland historians Gerrit Van Schelven and Peter Moerdyke. Although a useful, rough guide to the collection was produced, much of the collection was left undocumented. The collection itself, however, was very rich, with original Van Raalte letters, Civil War documents, and a treasure trove of other primary historical material. Van Schelven, who managed the community's semi-centennial in 1897, and Moerdyke, who was part of the staff in the museum's early days, had assembled rich resources that would prove invaluable to future generations.

At Hope College, circumstances were much better. Space had been dedicated to the archival collection and the materials were consistently cared for. When President Irwin Lubbers established the college's archives in 1952, retired librarian Janet Mulder was appointed to organize and manage the collection. Following her retirement in 1968, Bruins filled the gap on a volunteer basis until Andrew Vander Zee was made college archivist in 1970, a post he held until the formation of the Joint Archives and my appointment as its first archivist.[5]

Finally, Western Theological Seminary's archives were managed on an ad hoc basis. Bruins devoted attention to the collection after his

4 Nyenhuis file in Hope College Collection, Joint Archives of Holland; hereafter cited as JAH.

5 *Holland Sentinel*, 14 May 1975.

appointment to the Hope College faculty, duplicating the work that he did at the college and museum to preserve their materials. Dr. John Luidens followed Bruins as a part-time archivist for the seminary until the three archives were brought together in 1988. Luidens continued to assist at the Joint Archives for several years, until his death in 1994.[6]

In November 1987 the *Holland Sentinel* announced the formation of a "Joint Archives Council" that included three representatives from each of the three institutions. The members brought to their work on the Council a strong interest in preserving the historical record that can be found in archival collections. "Plans are to house the collections of the Holland Historical Trust, Hope College, and Western Theological Seminary in the Van Wylen Library sometime after July 1, 1988, and to hire a full-time archivist to begin work by July 1," commented Bruins.[7] Holland's mayor, Philip Tanis, declared the effort a "bargain rate solution" to the problems of providing professional care, preservation, and public access.[8]

A search drew some thirty candidates, who were narrowed down to a final pool of three. After extensive on-site interviews with all three candidates, I was appointed by the Joint Archives Council as the first archivist of the new archival program on 20 May 1988. My duties began in mid-August.

My first objective was to bring the archival collections together in the new space on the lower level of the Van Wylen Library, which was accomplished by the end of September. I developed a three-phase development plan for the Joint Archives which was implemented during my first years in the position:

1. Phase one—physical control, mission statement, collecting policy, standardized arrangement and description, a brochure, and National Historical Publication and Records Commission grant development;
2. Phase two—bibliographic and intellectual control, develop-

6 Dr. Luidens can be seen in a picture that was professionally produced and featured on the first brochure published shortly after the opening of the archives. He is seated at a table in the reading room of the Joint Archives of Holland. One of the first student staff members, Rebecca O'Shesky, and I can also be seen in the photo. Luidens was one of the first volunteers at the Joint Archives.

7 *Holland Sentinel*, 24 November 1987.

8 *Holland Sentinel*, 23 January 1988.

ment of finding aids, collection guides and indexes, computer automation, an active acquisition program;
3. Phase three—collections development, records management, translation program, continued development of items in phases one and two.[9]

Before moving to Holland, I wrote to Bruins, "Computerization of our efforts from the beginning is important in order to avoid [the] duplication of effort inherent in starting with a paper system."[10] In order to raise the profile and identity of the new effort, I proposed that the new cooperative institution be formally named "The Joint Archives of Holland" rather than the Joint Archives Program; my proposal was approved by the Council.[11] In September 1990, "History Research Center" was officially added to the name as a subtitle to highlight even better the function of the Archives.[12]

Since there were limited resources to start the new program, Van Wylen Library Director David P. Jensen agreed to underwrite several part-time student assistants for the Archives. The work of these students proved to be of great value: undergraduates Krystal Van Wulfen, Rebecca O'Shesky, and others over the next decade and a half tackled various tasks under the direction of the archivist, ably assisting in the development of collection management and public access. Dr. Luidens also agreed to stay on to assist with the work. He spent time at the Joint Archives almost weekly for the first two years.

Providing solid leadership throughout the initial development, search process, and the years that followed, Elton Bruins chaired the Joint Archives Council from the very beginning. The Council's team of nine provided directional support for the archival program and reviewed reports and updates at its regular meetings. For the first two years, the Council operated with an exceptional amount of unanimity.

In those first two years, policies were put in place to provide orderly access to the new Archives. A photo use schedule was adopted, and limited regular hours were established. For the first year, the facility

9 "Target Development—3 Phases," document presented to the Joint Archives Council members by Larry Wagenaar during the interview process (Hope College Collection, JAH).

10 Larry J. Wagenaar to Elton Bruins, 15 July 1988 (Hope College Collection, JAH).

11 Report of the Archivist, 16 September 1988 (Hope College Collection, JAH).

12 Ibid., 21 September 1990.

was open only from 1:00 to 4:30 p.m. to allow time in the mornings for staff to organize and process collections, connect with donors of material, and provide support services to the member institutions as needed. Opening the Archives in the evening and on Saturday was attempted, but did not prove satisfactory in the long run. The Archives was open by appointment in the morning until 1996, when the addition of Lori Trethewey as secretary for the Archives finally made full day hours possible.[13]

Although the Joint Archives of Holland opened its doors on 3 October 1988, the formal dedication of the facility occurred on 18 November. Present were leaders of the three participating institutions: John H. Jacobson Jr., President of Hope College; Marvin Hoff, President of Western Theological Seminary; and Clay Stauffer, President of the Board of the Holland Historical Trust. Mayor Tanis was also on hand for the ribbon cutting. Distinguished Dutch-American scholar Robert P. Swierenga of Kent State University gave the keynote address, "Dutch Immigration to Michigan and the Middle West."[14] In 1996 Swierenga joined the faculty of Hope College as the Albertus C. Van Raalte Research Professor at the A. C. Van Raalte Institute, which had been established in 1994; he was appointed concurrently as Adjunct Professor of History.

Development and growth happened quickly in the first years of the Joint Archives and the program gained recognition in the local and college community, as well as more broadly in the Reformed Church in America and Dutch-American studies circles. The first large donation was from First of America Bank in January 1989. A hidden prize, unknown to anyone, surfaced during an initial inventory of the bank's historical ledgers and other records. The minutes of the Hope College Council (later known as the Board of Trustees) from its founding in 1866 to 1929 were discovered among the leather-bound books held in a dank storage room adjacent to the bank's drive-through.[15] This would be the first of many unique finds that were added to the collections in the coming years.

[13] Ibid. Although it was expected that appointments would be made, it was the common practice to serve visitors, especially out-of-town researchers, if they came to the door.

[14] Joint Archives of Holland press release, 14 November 1988 (Hope College Collection, JAH). A program from the dedication is also located in the JAH history collection.

Supposedly lost material was now coming in as word of the Joint Archives spread, although Bruins, the Council, and I initially focused on determining what was really in the archival collections, stabilizing their storage in acid-free containment that would not damage the historical material, and developing bibliographic control of the collections so researchers and staff could find documents and artifacts. Prior to this point, the finding aids were very limited, and the collections, especially the museum's materials, were in a state of disarray.

A numbering system was adopted that was consistent across the collections. Movement of the materials into acid-free folders and inert plastic sleeves (for fragile items and photographs) proceeded steadily, and documenting the contents of the collections was also a priority. Along with these efforts at physical control of the collections came the completion of other aspects of first-phase development: a mission statement and collecting policy, public brochure, and standardized arrangement and description techniques.[16]

A major accomplishment of the first year involved the production of a detailed "Guide to the Collections," which was published in 1989. This was followed by a "Guide to Supplemental Collections," such as the Archives's extensive photo collections. A few years later, these were placed online as the internet became popular. By the end of the 1990s complete collection registers, with detailed container lists, were available online.

As the focus on internal control, documentation, and public access continued, the Joint Archives also emphasized public outreach. Since archival institutions often have little public profile, Bruins and I were determined to provide a public face for the cooperative archival effort. In April 1989, less than one year after the Joint Archives opened its doors, the *Joint Archives Quarterly* newsletter was published: it included news of the collection, upcoming events, historical stories, and other content designed to make friends and the public aware of this new resource.[17] In the fall of 1990, I began writing a column for the *Holland Sentinel*. The staff also was often consulted by the local news media on historical issues.

Public programs were emphasized as a way to draw people to the Joint Archives. The events included such diverse topics as the *S.S.*

15 Joint Archives of Holland press release, 5 January 1989.

16 Report of the Archivist, 20 January 1989 (Hope College Collection, JAH).

17 Report of the Archivist, 1 May 1989.

South American, the Civil War in our Hometown, Archival Skills for Churches, and the Care of Historic Photos. An annual Spring Speaker series was established to bring in well-known persons, such as former Archivist of the United States Robert Warner, Dutch-American scholar Suzanne Sinke, and many others. The Joint Archives also hosted several conferences, including the Biennial Conference of the Association for the Advancement of Dutch-American Studies in 1991 and 1997 and the Historical Society of Michigan's State History Conference in 1997.

In addition to its own public programming, the Archives became more actively involved in the Holland Area Historical Society (HAHS) in late 1989. The Society was a local non-profit organization that held monthly meetings on historical topics, from September through June each year. By the late 1980s, HAHS had dwindled to about thirty members. I saw an opportunity to rebuild interest in the Society and perceived a real benefit for the new Archives if we would provide the support needed to make such programs occur. I therefore agreed to serve the Society as secretary-treasurer, a post later changed to volunteer director.[18] Although HAHS continued to have its own board and leadership, the Joint Archives assisted in coordinating meetings, locating facilities, developing an annual flier, and providing regular communication with Society members. By the mid-1990s, membership in HAHS had grown ten-fold, to over three hundred members. It was a true win-win arrangement, providing steady support and growth to the Society and key exposure to the Joint Archives of Holland.

Attempted Expansion of the Joint Archives

The number of visitors undertaking research at the Joint Archives reflected consistent increases from its formation in 1988 until 2002. But the development of the Joint Archives was not always smooth after its dramatic launch and growth in its first years. One challenge to the expanding vision for the Joint Archives developed when I sought to make the Joint Archives of Holland the repository for some Reformed Church in America archives. Already during my first year I had put this idea forward, but in May 1990 I reported:

> I have approached the Reformed Church in America with the possibility of becoming a regional archive of the RCA in the Midwest. As you might recall this was an objective which was

[18] Ibid., 19 January 1990.

> mentioned by Dr. Swierenga at our dedication dinner. It has been referred to the Historical Commission of the RCA. Russell Gasero, archivist of the RCA at New Brunswick, has voiced his opposition to our becoming a regional archive and will be calling for a major capital commitment by the church to his operation. We may be able to impress the church with our ongoing operation, good facility, and staffing while providing a service at a very reasonable cost.[19]

The Joint Archives of Holland had been operating *de facto* as a regional archive for RCA materials because we were caring for the archival collection of Western Theological Seminary, and WTS had been collecting local church records through a less formal arrangement with the denomination. It seemed logical to me for the church to use the talents of the Joint Archives staff to collect, maintain, and make available collections from churches in the Midwest region in a facility much closer to these congregations. Throughout the early 1990s, I explored the idea of a regional RCA archive in Holland, but in 1996 I began formal negotiations with Kenneth Bradsell, a senior executive of the RCA. There were others, however, including the denomination's archivist, the president of New Brunswick Theological Seminary, and some members of the RCA Commission on History, who argued that the RCA archives should continue to be held in a central location near the RCA headquarters in New York City. To the keen disappointment of myself and others, that position ultimately prevailed.[20]

Nonetheless, collection of congregational records (under the prior informal arrangement) and non-congregational records continued successfully throughout this period, including major efforts to collect the personal papers of RCA missionaries (an important resource that was not a significant focus of the New Brunswick archives), sermon collection projects, involvement in a book celebrating the churches in the Holland Classis of the RCA, and support and training for churches wanting to preserve their collections. Expansion of these collections benefited from Bruins's extensive connections in the church, our

19 Report of the Archivist, 1 May 1990.

20 The first formal approach to the RCA is mentioned in the 1 May 1989 Report of the Archivist. My regular reports for 1996-99 detail the progress of the negotiations and the final resolution of my proposal. Northwestern College in Iowa likewise holds some congregational records from its region and would also have become an RCA regional archive under my proposal.

regular visits with missionaries and churches, and my oral history fieldwork.

Challenges to the Founding Vision

Although success was elusive in our efforts to add a fourth institutional member to the program by becoming a regional archive for the Reformed Church, we faced a much larger challenge to the Joint Archives of Holland after Ann Kiewel was installed as the new Director of the Holland Historical Trust/Holland Museum in 1990.

Kiewel's predecessors—legendary museum director Willard C. Wichers and his successor Reid Van Sluis—wholeheartedly endorsed the concept of providing unified preservation and access to the archival collections by developing the Joint Archives model. The appointment of Kiewel as a development officer to lead a major capital campaign to redevelop the old United States Post Office on the corner of River Avenue and 10th Street as a museum ultimately resulted in the resignation of Van Sluis in mid-1990 and the installation of Kiewel as the new museum director. This change had dramatic implications for the relatively new Joint Archives as it entered its third year of operation.

Unlike her predecessors Wichers and Van Sluis, Kiewel approached museum management with the belief that the purpose of the archival collection was solely to support exhibit design. It was her view that public access was not desired and should even be discouraged. It was also her intention that any purpose other than supporting exhibits at the museum should not be included in their annual fee as part of the Joint Archives.[21]

Problems began for the Archives at the 21 September 1990 meeting of the Joint Archives Council, the first meeting Kiewel attended as the successor to Wichers on the Council. Beginning the next year, a cycle of objections to a wide variety of the Archives's actions, practices,

[21] These positions and others were regularly voiced by Kiewel in meetings and in her correspondence, especially when contracts were up for renewal following the move to a contract for services in 1994. One of the many times it was discussed is included in the notes from Wagenaar's meeting with Provost Jacob Nyenhuis on 7 March 2000 when the contract was again due for renewal: "Discuss Ann Kiewel's letter [and our] response to cost questions. . . . This is the clearest comment, and the first in writing, which specifically threatens the possibility of removing the Trust's collection from the JAH" (Hope College Collection, JAH).

and procedures occurred on a regular basis. Each time, the Archives staff addressed every concern by preparing new reports, conducting additional dialogue on collection matters, or tracking new collection statistics. These challenges continued until the Holland Museum removed its collection from the Joint Archives in 2003.

Despite these difficulties, the Joint Archives continued to grow. After a failed first attempt, the Archives won approval for a two-year grant from the National Historical Publications and Records Commission in 1990.[22] This grant allowed the Archives to add Craig Wright to its staff as its first Collections Archivist. The main task of Wright, and his successors in the position, was to lead the processing of the archival collection. He brought skills from his training at one of the leading archival schools in the country and was able to exceed the grant's goals and processing needs set for this period. A follow-up one-year grant from the NHPRC allowed the work to continue, but was not fully secured before Wright departed for a new position. Jennifer Smith Holman succeeded him in 1993 as the Archives's second Collections Archivist, serving in that capacity until 1996.

Although grant funds were very helpful, they were not a source of permanent funding. The cooperative structure of the Joint Archives also meant that the Archives was limited by the fiscal constraints of the partner with the weakest financial circumstances. These constraints, when combined with the new opposition of Museum Director Ann Kiewel to the original vision for the joint program, made it apparent not only that the Collection Archivist position was in serious jeopardy, but also that the survival of the Joint Archives itself was threatened.[23]

A New Operational Model

In response to this threat, Bruins and I met to discuss a new model that would sustain the viability of the Joint Archives. By moving from a jointly-managed approach with a governing council to one where Hope College made the Joint Archives an official department of the college and provided contract archival services to the other institutions, the Archives could be put on firm financial ground. It

22 Joint Archives of Holland press release, 22 June 1990.

23 Report of the Archivist, 1 October 1992 (Hope College Collection, JAH). It became apparent from comments at this Council meeting and many others that the Holland Historical Trust would not fund any increase in their fee beyond inflationary increases.

would specify the services provided to the member institutions, allow for funding from new sources, and preserve the position of the critical second archivist on the staff. After significant negotiations, especially with the museum, the new contract-for-services model went into effect on 1 July 1994.[24] This move ensured the survival of the Joint Archives of Holland regardless of the actions of any of its member institutions. Other results of this move were the higher integration of the Archives into the college community and its educational mission, including the addition of the two archivists to the faculty of the college, and a change in reporting for the director from the Joint Archives Council to the college provost. Although the Joint Archives Council continued to exist for a short time after the move, it was later disbanded.

The shift to a college department had dramatic effect on the Joint Archives of Holland. With greater financial security and higher integration into the college campus, the Archives was finally able to hire its own students, acquire updated computer and copier equipment, and more aggressively support students in their research and instructional needs.

Throughout the mid-1990s, the Joint Archives grew and flourished. A team of volunteers was developed, many of whom continue serving the Archives to this day. The Archives took over the Hope College Oral History Project and focused on a particular theme each year. Record numbers of researchers were regularly reported. At the time of JAH's founding, thirty visitors a month working in the collections was typical, with a few hundred in its first year. By April 1992, however, staff counted 116 research visits in just one month,[25] with overall annual counts approaching one thousand. By fiscal year 2001-02, the last full year the museum's archives was still on site, the patron count was 1,351.[26]

As cooperative relationships grew in the wake of the organizational change, additional financial resources were also secured. Revenues from new sources of support, including cooperative service

24 Archival Services Agreement with the Holland Historical Trust, 15 September 1994 (Hope College Collection, JAH). Although the conversion to a contract-for-services model began on 1 July, the Holland Historical Trust did not sign its contract until September. A contract between Hope College and Western Seminary was signed before the change took effect.

25 Joint Archives of Holland press release, 5 March 1992.

26 Annual Report that cites usage statistics for fiscal year 2001-02 (Hope College Collection, JAH).

and collecting agreements with Robert Schuller's Crystal Cathedral, Amway, and others, were placed in an Archives Advancement Account held by the college. These new funds combined with funds previously raised allowed the Archives to hire its first secretary/receptionist. Lori Trethewey accepted this position in December 1995; her addition allowed the Joint Archives to formally expand its hours from afternoons only to 9:00 a.m. to 5:00 p.m., beginning in January 1996.[27] A nearly 30 percent increase in research visits was a direct result of this move.[28]

Other opportunities also emerged. In January 1995, Holland Mayor Albert H. McGeehan, City Clerk Jodi Syens, Ann Kiewel, and I met in the mayor's office to discuss how to celebrate Holland's sesquicentennial in 1997.[29] This developed into a planning committee with a variety of community representatives. The Joint Archives and its staff played a significant role in a variety of activities: the development of an official calendar; a major oral history project to collect "150 stories for 150 years"; a new biography of the community's founder Albertus C. Van Raalte, co-authored by Jeanne M. Jacobson, Elton J. Bruins, and me; and assisting with the major events and other activities. The Sesquicentennial Celebration also provided the side benefit of a new logo for the Joint Archives. One of the logo designs considered for the sesquicentennial was reworked into a new three-panel logo for the Joint Archives of Holland.

After three years as Collection Archivist, Jennifer Holman left the Archives in the summer of 1996. In January 1997, Geoffrey Reynolds became the third individual to serve in the position. He immediately undertook work on the collection, coordinating the student staff and stable cadre of dedicated volunteers.

The end of the decade brought many milestones to the archival program. The Guy Vander Jagt Congressional papers—secured earlier in the decade[30]—received the attention of two summer archival interns

[27] *Joint Archives Quarterly*, winter/spring 1996.

[28] Joint Archives of Holland press release, 5 March 1996.

[29] Report of the Director, 15 March 1995.

[30] GVSU President Arend D. Lubbers maintained that Rep. Vander Jagt had promised his papers to the University although Vander Jagt, a Hope College alumnus, had earlier indicated to his alma mater that his papers would be part of the college's archives. Jim Sparling, then Vander Jagt's chief of staff, was able to resolve the issue by placing Vander Jagt's congressional papers in the Hope College Collection of the Joint Archives and his papers from his work as leader of the National Republican Congressional Committee at GVSU.

in the middle of their professional archival training. Rep. Vander Jagt's original six hundred-plus linear feet of papers were processed down to 244, and when finished, the Vander Jagt Collection was opened with a special program, address, and luncheon in the fall of 2000.[31]

Although fundraising was difficult, given the inter-institutional nature of the archival program, the Joint Archives was able to do an annual year-end appeal, which raised some funds. On a larger scale, Hope Advancement staff member John Norden, Nyenhuis, and I visited on several occasions with Dr. Henri Theil, a retired economist, and his wife, Eleonore, in Florida. Dr. Theil was particularly interested in combining the Archives and the Van Raalte Institute in a single facility.[32] A few years after Dr. Theil's death on 10 July 2000, his wife provided a major gift to the college that enabled the Joint Archives of Holland and the A. C. Van Raalte Institute in 2004 to move into a newly renovated building on 10th Street, which was renamed the Henri and Eleonore Theil Research Center in their honor.

In March 2001, I announced my decision to leave the Joint Archives of Holland to lead the Historical Society of Michigan, the oldest cultural organization in the state. Collections Archivist Geoffrey Reynolds was named the new Director of the Joint Archives on 1 July 2001.

Within days of Reynolds's appointment, the Holland Museum formally made its decision to pull its archival collection out of the Joint Archives and to relocate it in the basement of the main museum building. This move was made possible by an earlier decision by the City of Holland to lease the empty Holland Armory to the Museum for one dollar per year, opening up space in the cramped main building. In January 2003, the Holland Museum's archival collection was removed from the care of the Joint Archives staff. As a result, user statistics at the Joint Archives dropped by nearly 250 people in the next year, representing over 20 percent of its patronage.

In the wake of this major change, the Joint Archives of Holland, under Geoffrey Reynolds's leadership and in coordination with

[31] Vander Jagt Collection Opening, 16 November 2000 (Hope College Collection, JAH).

[32] After reading in *News from Hope College* about Bruins's proposal for a joint facility, Dr. Theil telephoned Bruins to express his keen interest in this idea. In March 2000, during a visit by Provost Nyenhuis with Dr. and Mrs. Theil in Florida, Dr. Theil made the commitment to provide funding for a building for the two entities (Nyenhuis file in Hope College Collection, JAH).

Assistant Provost Alfredo M. Gonzales, developed a revised mission statement and collecting policy.[33] It reaffirmed the institution's commitment to its remaining institutional partners and its continued service to researchers and the general public.

Conclusion

On 9 November 1998 the Joint Archives of Holland celebrated its tenth anniversary. Keynote speaker Sandra Clark, Director of the Michigan Historical Center, spoke about "Michigan's History at Risk." Preserving history and dedicating effort to ensure that the documentary heritage of our past survives can, at times, be a precarious endeavor. The work of Elton Bruins over the past four decades, along with the efforts of many others over the years, has demonstrated that a consistent commitment to preserving records of our individual and collective past is vital to the preservation of the history of our community and our state. Although the Museum and the Joint Archives now maintain separate collections, both entities continue to gather documents and artifacts that help to preserve our collective history.

Despite the loss of the museum's archives, the Joint Archives continued to expand. The space vacated by the Museum's collection made it possible to explore new avenues for adding to the collections of the College and the Seminary. Even more exciting was the October 2004 move into the new Theil Research Center. This location not only brought the Joint Archives of Holland together with the Van Raalte Institute, it also brought the Archives together with its visionary, Elton Bruins. With his office just a few steps from the Archives reading room and its rich collections, the Archives now benefits even further from his knowledge and expertise. His extensive files on Van Raalte and other aspects of local history are also now readily accessible to Archives staff. The union of the Joint Archives and the Van Raalte Institute in this new facility represents a visible symbol of the unified vision that Elton Bruins articulated some three decades ago. Thanks to his legacy of vision and hard work, the preservation of the documentary heritage of our past will surely survive and flourish.

[33] Mission Statement and Collection Purposes for the Joint Archives of Holland, 13 February 2003 (Hope College Collection, JAH).

Index

The Historical Series of the Reformed Church in America

Recent Books

Allan J. Janssen
Constitutional Theology: Notes on the Book of Church Order *of the Reformed Church in America*
An absolutely indispensable aid to anyone responsible for the governance of the church, whether deacon, elder, minister, or denomination executive. Personnel and churches could be prevented from floundering, time in classes and synods could be saved, if only these guides for living together were followed, rather than approaching issues on an ad hoc basis. The wisdom of centuries has gone into this guide for governance. Janssen reaches beyond the pragmatic to show the underlying theology that governs our living in consistories, classes, and synods. Pp. xii, 321, index. 2000. $25.

Gregg A. Mast, editor
Raising the Dead: Sermons of Howard G. Hageman
Perhaps one of the most erudite and eloquent preachers of the latter half of the twentieth century, from his pulpit in the North Reformed Church in Newark Hageman was in demand as preacher and lecturer, as well as a professor of preaching, and later president, at New Brunswick Theological Seminary. Two series of sermons on Christ's seven last words open the book, followed by seven Christmas sermons, six for Easter, and four each for Ascension and Pentecost. While Hageman's eloquence was a gift improbable to teach or imitate, nonetheless these sermons will stimulate and excite all who care about great preaching. Pp. xxix, 241. 2000. $20.

James Hart Brumm, editor
Equipping the Saints: The Synod of New York, 1800-2000
The editor describes the convening of the Synod of New York, while Christopher Moore moves us from the early days in the mill to the present millennium. Betty L. King describes the historic St. Thomas Reformed Church

in the Virgin Islands, while Anna Melissa James describes the experience of black people in the Reformed Church in America. Scott Conrad and Stephen Hanson describe the different perspective of the northern reaches of the synod in the Classis of Mid-Hudson. Herman D. De Jong describes the changes in the Classis of Queens, while Michael Edwards offers practical perspectives on urban ministries. John E. Hiemstra describes the remarkable growth of the Asian church in the synod, while Russell L. Gasero offers a pictorial view. There is also a chronological list of congregations (which at one time ranged through New Jersey to Illinois to Oklahoma). Pp. xii, 185, illustrations, index. 2000. $16.

Joel R. Beeke, editor
Forerunner of the Great Awakening: Sermons by Theodorus Jacobus Frelinghuysen, 1691-1747
The robust pietism of Frelinghuysen and his preaching seeking an experientially defined conversion is acknowledged as the beginning of the Great Awakening. An excellent introduction to Frelinghuysen is offered by Joel R. Beeke. Twenty-two sermons are included, intended to bring the hearer to an intimate awareness of sin and peril, through God's grace in conversion. The sermons offer an original source for understanding the Awakening. Pp. xliii, 339, 6 x 9". 2000. $28.

Russell L. Gasero
Historical Directory of the Reformed Church in America, 1628-2000
This newest edition of the historical directory contains the six thousand ordained ministers serving in over tweny thousand individual areas of service in more than seventeen hundred congregations. The listings of ministers, missionaries, and churches follows that of the directory of 1628-1992. Pp. xvi, 720, 6 x 9". 2001. $70.

Eugene P. Heideman
From Mission to Church: The Reformed Church in America Mission to India
The story chronicles the period from the beginning of the mission under John Scudder in 1819 to 1987. Beginning with a focus on evangelism with the initiative in the hands of missionaries and mission societies, the organization of the Classis of Arcot puts the churches into relationship with the church in America. At the same time there is a growth of institutions in education and medicine. With the independence of India and the formation of the Church of South India in 1947, mission is seen as partnership, with the mission playing a supporting role to a self-determining church. The history is an honest portrayal of both failure and success. Pp. xix, 748, illustrations, maps, bibliography, index. 2001. $50.

James I. Cook, editor
The Church Speaks, Vol. 2: Papers of the Commission on Theology Reformed Church in America, 1985-2000
Includes "The Use of Scripture in Making Moral Decisions." Under "Church and Faith" are papers on liberation theology, the Nicene Creed, confirmation,

conscience clauses, and the uniqueness of Christ. "Church and Sacraments" includes consideration of children at the Lord's Table, while "Church and Ministry" treats the role and authority of women in ministry, the laying on of hands in ordination, the commissioning of preaching elders, moral standards for church offices, and constitutional inquiries. "Church and Witness" considers the relationship to Muslims and the farm crisis and "Church and Sexuality" considers homosexuality. Pp. xix, 315, appendix, scripture index, name index, subject index. 2002. $28.

John W. Coakley, editor
Concord Makes Strength: Essays in Reformed Ecumenism
Herman Harmelink III revisits the first volume in this series; Lynn Japinga describes our hesitant ecumenical history; Paul R. Fries discusses the theological roots of our ecumenical disposition; and Karl Blei gives a broader view of Reformed ecumenism. Discussed are full communion, Roman Catholic dialogue, the Joint Declaration on Justification, a Reformed-Catholic future, Reformed and evangelical and Eastern Orthodox, plus an attempt to see the future by Dale T. Irvin and Wesley Granberg-Michaelson. Pp. xvii, 194, index. 2002. $19.

Robert P. Swierenga
Dutch Chicago: A History of Hollanders in the Windy City
From the very beginnings of Dutch immigration to Chicago, Swierenga traces the development primarily of Dutch Calvinists, but also of the smaller numbers of Jews and Roman Catholics. The role of the church and Christian schools, as well as mutual aid societies, social clubs, truck farming, garbage and cartage, stores, services, and ethnic politics are covered in detail. Five appendices include garbage and cartage companies, churches, schools, missions, societies, clubs, and church membership. Pp. xx, 908, illustrations, maps, tables, bibliography, index, 6 x 9", hardcover, dust jacket. 2002. $49.

Paul L. Armerding
Doctors for the Kingdom: The work of the American Mission Hospital in the Kingdom of Saudi Arabia
Drawing upon original source materials from the missionary doctors and nurses involved, Armerding creates a compelling narrative of these men and women who witnessed to the love of Christ through the words and deeds of their medical mission. The book has been translated into Arabic and published by the King Abdulaziz Foundation in Riyadh, Saudi Arabia. The principal doctors cited in the book were featured in *Saudi Aramco World*, May/June 2004. Lavishly produced. Pp. 182, illustrations, glossary, gazetteer, maps, bibliography, 8½ x 10¼", hardcover, dust jacket. 2003. $39.

Donald J. Bruggink and Kim N. Baker
By Grace Alone: Stories of the Reformed Church in America
Intended for the whole church. After a consideration of its European background in an introductory chapter "Reformed from What?," the story of the Dutch and their church in the New World from the early seventeenth

century to the present is told with attention paid to relationships to Native and African Americans at home and missions abroad. The movement of the church across the continent and immigration to Canada, as well as its ecumenical involvement, leads to a challenge for the future. Additional personal interest stories in sidebars, as well as time lines and resources, accompany each chapter. Pp. ix, 222, illustrations, index, 8½ x 11". 2004. $29.

June Potter Durkee
Travels of an American Girl
Prior to WWII, June accompanied her parents on a trip through Europe to the Middle East and India. Her father, F. M. "Duke" Potter, was for thirty years a major force in mission policy and administration. The world and the missionaries, as seen through the eyes of a precocious ten year old who polished her account at age twelve, makes delightful and insightful reading. Pp. xv, 95, sketches, illustrations. 2004. $14.

Mary L. Kansfield
Letters to Hazel: Ministry within the Woman's Board of Foreign Missions of the Reformed Church in America
A collection of letters, written by overseas missionaries in appreciation of Hazel Gnade, who shepherded them through New York on their departures and returns, inspired this history of the Woman's Board. Kansfield chronicles how a concern for women abroad precipitated a nineteenth-century "feminism" that in the cause of missions, took women out of their homes, gave them experience in organizational skills, fundraising, and administration. Pp. xiii, 257, illustrations, appendices, bibliography, name index, subject index, 8½ x 11". 2004. $29.

Johan Stellingwerff and Robert P. Swierenga, editors
Iowa Letters: Dutch Immigrants on the American Frontier
A collection of two-hundred-fifteen letters between settlers in Iowa and their family and friends in the Netherlands. Remarkable is the fact that the collection contains reciprocal letters covering a period of years. While few have heard of the Buddes and Wormsers, there are also letters between Hendrik Hospers, mayor of Pella and founder of Hospers, Iowa, and his father. Also unusual is that in contrast to the optimism of Hospers, there are the pessimistic letters of Andries N. Wormser, who complained that to succeed in America you had to "work like a German." Pp. xxvii, 701, illustrations, list of letters, bibliography, index, 6 x 9", hardcover, dust jacket. 2005. $49.

James C. Kennedy and Caroline J. Simon
Can Hope Endure?: A Historical Case Study in Christian Higher Education
Hope was founded as a Christian college. How it has endured to the present without slipping either into secularism or a radical fundamentalism is the account of this book. The course has not always been steady, with factions within the school at times leaning either to the left or right. The account can perhaps be instructive in maintaining Hope's traditional centrist position. Pp. xvi, 249, bibliography, index, 6 x 9". 2005. $28.

LeRoy Koopman
Taking the Jesus Road: The Ministry of the Reformed Church in America among Native Americans
The ministry began in the seventeenth century, carried on by pastors who ministered to their Dutch congregants and native Americans. After the Revolutionary War, ministry moved from pastors to missionaries, increasing in activity following the Civil War. Koopman does not shy away from multiple failed government policies in which the church was often complicit, but he also records the steadfast devotion of both missionaries and lay workers who sought to bring assistance, love, and the gospel to native Americans. Pp. xiv, 512, illustrations, appendices including pastors, administrators, other personnel, and native American pastors, index, 6 x 9", hardcover, dust jacket. 2005. $49.

Karel Blei
The Netherlands Reformed Church, 1571-2005
translated by Allan J. Janssen
Beginning with the church's formation in 1571 during the upheavals of the Reformation, Karel Blei's *Netherlands Reformed Church* follows a dynamic path through over 400 years of history, culminating in the landmark ecumenical union of 2004. Blei explores the many dimensions of the Netherlands Reformed Church's story including the famous splits of 1834 and 1886, the colorful and divisive theological camps, and the hopeful renewal of the church in the mid-twentieth century. Also included are incisive explorations of new confessions, church order, and liturgical renewal. Pp. xvi, 176, index, 6x9", 2006. $25.00

Janel Sjaarda Sheeres
Son of Secession: Douwe J. Vander Werp
Janet Sjaarda Sheers has written a moving, sympathetic, and exciting biography of Douwe Vander Werp, one of the key figures in the Netherlands *Afscheiding* of 1834 and a principal minister in the early development of the Christian Reformed Church. Credited with having founded ten congregations, Vander Werp was a man zealously committed to his understanding of God's Word and its implications for his life, even when it required the painful sacrifice of three secessions. Sheeres's sociological observations add interesting insights into Vander Werp's fascinating and fractious times. *Son of Secession* is a challenge to our understanding of the historical origins of the Christian Reformed Church, as well as that church today. Pp. xxii, 210, Appendices, bibliography, index, 6 x 9", 2006. $25.00.

Allan J. Janssen
Kingdom, Office, and Church: A Study of A. A. van Ruler's Doctrine of Ecclesiastical Office.
A. A. van Ruler is one of the most influential twentieth-century theologians from the Netherlands. One of the many challenging aspects of his work is his theology of the kingdom of God and its relationship to the church and its ecclesiastical offices. Allan J. Janssen draws on extensive pastoral and ecclesial

experience as well as closely reasoned analysis to set forth the implications of van Ruler's theology for the church today. Christo Lombard of the University of the Western Cape writes: "When theologians grappling with the realities of the new millennium are re-discovering the exciting and challenging work of one of the most original theologians of our time . . . anyone interested in the way forward for the church in an age of post-modernity and globalization, should read Dr. Janssen's book, based on meticiulous scholarship and a passion for God's work in and through us as God's partners." Pp. xvi, 319, bibliography, index, 6 x 9", 2006. $35.00.

Corwin Smidt, Donald Luidens, James Penning and Roger Nemeth
Divided by a Common Heritage: The Christian Reformed Church and the Reformed Church in America at the Beginning of the New Millenium.

Comparisons are based on surverys of the positions of ministers and laity of the two denominations on a wide variety of religious, social and political issues.

"Ecclesiastical introspection can lead to banal, partial analysis. But not in this book from four social scientists who have taken a long and discriminating yet loving look at their own denominations. . . . For members of the Christian Reformed Church and the Reformed Church in America, the book offers sympathetic insight into the present character of both denominations and their prospects for the future." Mark A. Noll, University of Notre Dame.

"In helping us to understand our past separate existence, the authors lay the groundwork for honest discussions of the future relationship between the RCA and CRC." Dennis Voskuil, Western Theological Seminary, Pp. xiv, 226, bibliography, index, 6 x 9" paperback, 2006, $24.00.

James A. De Jong
Henry J. Kuiper: Shaping the Christian Reformed Church, 1907-1962.

"There was no one more important than H. J. Kuiper in shaping the Christian Reformed Church as it moved out of its immigrant phase in the second quarter of the twentieth century. In this close study, one both empathetic with its subject and professionally executed, James De Jong helps us understand Kuiper in all his roles–as forceful journalist and ecclesiastical politician but also pastor, liturgical reformer, hymnologist, promoter of city missions–and always champion of Reformed orthodoxy. A window into the mind and spirit of a man, a denomination, and a social world now past but still influential." James Bratt, Professor of History, Calvin College.

The author, James A. De Jong, was president of Calvin Theological Seminary from 1983 to 2002. His specialty is historical theology and church history. Pp. xviii-270, bibliography, index, 6 x 9" paperback, 2007, $28.00.